R. Albritton

16.95N

The Capitalist State

D11194454

The Capitalist State

Marxist Theories and Methods

BOB JESSOP

Martin Robertson · Oxford

© Bob Jessop, 1982

First published in 1982 by Martin Robertson & Company Ltd.,
108 Cowley Road, Oxford OX4 1JF.

All rights reserved. No part of this publication may be reproduced, stored in
a retrieval system, or transmitted, in any form or by any means, electronic,
mechanical, photocopying, recording or otherwise, without the prior written
permission of the copyright holder.

Except in the United States of America, this book is sold subject to the
condition that it shall not, by way of trade or otherwise be lent, re-sold, hired
out, or otherwise circulated without the publisher's prior consent in any form
of binding or cover other than that in which it is published and without a
similar condition including this condition being imposed on the subsequent
purchaser.

British Library Cataloguing in Publication Data
Jessop, Bob
   The capitalist state: Marxist theories and
   methods.
   1. Capitalism
   I. Title
   330.12′2   HB501
   ISBN 0-85520-269-6
   ISBN 0-85520-268-8 Pbk

Typeset in 11/12 pt IBM Press Roman by Freeman Graphic, Tonbridge
Printed and bound in Great Britain

In Memoriam:

Nicos Poulantzas

Contents

Contents

Preface

This book has been an unconscionably long time in the making. My interest in theories of the state and state power dates back some twelve years or more and my interest in epistemological and methodological issues in theory construction is even longer-lived. But the immediate stimulus to undertake a theoretical investigation into recent Marxist analyses of the capitalist state came from two discussion groups in which I have been involved during the last five years: the Conference of Socialist Economists group on the capitalist state and the 'Problems of Marxism' seminar at the University of Essex. Some preliminary results of this investigation were published in the *Cambridge Journal of Economics* in 1977 and I have since published several other papers on various aspects of postwar Marxist theories of the state, law, and politics. Nonetheless the greatest part of the current book is newly published here and the book as a whole draws together for the first time the principal theoretical and methodological conclusions of my various studies to date on these matters.

In general terms the present study focuses on postwar European Marxist theories of the capitalist state and its middle chapters consider three major approaches to this topic. It is not concerned with earlier Marxist analyses of the capitalist state and politics, however significant they might have been at the time in theoretical discussion and/or political strategies, unless they have also been directly influential in the development of the postwar European work considered in this volume. Among the important studies that are ignored due to this self-imposed restriction are the work of Austro-Marxist theorists such as Max Adler, Otto Bauer, Rudolf Hilferding, and Karl Renner, German Social Democrats such as Eduard Bernstein and Karl Kautsky, advocates of council communism such as Anton Pannekoek and Herman Goerter, and leading communist theorists such as Karl Korsch, George Lukacs, Rosa Luxemburg, and Leon Trotsky. How-

ever, since almost all self-professed Marxist theories seek some justification (if not the exclusive right to the mantle of Marxism) in their
interpretation of the work of Marx and Engels and its continuation
by such figures as Lenin or Gramsci, I devote the first chapter to a
brief assessment of the contribution of the two founding fathers and
also discuss the studies of Lenin and Gramsci in subsequent pages. In
the first chapter I consider the work of Marx and Engels from two
interrelated perspectives: its substantive content and its underlying
theoretical method. In relation to the latter I argue that Marx provides the foundations for a realist scientific method in his 1857
Introduction and relates this to problems of state theory and political practice in his 1875 *Critique of the Gotha Programme.* In order
to distinguish this theoretical method from others, I refer to it as the
'method of articulation'; but it is worth emphasising at the outset
that I believe this approach involves nothing more than the correct
application of a realist scientific method to the field of political
economy. In terms of its substantive content I deny that it is possible
to distil a single, coherent, unitary Marxist theory from the various
studies that Marx and/or Engels presented concerning the state and
political action. Instead they offered a variety of theoretical perspectives which co-exist in an uneasy and unstable relation. It is this very
plurality of viewpoints and arguments that provides the basis for the
subsequent diversification of Marxist state theories.

In the three central chapters of this book I consider three recent
Marxist approaches to the capitalist state. The discussion has a dual
orientation. For, in addition to a critical review of the merits and
demerits of the substantive arguments of these approaches, I also
consider how far their proponents follow the methodological procedures specified by Marx. The order of presentation reflects this dual
concern. For, although there is much to recommend in the substantive arguments of all three approaches (as well as more or less significant areas for criticism), the different methods of theory construction
which are predominant in each approach are certainly not of equal
merit. Thus I deal first with theories that resort to the unsatisfactory
method of subsumption, proceed to theories that adopt the method
of logical derivation, and conclude with theories that follow more or
less closely the realist scientific method of articulation.

It is the orthodox communist theory of state monopoly capitalism
that provides the focus of the second chapter. The preparation of
these pages was particularly interesting because it forced me to re-
think my own dismissive attitude as well as to question other, more
widespread criticisms. For, although the great bulk of 'stamocap'

analysis is dull and repetitive as well as being committed to untenable forms of economic reductionism, there is sufficient interesting and original work to merit an extended treatment. It is also worth noting that there are important parallels between 'stamocap' theories in their 'monopoly-theoretical' version and American analyses of the 'military industrial complex' or the 'corporate state' in the USA; and that major similarities can be found between 'stamocap' theories in their 'capital-theoretical' version and arguments such as those of Galbraith concerning the 'technostructure' in the 'new industrial state' or of James O'Connor concerning the sources of the 'fiscal crisis of the state' (Galbraith, 1967; O'Connor, 1973). This means that, although theories of state monopoly capitalism are nowhere near as influential in countries with a weak communist movement (such as the USA, Canada, and Britain) as they are in countries where communists are a significant political force (such as the Soviet bloc, France, and Italy), many of the criticisms levelled at these theories are germane to other theoretical and political analyses which emphasise the close links between monopoly capital and the state. Finally, because state monopoly capitalism theories enjoy significant political influence in several countries but are also deeply flawed theoretically, they have provided a major stimulus to the development of other approaches which aim to transcend these limitations.

One such approach is the so-called *Staatsableitungdebatte* or 'state derivation debate', This comprises the subject matter of the third chapter. Here I deal with the whole range of explicitly Marxist theories concerned with the logical derivation of the form and/or functions of the capitalist state. Although the main points of this approach are already familiar in Britain through the work of Holloway and Picciotto, the breadth of the debate and its recent development is less well-known. Nor is there much real appreciation of the precise methodological implications of the derivation approach among its opponents or, indeed, its proponents. More generally the substantive arguments of the *Staatsableitungdebatte* are almost wholly unknown in the USA and its methodological approach is quite alien to the empiricist tradition that dominates American Marxism as well as more orthodox, pluralist social sciences. Since there is much of real theoretical and methodological worth in this approach it is particulariedly important to make it accessible to a wider audience. Thus, in addition to considering the whole range of West German and British attempts at a derivation of the form and/or functions of the capitalist state, special attention is also paid to the method of derivation and its affinities with the method of articulation.

In the fourth chapter I deal with the theoretical and political work of Gramsci and the neo-Gramscian school. By far the largest part of this chapter is devoted to the contribution of Poulantzas but I also consider the 'discourse-theoretical' analyses of Laclau and Mouffe. A superficial familiarity with the early work of Poulantzas has bred a certain contempt among English-speaking readers — especially those who interpreted it in terms of the sterile and misleading 'structuralist-instrumentalist' debate with Ralph Miliband. My own presentation attempts to bring out the real structure of Poulantzas's argument and to trace his theoretical evolution. The critique of Laclau and Mouffe is necessarily provisional since the principal results of their enquiries have still to be published. But the 'discourse-theoretical' approach is so distinctive and important in its novel interpretation of Gramsci's account of hegemony and has influenced my own approach to such an extent that a provisional review and assessment is required. Both Poulantzas and Laclau and Mouffe adopt the method of articulation in at least some respects and this chapter concludes with a brief account of its application in these and related analyses of the state.

The final chapter builds on the criticisms of the above-mentioned approaches and presents a set of guidelines for a theoretically-informed account of the state in capitalist societies. It begins with an extended discussion of articulation as the most appropriate method of constructing such accounts and relates it to the realist interpretation of scientific method. The bulk of the chapter then introduces in a preliminary and exploratory fashion some protocols for the analysis of the state as a complex institutional ensemble of forms of representation and intervention and of state power as a form-determined reflection of the balance of political forces. In this way I eventually return to the concerns of the first chapter and show how the methods of research and the methods of theoretical presentation advocated by Marx have continuing validity and provide the most appropriate basis for a fresh assault on the problems of constructing an adequate account of the state.

Even this brief outline shows that at least four possible topics are ignored. Firstly there is no extended criticism of the so-called 'instrumentalist' approach which has been so influential in Marxist work as well as more orthodox investigations. In its sociological version 'instrumentalism' establishes the nature of the state from the class affiliation of the state elite; in its politological version it does so in terms of the immediate economic interests advanced by specific policy decisions and 'non-decisions'. In neither version does instrumentalism offer a coherent account of the distinctive properties of state power nor provide an adequate explanation for its limitations. As a general approach it has been subject to extensive criticism elsewhere and it is also considered *en passant* below. Similar considerations led me to neglect the debate between 'neo-Ricardian' and 'fundamentalist' theorists over the nature and causes of state economic intervention. The basic terrain of this debate is economic rather than political and, in so far as it deals with the state apparatus and state power, it adopts an instrumentalist ('neo-Ricardian') or complex reductionist ('fundamentalist') view. Thus, although I do not deal with this debate directly, both sides are criticised by implication (for a useful review of the economic issues at stake in the debate, see Fine and Harris, 1979, pp. 3–92).

Thirdly, given that this book is concerned with postwar European Marxist analyses of the state, it might seem odd to have devoted so little space to Italian theorists. In a more general review of postwar Marxism this neglect would be unforgivable but it is justified in terms of the particular focus and ambit of the current work. For Italian contributions to Marxist political analysis are often very philosophical in character and/or strongly Italocentric in their theoretical and strategic concerns. It would certainly be desirable to discuss elsewhere Marxist solutions to the traditional problems of political philosophy, such as the nature of democracy, liberty, equality, constitutional rights, and the rule of law; and, in a work less concerned with abstract methodological issues and the general characteristics of the capitalist state, it would be appropriate to consider the attempts of Italian Marxists to update and apply the work of Gramsci to the current situation in Italy. But issues of political (as opposed to state) theory lie beyond the scope of the present text and the most original and far-reaching developments of Gramsci have occurred outside Italy (see chapter 4 below). Nonetheless I hope to settle accounts with Italian theories of the state and politics at a later date. (Meanwhile those interested in such matters should consult, *inter alia,* Altvater, 1977; Altvater and Kallscheuer, 1979; Bobbio *et al.,* 1976; *Critica Marxista,* seriatim; Mouffe, ed., 1979; Mouffe and Sassoon, 1977; Negri, 1977; and Sassoon, ed., 1982.)

Finally it is worth recording that I deliberately ignore American contributions to the analysis of the state. Most of these theories are heavily imbued with instrumentalism and/or adopt crude forms of reductionism and thus merit no more attention than their European counterparts. Those few analyses that escape this criticism generally owe so much to the other European approaches considered here and/ or bear such marked similarities to them that a separate review is not required. More generally it would be an interesting exercise to consider how far the absence of a well-developed 'state tradition' in Britain and the USA and the corresponding dominance of liberal, pluralist conceptions of government and citizenship has led to the extraordinary weakness of Marxist theories of the state in these countries.

In undertaking a research project of this kind one inevitably incurs a large number of intellectual and material debts. This particular study is no exception. It is impossible to mention all those who have influenced me in conferences, seminars, and personal discussion (let alone through the published word) but I am acutely aware of debts in this respect to David Abraham, Kevin Bonnett, Joachim Hirsch, John Holloway, Ernesto Laclau, David Lockwood, Sol Picciotto, Claus Offe, Nicos Poulantzas, Harold Wolpe, and Tony Woodiwiss. To Claudia von Braunmühl and Jutta Kneissel I would like to extend public thanks for their hospitality during a six-week visit to the University of Frankfurt to examine German state theory at first hand; and to Hans Kastendiek I would like to extend similar thanks for introducing me to the work of the *Prokla* group at Berlin. To the students in my seminars on theories of the capitalist state I offer my sympathies as the guinea pigs for the development of my approach over the last four years. Since the arguments presented here often differ from those held by friends and colleagues whose influence I have just acknowledged, it is particularly important to issue the usual disclaimers and stress that the ultimate responsibility for the study rests firmly with me. I would also like to thank Lawrence and Wishart for permission to use material from an earlier article on 'Marx and Engels on the State' in the book on *Politics, Ideology, and the State,* edited by Sally Hibbin and published in 1978. For those interested in such matters I did my own typing, xeroxing, collating, and so forth, and Janet Godden offered valuable advice at the copy-editing stage. My children and wife distracted me from these endeavours more than I should have allowed were I to meet the ever-retreating deadlines set by Martin Robertson and I would like to thank my publishers for their great patience and my family for reminding me that there is more to life than a concern with theories of the state. I have dedicated this book to the memory of Nicos Poulantzas whom I met for the first time some few months before his tragic death and who encouraged me to be critical in my approach to his work as well as that of others.

Bob Jessop
12 October 1981

Abbreviations

The following abbreviated references to texts or collections are employed:

C1   Karl Marx, *Capital* vol 1
C3   Karl Marx, *Capital* vol 3
CCC   Nicos Poulantzas, *Classes in Contemporary Capitalism*
CD   Nicos Poulantzas, *Crisis of the Dictatorships,* 2ed.
FD   Nicos Poulantzas, *Fascism and Dictatorship*
LCW   V. I. Lenin, *Collected Works* (Moscow, 1960–1970)
MECW   Karl Marx and Friedrich Engels, *Collected Works* (London, 1975–)
MESW   Karl Marx and Friedrich Engels, *Selected Works* in 3 volumes (London, 1969–1970)
PPSC   Nicos Poulantzas, *Political Power and Social Classes*
SCW   J. Stalin, *Collected Works* (Moscow, 1953–56)
SPS   Nicos Poulantzas, *State, Power, Socialism*
TSV3   Karl Marx, *Theories of Surplus Value*, vol 3

The following abbreviations are also adopted:

AK   Arbeitskonferenz
CDU   Christlich-Demokratische Union
CME   capitalisme monopoliste d'état
CMP   capitalist mode of production
ISA   ideological state apparatus
PCF   Parti communiste français
PCI   Partito Comunista Italiano
PKA   Projekt Klassenanalyse
RSA   repressive state apparatus
SMC   state monopoly capitalism
SMK   staatsmonopolistischer Kapitalismus
STR   scientific and technical revolution
TRPF   tendency of the rate of profit to fall

1

Marx and Engels on the State

It is a commonplace that Marx did not produce an account of the state to match the analytical power of his critique of the capitalist mode of production in *Das Kapital*. Indeed, although this great work was to have included an extended treatment of the state, Marx did not succeed in committing it to paper. Instead his legacy in this respect comprises an uneven and unsystematic collection of philosophical reflections, journalism, contemporary history, political forecasts, and incidental remarks. It was left to Engels to develop a more systematic account of the origins and nature of the state and to discuss the general relations between state power and economic development. However, while it was Engels rather than Marx who first adumbrated a class theory of the state, the 'General' was no more successful than Marx himself in developing this insight into a complete and coherent analysis of the capitalist state.

This commonplace should not be taken to imply that Marx made no lasting contribution to political analysis. On the contrary it is as much for his theory of proletarian revolution as for his critique of political economy that Marx can be considered to have founded Marxism and continues to have an exceptional posthumous influence. Likewise Engels is as well known for his work on the state and politics as he is for his indictment of early English capitalism or his philosophy of 'scientific socialism'. Hence in this introductory chapter I intend to review the development of the historical materialist approach to the state and politics in the work of Marx and Engels and to consider how different elements and arguments are combined at different stages in their studies. Rather than attempt to distil a single 'essential' Marxist theory of the state I emphasise the discontinuities and disjunctions in their work and try to show how its very incompleteness and indeterminacy account for the wide range of so-called Marxist theories of the state developed during the last

1

hundred years. We begin with a brief review of the early approach of Marx to the question of the state.

THE EARLY MARX

Since the publication of the 1844 manuscripts in 1927 there has been a lively debate among Marxists and Marxologists alike concerning whether or not Marx effected (or experienced) a radical break during the course of his intellectual development. This debate is generally focused on the basic epistemological and philosophical pre-suppositions of the *Manuscripts* and *Das Kapital* and it has been much complicated by the still more recent republication in 1953 of the hitherto unremarked *Grundrisse*. But it is also concerned with the relative continuity or discontinuity of Marxian concepts and principles of explanation in the analysis of specific topics in the domains of economics, politics, and ideology. That the two levels of debate are closely related can be seen particularly clearly in the present context from the Hegelian-centred reading of Marx rendered by Avineri, who seeks to establish the deep-seated continuity of the social and political thought of Marx by tracing the themes of his early work on Hegel's political philosophy through the vicissitudes of Marx's subsequent theoretical development (Avineri, 1968, *passim*). It is beyond the scope of this chapter to discuss the general issues involved in this debate but it is clearly essential for us to confront the particular question of continuity in the Marxian analysis of politics and the state.

This question is overlain by another. For there is also a major dispute concerning whether the Marxian analysis of politics is an original theoretical product or whether it is largely borrowed from the works of Machiavelli, Montesquieu, and Rousseau. Thus Colletti argues that Marx had already developed a near definitive theory of state power before the 1844 manuscripts started him on the long march to his most important theoretical discoveries. In particular Colletti argues that the *Critique of Hegel's 'Philosophy of Law'* (1843) and the *Introduction* to a proposed revision of that critique (written in 1843–44) embody a mature theory which neither the older Marx, Engels, nor Lenin would substantially improve upon in the least bit. And he also argues that this so-called mature Marxist theory was heavily indebted to Rousseau for its critique of parliamentarism, the theory of popular delegation, and the need for the ultimate suppression of the state itself. From this Colletti concludes that the originality of Marxism must be sought in the field of social and economic analysis rather than in its politics (Colletti, 1975, pp. 45–48; and for Colletti's views on the theoretical importance of Marx's social and economic analyses, *idem*, 1969, pp. 3–44, 77–102).

In contrast Blackburn has argued that the real focus of the work of Marx and Engels was political rather than philosophical or economic and that their decisive contribution was the theory of proletarian revolution. And he insists most strongly that in no field has Marxism been more original than in political theory and that Marxists either discovered or thoroughly reworked every important political concept. For the historical materialist concepts of class, party, revolution, bureaucracy, state, nation, etc., are not in the least anticipated in the work of earlier political theorists and philosophers. This leads Blackburn to a different periodisation of the development of Marxian political analysis. Thus, whereas Colletti finds a mature and near-definitive theory in the 1843 *Critique,* Blackburn argues that Marx did not even commit himself in outline to the proletarian revolution until 1844 (in the *Introduction*) and was still employing political concepts that were 'spare and rudimentary' in the *Communist Manifesto* some four years later. Moreover, although Marx and Engels were able to develop these concepts through their involvement in the First International, their intervention in the development of the German workers' movement, and their observation of French politics (especially the Paris Commune), they could not complete their theory of proletarian revolution even if they were able to distinguish it from Blanquism and 'democratic faith in miracles'. He concludes that it was not until the events of 1905 and 1917 in Russia that other revolutionary Marxists could substantially (albeit not finally) accomplish this task (Blackburn, 1976, *passim*).

What evidence can be adduced for these radically different views of the trajectory followed by Marx in developing his political theory? In the rest of this chapter I argue that the evidence is far from consistent and unambiguous because neither Marx nor Engels presented a definitive analysis of the state and politics. Instead we find a wide variety of themes and approaches which are capable of independent (and in part contradictory) theoretical development but which are typically combined in various ways by Marx and Engels in their empirical studies of particular societies and political conjunctures. These themes and/or approaches occasionally receive an exclusive and one-sided treatment but they are generally articulated in a way that ensures their mutual qualification in a state of theoretical tension. But it is also true that we can trace a gradual transformation of these different elements and the manner of their combination so that the Marxian theory of the state and politics undergoes substantial development from the 1840s to the 1880s. It remains ill-formulated and inconsistent throughout its development but the final version is much more adequate theoretically. But, before presenting our reconstruction of the final Marxian approach, let us first consider the early political writings.

The *Critique of Hegel's 'Philosophy of Law'* is the central work of political theory written by Marx in the period before he became a communist. It is mainly concerned with a criticism of Hegel's method of dialectical logic rather than with a direct examination of Hegel's doctrine of the state (on the latter, see the important account given in Avineri, 1972). Marx first shows how this method results in an apologia for the Prussian constitution and system of government on the thoroughly idealist grounds that it is the 'empirical existence of the truth', the self-incarnation of God in the world (Marx, 1843a, pp. 3–40 and especially 38–40). He then proceeds to examine Hegel's own prescription concerning the mediation between the separate spheres of state and civil society to be effected through the monarchy, the executive, and the legislative assembly. It is here that Marx develops a general critique of the separation of the state and civil society and argues that this separation cannot be resolved either through the rule of a universal and neutral bureaucracy or the election of a legislative assembly to govern in the interests of the people (Marx, 1843a, pp. 20–149).

Thus, although Marx agrees with Hegel that there are two distinct spheres in modern society and that civil society is a sphere of egoism or self-interest, he also denies that this separation is immanent or inevitable and that the state can transcend the war of each against all and secure the common interest of all its citizens. In opposition to the claim that the institutional separation of the state is the logical complement to the self-particularisation of the universal Idea, Marx argues that the state becomes fully differentiated only in definite historical circumstances which he identifies mainly in terms of freedom of exchange in commerce and in landed property (Marx, 1843a, pp. 16–17 and 32). And, whereas Hegel claims that the bureaucracy in the modern state is a 'universal class' whose necessary and objective function it is to realise the 'universal interest', Marx argues that the egoism of civil society implies that any concept of a 'universal interest' is necessarily a pure abstraction (Marx, 1943a, pp. 45–46). Nor does the agreed fact that the state assumes an independent material form mean that it can therefore transcend the generalised particularism of civil society. Instead the state itself becomes shot through with crass materialism and the bureaucracy simply becomes one particular interest among others. Indeed Marx notes that the various independent groups in Prussian civil society struggle to maintain their interests against the encroachments of the bureaucracy but also need the latter to act as the guarantor of their interests against other groups. In turn the officials tend to appropriate state power as their private property and use it to further both their corporate and individual interests (*ibid.*). Moreover, since state power is used to protect the rights of property (especially those of the Junker class), the Prussian state actually functions to reproduce the war of each against all in civil society (Marx, 1843a, pp. 98–99 and 108). Accordingly the citizens of the modern state are involved in an alienated and estranged form of public life since its constant penetration by private egoism ensures that the universal interest remains abstract and illusory (Marx, 1843a, p. 46 and *passim*).

Marx also comments on two proposed solutions to these problems. He argues that neither the introduction of a recharged organic feudal order with representation based on estates nor, indeed, the further development of the bourgeois democratic republic based on universal suffrage can overcome this estrangement through the re-integration of the public and private lives of the citizens. For, in opposition to Hegel's proposal that each social class be legally incorporated as a basis for political representation and for the fusion of the public and private spheres, Marx argues that this would involve the refeudalisation of modern society and destroy the individual freedoms and formal equality of private citizens (Marx, 1843a, pp. 72–73 and 79–81). He also argues that estates or corporations of this kind would not materially represent the universal interest but would simply reproduce the antagonisms of civil society inside the state (Marx, 1843a, pp. 90–91). In addition Marx criticises Hegel's proposals for the popular election of deputies on the twin grounds that such deputies would employ public office to further private interests and that they would dominate rather than represent the people (Marx, 1843a, pp. 122–123). This means that the parliamentary republic is necessarily limited as a form of popular control because it is inserted into a state whose claim to represent the interest of all its citizens must remain illusory so long as civil society is dominated by the egoism engendered by private property and competition. Thus, if real democracy and the universal interest are to be realised, private property and the abstract state must be abolished.

These themes are elaborated by Marx in his contemporaneous essay *On The Jewish Question*. This is a critique of the ideas of

Bruno Bauer regarding Jewish emancipation and compares the nature and effects of religious and political emancipation. Marx argues that the modern state abolished the political significance of religion, birth, rank, education, and occupation through the institution of formal equality among its citizens; but it could not abolish their continuing social significance in the reproduction of substantive inequalities. Thus, although the modern state and civil society are structurally distinct, it is the egoism of civil society that shapes political activity (Marx, 1843b, pp. 153 and 164). Accordingly Marx concludes that the emancipation of man requires more then the concession of formal political freedom. It can be completed only when the individual activities of men are reorganised to give full expression to their social and public nature (Marx, 1843b, pp. 167–168).

This stress on human emancipation is articulated with class struggle for the first time in the *Introduction to a Contribution to the Critique of Hegel's 'Philosophy of Law'*. In this brief essay Marx discusses the uneven development of philosophy and society in Germany (noting that social development lagged behind philosophical) and argues that complete emancipation is possible only on the basis of a proletarian revolution. For, since the nascent proletariat is subject to all the evils of modern society, it can achieve its own emancipation only through the total elimination of all exploitation and oppression (Marx, 1844a, pp. 185–187). Moreover, given the wholly miserable conditions in which the proletariat lives, all that is required for the German revolution to occur is the widespread diffusion of the critical philosophy of the whole man (Marx, 1844a, p. 187). In short, while the proletariat has nothing to lose but its chains, it stands to gain the whole world not just for itself but for mankind in general.

We are now in a position to assess the contributions of the young Marx to the analysis of politics and the state. It should be apparent that these studies do not amount to a near-definitive theory of the state apparatus or state power and, indeed, since they take the form of critiques and are very much preliminary analyses, it is unreasonable to expect them to do so. At best they reproduce and elaborate certain elements of anti-statism current at the time and also present a series of acute observations on the nature of bureaucratic rule and political representation. In this respect it should be noted that, although these ideas clearly owe much to the work of other radical liberal democrats, the young Marx locates them in a problematic which is inspired by Hegel rather than Rousseau. In addition to his analyses of the modern state Marx also examines the question of revolution. His emphasis on the role of the proletariat in this context is original but its initial presentation is still much influenced by the Hegelian approach. Indeed, since Marx had not yet developed the fundamental concepts of historical materialism, it is difficult to see how these studies could seriously be described as works of mature Marxism.

In support of this conclusion we should note that the entire theoretical discussion is cast in a philosophical framework and that many of the key economic and political concepts are heavily imbued with philosophical overtones. For, not only are class differences assimilated to those of rank, religion, and education and discussed in terms of an undifferentiated and non-specific conception of private property and human egoism, but the relation between the state and civil society is also analysed mainly in terms of such oppositions as 'universal-particular' and 'real-abstract'. Likewise the proletariat is seen largely as an underclass (even a lumpen-class) precipitated in the course of a general social disintegration and its emancipation is seen in terms of the final liberation and fulfilment of an essentially social man who has hitherto lived in conditions of unfreedom and/or self-estrangement (see especially Marx, 1843b, pp. 167–168, and 1844a, p. 187). It is certainly true that Marx consistently argues that this final stage in human emancipation requires the abolition of private property and the abstract state and the introduction of social co-operation and true democracy. But he does not attempt to delineate the future society nor to specify how the transition will be effected. In short a careful reading of these early studies does not support the claim that they contain an elaborate and adequate theory of the modern state and the dynamics of proletarian revolution. This is not to deny that subsequent Marxist theorists have attempted to build on his early insights on the nature of the state – especially in relation to the institutional separation or 'particularisation' of the modern state and its phenomenal form as the institutional embodiment of the universal interest (see chapter 3). It is to suggest that their significance for Marxism in this respect is almost wholly prospective and that, had Marx died in 1844, they would merit no special attention today.

TOWARDS A CLASS THEORY OF THE STATE

In general Marx's earliest theoretical work treats the state as an irrational abstract system of political domination which denies the social nature of man and alienates him from genuine involvement in public life. It also sees the state elite as the representative of private interests and, indeed, argues that the bureaucracy attempts to appropriate state power in its own interest. None of this suggests that Marx had yet developed a class theory of the state (let alone one articulated with the political economy of capitalism). For, although his contemporary political journalism on such matters as the 'wood-theft' law and the plight of the Moselle peasants alludes constantly to the use of state power to advance particular economic interests (Marx, 1842, pp. 224–263; 1843c, pp. 332–359; general reviews are presented in Draper, 1977, pp. 168–192, and Phillips, 1980, pp. 5–22), Marx does not integrate these remarks with his view of the Prussian state as a system of political domination to produce an account of the state as an organ of class rule. This is hardly surprising. For, not only was Marx still working within the Hegelian-Feuerbachian approach of his student days in Berlin, but for most of this time he was living in the Rhineland province of Prussia. If his general theoretical view meant that Marx continued to discuss political matters in terms of the opposition between state and civil society rather than class struggle, the fact that the Rhineland was the centre of German industrialism and bourgeois liberalism and was nonetheless oppressed by a strong, feudal state meant that this approach could be applied to contemporary issues without too much difficulty. This should not be taken to imply that Marx was uncritical in his use of the Hegelian framework. For he used the methods of Feuerbachian transformative criticism to reveal the need for the abolition of private property and the abstract state as necessary preconditions for the full realisation of democracy and human emancipation. But this commitment was not articulated with a class perspective and remained essentially jacobin in its over-riding concern with popular-democratic struggle.

In contrast Engels undertook a different theoretical path. Indeed, although he was active in the young Hegelian movement with Marx and became a communist in 1842, it was his stay in Manchester from 1842 to 1844 that was the fundamental formative influence on his understanding of political economy and that enabled him to anticipate the Marxian class theory of the state. Thus, as early as 1843 (while Marx himself was engaged in political journalism and his critique of Hegel), Engels had already written his *Outlines of a Critique of Political Economy* as well as several articles on the social question in England. Moreover, while Marx was busy on his 1844 Paris manuscripts, Engels formulated a preliminary version of the class theory of the state in his articles on the English Constitution and his classic work on *The Condition of the Working Class in England*. In these studies Engels argues that it is property – specifically the middle class — that rules in England and he describes how 'the bourgeoisie defends its interests with all the power at its disposal by wealth and the might of the State' (Engels, 1844b, p. 501). Thus, in addition to an examination of the institutional channels through which the political domination of the middle class is secured within the state apparatus, Engels also discusses the class nature of legislation, the common law, the poor law, and philanthropy (Engels, 1844a, pp. 489–513, and 1844b, pp. 562–583). Despite the clarity and the vehemence of these analyses, however, Engels does not elaborate them to produce a general 'class-theoretical' account of the state. This had to await the collaboration of Marx and Engels in the following years.

The first general formulation of the new approach is found in *The German Ideology* which was co-authored in 1845–1846 but was not published in full until 1932. It was subsequently elaborated in the *Manifesto of the Communist Party* and many other political analyses. However, while it is customary to talk about *the* Marxist class theory of the state, these studies do not contain a unitary and coherent analysis. Instead Marx and Engels present a complex array of ideas and arguments unified (if at all) through their common concern with the relations between class struggle and state power within the general framework of historical materialism. Since it is beyond the scope of this introductory chapter to give a full account of these ideas and arguments, we will concentrate on the main themes to be found in the various Marxian and/or Engelsian analyses of the state.

ECONOMIC BASE AND POLITICAL SUPERSTRUCTURE

One of the most prominent themes is the argument that the form of the state is a reflection of the economic base of society and that its interventions are a reflection of the needs of the economy and/or of the balance of economic class forces. This interpretation of politics in terms of a 'base-superstructure' model is most clearly stated in *The German Ideology, The Poverty of Philosophy,* the *Preface to a Contribution to the Critique of Political Economy,* the third volume of *Das Kapital,* the second part of *Anti-Dühring,* and Engels's letters on historical materialism. In the first of these works, for example, Marx and Engels argue that the state develops with the social division of labour and is the form in which the ruling class asserts its common interests. They also argue that political struggles within the state are merely the illusory forms in which the real struggles of antagonistic classes are fought out (Marx and Engels, 1845–1846, pp. 46–47).

Marx presents similar ideas in *The Poverty of Philosophy* in his observations on the method of political economy (Marx, 1847, pp. 161–
178). Likewise, in the famous 1859 summary of his general approach,
Marx suggests that the relations of production are the real foundation on which rises a legal and political superstructure and to
which correspond definite forms of social consciousness (Marx,
1859, pp. 503–504). This view is further developed in various parts
of *Das Kapital* and is forcefully re-stated when Marx examines the
genesis of capitalist ground-rent. For he argues that:

(i)t is always the direct relationship of the owners of the conditions of production to the direct producers — a relation always naturally corresponding to a
definite stage in the development of the methods of labour and thereby its social
productivity — which reveals the innermost secret, the hidden basis of the entire
social structure, and with it the political form of the relation of sovereignty and
dependence, in short, the corresponding specific form of the state (Marx, 1894,
p. 791).

The same theme is taken up by Engels in his attack on Dühring's
argument that direct political force is the primary determinant of the
economic situation and that the reverse relationship is purely secondary in nature (Engels, 1878, pp. 217–255). And it is often repeated
in Engels's letters on economic determinism (Marx and Engels, 1975,
pp. 394–396, 397–401, 433–445, and 441–443).

     This theme was described by Marx in his 1859 *Preface* as a guiding
thread for his studies and no doubt Engels would acknowledge this
too. But it is a thread which is split and frazzled. For it is subject to
various twists in their work and is often interwoven with other ideas
and themes. At its most extreme this theme could be taken to imply
that the state is a pure epiphenomenon of the economic base with no
reciprocal effectivity and that there is a perfect correspondence
between base and superstructure. This version is not stated explicitly
anywhere in the work of Marx and Engels although certain formulations are susceptible to such a construction. Instead they tend to
argue that different forms of state and state intervention are required
by different modes of production and that the nature of state power
is determined by the changing needs of the economy and/or by the
changing balance of class forces at the economic level. This view is
elaborated in relation to various stages in capital accumulation —
with different forms of state and state intervention required at different stages in its development. For example, Marx comments at
some length on the role of the absolutist state during the transition
from feudalism to capitalism, notes that the state is less interven-

tionist during the hey-day of liberal, *laissez-faire* capitalism, and becomes more active again with the socialisation of the capitalist relations of production (Marx, 1858, p. 651; *TSV*3, pp. 467, 468–469, 470, 491–492; *C*1, pp. 252–286, 667–725); and Engels also notes that the progressive socialisation of the productive forces requires a matching degree of socialisation of relations of production and adds that, in so far as this cannot be achieved through the joint-stock form of company, the state will be obliged to take over or establish production in major areas (Engels, 1878, pp. 384–387). It is also elaborated in relation to the development of the balance of class forces in struggle as this alters under the impact of the continuing reorganisation of the capitalist labour process (e.g., Marx and Engels various comments on the passage of factory legislation). In this context Engels also notes that, *as a rule,* the state cannot oppose the long-run development of the forces of production since this would generally result in the collapse of the power of the state (an argument developed most cogently in Engels's study of the unification of Germany and its subsequent economic and political development under Bismarck: see Engels, 1888, *passim,* and Engels 1878, pp. 253–254).

That such arguments are not wholly satisfactory is apparent from the qualifications that Marx and Engels themselves often made in their political analyses and their recognition that the correspondence between base and superstructure was a general rule rather than global. But this did not prevent the widespread adoption of simple economism in the Second International nor the development of more complex forms of economic reductionism by the 'capital logic' variant of the *Staatsableitung* school (see chapter 3). The theoretical difficulties involved in an exclusive, one-sided emphasis on economic determinism can be stated quite easily. For such a position implies that the economic base is ultimately (if not immediately) self-sufficient and that its spontaneous development is the sole determinant of social evolution. If it is once conceded that the reproduction of the economic base depends on factors outside its control, it follows that its nature and dynamics cannot provide a sufficient explanation for those of society as a whole. This creates insuperable problems for any attempt to prove a simple correspondence between the relations of production and juridico-political relations and/or between economic classes and political forces. It also implies that political action cannot alter the economic base and/or the nature of class relations until economic factors themselves permit or require such an alteration. At most this position allows for temporal deviations in economic development through the introduction of 'leads' or 'lags' between base and superstructure and/or between different levels of the class struggle. It cannot concede more without becoming inconsistent. However, although Marx and Engels emphasised the role of the economic base (*sic*) in social development (especially when engaged in criticism of Hegelian idealism or Dühring's 'force theory'), they do not adopt a monodeterminist line. Instead they are sensitive to the problems involved in economic reductionism and attempt to avoid them through a mixture of qualifications and resort to alternative modes of analysis.

THE STATE AS AN INSTRUMENT OF CLASS RULE

In this respect it is important to consider the recurrent thesis that the state is an instrument of class rule. This approach can be assimilated to economic reductionism through the assumption that the economic base determines the balance of political forces in the struggle for state power as well as the institutional form of the state as an instrument over whose control political struggle is waged. But it can also be developed in a voluntarist direction focusing on the more or less independent role of political action in the transformation of the economic base and the conduct of class struggle. This means that it is essential for us to examine the precise interpretation (if any) which Marx and Engels themselves placed upon the instrumentalist thesis.

In its least developed form the instrumentalist approach merely involves the claim that the state is not an independent and sovereign political subject but is an instrument of coercion and administration which can be used for various purposes by whatever interests manage to appropriate it. In this sense Marx had already developed such a view in his 1843 *Critique* and his articles on the 'wood-theft' law and similar matters. But it was Engels who first combined this instrumentalist view with the claim that it was a specific class which controlled the state apparatus and used this control to maintain its economic and political domination. This view is further developed in *The German Ideology,* in which Marx and Engels note that the state is the form in which the individuals of a ruling class assert their common interests (Marx and Engels, 1845–1846, p. 90); and again in the *Manifesto,* in which they note that the executive of the modern state is but a committee for managing the common affairs of the bourgeoisie (Marx and Engels, 1848, p. 486). Similar remarks occur throughout the subsequent political analyses of Marx and Engels and much of their work is concerned to reveal the various ways in which the modern state is used as an instrument for the exploitation of wage-labour by capital and/or the maintenance of class domination in the political sphere.

Moreover, in developing this instrumentalist approach, they also make a fundamental contribution to the analysis of class struggle. For both Marx and Engels are interested in the specific forms and the peculiar dynamics of such struggle at the political level in different social formations as well as in the essential class antagonism evident at the heart of a pure mode of production. Thus, although they sometimes assert or imply that political class struggle is a simple reflection or, at best, a tendential reflection of the economic conflict between capital and wage-labour, they also frequently refer to the many complexities introduced through the presence of other classes and social forces and to important discontinuities between different levels of class struggle. In this respect it is most instructive to compare the general theory of class struggle offered in the *Communist Manifesto* with the concrete historical analyses presented in the work of Marx and Engels on France, Germany, and England. In the former we find a general account of the progressive polarisation of class forces consequent upon the consolidation of the capitalist mode of production and a paradigm of the gradual but inevitable transformation of narrow, localised economic class struggles into a broad-ranging, unified political class struggle to wrest control of the state as instrument from the ruling bourgeoisie. In the latter we find a wealth of descriptive concepts specific to the political class struggle and its various modalities and a whole series of attempts to grapple with the conjunctural specificity of the struggle for state power. Thus Marx and Engels discuss the relations obtaining among different class fractions, the role of class alliances, the role of supporting classes such as the smallholding conservative peasantry and the lumpenproletariat, the relations between classes in charge of the state and economically dominant classes, and so forth (cf. Poulantzas, *PPSC,* pp. 229–253). They also examine the role of political parties in the representation of class interests in the struggle for control of the state apparatus and compare it with the effects of Bonapartism and other forms of executive rule. In short, at the same time as their analyses of political class struggle reveal the complexities of state power, they also affirm the importance of that struggle in securing control of the state apparatus and shaping its operation. This leads further credence to the instrumentalist approach.

The frequency of such arguments is reflected in subsequent studies. For the instrumentalist approach is particularly common in exegeses of the Marxian theory of the state and is widely adopted in more recent Marxist studies. In its pure form it is evident in analyses that reduce the class character of the state to the sociological question of the class affiliation of political elites and/or the politological question of the particular economic interests immediately advanced by government decisions and 'non-decisions'. In association with more or less complex forms of economic determinism it can be found in 'neo-Ricardian' analyses of economic policy-making and implementation as well as in various works stemming from 'state monopoly capitalism' theorists. Thus neo-Ricardians theorists have often focused on the instrumentality of the state for and on behalf of capital through its interventions to maintain or restore profits at the expense of wages (e.g., Boddy and Crotty, 1974; Glyn and Sutcliffe, 1972; and Gough, 1975). Likewise 'stamocap' theorists claim that the state and monopolies have 'fused' into a single mechanism which acts on behalf of monopoly capital in the twofold attempt to secure the political and ideological conditions necessary to capital accumulation and to secure various economic conditions that can no longer be realised through the operation of market forces (see chapter 2).

Interpreted in a different manner this instrumentalist view also underlies the reformism of social democratic movements. These tend to see the state apparatus in liberal parliamentary regimes as an independent, neutral instrument which can be used with equal facility and equal effectiveness by all political forces and they have therefore concentrated on the pursuit of electoral victory as the necessary (and sometimes even the sufficient) condition of a peaceful, gradual, and majoritarian transition to socialism. In certain respects this 'social democratic' conception of the state as instrument is also evident in the growth of right-wing 'Eurocommunism'[1] and, indeed, some of the arguments advanced by Engels in relation to

[1] Eurocommunism developed as a political strategy concerned with a democratic road to democratic socialism in the advanced capitalist societies. Within this broad strategic orientation it is possible to distinguish two currents: left and right. Rightwing Eurocommunists tend to view the transition as gradual and progressive, based on an anti-monopoly class alliance under the leadership of the communist vanguard party, and oriented to the strengthening of parliamentary control over the state and economic systems in association with certain measures of trade union participation in plant management and economic planning. Leftwing Eurocommunists tend to view the transition as a long series of ruptures and breaks, based on a national-popular, broad democratic alliance involving new social movements as well as class forces and organised in a pluralistic manner, and oriented to the restructuring of the state and economy so that there is extensive democracy at the base as well as an overarching, unifying parliamentary forum. In this sense rightwing Eurocommunism has marked affinities with orthodox analyses of state monopoly capitalism and leftwing Eurocommunism owes more to the influence of Gramsci's account of hegemony as 'political, intellectual, and moral leadership'.

the electoral progress of Social Democracy in Germany give credence to this conception (see the discussion of Engels's 'political testament' in Przeworski, 1980, *passim*).

In a different guise again instrumentalism is also common among Marxist social and political scientists engaged in theoretical combat with various liberal and pluralist positions. A classic work in this context is Ralph Miliband's study of *The State in Capitalist Society* — although it would be wrong to suggest that Miliband is committed to a simple instrumentalist position (see Miliband, 1969, pp. 23–67, and *idem*, 1977, pp. 66–74). But, as the debate between Miliband and Poulantzas indicates, there is little agreement that instrumentalism is the most adequate approach to a Marxist analysis of the state and politics.

Indeed a close examination of the work of Marx and Engels themselves should be sufficient to disclose several problems with such an approach. Firstly there is some uncertainty in its formulation. For Marx and Engels generally allude to the simple instrumentality of the state in aphorisms and metaphors rather than in more extended and concrete analyses; in other contexts they employ different formulations and contrary arguments. In the second place, if one accepts a simple instrumentalist approach, it is difficult to account for the different forms of the state as well as to explain why it is necessary to smash or transform the state apparatus rather than seize its control. In general Marx and Engels resolve the problem of different forms (and the attendant problem of dismantling one form so that it can be replaced with another) in terms of changes in the economic base and/ or in the balance of class forces. But it is difficult to square such solutions with the view that the state is an essentially *neutral* instrument in so far as they imply that its class character is determined at least in part through the correspondence between its form and the economic infrastructure and/or that its accessibility and 'use-value' can be modified through changes in its institutional structures. Thirdly, while a simple instrumentalist view implies that the state apparatus is non-partisan and passive in its personnel and orientation, as early as the 1843 *Critique* Marx had referred to its penetration by competing private interests (Marx, 1843a, pp. 3–129). Fourthly, if the state is a simple instrument of class rule, it is necessary to explain how the dominant mode of production is successfully reproduced when the economically dominant class does not actually occupy the key positions in the state system. This situation is noted by Marx and Engels themselves in relation to the political rule of the landed aristocracy on behalf of capital in the nineteenth-century Britain (Marx and Engels, 1962, pp. 423–427). The same problem is raised when the state apparatus acquires an extensive measure of independence from the dominant class owing to a temporary equilibrium in the class struggle. This situation is alleged to have occurred in the absolutist state in connection with a temporary equilibrium between feudal lords and ascendant bourgeoisie, the Second French Empire under Louis Bonaparte in connection with a temporary equilibrium between a declining bourgeoisie and an ascendant proletariat, and the German Reich under Bismarck in connection with a temporary equilibrium involving the feudal nobility, an ascendant bourgeoisie, and an ascendant proletariat (see particularly: Marx and Engels, 1845–1846, p. 90; Marx, 1852, pp. 128–129, 139, 172–173, and *passim*; Marx, 1871, p. 208; Engels, 1872, pp. 348–349; Engels, 1878, pp. 417–421; and Engels, 1884, pp. 328–329; for a detailed account of such analyses of this autonomisation of the capitalist state, see Draper, 1977, pp. 311–590). Indeed, whereas the simple instrumentalist thesis would seem to suggest that the dominant class is generally in immediate and overall control of the state system, it is evident from the many political studies of Marx and Engels that the bourgeoisie rarely occupies such a position in any capitalist society and that it is so vulnerable to internal disunity and fractioning that it lacks the political capacities to rule in its own name and/or to its own long-term interest. The *locus classicus* for such an argument is Marx's celebrated interpretation of *The Eighteenth Brumaire of Louis Bonaparte* (1852, *passim*) but it can also be found in other studies (for a valuable symptomatic reading of relevant texts supporting this interpretation, see: Poulantzas, *PPSC*, pp. 258–262). These views are so prevalent in the various *pièces de circonstance* penned by Marx and Engels that exegetists are frequently obliged to refer to the existence of *two* Marxian theories of the state: an instrumentalist account and an account of the state as an independent force 'standing outside and above society' (e.g., Maguire, 1978, pp. 24–27 and *passim*; Miliband, 1965, pp. 278–296; and Hunt, 1974, pp. 121–130). This suggests the need for a thorough reappraisal of the instrumentalist reading of the Marxian theory of the state and its subsequent development by latter-day Marxists.

THE STATE AS A FACTOR OF COHESION

In this context we should consider the argument that the state is the factor of cohesion in the social formation. This perspective is closely identified nowadays with the anti-instrumentalist arguments of

Poulantzas (see chapter 4, pp. 153–191) but it is also evident in the classic Marxist texts. Thus Marx and Engels argue in *The German Ideology* that an institutionally separate state emerges *before* the development of class antagonism to manage the common affairs of the members of gentile society. Such an institution is socially neces- sary because of the mutual interdependence of the individuals in any society with a complex division of social labour (Marx and Engels, 1845–1846, pp. 46–47). It should be noted that, although this argu- ment is continuous with the Hegelian framework of 'state-civil society' and 'public-private', it is also articulated with concepts relat- ing to class analysis. This is apparent from the subsequent argument that the public power of gentile society is over-determined in its operation by the emergence of class conflict rooted in an antagonis- tic mode of production. Thereafter the socially necessary institution becomes a class institution as well and the state must be sensitive to the complex relations between the common interest and class interests. In this respect Marx and Engels suggest that the conquest of state power presupposes the successful representation of a class interest as the general interest and thereby anticipate much subsequent Marxist analyses of 'hegemony' in the sense of 'political, intellectual, and moral leadership' aimed at winning the 'active consent' of the domi- nated sectors to the rule of capital (Marx and Engels, 1845–1846, p. 60).

These ideas are taken up in later studies by both founding fathers but are not re-stated with the same clarity and simplicity until Engels presented his general observations on the origins of the state. Thus Marx refers to the English factory acts as essential not only for the physical survival of the working class but also for its reproduction as variable capital but notes that this legislation to secure the interests of capital as well as the conditions for general social reproduction had to be enacted against substantial bourgeois opposition (Marx, 1867, pp. 264–280). Engels discusses the housing question in Ger- many in analogous terms (Engels, 1872, pp. 323–324 and *passim*). Likewise Marx notes in *The Eighteenth Brumaire* that the political need to restore social order in France as a precondition of the con- tinued social power and economic domination of the bourgeoisie induced it to abandon its control over the state apparatus through parliament in favour of a strong executive under the personal sway of Louis Bonaparte (Marx, 1852, pp. 128–129, 139, 171, 175–176, and *passim*). Finally, in his general treatise on *The Origins of the Family, Private Property, and the State*, Engels argues that the state is necessary to moderate the conflicts between antagonistic classes and keep them within the bounds of social order. This is a complex functional requirement. For, while the state must appear to stand above society and keep class antagonisms in check, it is normally the state of the most powerful, economically dominant class. As a rule its class function predominates over its socially necessary function but abnormal or exceptional periods occur when the warring classes are so nearly equal in strength that the state apparatus, as apparent mediator, acquires for the moment a certain independence from the immediate (or, indeed, indirect) control of these classes (Engels, 1884, pp. 326–329). The role and effects of such an independent state power in maintaining both social cohesion and capital accumulation need to be examined case by case.

This approach lends itself to various lines of development. Thus Bukharin attempted to develop a scientific analysis of the state in his general sociological work on *Historical Materialism.* He treats society as a system of unstable equilibrium inside which the state functions as a 'regulator' and attempts to manage or absorb contradictions between the productive forces and production relations and/or between the economic base as a whole and the various elements of th superstructure. In this sense Bukharin provides a mechanistic account of the emergence of 'organised capitalism' or 'state capitalism' which anticipates in certain respects subsequent work on 'state monopoly capitalism'. In addition to the role of the state in maintaining this unstable equilibrium in the face of disturbances that are allegedly determined in the last instance through the development of the forces of production, Bukharin also refers to the role of a normative system which requires individuals to subordinate their particular interests to those of the (class) society as a whole (Bukharin, 1921, pp. 150–154, 157–158, 229, 262–267, 274, and *passim*; for reviews of Bukharin's theory of equilibrium, see Cohen, 1975, pp. 107–122, Gramsci, 1971, pp. 419–472, and Hoffman, 1972, pp. 126–136). Gramsci is also concerned with the problem of cohesion and the role of the state in maintaining some correspondence between base and superstructure: but his approach is far less mechanistic and eschews Bukharin's determinism. For Gramsci is especially interested in the ideological and political practices through which the dominant class (or class fraction) maintains its class hegemony through the articulation of the narrow 'economic-corporate' interests of subordinate classes and/or the 'national-popular' traditions of the masses with its own long-term class interests so that the various dominated classes and groups consent to their economic exploitation and political oppression (see Gramsci, 1971, *passim*). This approach has been further developed in neo-Gramscian studies such as those of Poulantzas or Laclau and Mouffe. Thus, in rejecting economism and class reductionism and attempting to develop an account of the 'non-necessary correspondence' between base and superstructure, Laclau and Mouffe argue that the unity or cohesion of a social formation are the product of specific ideological and political practices mediated through the role of the state and/or private institutions (see Laclau and Mouffe, 1981, pp. 17–22). Moreover, whereas other theorists tend to treat cohesion as the contingent effect of state intervention, Poulantzas initially defined the state in terms of its necessary and objective function in the reproduction of social cohesion. This approach was associated with an inclusive conception of the state as comprising all those political and ideological apparatuses through which cohesion is maintained. It also implies that, in so far as the state secures the global cohesion of the social formation so that the process of capital accumulation can proceed unhindered at the economic level and regardless of whether or not the state acts in the immediate, short-term economic interests of the dominant class, it is nonetheless a class state (see Poulantzas, *PPSC, passim*; for an account of his ensuing theoretical development, see chapter 4 below).

This approach not only involves serious theoretical difficulties when it is developed in a one-sided manner but it can also produce rather odd results even in less extreme formulations. Thus, although Poulantzas adopted a functionalist and essentialist definition of the state focusing on its role in the maintenance of social cohesion, he presents several case studies which show that cohesion is a contingent rather than necessary effect of state power. Likewise, although he includes all those apparatuses which contribute to cohesion within his overall definition of the state, his own studies reveal that there are significant differences between liberal and fascist regimes in the boundaries of the 'public' and 'private' and in the articulation between repressive and ideological state apparatuses (see Poulantzas, *FD, passim*). Yet it is far from clear how such differences can be squared with his all-inclusive definition of the state. These inconsistencies in the work of Poulantzas seem less significant, however, when compared with the one-sided arguments developed in other theoretical and political analyses. For, unless one insists with Marx and Engels on the complex and contingent articulation of the socially necessary and the class functions of the state, concern with the role of the state in maintaining social cohesion can easily lead to the conclusion that it can 'reconcile' class conflict by acting as a neutral mediator and peace-maker. This essentially Jacobin or social democratic conception was criticised by Marx himself in *The Eighteenth Brumaire* (Marx, 1852, p. 130). Likewise, in opposition to the bourgeois and petit bourgeois politicians who equate social cohesion with class reconciliation, Lenin stresses that 'order' involves the oppression of one class by another and the systematic denial of means and methods of struggle to the oppressed class. Indeed, owing to his neglect of the 'socially necessary' moment of the state, Lenin argues that, had it been possible to reconcile classes, the state would never have arisen nor been able to maintain itself (Lenin, 1917g, p. 387). Nonetheless, without accepting Lenin's class reductionism and his all too one-sided emphasis on the repressive role of the state, we can still view the state as an organ of class domination and examine how various forms of representation and intervention help to sustain a balance of political forces simultaneously compatible with social cohesion and the accumulation of capital. There is certainly no necessity in moving from a recognition of the role of hegemony as well as coercion in social reproduction to the conclusion that the state is neutral and able to conjure away the material bases of class antagonism.

THE STATE AS AN INSTITUTIONAL ENSEMBLE

Finally it is necessary to consider the presupposition of all the themes and arguments outlined in the preceding pages. For we have not yet established the Marxian definition of the state and examined its implications for political analysis. Indeed, although the point is often ignored in exegeses of Marxian political theory, the themes and arguments reviewed above presuppose a definition of the state rather than provide it. Hence the assertion that the state is an epiphenomenon (simple or complex) of an economic base is a theoretical proposition; the claim that the state is an instrument of class rule is best interpreted metaphorically rather than literally and is at best inexact as to the nature of the instrument; and the view that the state is a factor of cohesion performing socially necessary as well as class functions could be seen as an empirical generalisation. In short these approaches might usefully be interpreted as adjectival rather than substantive, as predicates rather than subjects as propositional rather than definitional, as synthetic rather than analytic. This is not to downgrade these approaches but to insist that we reconsider their theoretical status within the Marxian system. In turn this means that we must examine how Marx and Engels actually defined the state itself.

The institutional separation of state and civil society was taken for granted by Marx and Engels in their earliest writings and they did not concern themselves at length with its genesis until *The German Ideology*. In this work they still take the form of this separate entity for granted and merely allude to its control of military force and its connections with the legal system. In general Marx and Engels view the state as a 'public power' that develops at a certain stage in the social division of labour and that involves the emergence of a distinct system of government which is separated from the immediate control of the people over whom it exercises authority. A degree of economic surplus is needed to support this 'public power' and its realisation of socially necessary and/or class functions. In terms of the latter Marx and Engels identify the emergence of the state (or its overdetermined transformation from an organ of gentile society into an organ of class domination) with the rise of private property in the means of production and/or the emergence of modes of production based on the exploitation of one class by another. They generally refer to its control of the means of coercion and often employ ostensive definitions which offer a more or less complete list of the institutions that comprise the state.

Thus, in his justly celebrated study of *The Eighteenth Brumaire of Louis Bonaparte,* Marx refers to the French state as '(this) executive power, with its enormous bureaucratic and military organisation' and proceeds to discuss its forms of representation and their transformation (Marx, 1852, p. 185). Likewise, in his address on *The Civil War in France,* he identifies the French state as '(the) centralised state power, with its ubiquitous organs of standing army, policy, bureaucracy, clergy, and judicature' (Marx, 1871, p. 217). And, in *Critique of the Gotha Programme,* Marx refers to the Prussian state as 'a state which is no more than a military despotism and a police state, bureaucratically carpentered, embellished with parliamentary forms and disguised by an admixture of feudalism' (Marx, 1875, p. 356). Several similar ostensive definitions are offered by Engels in his various studies of England, Germany, and other countries. In addition, in his general treatise on the origins of the state, Engels identifies its defining attributes as organisation on a territorial basis, specialised coercive apparatus or force, taxation, administrative staff, and, as a rule, political rights graded on the basis of property (Engels, 1884, pp. 155–156). But it is the less well-specified definitions that provide the framework within which Marx and Engels develop their arguments about the concentration and centralisation of power in the modern military-bureaucratic state and their analysis of the changing balance of political forces in various forms of state in nineteenth-century Europe.

There have been few attempts to develop a Marxist theory of the state based on a narrow institutional definition similar to those of orthodox social and political science. Such an approach has obvious theoretical difficulties for historical materialism since it tends to treat the state as a 'thing' in isolation from other institutions and/or as a separate instance engaged in external relations with other structures. This means that the 'relative autonomy' of the state becomes total and the complex internal relations between the different levels of a social formation dominated by a determinate mode of production are ignored. In short, given the orthodox account of the relations between economic base and political superstructure or, indeed, more sophisticated accounts of the internal relations among various structures in a social formation, it is evident that most Marxist analyses will eschew a straightforward institutional approach.

Nonetheless many studies adopt an institutional definition in association with an instrumentalist approach in the false belief that this is sufficient to establish the class nature of state power. This is particularly clear in the opening chapters of Ralph Miliband's analysis of *The State in Capitalist Society*. For, although he emphasises that the state is not at all a unitary thing but instead comprises a number of institutions which interact as parts of a 'state system', it is the activities of the people who occupy the leading positions in these institutions and thus constitute the 'state elite' that are said to determine the class nature of state power (Miliband, 1969, pp. 49, 54, and *passim*). In later chapters, however, Miliband emphasises the veto power of 'business confidence' entailed in the institutional separation of the economic and political – a power that is independent of interpersonal connections – and also discusses the role of ideological practices rooted in civil society in shaping the political agenda (ibid., pp. 151–153, 179–264). In this way Miliband points beyond institutionalism and instrumentalism and adumbrates an analysis of the 'form-determination' of state power that stops well short of ascribing an *a priori,* essentially capitalist character to the state in capitalist societies.

Such an *a priori* approach is found in the economic reductionism of the 'capital logic' variant of the form derivation school and its analysis of the state as 'an ideal collective capitalist'. It is also evident in the work of those who seek to prove the class character of the state in terms of its very organisational structure. Thus, in rejecting the view that the state elite must act willy-nilly in favour of capital owing to over-riding external economic constraints as well as in rejecting the claim that it is sufficient to change the class background and attitudes of this elite to change state policies, several theorists argue that there is an in-built 'structural selectivity' that does not simply introduce a bias into the policy-making process but actually ensures that the state will only produce pro-capitalist policies (e.g., Offe, 1972; but see also Offe's more recent work for a retreat from this hardline position). Yet another form of essentialism can be found in the recent debate on the nature of the dictatorship of the proletariat and its implications for political strategy in the workers' movement. Thus, in opposition to the sort of instrumentalism that often underlies the right-wing Eurocommunist refusal of the dictatorship of the proletariat, Balibar has argued that state power is always the political power of a single class, which holds it in an absolute way, does not share it with any other class, and does not divide it up among its own fractions. He also argues that the state power of the ruling class is embodied in the development and operation of the state apparatus which therefore has an absolute and unequivocal class character, cannot be used in neutral fashion, and must be 'smashed' as an essential precondition of the transition to socialism (Balibar, 1977, pp. 64–77; for a critique, see Jessop, 1978b). Unfortunately, although such essentialist approaches may be valuable in polemical discourse about party strategy (and even this concession is debateable in the light of the recent history of the PCF), they are most inappropriate to analyse the complex and contingent articulation of different apparatuses into a more or less unified state system or to assess the various effects of state power on the reproduction of bourgeois political domination as well capital accumulation. In this respect it would be preferable to adopt an institutional approach in combination with a firm grasp of Marxist political economy and an historical appreciation of the nature of class and popular-democratic struggles.

It is significant that Marx and Engels themselves do not offer a conclusive, abstract definition of the state similar to those presented for commodity, value, organic composition, etc., in *Das Kapital.* For, while Marx is concerned with the analysis of a pure mode of production at high levels of abstraction in the latter work, it is concrete social formations with which he and Engels are concerned in their various political studies. This has fundamental implications for their analysis of the state in capitalist societies. For, as Marx himself argues in his well-known 1857 *Introduction* to the method and concepts of political economy, 'real-concrete' phenomena cannot be grasped in themselves but must be reconstituted in thought as the 'complex synthesis of multiple determinations' (Marx, 1857, p. 101).

This implies that the state is both the point of departure and the point of arrival in political analysis since it can only be comprehended after a complex process of theoretical analysis and synthesis. It means that one cannot take the state as an unproblematic empirical given nor reduce it to one of its multiple determinations. Thus, if the narrow institutional approach and the view of the state as a unitary subject share the assumption that the state is a given, both economic and class reductionism take a one-sided approach and define the state only in relation to the mode of production or to the class struggle. This does not mean that it is illegitimate to focus upon particular determinations of the state apparatus and/or state power; nor that it is illegitimate to focus on specific effects of the state and its interventions on other elements of the social formation or the pure mode of production. But it does mean that such abstract and restricted forms of analysis are not equivalent to a concrete analysis of specific forms of state or state power in determinate conjunctures.

This is emphasised by Marx in his *Critique of the Gotha Programme* of the German Social Democratic Party. For he argues that, while one can generalise about 'present society' across national boundaries, it is impossible to do so about the 'present state'. Thus, whereas capitalism could be found in all 'civilised countries' and varies only in its degree of development, the form of state changes with each country's border and differs between the Prusso-German empire and Switzerland, between England and the United States. However, although Marx concludes that ' "*the* present state" is thus a fiction', he also argues that modern states share certain essential characteristics. This follows from the fact that, despite their motley diversity of form, states in the civilised countries all stand on the ground of modern bourgeois society. This means that one can talk of 'present states' in contrast to the future when their present root, bourgeois society, will have died off (Marx, 1875, p. 26). But it is still necessary to examine each state in its own terms rather than treat all capitalist states as identical because of their common foundation. Thus Marx points out that the failure of the SPD to grasp the fictitious character of 'the present state' leads to a 'riotous misconception' of the Prusso-German empire to which the Social Democrats addressed their demands. In turn this means that their political programme and strategy are dishonest and unworkable (1875, pp. 25 and 27). In short both the 1857 *Introduction* and the 1875 *Critique* suggest that it is incorrect to adopt an essentialist approach to the state and that one must always engage in a complex process of analysis and synthesis in order to comprehend 'present states' and change them.

CONTINUITY AND DISCONTINUITY

We have examined in broad terms the various themes and arguments of the mature theory of the state adopted by Marx and Engels. But this review still leaves certain questions unanswered. I have suggested that these themes remain unchanged (except in their articulation with each other) from *The German Ideology* to the final texts on the state. Yet I also argued that it was unreasonable to expect the young Marx to have developed a mature Marxist political theory in his critical remarks on Hegel and Bauer since he had not yet developed the central concepts of his mature political economy. Does this imply that there should be some discontinuity in the development of the Marxian theory of the state? Conversely, in his *The Civil War in France,* Marx repeats the demand for the abolition of the abstract state and the creation of real democracy. Does this imply that Marx has returned to the themes and arguments of his Hegelian-Jacobin youth? In short we must ask whether there are major elements of continuity and/or discontinuity that our rapid overview of Marxian state theory has distorted or ignored.

It must first be emphasised that the Marxian analysis of state power was throughout this period basically 'class-theoretical' rather than 'capital-theoretical' in orientation. For Marx and Engels were generally concerned with political class struggle focused on control of the state apparatus and its use in the repression of the dominated classes and/or the consolidation of bourgeois power. They were less often concerned with the integration of the state into the circuit of capital or the effects of state power on the reproduction of capital at the economic level. Marx discusses such topics in detail only in *Das Kapital* and even then confines the analysis to primitive accumulation, social legislation, and banking. Likewise, in his analysis of *The Role of Force in History,* Engels examines the role of the Prussian state under Bismarck in the creation of a national market and certain other conditions necessary to accumulation in Germany (Engels, 1888, 378–381 and 398–400). He also notes in *Anti-Dühring* that 'the modern state . . . is only the organisation that bourgeois society takes on in order to support the general external conditions of the capitalist mode of production against the encroachments as well of the workers as of individual capitalists' (Engels, 1878, p. 386). It could thus be said that Engels anticipated the work of the 'capital logic' school on the state as an 'ideal collective capitalist'. But neither he nor Marx elaborate these insights into a coherent, general theoretical account of the capitalist state premised on the nature and dynamics of the capitalist mode of production. And, although it is true that Marx had intended to write on the state in *Das Kapital,* this does not alter the overall lack of such an account elsewhere in their work on political economy. It is for this reason that there may well be more continuity in the Marxian analysis of the state than Marx and Engels themselves may have intended or wished.

In this connection it should also be noted that Marx and Engels do mention the forms of state and law that correspond in various ways to the dominance of the capitalist mode of production. Thus both men discuss the emergence of Roman law and the juristic world outlook with the growth of capitalism and demonstrate how legal equality in the realm of circulation and exchange underwrites the domination of capital over wage-labour in the sphere of production (Marx, 1867, pp. 172 and 547; Engels, 1886a, pp. 370–372; Engels, 1886b, *passim*; and Marx and Engels, 1975, pp. 355 and 399). Likewise both argue that the development of the capitalist mode of production permits and/or requires changes in the state apparatus. In particular they refer to the centralisation of power in the modern state and the correspondence between capitalism and the parliamentary republican regime (e.g., Marx and Engels, 1848, p. 486; Marx, 1850, *passim*; Marx, 1852, *passim*). But these arguments are part of the 'base-superstructure' tradition and are not elaborated into a coherent 'capital-theoretical' account of the state as envisaged by the West German 'form derivation' theorists. Indeed Marx and Engels relate most of these political tendencies in the modern state to the changing balance of political forces as well as to the economic base and thereby give these analyses a 'class-theoretical' as much as a 'capital-theoretical' slant.

More significant for the overall development of the Marxian approach is the analysis of the Paris Commune presented in Marx's address on *The Civil War in France.* This text represents a major advance in his analysis of the state and revolution. In all three drafts of this study Marx stresses that, while the ruling classes and their different rival fractions can simply lay hold of the existing state apparatus and wield it as a ready-made agency for their own political purposes, it is essential for the working class to smash its repressive machinery and to reorganise the way in which its socially necessary functions are secured (Marx, 1871, pp. 244–250). The centralised state power of the modern state is said to be the organ of bourgeois domination in France even when it is not directly controlled by bourgeois deputies in Parliament. In most political upheavals in nineteenth-century France one had seen merely the dwarfish struggles between parliamentary and executive state forms, culminating in Bonapartism as the supreme expression of bourgeois class domination. But the Communards were not in revolt against this or that − legitimist, constitutional, republican, or imperialist − form of state power; their revolution was aimed against the state itself so that the people could resume control of its own social life (Marx, 1871, p. 250). This is a revolution that can only be carried out by the proletariat since only they have the incentive and power to do away with all classes and all forms of class rule. Indeed, whereas the state apparatus is the general organ of political class domination, the Commune is the political form and means of the social emancipation of labour. For the political instrument that has been used to secure the enslavement of the working class cannot also be employed as the political instrument of their self-emancipation. This requires a revolutionary new form of political organisation which ensures that the people control its own social life through direct and continuous involvement in all facets of government.

Now, although this crucial text is replete with instrumentalist metaphors, its basic thrust is strongly anti-instrumentalist. Indeed Marx implies that the state is a system of political domination whose effectiveness is to be found in its institutional structure as much as in the social categories, fractions, or classes that control it. In turn this implies that different forms of state have different effects on the balance of class forces and the course and outcome of political struggle. Thus the analysis of the inherent bias of the system of political representation and state intervention is logically prior to an examination of the social forces that manage to wield state power at a given point in time. This represents a basic shift in theoretical focus and illustrates a point made elsewhere by Engels in connection with historical materialist analyses of ideology: 'form is always neglected at first in favour of content' (Engels, 1886b, p. 435). Likewise, in writing a fresh preface to *The Communist Manifesto* in 1872 (one year after the Paris Commune), Marx and Engels emphasise that the general principles it lays down are as correct as ever but add that it has since been proved by the Commune that 'the working class cannot simply lay hold of the ready-made state machinery and wield it for its own purposes' (Marx and Engels, 1872, p. 102). This fundamental insight is also stressed in Lenin's remark in *The State and Revolution* that the bourgeois democratic republic is the best possible political shell for capital and that, once it has gained possession of this shell, capital establishes its power so securely that no change of persons, institutions, or parties can shake it (Lenin, 1917g, p. 393).

It is also taken up in recent work on the form and functions of the capitalist state (see chapter 3) as well as in the later studies of Poulantzas on state power as a form-determined condensation of political forces (see chapter 4). Unfortunately Marx himself does not develop this new approach in other political studies nor does Engels do more than repeat the arguments in his subsequent work. But it should be clear that, although certain of the ideas first presented in the 1843 *Critique* and 1844 *Introduction* are reproduced in this analysis of the Paris Commune, they have been radically transformed through their articulation with the concepts and principles of Marxian political economy. For the 'abstract state' is now seen as an organ of political class domination rather than an expression of the political self-estrangement of private individuals; the 'universal class' is no longer seen as a poverty-stricken mass precipitated through the acute social disintegration of modern society during the process of primitive accumulation and is now recognised as a wage-labouring class economically exploited through determinate relations of production by capital; and 'real democracy' is no longer premised on the reintegration of the schizoid 'public' and 'private' lives of modern man but on the class dictatorship (in the sense of a specific *form* of state as well as a specific social basis) of the proletariat in alliance with the urban petit bourgeoisie and rural peasantry. In short, far from marking a simple return to the radical-liberal blue-print of his political youth, this text sets the keystone in the arch of Marxian revolutionary theory.

MARX AND ENGELS ON METHOD

We have now examined the youthful philosophical reflections of Marx, the adumbration of a class theory of the state by Engels, its subsequent development by both men, and the final (albeit unfinished) approach implied in their comments on the Paris Commune. But I have not tried to establish *the* Marxian theory of the state. Indeed an attempt of this kind has been deliberately and studiously avoided throughout our review. In part this stems from the observation that Marx and Engels adopted different approaches and arguments according to the problems with which they were concerned from time to time and did not themselves attempt any systematisation of their various forms of analysis. But it also stems from my belief that it is impossible to establish a unitary and coherent theory of the state in general on the basis of the methods and principles of the Marxian critique of political economy.

It is true that Engels wrote a general treatise on the state but its exact theoretical status should be established before we conclude that a general theory of the state is possible. For Engels presents an historical account of three different paths of state formation (in Greece, Rome, and Germany) rather than a single theory of the origins of the state in general. And he then proceeds to discuss only the most abstract determinations of the state and state power rather than to give a complete account. This coincides with the arguments propounded by Marx in his 1857 *Introduction* concerning the method of political economy. For he insists that production in general does not exist in the real world but can still be a valid object of analysis in so far as it brings out and fixes the common element in all production and thus saves repetition; but, since production is always production at a definite stage of social development, it is always necessary to analyse production in each epoch as a complex synthesis of general and specific elements. In the same way it can be argued that the state in general is also a rational abstraction but can still be useful in theoretical work to the extent that it brings out the common elements and foundations of all states. Indeed, as Marx himself points out in his 1875 *Critique,* 'the present state' is a valid abstraction based on the essential characteristics of the motley diversity of all bourgeois states. But such conceptions must always be complemented and combined with many other determinations in order to produce an adequate account of concrete forms of state and state power. Thus, although Engels provides certain basic elements in a Marxist account of the state, his work does not (and cannot) amount to a definitive and exhaustive theory of the state. Only through the synthesis of many different determinations can one move from the abstract to the concrete and this involves the articulation of quite different principles of explanation and modes of analysis. For to attempt to produce a theoretical account of a specific state in a given conjuncture on the basis of a single causal principle is to engage in the most extreme form of reductionism or essentialism. In short, while a theoretical account of specific states is possible, no single theory of the state can be constructed without rejecting the basic premises of historical materialism.

This conclusion can be illustrated through the work of Marx and Engels themselves. Most of their political writings were produced to describe specific political events and to situate them in a specific historical context; and/or to provide a theoretical basis for the identification of political class interests and an appropriate mode of intervention in the class struggle. They draw on several different principles of explanation and combine different themes and approaches. They offer a series of acute generalisations and present a number of valuable practical concepts for conjunctural analysis. They focus upon the organisation of the state apparatus as well as the appropriation and organisation of state power. But they do not offer a systematic and coherent theory of the state based on any one given causal principle or major theme. It is the exegetists who have blocked further advance in the Marxist analyses of the state and state power through their desire to present a simple theory of this kind. This is particularly evident in the facile way in which many subsequent Marxists have seized upon the instrumentalist metaphor to exposit *the* Marxist theory of the state or, alternatively, reduced the state to a more or less complex epiphenomenon of an economic base. Nor is this criticism just a sign of academicism or theoreticism. For, as Marx himself argues in his 1875 *Critique,* errors of analysis concerning the 'present state' are linked to errors in political practice. It follows that no one can afford to ignore the specificity of the state apparatus and state power in the pursuit of objectives that are politically mediated and/or conditioned.

However, whilst it is important to notice the many complexities of the current situation and to adapt strategy and tactics to changing forms of state and the ever-changing balance of political forces, it is also essential to remember the most abstract determinations of the 'present state' and assess their implications too. Thus Marx stressed that, regardless of the specific forms of the modern state, it stood on the ground of capitalist relations of production. He also stressed elsewhere that it was the historic mission of the communist movement to abolish not merely the present capitalist state but also to end the separation of the state and civil society in all its forms. This suggests that an adequate theoretical analysis of the state must consider not only its economic determinations but also those rooted in the distinctive organisation of the state as well as in the social division of labour between officialdom and people. That Marx himself was interested in such issues is evident not only from his early remarks on the separation between the state and civil society (in addition to Marx, 1843a and 1843b, see especially the comments on state and administration in Marx, 1844b, pp. 192, 197–200) but also from his argument that the Paris Commune involved an assault on the very form of the state rather than one or another variant of the state form (Marx, 1871). It is also clear from his little-remarked discussion of the conditions and manner in which Louis Bonaparte succeeded (albeit temporarily) in displacing the principal contradiction in France from the opposition between bourgeoisie and proletariat to the opposition between officialdom and people (Marx, 1858b, *passim,* for commentary, see Draper, 1977, pp. 453–463, and Gulijew, 1977, pp. 41–42). That these comments are secondary in terms of the general thrust of the founding fathers' work on the state and, in relation to Marx's observations on the 'rule of the praetorians', little-remarked, does not mean that they can safely be ignored in the development of state theory. Indeed, as is argued in the concluding chapter, it is vital to include such determinations in a full analysis of the state. But we must first consider how the approaches that received greater emphasis in the work of Marx and Engels have been taken up and deployed in more recent Marxist theories.

2

State Monopoly Capitalism

'State monopoly capitalism' is the central organising concept of orthodox theories of the modern state advanced in the Soviet bloc and many western communist parties. These theories claim to explain the specific economic and political characteristics of the current stage of capitalism in terms of the fundamental contradictions and laws of the capitalist mode of production and their overdetermination through the development of the socialist world system. They also claim to produce correct conclusions about the strategy and tactics appropriate to a communist revolution in the conditions of advanced capitalism. However, while the 'state monopoly capitalism' approach is quite widely shared among communist parties, its application is also subject to wide variation. Indeed it would not be far-fetched to suggest that 'stamocap' theory is a shibboleth which disguises a broad range of assumptions, central concepts, principles of explanation, and political conclusions. Thus we must consider both the common ground and the variations to arrive at an adequate theoretical and political assessment of this approach.

State monopoly capitalism is usually treated as a distinct stage of capitalism characterised by the fusion of monopoly forces with the bourgeois state to form a single mechanism of economic exploitation and political domination. Moreover, even when such a formula is not used, there is still great emphasis on the growth of a close, organic connection between monopoly capital and the state. This development is supposed to advance the struggle to consolidate the economic and political domination of monopoly capital in the face of opposition from the oppressed classes and/or competition from the socialist world system during the general crisis of capitalism. Certain stamocap measures and tendencies can be discerned in the two world wars and the intervening depression but the full system was finally instituted only in the mid-fifties in response to a further intensifica-

32

tion of the so-called 'general crisis of capitalism'. In this context it is argued that state intervention has become a normal and, indeed, dominant element in the reproduction of capitalism. Moreover, whereas the state once acted as a committee for managing the affairs of the whole bourgeoisie, now it is said to intervene on behalf of monopoly capital to the total (or near total) exclusion of other fractions of capital. Thus, as well as its alleged functions in increasing the rate of exploitation of wage-labour and relieving the monopolies of essential but unprofitable economic tasks, the state is also supposed to exploit other classes and bourgeois fractions through its fiscal and budgetary policy and to reorganise all spheres of social life to maintain monopoly power and profits. However, although these changes allegedly result in the exploitation and oppression of virtually all the people, they are also said to prepare the material basis for the transition to socialism and to reveal the reactionary nature of imperialism. In turn this justifies the claim that the most suitable revolutionary strategy is an anti-monopoly, popular-democratic alliance embracing small and medium capital as well as the petit bourgeoisie and working class. For this should isolate monopoly capital and enable the conquest of state power in preparation for a peaceful and progressive transition to socialism and communism.

THE PRECURSORS OF 'STAMOCAP' THEORY

Its proponents often invoke Lenin as a pioneer of stamocap theory. However, while this might well establish the Marxist-Leninist orthodoxy of the 'stamocap' approach, there is little historical or theoretical warrant for this claim. For, although Lenin does mention 'state monopoly capitalism' in his work during the closing years of the First World War, he does not treat it as a distinct stage of capitalism, nor does he provide anything but a conjunctural explanation for it (see below). Conversely there are other Marxists who did anticipate and/or directly contribute to stamocap theory before its rediscovery and development in the 1950s. Thus, before examining the more recent studies, we shall consider the precursors of postwar stamocap theory.

The principal contribution of Lenin to the critique of political economy is found in his studies of imperialism and its implications. But, as in the earlier study of Hilferding on finance capital (1909), Lenin focuses on what one might term 'bank monopoly capitalism' rather than 'state monopoly capitalism'. For the five essential traits in his account of imperialism are the rise of monopolies, the fusion of bank and industrial capital, the export of capital, international cartels and trusts, and the territorial division of the world among the great capitalist powers (1916b, pp. 105–106; 1917b, p. 266 and *passim*). Lenin describes how the activities of different capitals are coordinated through banks and cartels by a new financial oligarchy and implies that the state is superfluous in this respect; indeed, on one occasion, he argues that the big banks themselves would become the 'state apparatus' necessary for socialist accounting in the transition period (1917h, p. 106). In general, Lenin treats the state as an essentially repressive instrument of political domination and so, apart from the use of extra-economic compulsion in the (re-)partition of the world through colonial annexations and imperialist wars, he hardly mentions its economic role. Moreover, when he turns to the political rather than the economic aspects of imperialism, he merely emphasises the reactionary nature of the state as monopoly capital tries to maintain its rule during a final period of capitalist stagnation and decay (1915a, pp. 301–302; 1916a, p. 43; 1916b, pp. 105–106; 1917b, pp. 268, 276–285, 301; 1917g, p. 410; 1918f, p. 239).

In contrast with his endless references to imperialism, Lenin does not discuss 'state monopoly capitalism' in any detail. It is typically seen as the product of increased, war-time state intervention to procure military supplies, overcome economic disorganisation, and relieve famine and/or as the result of a general acceleration of imperialist trends in war-time (1917a, p. 267; 1917c, pp. 73–74; 1917d, p. 240; 1917f, pp. 357–359; 1917i, p. 170; 1918e, p. 385; alternatively, 1917c, p. 205; 1917e, p. 403; 1918b, p. 22; 1918c, pp. 293–294, 298; 1919a, p. 170). And, although he makes his *only* reference to the fusion of capital and the state into a single mechanism in relation to German imperialism (1917e, p. 403) and generally cites Germany as the most advanced stamocap society (1917f, p. 357; 1918c, pp. 293–294; 1918d, p. 339; 1918e, pp. 385–386), Lenin's main focus is on the opportunity to build socialism in revolutionary Russian by extending the existing state sector and war-time controls (1917c, pp. 73–74; 1917f, *passim*; 1917g, pp. 442–443; 1918c, pp. 293–295; 1918d, pp. 334, 339; 1918e, pp. 385–386). When this gradualist strategy is rejected in favour of full-blooded 'War-Communism' after mid-1918, he effectively drops the stamocap issue. Thus, while Lenin does refer to 'state capitalism' again in defending the New Economic Policy against the Left Opposition some three years later, his focus has shifted from war-time changes in imperialism to the propriety of introducing state-sponsored, private capitalism en route to socialism in Russia (1921a, p. 345; 1921b, p. 491; 1921c, p. 58;

1922, pp. 278–279, 310–311). Despite certain verbal continuities, this issue actually has little to do with stamocap.

Nor does Lenin develop his ideas on the transition much beyond the arguments of Hilferding or Bukharin. Each argues that the concentration and centralisation of control under finance capitalism facilitates the seizure of the commanding heights of the capitalist economy; and that the techniques of administration and control implemented by the banks and/or the state can be employed during the transition to socialism (Hilferding, 1909, pp. 503–505; Lenin, 1917b, p. 205; 1917d, pp. 306, 310; 1917f, pp. 357–359; 1917g, pp. 426–427, 442–443, 473; 1917h, pp. 105–109; 1918c, pp. 294–295; and Bukharin, 1920, pp. 64–65, 116–118). But Lenin, following Bukharin, also argues that it is impossible to effect this transition without smashing the imperialist state and establishing new forms of political domination (Bukharin, 1916, *passim*; 1920, pp. 114–121; Lenin, 1917f, p. 357; 1917g, *passim*; 1918d, p. 339). Thus, not only did Lenin argue during the Kerensky regime that the change from the old 'reactionary-bureaucratic' state-form in the stamocap system to a new 'revolutionary-democratic' form would bring socialism visibly closer to fruition, but, following the Bolshevik revolution, he also proceeded to argue that the transition to socialism could be achieved simply through the substitution of the Soviet type of state for the capitalist type in a system of state monopoly capitalism (1917f, pp. 357–358; cf. 1918d, pp. 339, 342, 351; 1921b, p. 491). It is in this context that Lenin remarks that Germany and Russia embody between them in 1918 all the conditions necessary for socialism – the productive, economic, and socio-economic conditions in Germany, the political conditions in Russia (1918d, p. 340).

Overall Lenin's views on stamocap differ little from his general account of imperialism. Rather than presenting it as a separate stage of imperialism, he considers it either as a war-time variant and/or as a highly regulated variant. Nor does he provide a distinctive theoretical explanation for its emergence but instead describes it as a conjunctural phenomenon and/or as the ultimate embodiment of imperialist tendencies. Indeed his general analyses of imperialism also tend to describe rather than explain its principal attributes. Thus, although Lenin does link the emergence of monopolies to the operation of free competition, the concentration of industrial and banking capital, the socialisation of production, economic crises, and the growing mass of capital unable to find a field for profitable investment (1915a, pp. 301–302; 1916b, pp. 106–107; 1917b, pp. 197,

205, 209, 213–215, 276, 302–303), none of these explanatory factors is discussed in depth or at length. Instead Lenin is far more concerned to assess the ever-changing current situation and its implications for revolutionary strategy than he is to identify and elaborate the fundamental laws of motion of imperialism. Nor does he explore the economic nature and functions of the imperialist state – let alone the specific connections between monopoly capital and the state in state monopoly capitalism. In short, although Lenin can certainly be credited with introducing the idea (or, better, the label) of 'state monopoly capitalism', it would be quite wrong to identify him as its first and foremost theoretician.

Engels is also cited as a major source for stamocap theory on the grounds that he discusses 'state capitalism' in his critique of Eugen Dühring. He bases its development on the growing contradiction between the forces and relations of production and suggests that the progressive socialisation of productive forces requires a corresponding alteration in production relations. Initially, as Marx himself emphasised, this occurs in the form of the joint-stock company (*C3*, pp. 436–438). But Engels suggests that the joint-stock form could also prove too limited and that the state would therefore be forced to take over or establish production in important areas. He also notes that state capital paves the way for the eventual management of all productive forces by society itself (1878, pp. 384–387). Thus Engels attempts to found the necessity of state capitalism as a transitional form in the contradictions of capital accumulation. But he does so in terms of the forces/relations contradiction that holds for all modes of production rather than in relation to laws of motion specific to capitalism as such. His evolutionist approach thus lends itself to the view that the transition is inevitable and/or can be accomplished without any radical transformation in the nature of the state.

In contrast, although he anticipates many of the principal ideas of postwar stamocap theory, Bukharin's studies of 'state capitalism' are never cited. Until he is rehabilitated by the Soviet authorities his past conflicts with Lenin and Stalin will presumably continue to make him a 'non-person' theoretically as well as politically (cf. Cohen, 1975, pp. 22–25, 44–43, 270–336). Nonetheless Bukharin examines not only the international dimensions of imperialism but also its economic and political implications at home. He argues that state capitalism represents the historical and logical completion of finance capitalism. The state is no longer the simple guarantor of the general conditions of economic exploitation but has itself become directly involved in such exploitation on behalf of finance capital. The main forms of this development are state monopolies in production and trade, mixed enterprises based on public and private capital, and state control of credit. In all these cases the state acts as the highest organisational embodiment of finance capital and also coordinates the activities of lesser organisations (1917, pp. 108, 129, 149–150, 158; 1920, pp. 37–38). This transformation in the economic role of the state is reflected in the decline of parliamentarism and the concentration of political power (1917, pp. 124–128). Moreover, not only does the state reorganise the relations between enterprises, it must also reorganise the relations among classes. Thus, in addition to its expansion of the military and police apparatus and the absorption of institutions such as the church, the press, and education, the state also integrates trade unions and working-class parties and turns them into agencies of social control (1916, pp. 105–106; 1920, pp. 40–41). This 'leviathan state' thus fuses economic and political power into one colossal state-capitalist trust which carries on capitalist competition in the form of imperialist wars and colonial annexations. The growth of state capitalism shows that the time is ripe for a transition to socialism; and the impulse towards war creates the conditions for successful revolution as well as further accumulation (1917, pp. 144–160, 167; 1920, pp. 30–32, 162–173). In this context a transition to socialism demands not only the nationalisation of capitalist trusts but also the creation of new forms of proletarian economic and political domination (1916; 1920, pp. 114–132 and 150–152).

Despite his many insights into state capitalism, Bukharin's views also involve several theoretical problems. Thus he implies that state capitalism can eliminate capitalist anarchy within a society and also externalise competition and contradictions in the form of imperialist rivalry and war. Bukharin thus moves close to social democratic ideas of 'organised capitalism' and still retains a catastrophist analysis of the causes of revolution. Conversely he ignores the real limits to state intervention and the various forms of class struggle within the nation-state. This neglect is related to Bukharin's tendency to absolutise state power and treat the state as an all-embracing, omnipotent organisation which embodies the collective will of capital (e.g., 1917, p. 129; cf. Cohen, 1975, pp. 31–34 and 39). But this is inexact even in a total war economy and it is still less adequate as an account of the state in other conditions. Despite these difficulties, however, Bukharin's work more clearly and more fully anticipates recent studies of stamocap than does that of Engels, Hilferding, or Lenin.

After these early contributions, 'state monopoly capitalism' largely disappeared from theoretical view in the interwar period in favour of more general discussions of imperialism (although, as Roberts, 1977, has shown, even the latter concept remained undeveloped). This disappearance could be linked to the prevailing political priorities of the Comintern as well as to the partial economic disengagement of the state after the First World War. Thus, although 'war-time state monopoly capitalism' figures to a certain extent in Comintern theses during the earlier years of the postwar revolutionary crisis (dated 1917–1923), the ensuing period of so-called 'relative stabilisation' (dated 1924–1928) saw less concern with direct economic intervention by the imperialist state. Moreover, since Russia was now committed to building 'socialism in one country' and its leaders were still convinced that capitalism was in its death-throes as a result of the 'general crisis of capitalism', the Comintern was less concerned to wage an open revolution against moribund western imperialism than to contest the succession with social democracy. Hence the Comintern focused less on the ties between monopoly capital and its state than on the role of social democracy as the principal economic and political support of capital as a whole. Thus, although there are certainly frequent references to the subordination of the imperialist state to the financial oligarchy and to its use of extra-economic force as well as occasional references to state capitalist tendencies, there is no attempt to distinguish a separate stamocap stage in the terminal years of capitalism. Much more emphasis was given to the alleged fusion of social democracy (or at least its leaders) with the capitalist state than to any fusion of monopoly capital and the state into a single mechanism. This concern with social democracy as a prop of capitalism was already evident before the Bolshevik Revolution, intensified thereafter, and culminated in the charge of 'social fascism' levelled during the so-called 'third period' (1928–1935) against all social democratic movements in the West (for documentation, see Degras, 1956–1965, three vols., *passim*; for useful commentaries, see Borkenau, 1938; Braunthal, 1967; and Claudin, 1975). Admittedly, there was renewed interest in issues of state intervention with the development of the international economic crisis in the 'thirties. But, although there was increasing mention of state capitalist and/or state monopoly capitalist tendencies, there is still no attempt to distinguish between simple and state monopoly capitalism as stages within imperialism. Instead the growth of state intervention is typically understood as a final, abortive attempt to overcome the general crisis of capitalism and its economic effects (for a magisterial review of Soviet attitudes to western capitalism in the interwar period, which unfortunately appeared too late to be considered in any detail here, see Day, 1981, *passim*).

Thus Varga, the influential but maverick Hungarian economist, suggested that monopoly capitalism was turning into 'state war-monopoly capitalism' as preparations for the next imperialist war came to dominate efforts to resolve the economic crisis (1934, p. 68). This was reflected in the growth of the state budget, state control of foreign trade, state regulation of credit, state intervention in the labour market, and state determination of prices (1934, pp. 68–70). Measures to overcome the crisis artificially were associated with a growing struggle among different strata of the ruling class to influence state policy but its overall effect was to redistribute the national income in favour of monopoly capital (1934, pp. 63–70). The bourgeois response was also overdetermined by the rapid maturation of the general crisis – leading to the collapse of mass support for the capitalist system and political splits in the dominant classes. This accelerates the tendential fascisation of the capitalist state under the aegis of social democracy ('social fascism') and/or pure fascism based on the petit bourgeois and peasant masses (1934, pp. 139–162). But, since the fascist dictatorship is the final form of bourgeois rule and is itself crisis-ridden and self-contradictory, Varga concludes that a united front against fascism could soon win in the struggle for socialism (1934, pp. 163–173).

Indeed, once we turn from the analysis of stamocap as such to the Comintern's views on fascism after the close of its 'third period', certain themes that anticipate postwar stamocap studies become clear. Thus the new definition of fascism as 'the open, terrorist dictatorship of the most reactionary, most chauvinistic and most imperialist elements of finance capitalism' (Dimitroff, 1935, p. 10) presages the later stress on the exclusive appropriation of state power by monopoly capital to the detriment of other bourgeois fractions as well as the dominated classes. This analysis led to the strategy of a popular front against the fascist dictatorship – embracing non-monopoly capital as well as the subordinate classes, having at its heart a united front of social democratic as well as communist forces, and committed to a bourgeois-democratic restoration rather than an immediate transition to socialism. This strategy clearly anticipates the anti-monopoly alliance committed to 'advanced democracy' proposed in postwar stamocap theories. Conversely, after the adoption of these theories, fascism itself has been redefined as a specific form of state monopoly capitalism (e.g., Eicholz and Gossweiler, 1968, pp. 210–227; Hemberger *et al.,* 1965, pp. 60–72; Reinhold *et al.,* 1972, pp. 48–58).

POSTWAR 'STAMOCAP' THEORIES

Stamocap theories were first seriously and widely developed in the mid-1950s in an effort to account for the continued expansion of capitalism during the so-called 'second stage of the general crisis'. Initially these theories treated stamocap as a last-ditch attempt to shore up capitalism during its general crisis through the direct, personal subordination of the state to the financial oligarchy resulting in specific policies favouring monopoly capital and in a general militarisation of the economy in the interests of monopoly profit maximisation. Moreover, since this entailed ruin for the peasant and artisan classes as well as impoverishment for the proletariat and since palliative measures and self-contradictory attempts at capitalist 'planning' could not indefinitely prevent economic collapse, socialist revolution would be achieved through an anti-monopoly alliance under communist leadership in conditions of peaceful coexistence between the two world systems. Subsequent theoretical developments shifted attention towards state monopoly capitalism as a new stage of capitalism compatible with continued accumulation, allowed for the relative autonomy of the state to secure the collective interests of (monopoly) capital against those of particular capitals, considered the new forms of state intervention in the expansion of capitalism, and discussed the contribution of science and technology to postwar growth within the framework of capitalist relations of production. Increasing attention was also paid to the fiscal exploitation of pre-capitalist classes and the prefigurative character of capitalist planning for the transition to socialism. But, despite this remarkable sophistication and specification of stamocap theory, little change is evident in its political conclusions until the growth of 'Right Eurocommunism' induced a reappraisal of the Soviet Union as a model of advanced socialism and as the 'world-historical' representative of the working class (for a brief contrast between right and left variants of Eurocommunism, see p. 14 above).

At the end of the Second World War it was believed that the defeat of fascism and revolutionary solidarity with Russia would provide favourable conditions for a worldwide, socialist revolution and that this would be precipitated by economic collapse. Thus, although some analyses in the immediate postwar period suggested that the increased wartime economic role of the state would remain, that it could organise, regulate, and stimulate production on behalf of capital as a whole, and, indeed, that a new stage had emerged in the development of capitalism (above all, see Varga, 1946, *passim*), they were strongly criticised for abstracting from the general crisis of capitalism and its competition with the socialist world system, treating the state as classless and/or able to stand above the monopolies, mistaking state monopoly capitalist tendencies for the development of a new stage, and attempting a purely economic analysis without regard to the changing political context (for documentation, see Ostrovityanov, 1948, *passim*; for useful commentary, Barghoorn, 1948; Nordahl, 1974, pp. 239—251; Schlesinger, 1949; Tikos, 1965, pp. 80—93). The emergent Cold War reinforced the sterile dogmatism of Soviet theory and its subordination to the zigs and zags of political strategy. Indeed, from the early 1930s (Barber, 1976, 1979, *passim*), the views of Stalin and the political leadership were imposed forcefully and forcibly in all areas. In political economy these stressed the destruction of a single world market, the collapse of internal markets, the impossibility of real planning under capitalism, the end of 'relative stability' for the West, the growth of stagnation and decay, an absolute impoverishment of the working class, the inevitability of wars among the imperialist powers, and the growing competition between the two world systems (see Stalin, 1930, pp. 250—253; 1934, pp. 290—300; 1939, pp. 335—344; 1952, pp. 467—473; cf. the Stalinist textbook, Ostrovityanov *et al.*, 1955, pp. 332—373, 410—411). The basic law of modern capitalism was said to be the monopolies' striving for the maximum profit on a world scale and the state was supposed to have been directly subjugated by the monopolies in the attempt to maintain their economic and political domination (Stalin, 1952, pp. 473—478; cf. Ostrovityanov *et al.*, 1955, pp. 197—302, 324—326, 331). Economic studies in this period involved ritual incantations of Stalinist dogmas and/or empirical analyses of various postwar developments. Whenever it proved necessary to reconcile these procedures, recourse was made to temporary, accidental, and *ad hoc* features of the current situation, such as postwar reconstruction, militarisation of the economy, overdue renewal of fixed capital, and working class disunity (e.g., Ostrovityanov *et al.*, 1955, pp. 366—367). This situation prevailed until the 20th Congress of the CPSU initiated an open, albeit posthumous, break with Stalin's political economy along with his dictatorship (see Khruschev, 1956a, pp. 11—21; 1956b, *passim*; and, for a major and popular text laying to rest many Stalinist economic dogmas, Varga, 1963, *passim*).

For, although a few studies adumbrating new lines of theoretical enquiry had been started or published before 1956 (e.g., Kusminov, 1955; Gluschkov, 1955; Zieschang, 1956), the principal spur to renewed public discussion of state monopoly capitalism was the 20th

Congress and its break with Stalinism. A further stimulus emerged with the apparently successful interventions to resolve the 1957–58 crises in the dominant capitalist metropoles. This is not to argue that all party control over political economy ceased forthwith in 1956 (far from it) but it is to note the liberating effect of the Congress on the intellectual climate. Following the Congress there appeared a spate of works dealing with the transformation of contemporary capitalism and suggesting that state monopoly capitalism really did signify a qualitatively new stage of imperialism (e.g., Cheprakov, 1956; Varga, 1958; Kuusinen, 1961; Zieschang, 1956). These new theories were then ratified and expounded in various communist conferences and included in new editions of party programmes and textbooks (cf. reports in *World Marxist Review, seriatim*).

The subsequent development of stamocap theory renders any simple account impossible owing to its political zig-zags, totalising ambition, multilateral development, and increasing sophistication. Moreover, even if we focus on the principal themes of mainstream stamocap analyses, several schools or tendencies can be distinguished. These stem from important differences in theoretical starting-point. Thus studies that proceed from Lenin's analysis of imperialism tend to explain state monopoly capitalism in class-theoretical terms. In particular they invoke the imperatives of maintaining the domination of monopoly capital over other fractions, classes, etc., in a moribund imperialism and/or of promoting the military might and economic strength of capitalism in its struggle against socialism (itself seen as the representative of the working class on a world-historical plane). Often such works also tend to suggest the causal primacy of the power strivings of monopoly capital and/or the dominant role of extra-economic force in the present stage of capitalism. In contrast those stamocap analyses that start out from Marx's critique of political economy tend to be capital-theoretical and to suggest the causal primacy of the basic laws of motion of capitalism. Most of these studies focus on the growing socialisation of the forces of production and/or on the tendency of the rate of profit to fall and the political mobilisation of counter-tendencies. The increasing role of the state in crisis-management is also emphasised here. In addition French stamocap theory invokes the overaccumulation of private monopoly capital and its devalorisation through the state. There are also many factors and themes that receive more or less equal emphasis regardless of the particular theoretical tradition from which stamocap is studied. Nor should it be assumed that these traditions are mutually exclusive. Indeed many texts attempt to combine them and thus produce more general, if somewhat eclectic, accounts of the origins, nature, and significance of state monopoly capitalism.

THE GENERAL CRISIS OF CAPITALISM

Imperialism and the 'general crisis of capitalism' occupy a central position in most theories but should not be conflated. For, whereas the development of imperialism is located in the closing decades of the nineteenth century and is explained in terms of tendencies inherent in capitalism, the 'general crisis' is provoked by the Bolshevik Revolution and unfolds according to the dialectical interplay between capitalism and socialism. The 'general crisis' affects all areas — economic, political, and ideological — of capitalism; leads to its general decline as a viable world system; and drives it forward to the 'threshold of socialism'. It results from the intensification of all the fundamental contradictions of capitalism: especially those between the forces and relations of production, capital and labour, imperialist metropoles and dependent peripheries, and inter-imperialist rivalries. But these contradictions are overdetermined by the fundamental contradiction of the present world epoch: the division of the world into two opposed social systems, the struggle between them, and the inexorable forward march of socialism. For it is the dialectical interplay among the internal contradictions of metropolitan imperialism, the crisis of (neo-)colonialism and the growth of national liberation movements, and the increasing strength of the socialist bloc that conditions the fate of capitalism on a world historical plane. It is these same phenomena and their development that enable one to periodise the general crisis (cf. Heininger, 1975, p. 27).

Thus the first stage of the general crisis was initiated with the 'Great Socialist October Revolution'. This is supposed to have led to the first ever shrinkage in the world market for capitalism; to an intensification of worldwide revolutionary struggles, colonial and national liberation movements; and to the deepening of economic crises culminating in the Great Depression, fascism, and world war. The latter in turn initiated the second stage of the general crisis with the growth of a socialist world system in Europe and Asia and a further loss of markets; a renewed upswing in national liberation struggles; and the introduction of neo-colonialism and the strengthening of state monopoly capitalist tendencies in the vain effort to prevent the collapse of imperialism. The third stage emerged during the mid-1950s as the continued expansion of the socialist bloc allegedly transformed it into the dominant pole in the contradiction between the two world systems. Particularly influential here were Soviet achievements in the scientific and technical revolution (e.g., the 'Sputnik shock', atomic weapons, and economic growth); communist victories in Korea, Indochina, and Cuba; and the increasing collapse of the colonial system. There was also growing instability within the imperialist metropoles and a new upswing in class struggle. In response there occurred the final consolidation of state monopoly capitalism in the leading capitalist societies and the growing internationalisation of capitalist relations in an abortive attempt to rescue the moribund capitalist world system through state intervention and more effective imperialist exploitation. But in the long-term they bring it ever closer to the threshold of socialism and so prepare the material base for the coming revolution (e.g., Autorenkollektiv, 1975; Gerns, 1974; Haak *et al.*, 1973, pp. 213–239; Heininger, 1975; Jung and Schleifstein, 1979, pp. 26–28; Klein, 1974, pp. 5–89; Inosemzew *et al.*, 1972, pp. 13–118; Kozlov, 1977, pp. 375–394; Reinhold *et al.*, 1971, pp. 124–125; Varga, 1961, pp. 34–81, 112–116, 144–147; Wygodski, 1972, pp. 496–511).

Some recent studies claim to discern the birth of a new phase of the third stage of the general crisis. They link this to continued expansion of the socialist world system, fresh victories for the Soviet policy of peaceful coexistence, weakening of the principal imperialist powers owing to the raw material and energy crises, crises in the relations among the USA, EEC, and Japan, growing instability and stagflation, and a sharp upturn in economic class struggles. This new phase is coupled with strenuous attempts by the monopolies to step up the rate of economic exploitation and to move to more authoritarian forms of rule. In France this is expressed in the assertion that the system of state monopoly capitalism itself has entered crisis (e.g., Boccara, 1977, pp. 315–344, 391–414, and 471–498) but arguments that a new phase in the third stage of the general crisis has occurred and/or that the stamocap system itself is in deep crisis are also expounded in other traditions (e.g., Gerns, 1974, pp. 17–41; Heininger, 1975, pp. 34–46; Jung and Schleifstein, 1979, p. 32; Klein, 1974, pp. 65–87; *World Marxist Review, seriatim*). There have also been some half-hearted suggestions that we are now witnessing the onset of a *fourth* stage in the general crisis but these have been criticised for faulty periodisation (see the discussion in Gerns, 1974, pp. 41–42, and Heininger, 1975, pp. 35–36). However, whether they posit a new stage or merely a new phase in the general crisis, these theorists draw political conclusions identical to those who simply consider its overall nature. In all cases the analyses advocate strategies based on anti-monopoly, popular-democratic alliances organised under working class hegemony and articulated with an alleged Soviet policy of peaceful co-existence and economic competition between the two world systems.

THE 'MONOPOLY-THEORETICAL' TRADITION

The Leninist tradition is particularly strong within Russian and German analyses. Thus the growth of stamocap is usually situated in the context of the general crisis of capitalism and there is a strong emphasis on its moribund, reactionary character in comparison with the socialist bloc. In this respect particular weight is attributed to the specific qualities of imperialism and the striving of the monopolies for the maximum possible profit. Thus it is argued that the process of free competition under liberal capitalism inevitably leads to the concentration and centralisation of industrial and banking capital and so results in the increasing dominance of monopolies and their union into finance capital (e.g., Haak *et al.*, 1973, pp. 145–165, 234–246; Inosemzew *et al.*, 1972, pp. 120–138, 206–222; Kozlov, 1977, pp. 316–336; Kuusinen, 1971, pp. 294–310; Oelssner, 1971; Ryndina and Chernikov, 1974, pp. 165–195). Sometimes these tendencies are also related to the socialisation of the forces of production and/or technological changes that increase the amount of capital needed for the production of given commodities (e.g., Katzenstein, 1974, pp. 95–96). Moreover, although monopolies emerge from free competition, they represent the negation of such competition. For monopolies exploit their dominant position in production and/or markets to secure for themselves long-term profits above the average rate in the economy as a whole. And, while it is often conceded that monopoly price formation is ultimately subject to the law of value, it is always the role of such super-profits in consolidating the dominance of monopoly capital that is stressed (e.g., Hess, 1974, pp. 829–833; Inosemzew *et al.*, 1972, pp. 164–184; Kozlov, 1977, pp. 321–326, 447–468; Schenajew, 1973, pp. 121–128). In this context some texts conclude that the increasing use of extra-economic coercion and the exploitation of monopolistic positions means that the allocation of profits among individual capitals depends on their political and economic power rather than their relative size or efficiency (e.g., Schirmeister, 1970, pp. 564–565). Other texts conclude that the use of state power to underwrite the collective power and profits of monopoly capital implies a *primacy of politics* over economic factors such as the law of value and/or pure market forces in the dynamic of imperialism (e.g., Hemberger *et al.,* 1965, pp. 142–143 and *passim*). But, whether or not such a political primacy is emphasised, it is always argued that the state has become crucial in securing monopoly domination.

Thus monopolies strive to coordinate their economic power with the political power of the state in order to gain 'state monopoly profits' and protect their power positions. Initially this takes two principal forms: exploitation of state revenues (e.g., state credit, public debts, collective consumption) and the use of extra-economic compulsion (e.g., quota-setting, forced cartellisation, tariffs). In this manner the imperialist state is employed to redistribute the total national income to the advantage of monopoly capital and to maintain various conditions favourable to its economic and political domination. Subsequently such methods are extended and reinforced through the development of a public economic sector, economic programming, state-monopoly regulation of the relations between capital and labour, and international state-monopoly organs and activities (e.g., Haak *et al.,* 1973, pp. 257–264; Hemberger *et al.,* 1965, pp. 249–283; Inosemzew *et al.,* 1972, pp. 383–462; Kozlov, 1977, pp. 398–420; Reinhold *et al.,* 1971, pp. 241–333; Ryndina and Chernikov, 1974, pp. 204–213; Varga, 1961, pp. 112–116). This is reflected in the growing fusion, coalescence, or merger of monopolies and state into a single mechanism of exploitation and oppression. Moreover, just as monopoly capitalism is personified in the rise of a financial oligarchy, stamocap sees the personal union of the state elite and the financial oligarchy (e.g., Kozlov, 1977, p. 415; Reinhold *et al.,* 1971, pp. 127, 179, 183; Ryndina and Chernikov, 1974, pp. 204; Lewin and Tumanov, 1977, p. 22).

These processes continue throughout the course of imperialism (or, at least, the general crisis) until they culminate in a complete system of state monopoly capitalism and the single state-monopoly mechanism essentially determines the whole reproduction process. With the third stage of the general crisis this system is supposedly fully consolidated. For it is now established rather than tendential, permanent rather than temporary, total rather than partial, preemptive rather than reactive, long- rather than short-term in outlook, and international rather than national (Hemberger *et al.,* 1965, p. 137; Lewin and Tumanov, 1977, pp. 37, 49–50; Reinhold *et al.,* 1971, pp. 95–96). Moreover, whereas the simple monopoly state intervened mainly through extra-economic force and stayed separate from its material base, the stamocap state is an economic power directly integrated into the economic base and organically bound to it in the closest possible manner (Hemberger *et al.*, 1965, pp. 137–139; Inosemzew *et al.*, 1972, p. 389; Reinhold *et al.*, 1971, p. 100; Ryndina and Chernikov, 1974, p. 201). This implies a partial transformation of the laws of motion of capitalism (something already apparent in simple monopoly capitalism as compared with competitive capitalism) but it does not mean that the system ceases to be capitalist nor that the inevitable breakdown of capitalism and its transition to socialism can be avoided (Hemberger *et al.*, 1965, pp. 137–139; Haak *et al.*, 1975, pp. 266–269; Inosemzew *et al.*, 1972, pp. 389–390, 463–506; Klein, 1974, pp. 136–159).

Such analyses are combined with an emphasis on the class struggle on a national and international scale. The development of stamocap is also provoked by the desperate efforts of the monopoly bourgeoisie to maintain their power in the face of the forward march of the working class in alliance with all anti-imperialist, democratic forces and the growing strength of the socialist world system. For, not only is it no longer possible to solve economic problems in the interests of monopoly capital without state involvement, but inward political repression and outward military aggression are also increasingly dependent on control of economic resources. This is reflected in active state promotion of the scientific-technical revolution and its industrial and/or military applications. It is also reflected in the overall militarisation of the economy based on arms production and the growth of a distinct stamocap sector in the military-industrial complex. However, while the failure of state monopoly capitalism to realise the full potential of the 'STR' (scientific-technical revolution) reveals its out-dated character in comparison with the benefits derived from effective socialist planning, the militarisation of the economy reveals how parasitic and corrupt capitalism has become. This provides further proof of the need for its revolutionary overthrow and the resulting emancipation of all of mankind (e.g., Haak *et al.*, 1975, pp. 247–251; Hemberger *et al.*, 1965, pp. 440–496; Inosemzew *et al.*, 1972, pp. 475–492; Reinhold *et al.*, 1971, pp. 462–502; Ryndina and Chernikov, 1974, pp. 218–228; and, specifically on the military-industrial complex, Pyadyshev, 1977, *passim*).

THE 'CAPITAL-THEORETICAL' TRADITION

In contrast to such Leninist (and often near-Stalinist) accounts, other Russian and German studies explain the development of stamocap in terms of the universal laws of motion of capitalism rather than the particularities of imperialism. While this approach is occasionally

coupled with the claim that no changes are required at any level in
Marx's argument to explain the rise, nature, and dynamics of monopoly or state monopoly capitalism, it is more often associated with
the view that some amendments are necessary to account for the new
forms in which the self-same universal laws are realised in the final
stages of capitalism. However, although they agree in rejecting the
need for an exclusive, *sui generis* theory of stamocap and in trying to
derive its underlying economic imperatives from the overall dynamic
of capital accumulation, these studies disagree on the most appropriate starting point for a general, 'capital-theoretical' analysis of this
phenomenon.

One important approach starts from the fundamental contradiction between the socialisation of the forces of production and the
private character of the relations of production. This has several
important implications. Thus, not only does the development of
these forces under the impulsion of capitalist competition result in
an explosive growth of productive capacities and a disproportionate
increase in fixed capital (particularly after the onset of the 'STR'), it
also intensifies the division of labour and the overall interdependence
of different branches of production. This implies in turn the need to
ensure continuity of production throughout the economy and considerably to increase effective demand to match the explosion in
productive capacities, as well as to smooth our fluctuations in demand.
It also implies that the conditions for the maintenance of the system
as a whole become immediate preconditions for the valorisation,
realisation, and accumulation of individual capitals. Indeed more and
more spheres of production make demands that exceed the capacities
of private capitals and thus need to be developed through state intervention. Therefore, in addition to its traditional involvement in the
provision of the general external conditions of production, the state
is involved in specific areas of production (especially those with a
highly developed social character, high fixed capital, above average
turnover time, long gestation period, uncertain valorisation, etc.).
Moreover, with the growth of the 'STR', the ties between the material and non-material spheres, between production and education,
information, research, and so on, become ever more close. All this
suggests the need for a corresponding socialisation of relations of
production to overcome the limits to capital accumulation imposed
by the nature of the capital relation itself and, since monopoly is the
highest possible developmental form of private capital, this need
must be met by the state. The growth of state monopoly capitalism
is thus a necessary adaptation of the relations of capitalist produc-

tion to the level of socialisation of production. Hence, if the liberal state was primarily concerned to establish the general social framework for capitalist production and the simple monopoly state combined this with intervention through fiscal, legal, administrative, and repressive means to influence the appropriation of profit in favour of monopoly capital, the 'stamocap' state is immediately integrated into the valorisation, realisation, and expanded reproduction of the total social capital. However, even though — and precisely because — it is an integral element of an increasingly self-contradictory capital relation, the state can only modify the forms in which its worsening contradictions appear. It cannot break through the limits imposed by these contradictions and ensure the harmonious, crisis-free development of capitalist society (e.g., Gündel *et al.*, 1975, pp. 7–16, 183–192, 317–327; Hess, 1971, pp. 57–58 and *passim*; Katzenstein, 1973, pp. 21–33; Schleifstein, 1973, pp. 385–391; Schwank, 1974, *passim*).

A cognate approach focuses less on the impact of the socialisation of production than the imperatives of crisis-management. Indeed a major stimulus in the growth of stamocap theory came from studies of changes in the economic cycle after the Second World War (e.g., Heininger, 1959; Gündel, 1961; Schmidt, 1959; Varga, 1958). Recent studies variously explain cyclical economic crises in terms of uneven development across different sectors, disproportions between exchange-value and use-value, the periodic excess of capital, the overproduction of commodities, working-class underconsumption, and the tendency of the rate of profit to fall. But, whatever the specific explanation(s) offered for cyclical crises, the course of these cycles is held to have changed fundamentally and permanently since the war. This is then explained in terms of the widespread use of state-monopoly measures and economic programming at both national and international levels. For, although state intervention cannot change the objective nature of capitalism and its laws, it can influence their forms of appearance and development. These stamocap measures range from contracyclical fiscal and monetary policies through state sponsorship of R&D, investment, and production to direct involvement in key areas of production through the growth of public enterprise. Special attention is paid to militarisation of the economy as a source of expansion along with state involvement in the 'STR'. Recent studies also stress the role of economic forecasting, regulation, programming, and incomes policies as the newest elements in stamocap contracyclical activities. But it is also emphasised that all these measures have only limited effect. Thus, if militarisation fosters demand in the military-industrial sector, it also transfers demand from civilian production, intensifies capitalist waste, and ultimately retards growth. Similarly the growth of state spending is said to cause upheavals in the monetary and/or financial area and, in the longer term, to produce stagflation, international currency crises, balance of payments difficulties, etc. Moreover, in so far as stamocap interventions promote the development of the productive forces, they aggravate the contradictions between the socialisation of production and the private appropriation of profit (cf. Boradjewski, 1974; Burdjalov, 1978; Haak *et al.,* 1975, pp. 313–319; Jung and Schleifstein, 1979, pp. 16, 59–61, 219–235; Kozlov, 1977, pp. 469–477; Menshikov, 1975; Ryndina and Chernikov, 1974, pp. 157–174; Stadnichenko, 1975).

THE FRENCH 'STAMOCAP' APPROACH

French theories initially followed the same developmental path as the dominant Soviet bloc studies but, beginning in the mid-1960s and under the influence of Boccara, the PCF took a new course. This turn was confirmed at an important congress on stamocap held at Choisy-le-Roi in 1966 (Conférence Internationale Choisy-le-Roi, 1966) and the distinctive French approach has since been much elaborated in *Économie et politique,* other party journals, and various monographs. Thus, whilst there are many similarities between French work on 'le capitalisme monopoliste d'état' (CME) and that developed in the Soviet bloc, there are also quite important differences. It is on the latter that we shall focus.

The fundamental theoretical basis of French CME theory is the 'law of overaccumulation-devalorisation' and its effects on the relations of private monopolies and the state. French theorists distinguish three main stages of capitalism (primitive, classical, monopoly) and divide the last stage into two phases (simple monopoly and state monopoly) (see Boccara *et al.,* 1976, vol. 1, pp. 18–24). The chief motor force behind transitions from one stage or phase to another is seen as the progressive development of the forces of production and the recurrence of structural crises as the prevailing relations of production cease promoting this development and begin to retard it (Boccara *et al.,* 1976, vol. 1, pp. 183–184; Boccara, 1977, pp. 306–414, 328–344, 401–403). It is in this context that overaccumulation and devalorisation are located. Overaccumulation derives from the law of the tendency of the rate of profit to fall and appears as an excess of capital relative to the available opportunities for the creation and realisation of surplus-value in a given situation. It can take an absolute or relative form, corresponding to conditions in which marginal profit is nil or below average respectively. And it can be eliminated through a change in the conditions of exploitation and realisation and/or through the devalorisation of some part of the total social capital so that it obtains a reduced, nil, or even negative share of total surplus-value (Boccara *et al.*, 1976, vol. 1, pp. 36–40; Boccara, 1977, pp. 42–47). The immediate response to overaccumulation is seen in attempts to increase the rate of exploitation and/or in brief recessions in which capital is devalorised and reorganised; but, underlying the resulting short-term cyclical fluctuations, the tendency towards overaccumulation continues and culminates in structural crises that threaten permanent stagnation unless there is a much more fundamental reorganisation of the relations of production (Boccara, 1977, pp. 131–132, 220–222, 236–239, 398–403). It is from such structural crises that new stages and phases of capitalism develop.

Thus, while simply monopoly capitalism arose during the structural crisis of overaccumulation experienced by classical, liberal competitive capitalism in 1873–1896, it underwent a similar crisis itself during the 1930s and was replaced by state monopoly capitalism. Moreover, just as the former transition was effected under the *auspices of finance capital* through the permanent devalorisation of non-monopoly industrial and money capital and through the export of capital (also treated as a form of devalorisation in relation to the home market), it is the massive and permanent devalorisation of part of the total social capital *through state intervention* that characterises the transition to state monopoly capitalism (Boccara *et al.*, 1976, vol. 1, pp. 19–23, 42–45, 149–151; Boccara, 1977, pp. 52–57, 220–225, 238–239, 294–314). But even the progressive effects of CME on the evolution of the forces of production and its function in enabling private monopoly capital to accumulate on the basis of devalorised state capital are supposed to have been more or less exhausted by the late 'sixties. This results in a structural crisis of state monopoly capitalism and, since it is held impossible to develop the full productive potential engendered by the 'STR' within a capitalist society, the only solution is to embark on the transition to socialism (Boccara *et al.*, 1976, vol. 1, pp. 82–97; vol. 2, pp. 62–67, 254–266; Boccara, 1977, pp. 237–266, 391–352, 391–414).

Thus CME is an historically circumscribed phase of the imperialist stage of capitalism and is characterised by the long-term, public devalorisation of state and non-monopoly capital in favour of private monopoly capital. Not only does it share certain properties with the preceding phase of imperialism (such as militarisation of the economy, political authoritarianism, and parasitism), it also has several novel or much reinforced features compared with simple monopoly capitalism (Boccara *et al.,* 1976, vol. 1, pp. 22–24). For the state has become an indispensable element in the reproduction of capital: not only through its institutional and political role but also through its immediate involvement in the formation of monopoly profits at the expense of the whole people (Boccara *et al.,* 1976, vol. 2, pp. 29–30). In this context particular attention is paid to (a) public finance of private investment and production, (b) the public sector, (c) public finance of individual and/or collective consumption, (d) public intervention in the circuit of money as revenue and/or as capital through taxation, the national debt, credit regulation, etc., (e) public programming and planning, and (f) export of public capital (Boccara *et al.,* 1976, 2 vols., *passim*; Herzog, 1972, *passim*). Of these features the first is considered the most important element in CME and all six are understood as forms of devalorisation whose effect is to counteract the overaccumulation of monopoly capital and to secure the conditions necessary for continued expansion at an advanced stage of socialisation of production. They are condensed in the public budget so that it is here that one can most easily discern the character, effects, and contradictions of state monopoly capitalism as it emerges, matures, and enters its crisis phase (Boccara *et al.,* 1976, vol. 1, pp. 46ff; vol. 2, pp. 210–215; Boccara, 1977, pp. 46–68).

CME theory strongly emphasises the contradictory and transitional nature of state monopoly capitalism. For the latter involves both the consolidation of monopoly domination over society and the intensive development of the material base for a transition to an anti-monopolist, advanced democracy and thence to socialism. The former aspect is most clear in the pillage of all dominated classes and strata (including the non-monopoly fractions of the bourgeoisie) through fiscal exploitation and state redistribution of the national income as well as in the state's involvement in increasing the rate of exploitation in the domain of production itself (Boccara *et al.,* 1976, vol. 2, pp. 210–253; vol. 1, pp. 366–381). Indeed, as state intervention in CME reinforces capitalism, it also reinforces the polarisation of class forces through the elimination of the traditional petit bourgeoisie and small and medium capital ('petits et moyens entreprises' or 'PME') and the organisation of the expanding wage-earning classes in opposition to the monopolies (Boccara *et al.,* 1976, vol. 1, pp. 218–253, 366–381). The domination of monopoly capital in all fields of social life justifies the strategy of anti-monopoly alliance and the struggle to instal anti-monopoly forces at the head of the state. Moreover, since the state must extend its intervention in the economy in order to adapt the relations of production to the growing socialisation of the productive forces, it develops an increasingly social character itself and can only function adequately when this is reflected in the effective, democratic participation of all the people in the exercise of its power. This is particularly clear in the deformation of nationalisation and economic programming that results from their subjugation to monopoly capital. But democratisation of the state will mean that the people as a whole can employ these mechanisms for socialist advance (Boccara *et al.,* 1976, vol. 2, pp. 333–347, 361–413; Boccara, 1977, pp. 77–106, 328–389, 436–446; Delilez, 1976; Goffard, 1976; Jourdain, 1966; Masson, 1976; Perceval, 1977a, 1977b; Quin, 1976).

A MAJOR BRITISH CONTRIBUTION

A significant theoretical contribution to stamocap theory has been recorded by two British theorists, Fine and Harris (1979, pp. 112–145). Their approach is capital-theoretical and analyses the CMP as a complex circuit of social capital. Productive capital is said to be determinant in the last instance but is articulated in complex fashion with other forms of capital in the production, distribution, and exchange of value. They argue that capitalism can be periodised as a mode of production in abstraction from specific social formations since the laws of motion of the CMP themselves give rise to distinct *stages* rather than continuous *trends* (p. 105). Thus, while modes of production are distinguished in terms of the fundamental relations of possession and control among producing and non-producing classes, stages in each mode are differentiated in terms of the specific *forms* of these basic relations and their social reproduction. In this context the succession between stages as well as modes is explained through the development of the forces and relations of production (pp. 108–109). This procedure is justified through reference to Marx's own method of periodisation in the analysis of feudalism: for he distinguishes three stages according to the form of appropriation of ground-rent (labour-rent, rent in kind, money rent) associated with the development of feudal relations of production and distribution (1979, pp. 110–112; cf. Harris, 1976b, pp. 4–6; both citing Marx, *C3,* pp. 790–802). Likewise Fine and Harris also distinguish three stages in the development of the CMP: laissez-faire, monopoly, and state monopoly capitalism.

Their analysis is not fully specified but its broad outlines are clear and compelling. Particular attention is paid to the increasing socialisation of the forces of production and the need for a matching socialisation of relations of production and social reproduction. The first stage of capitalism is laissez-faire. Its main characteristics are: the formal subsumption of wage-labour under the control of capital through capitalist organisation of *manufacture,* the dominance of *absolute surplus-value* (with opportunities for relative surplus-value confined to simple cooperation and division of labour in manufacturing), the expansion of capitalism through the *concentration* of capital (i.e., growth of re-invested individual capitals), the mediation of the law of value in production through *market forces* (i.e., laissez-faire and free competition), and the dominant position of *profits of enterprise* in the appropriation of surplus-value (pp. 112–113). This first stage is also marked by the significance of trade cycles in the rhythm of economic crises (owing to the dominance of commodity capital and commercial capital in the exchange process) and the concentration of class struggles on the extraction of absolute surplus-value and/or on local political repression (pp. 113–114). In contrast monopoly capitalism is said to involve: the real subsumption of wage-labour under the control of capital through capitalist organisation of *machinofacture,* the growing importance of *relative surplus-value* (based on increasing productivity through continual reorganisation of the labour process), the expansion of capitalism through the *centralisation* of capital (i.e., the gathering of many capitals under the control of a few capitals), the mediation of the law of value in production through the *private credit system* (i.e., the allocation of money capital among different branches of production is now overdetermined through credit relations organised by finance capital), and the dominant position of *interest* in the appropriation of surplus-value (p. 115). The rise of machinofacture stimulates the socialisation of productive forces and is reflected in the socialisation of production relations in such areas as the labour process (e.g., the separation of ownership and control leading to the growth of a managerial stratum in place of the individual entrepreneur-manager), the 'accounting' process in the sphere of realisation (e.g., monopolies, trusts, and cartels socialise the formation of prices and allocation of markets), and financial control (e.g., money capital is socialised through the development of private credit organised through finance capital) (p. 117). This stage is also associated with the significance of the TRPF and credit relations in the increasingly violent rhythm of crises (owing to the dominance of relative surplus-value and private credit) and the concentration of class struggles not only on the continual reorganisation of the labour process and/or the introduction of social reforms (encouraged by the development of trade union and political organisation grounded in the socialisation of production and concentration of wage-labour) but also on the management and attempted resolution of economic crises (pp. 120–121).

These problems are resolved through the increasing involvement of the state in the economic as well as social reproduction of capitalism (pp. 129, 132). For state monopoly capitalism (or 'SMC') derives from the attempts of the state to resolve economic crises through the further socialisation of the relations of production. Thus, although it shares many features of monopoly capitalism (such as machino-facture, relative surplus-value, centralisation, role of the TRPF), this particular stage is distinguished by direct state involvement in the circuit of capital (especially in the three forms of nationalisation, taxation, and state credit). Thus, not only does SMC involve direct state control of the labour process itself within an expanding nationalised productive sector and direct intervention in the 'accounting process' through price codes, indirect taxation, subsidies, etc., it also involves the state in the financial control of production through the creation and manipulation of credit in such forms as contracyclical demand management as well as the appropriation and redistribution of surplus-value through taxation and subsidies. Thus the essential features that distinguish SMC from the preceding stages of the CMP are the new forms taken by capitalist control of the economic process (nationalisation, state credit, etc.) and the dominance of taxation as a new, highly socialised form of the capitalist appropriation of surplus-value (pp. 121–122; see also Harris, 1976b, pp. 6–8, who focuses on nationalisation and taxation). It should also be noted that the development of SMC also modifies the operation of market forces (e.g., state competition policy or control of free collective bargaining) and of private credit (e.g., affecting the balance of competition in the supply and demand for money capital) and thus, while co-existing with elements of earlier stages, overdetermines their forms and effects (pp. 112, 124, 133, 136).

The transition to SMC is associated with changes in the nature of the state and political relations. Thus, while the laissez-faire stage requires the maximum restriction on working-class resistance to the extraction of absolute surplus-value and the minimisation of material concessions through the state (hence the lack of political rights for wage-labour and the localisation of state power in the interests of local capital) and the monopoly stage requires the active political representation of the working class to facilitate the transition from absolute to relative surplus-value extraction and the moderation of trade union and political struggles (reflected in factory legislation and the subordination of local to central government in the interests of monopoly capital), state monopoly capitalism requires the political containment of the working class so that the inevitable politicisation of economic struggles under SMC does not lead to struggles to win real political power for the working class and a transition to socialism (pp. 113–114, 118–119, 124–125; cf. Harris, 1977, pp. 121–122). This requirement is best met through the establishment of bourgeois social democracy in which political parties based on working-class support become part of the state apparatus and the locus of struggles is moved from the point of production (where the socialisation of the forces of production in conjunction with trade union organisation make the working class strong) to the political and ideological domain (where capital tends to be hegemonic and can impose sacrifices on the working class in exchange for a spurious control of government) (pp. 125–126). But Fine and Harris also emphasise that these developments in SMC pose serious economic and political problems for capital. For these changes cannot prevent continuing struggles to shift the role of the SMC state away from aiding the reproduction of capitalism towards its abolition. This is clear not only in struggles over the role of nationalisation and state involvement in the restructuring of production but also in such fields of social reproduction as the welfare state, education, and housing (pp. 124–132; cf. Harris, 1977, pp. 121–122).

Fine and Harris conclude their analysis of SMC with some comments on inflation as one of its major features. They relate inflation to state intervention in the credit system, as determined by political struggle among different fractions of capital and/or different classes; and they explain it as an effect of a growth in state credit (whether as capital or revenue) that exceeds the rate of accumulation (conditioned by, inter alia, the expansion of unproductive state expenditure) (pp. 135–145).

It should be noted that this analysis is conducted at the level of the pure mode of production and abstracts from the existence of various nation-states. This is quite deliberate. For Fine and Harris contrast the periodisation of the CMP in terms of changes in social relations and class struggle arising from accumulation in general with the periodisation of the world economy in terms of relations among nation-states and international competition (p. 148). In the latter respect they describe three stages: the first stage of capitalist world economy involves the internationalisation of commodity capital in the search for expanded markets, the second stage involves the internationalisation of finance capital in association with the development of the private credit system, and the third stage involves the internationalisation of productive capital in association with multinational corporations (pp. 147–148). It is the combined and uneven development of the CMP (along with its linkages with pre-capitalist modes) and the world economy that determines the evolution of imperialism as a concrete, world-historical phenomenon. This implies that Fine and Harris reject any attempt to identify imperialism as a distinct stage of capitalism and, *a priori,* SMC as a distinct phase of imperialism (especially if the latter is understood in its Leninist sense). For, whereas Lenin emphasised the dominance of monopoly capital and the internationalisation of finance capital, Fine and Harris note that contemporary imperialism is dominated by SMC and the internationalisation of productive capital (pp. 148–151). In turn this means that the role of the state and the nature of inter-imperialist rivalries have changed. Thus, whereas Lenin emphasised competitive colonisation and inter-imperialist wars to divide the world into markets and spheres for lending, now we find the state intervenes to promote internationalisation (subject to the constraints of social reproduction at home) and competition among multinational corporations for markets, financial areas, and production bases (p. 152). It is in this context that Fine and Harris discuss the growth of international state apparatuses. These are fundamentally concerned with guaranteeing the economic and social reproduction of accumulation in general but are overdetermined in their actions by the competition among different blocs of capital and, to a lesser but variable extent, political pressure from the labour movement (pp. 153–154 and 159–160).

'STAMOCAP' ANALYSES OF THE STATE

By now it should be obvious that these theories of state monopoly capitalism are not theories of the state as such: instead they focus on the latest stage of capitalism and the decisive role of the state in its reproduction. However, while it is important that the state intervenes more and more actively and extensively in the capitalist economy and may even have become partly integrated into the base, it is also important to examine the changes in the state superstructure that follow from the development of state monopoly capitalism. Yet, although this aspect has quite fundamental implications for the analysis of stamocap as well as for problems of political strategy, it has not been studied to the same degree nor in the same detail as the economic role of the modern state. Hence this section will outline only the major conclusions of 'stamocap' analyses of the state.

The dominant tradition is Leninist in two senses. For most studies treat the state as an essentially repressive mechanism of political domination (despite the increasing importance of its economic functions) and also locate its development in relation to the growth of imperialism and the general crisis of capitalism. Thus, following Lenin's threefold characterisation of imperialism as monopoly, parasitic or decaying, and moribund capitalism (1916b, p. 105; cf. 1917b, *passim*), the present epoch is seen as one in which political reaction and repression are reinforced as monopoly capital strives to maintain its power and profit in spite of growing polarisation, obsolescence, and resistance. For the development of imperialism during the 'general crisis' involves an increasing split between monopoly capital and all other fractions and classes within the capitalist camp as well as increasing competition between the capitalist and socialist camps; sees the worsening of the fundamental contradiction between the socialisation of the forces of production and the private appropriation of (monopoly) profits; and engenders growing resistance by anti-monopoly forces in metropolitan and (neo-)colonial societies alike. Thus, not only is the state obliged to expand its economic role in order to maintain the profitability of monopoly capital, it must also step up its political and ideological role to protect the political power of the latter (see, for example, Burlatsky, 1978, pp. 57–61; Haak *et al.*, 1973, pp. 202–205; Hemberger *et al.*, 1965, pp. 157–160, 215–220; Inosemzew *et al.*, 1972, pp. 781–794; Röder, 1976, pp. 76–85, 93–101; Schmidt, 1974, pp. 45–60).

This is reflected in specific changes in the structure as well as the functions of the capitalist state. Firstly, there is the celebrated coalescence between the monopolies and the state apparatus into a single mechanism of economic exploitation and political domination. This is most evident in *personal fusion* through the occupation of the commanding political heights by individuals with familial, economic, or ideological ties to monopoly capital. But it is increasingly reinforced by the need for close *functional coordination* between the state and the monopolies. Secondly, the party system is adapted to the requirements of monopoly capital; and political parties become major instruments of ideological control. This occurs through monopoly financing of parties, party conferences, election campaigns, etc., and is reflected in the growing centralisation and bureaucratisation of party organisations. Thirdly, the role of interest associations, lobbies, and, indeed, individual concerns has increased in all areas of policy-making. Through its direct and immediate contacts with politicians and officials, this lobby system is able to influence, if not dictate, internal and external policies alike. This is accompanied by a massive extension of monopoly control over the means of mental production such as education, advertising, and the mass media. Indeed, following the transition from the nightwatchman state with its limited franchise to the interventionist state with its popular suffrage, monopoly capital is obliged to intensify its ideological control over voters and a veritable 'ideology industry' has been created by the state and monopolies. Fifthly, the executive apparatus has been strengthened at the expense of parliament and the rule of law. This reflects the concentration and centralisation of economic power under the auspices of monopoly capital and is evident in the rise of presidentialism, the personal element in power, the subordination of parliament to the executive, increasing restrictions on basic democratic rights and freedoms, and the general militarisation of state power. Sixthly, the state itself has been reorganised with a massive growth in functionally-oriented ministries, special courts and tribunals, interdepartmental committees, quasi-government bodies, state-run economic institutions, etc., as well as in the police and military apparatus. These changes reflect the need for greater efficiency and coordination of the state's ever-expanding activities to maintain monopoly power and profits. Seventhly, alongside this growing concentration of economic and political power, we also find a complementary process of deconcentration and decentralisation of power to micro-economic and/or local political levels in order to refine the control of capital over even the smallest areas of surplus production or consumption and/or to facilitate the penetration of state control into all areas of social life. Finally, in addition to these changes within the nation-state, there has also been a marked growth in international state-monopoly apparatuses on the political as well as economic plane (see particularly: Lewin and Tumanow, 1977, pp. 22–26 and *passim*; also, Burlatsky, 1978, pp. 56–61, 71–78, 86–88; Delilez, 1977, pp. 77–98, 131–140, 159–180; Gollan, 1954, pp. 15–40, 83–101, 115–116; Harvey and Hood, 1958, pp. 24–27 and *passim*; Herzog, 1971, pp. 123–124; Jung and Schleifstein, 1979, pp. 63–67, 184–186, 194–203, 207–209, 223; Röder, 1976, pp. 86–101, 110–166; Schmidt, 1974, pp. 44–60; Schuster, 1976, pp. 24–35, 82–85, 96–105, 139–162, and *passim*; Tumanov, 1974, pp. 64–76, 85, 89).

At first sight these analyses are basically descriptive and seem to raise no serious theoretical issues. But the Leninist framework within which they are typically situated involved a number of problems (see below) which are reflected in stamocap discussions of the state as well as the role of monopolies. Thus, in so far as it is organically integrated with the economy, the state appears as a major productive force in its own right; but, in so far as it is still the institutional locus of extra- economic coercion, it appears as an instrument of class domination. Nor can this ambivalence be resolved simply through noting a dialectic between forces and relations of production on the political as well as economic level. Instead it is aggravated by the insistence that stamocap is characterised by a fusion between the state and monopoly capital to form a single mechanism of economic exploitation and political domination (even if, *pace* Stalin, this formal, descriptive account is complemented by the substantive claim that the state machine is subjugated to monopoly capital) (Stalin, 1952, p. 478). For, if stamocap really does involve a unitary single mechanism, how can anti-monopoly forces take the place of monopoly capital; and, if the state is an instrument, how can individual monopolies transcend monopolistic competition and subordinate the state to their collective interests? These and similar questions have been aimed at 'stamocap' theory and have evoked a measure of self-criticism.

Thus 'stamocap' analyses adopting the 'monopoly-theoretical' stance have come to place more emphasis on the reproduction of competition and conflict within the supposed 'single mechanism' and, indeed, now mention a new, 'state monopoly capitalist' form of competition distinct from both monopolistic and free competition. This centres on the private appropriation of super-profits created and/or redistributed through state intervention of an economic and/or extra-economic kind (see, e.g., Kuusinen, 1961, p. 326; Ryndina and Chernikov, 1974, p. 176; Schirmeister, 1970, p. 565; Varga, 1968, p. 53; and, from a more 'capital-theoretical' viewpoint, Katzenstein, 1974, p. 15; idem, 1974, pp. 99–100; Klein, 1965, p. 94; Schleifstein, 1973, pp. 383, 386–393; Schwank, 1974, pp. 90–94). Several 'capital-theoretical' texts have also noted that the increasing socialisation of the forces of production and the increasing distortion of normal market forces have intensified the contradictions between the interests of individual capitals and those of (monopoly) capital as a whole. Some theorists from both theoretical approaches go on to argue that these problems can be resolved through the coordinating role of a financial oligarchy unified by its central position within the network of cross-cutting monopoly interests and/or through the integrative and representative role of peak organisations in the 'lobby system' that expands *pari passu* with state intervention (e.g., Aaronovitch, 1956, pp. 144–149; Banaschak, 1964, *passim*; Hess, 1972, pp. 392–394; Hemberger *et al.*, 1965, pp. 180–195; Jung and Schleifstein, 1979, pp. 64–65, 223). Conversely other theorists from both traditions suggest that the state itself must have an enhanced measure of relative autonomy in the stamocap system. This is required so that it can intervene against particular capitals to promote the interests of (monopoly) capital in general (e.g., Fine and Harris, 1979, pp. 96–97; Gulijew, 1977, pp. 49–53; Jung and Schleifstein, 1979, pp. 206–209; Katzenstein, 1975, pp. 434–435; Lewin and Tumanow, p. 19; Varga, 1968, p. 55).

One of the most sophisticated arguments along these lines has been outlined by the PCF economist, Philippe Herzog. Rejecting the Stalinist principles of 'fusion into a single mechanism' and 'subjugation to the monopolies', he argues that the relation between the state and monopoly capital is more akin to a 'contradictory separation in unity' (Herzog, 1971, p. 125; cf. Masson, 1976, pp. 40–41; Perceval, 1977b, pp. 51–52; Quin, 1972, p. 10; Vernay, 1968, pp. 61–62). Herzog attributes the relative autonomy of the state to its institutional separation from the sphere of production and its distinct means and forms of intervention into economy and civil society. Especially important here are its legitimate monopoly over the means of coercion, its prerogative of setting to work the state apparatus, the relative independence of the administration and judiciary from the government, and the plurality of state apparatuses which allows room for political maneouvre (Herzog, 1971, pp. 108–111; cf. Hess, 1974, p. 384). Although he is somewhat ambivalent about the extent to which this autonomy is relativised and rendered illusory through the ultimate dependence of the state on continuing capital accumulation and/or its active incorporation into the accumulation process itself, Herzog argues strongly that state intervention always reflects the relations of forces among *all* classes, fractions, and strata (not just monopolies) and that the search for coherence among government policies means that its actions rarely, if ever, directly meet the demands of specific interests but are imposed on all interests (pp. 124–125). Indeed the state faces a 'double bind' situation. For, if it acts to resolve problems or contradictions exclusively on behalf of one fraction, it aggravates them for capital as a whole and thus ultimately for all fractions. Conversely, even if it intervenes in defence of the collective interests of capital, it still needs the political support of particular capitals to carry through its policies and cannot avoid favouring some capitals more than others. This means it will aggravate the internal divisions of capital and so disturb the equilibrium of compromise that sustains such policies (Herzog, 1971, pp. 105, 111; cf. Fabre, 1966, p. 156; Maier and Ivanek, 1962). Indeed the contradictions inherent in state intervention and the ever-changing relations of force mean that consensus is always partial, unstable, and provisional. But, in so far as monopolies stay economically dominant and can resist effectively when interests vital to their collective survival are threatened, then successive compromises mediated through a relatively autonomous state will reproduce its political domination (pp. 113–114).

Another novel approach bearing on the nature and functions of the stamocap state has been outlined by a West German theorist, Heinz Jung. He distinguishes two variants of stamocap: an 'étatist' variant based on extensive state intervention in the economy and the social-reformist integration of subordinate classes and a 'private' variant with market-oriented economic management and a strong state suited to the repressive integration of dominated classes. Thus, while he follows an orthodox 'stamocap' line in arguing that state intervention must grow in response to the socialisation of the forces of production and the development of disproportions between commodity production and effective demand and/or between the exchange-value and use-value aspects of social reproduction, Jung also notes that monopoly capital adopts different strategies within these constraints according to its place in the international system and the balance of social forces at home. In West Germany an 'étatist' bias has alternated with a 'private' bias but the latter has been dominant since 1972/73. There has been a turn towards an export-led accumulation strategy in which German hegemony abroad will combine with repression at home. This is reflected in shifts from contracyclical fiscal policies to monetary and credit policies, from direct to indirect taxation, from growth in the public sector to privatisation and spending cuts, from an active structural policy involving state investments in infrastructure, energy, R&D, etc., to passive support for market solutions emerging from the monopoly sector; at the same time the state must foster internationalisation in favour of West German capital and also reinforce its legal, police, and ideological apparatuses to control the repercussions of its policies on the home front. This shift in strategy was prompted by a crisis in earlier forms of 'social partnership' involving the SPD and unions and by the inability of more radical forces to exploit this crisis; but it is limited by the continuing need for social democratic support in the political arena. In short, while the state inevitably expands its activities in the 'stamocap' era, its precise forms, social bases, strategies, and effects can still vary significantly. Much work remains to be done here in 'stamocap' theory (cf. Jung, 1979, pp. 51–65).

SUBSTANTIVE CRITIQUE

The most vehement and telling criticisms of 'stamocap' theory have been directed at the 'monopoly-theoretical' approach inspired by Lenin and still frequently imbued with Stalinist residues. Indeed it is not uncommon to find 'stamocap' theory identified exclusively with this tradition. The problems with this approach are similar to those found in the original studies of Lenin and Stalin: their descriptive bias, the lack of clear and consistent principles of explanation, their polemical and agitational purpose, and their narrow subordination to the supposed requirements of the prevailing revolutionary strategy and tactics of the international communist movement as organised under Bolshevik dominance. Thus this tradition starts out from Stalin's definition of Leninism as the Marxism of the era of imperialism and proletarian revolution (Stalin, 1924, p. 91) and Lenin's definition of imperialism as monopoly, parasitic or decaying, and moribund capitalism (Lenin, 1916b, p. 105). This is reflected in the way in which the dominance of monopoly capital is taken for granted and monopolies are seen as subjects striving for domination economically in the form of the 'maximum profit', i.e., permanent above-average or super-profits, politically in the form of securing monopoly power vis-à-vis non-monopoly fractions, classes, and strata and/or the allegedly ever more powerful socialist camp. It is also apparent in the emphasis or the moribund character of imperialism (associated with the so-called 'general crisis of capitalism') and the immediate prospects for a transition to socialism (due to the material ripeness or, indeed, over-ripeness of the high socialised productive forces of capitalism). This means that the principal political priority is to develop the hitherto backward revolutionary consciousness of the working class and anti-monopoly forces and to struggle against the superannuated, decaying system of domination maintained by the monopoly bourgeoisie. In making these proposals the Leninist (-Stalinist) approach thus combines economic determinism (either in the form of a progressive development of the productive forces and/or in the form of a catastrophic economic collapse or inter-imperialist war of redivision) with political voluntarism (such that the reproduction of state monopoly capitalism and the transition to socialism depend on relations of coercion, manipulation, and ideological will). Now, while few would deny the need to examine the interaction of economic, political, and ideological factors, the 'monopoly-theoretical' approach does not seriously analyse the mediations involved between its economic determinism and political voluntarism but relies instead on their simple juxtaposition. This problem is aggravated by the subjectivist method of analysis of politics and ideology, i.e., their treatment as the outcome of relations among subjects endowed with consciousness and free will, leading to the systematic neglect of the social relations of political and ideological practice and the manner in which subjects are constituted through such practices and relations (see chapter 5).

The principal thrust of West German criticism has been aimed at the Leninist(-Stalinist) analysis of monopoly capital. Moreover, while such criticism is often inspired by the reductionist 'capital logic' variant of form-analysis (see chapter 3), it is frequently justified. Thus it is argued that Leninist studies do not attempt to derive the existence of monopolies from the general concept of capital, suggest that monopoly is the antithesis of competition, imply that Marx's analysis of capital applies only to competitive capitalism and that new concepts and laws are required to interpret monopoly and state monopoly capitalism, view monopolies as subjects striving for domination through resort to extra-economic coercion rather than as the *träger* (or 'carriers') of social relations of production, neglect the distinction between particular capitals and capital in general or fail to establish how monopoly or state-monopoly capitalism is transcended politically to consolidate the power of the monopoly bourgeoisie as a whole, attribute all manner of arbitrary, *ad hoc,* or conjunctural features to the essence of monopoly or state-monopoly capitalism without rhyme or reason, reduce capitalist exploitation to a problem of distribution by focusing on the exaction of monopoly profits rather than the creation of surplus-value in capitalist relations of production, and so on (see, e.g., Altvater, 1975, pp. 129–198; Jordan, 1974a, pp. 137–172; *idem,* 1974b, pp. 212–242; Neusüss, 1972; Projekt Klassenanalyse, 1972; *idem,* 1975, pp. 9–38, 97–148; Schubert, 1973, pp. 8–67; Wirth, 1972, pp. 194–197 and *passim*; *idem,* 1973, pp. 18–30).

However, while these criticisms apply to many stamocap analyses (particularly those given in the 1950s and 'sixties and, indeed, more modern party programmes and basic textbooks), they are not always germane to the most recent studies (especially those informed by a 'capital-theoretical' rather than a 'monopoly-theoretical' approach). For recent analyses have tried more or less successfully to derive the emergence of monopolies from the process of capital accumulation and/or to establish their specific conditions of existence, to provide a coherent Marxist analysis of monopoly price, monopoly profit, etc., and to relate it to prices of production, the average rate of profit, etc., to differentiate forms of competition from free through monopoly to state monopoly and to consider their effects on the realisation of the law of value, to examine the implications of the distinction between particular capitals and capital in general, and to consider the role of force and extra-economic compulsion in the context of the forms of economic calculation mediating the dynamic of capital accumulation (see, e.g., Hess, 1974, pp. 826–841; Huffschmid, 1975, pp. 4–92; Jung and Schleifstein, 1979, pp. 120–167, 219–235; Inosemzew *et al.*, 1972, pp. 179–185; Katzenstein, 1974, pp. 93–109; *idem*, 1975, pp. 93–129; Kozlov, 1977, pp. 447–468; Wygodski, 1972, pp. 43–260). These studies have begun to meet the more obvious and justifiable criticisms of the 'monopoly-theoretical' approach but it is still far from clear that such advances in the analysis of stamocap can be easily combined with the political conclusions of 'monopoly-theoretical' texts. For, whereas an adequate theory of monopoly capital must examine how the formation of monopoly prices and the realisation of monopoly profits are related to the circuit of the total social capital and, indeed, depend on the overall level of economic exploitation of wage-labour by capital, it is invariably suggested in all versions of stamocap theory that the principal contradiction is now located between monopoly capital (and its state) and all other fractions, classes, and strata rather than between capital in general and wage-labour. Nor do these studies yet answer the question whether monopoly or state monopoly phenomena justify an attempt to periodise capitalism into stages.

Another characteristically West German line of criticism concerns the relation posited in stamocap theory between the economic and the political. Thus, in addition to the expected hostility to the general failure to derive the specific form of the capitalist state from that of the capitalist mode of production and the associated error of commission in considering the state as a simple mechanism of monopoly dictatorship, strong objections are also raised to the 'monopoly-theoretical' emphasis on the 'primacy of the political'. For, in so far as stamocap is viewed as the product of the struggle to maintain monopoly power in the face of an ascendant socialist world system, then the principal source of change is located outside the

'CMP' itself in the sphere of international relations. Moreover, even when this problem is avoided through a stress on the aggravation of contradictions internal to imperialism, primacy is still granted to the political interests of the monopoly bourgeoisie as a whole. The development and nature of stamocap are not related to the dynamic of capital accumulation but to the character of monopoly capital as a class subject striving after domination through the use of extra-economic compulsion. This means in turn that the relations between the economic and the political are oversimplified: for example, the growth of state intervention is derived from the political needs of system maintenance and the economic limits to state power are neglected or underplayed (Wirth, 1972, pp. 100–111, 117–136, 194–197; *idem*, 1973 pp. 18–21; see also, Gerstenberger, 1976, pp. 82–85; Schubert, 1973, pp. 67–87; Tristram, 1974, pp. 98–136; Winkelmann, 1874, pp. 46–63).

It should be noted that this criticism is particularly meaningful within the sort of economically reductionist framework adopted by many theorists in the 'capital logic' wing of the 'form derivation' school. For, in so far as they approach the analysis of the capitalist state from the viewpoint of economic determination in the first instance or, more commonly, from an emphasis on the 'separation-in-unity' of the economic and political moments of the capital relation, they are bound to treat the assumption of the 'primacy of the political' as outrageous nonsense. Even where one does not share this particular critical standpoint (and, as argued in the next chapter, there are sound reasons for rejecting some of the arguments of the 'capital logic' school), it is still necessary to reject those interpretations of political primacy that start out from the assumption that monopoly capital, either severally or collectively, is an autonomous, free-willed subject motivated by its strivings for the maximum profit and political power. But, if one interprets the 'primacy of the political' to mean simply that the development of the CMP entails a displacement of dominance to the political level in securing economic reproduction (i.e., from the dominant role of market forces and free competition to the dominant role of state credit, taxation, state intervention, nationalisation, etc.), there is much that can be said in support of this interpretation on 'capital-theoretical' as well as 'class-theoretical' grounds. On more concrete and complex levels of analysis, it is also evident that international relations will influence the development of particular capitalist societies and that competition between the socialist and capitalist blocs is not insignificant in this respect.

If we now consider the 'capital-theoretical' tradition, different sorts of criticism are appropriate. For, although the most egregious difficulties of the 'monopoly-theoretical' approach are absent, there are still sufficient problems to justify critical comment. The whole tradition tends to suffer from various forms of economic reductionism. Most notable among these is the technological determinism evident in the importance attached to the so-called 'fundamental contradiction' between the socialisation of the forces of production and the private appropriation of (monopoly) profits. For this is often coupled with a claim that the forces of production develop more or less autonomously from the relations of production and prepare the material basis for an inevitable transition to socialism. When linked with the idea that the state has become part of the economic base as well as retaining certain superstructural functions, this also suggests that the state might have a class-neutral core of productive functions which permit its economic apparatus (if not the repressive apparatus) to be employed immediately and unchanged in the transition period (for more extended criticism, see Magaline, 1975, *passim*; Mandel, 1978, pp. 154–158; Poulantzas, *CCC,* pp. 102–106; Théret and Wieviorka, 1977, pp. 11–31, 113–118; Valier, 1976, pp. 88–158). Even when the more extreme forms of technological determinism are avoided, economic reductionism is still evident in the marked tendency to treat the response of the state to the various needs of capital reproduction as automatic and immediate. This particular Marxist form of functionalism is typically a by-product of single-minded concern with the economic determinations of state monopoly capitalism and is quite compatible with an emphasis on the economic limitations to state power. But, as some of the more sophisticated stamocap analyses of the state have recognised, such an approach cannot account for the self-evidently partial, incoherent, and provisional nature of state intervention, the complex forms of institutional and organisation mediation involved in policy formation and implementation, and the crucial role of the balance of social forces in determining the pattern of state intervention. This theoretical failing is reflected in the simplistic claim that monopoly capital has fused with the state to form a single mechanism of economic exploitation and political domination and/or enjoys an exclusive command over state power. Such views presuppose that monopoly capital comprises a unitary class subject and that the state is a neutral instrument that offers no institutional or organisational resistance to manipulation in the interests of monopoly capital. Yet it should be clear that monopoly capital is heterogeneous and internally divided,

is organically related to non-monopoly capital, and has no unambiguous boundaries demarcating it as a specific class fraction. Moreover,
in advocating the need for an anti-monopoly alliance in the transition
to socialism, proponents of 'stamocap' theory seem to concede that
the monopoly bourgeoisie enjoys a measure of support from other
class forces. Otherwise there would be no need for an alliance — the
working class alone could overthrow the state monopoly capitalist
system. The stamocap analysis of petit bourgeois support for fascism
and the emphasis on the current major role of social democratic
opportunism in sustaining monopoly domination certainly lend little
credence to the cruder versions of the 'single mechanism' thesis.

These problems are aggravated in the case of French CME theory
by a serious misunderstanding of the nature of crises of overaccumulation, the function of devalorisation, and the overall dynamic of
accumulation. This is readily apparent from a brief comparison of
the account provided in PCF literature with that offered by Marx in
Das Kapital. Thus, while Marx distinguishes absolute from relative
overaccumulation in terms of a total or merely sectoral incidence of
zero 'value-added' at the margin, CME theorists specify them purely
in terms of the degree of marginal profitability. This encourages
neglect of the role of the intersectoral mobility of capital as a solution to relative over accumulation as well as the role of extending
labour time and/or increasing productivity as solutions to either form
of overaccumulation. Moreover, whereas Marx discusses these and
other counter-tendencies as cyclical phenomena, PCF theorists tend
to treat overaccumulation as a (potentially) permanent or long-term
phenomenon and suggest that devalorisation could be an equally
permanent or long-term solution. Again, while Marx defines devalorisation simply as a reduction in the total social capital (variable
as well as constant) due to the depreciation, sterilisation, or destruction of part of the total (which part depending on the outcome of
competition) viewed in isolation from its subsequent valorisation,
'CME' theorists define it as the valorisation of a determinate portion
of the total social capital at less than the average rate of profit (possibly nil or even negative) so that the remainder (typically monopoly
capital) can enjoy an above-average rate. Thus, although Marx concludes that devalorisation results in an increase in the rate of profit
for the total social capital (given that the amount of surplus-value
remains the same), in the CME analysis it involves merely a redistribution of profit from the devalorised capital to the monopolies
rather than an overall increase in the rate of profit (since the total
social capital also remains the same). Now, while it would be wrong

to suggest that such transfers of surplus-value cannot occur (or, indeed, to suggest that the taxation system cannot be used to extend the revenue sources of monopoly capital into non-capitalist relations of production), it is clearly wrong to suggest that devalorisation of this kind, even on a long-term basis, is more effective as a solution to overaccumulation than the mobilisation of other counter-tendencies (especially relative surplus-value production through increased productivity). Indeed, if one examines the nature of state intervention in modern capitalism, it is clear that it is often directed less at ensuring that state capital gets less than average profit than at promoting the reorganisation of private as well as public capital through the mobilisation of these counter-tendencies and/or arranging the socialisation of production in the interests of greater accumulation in general. However, by looking only at the relationship between the state and monopoly capital to the exclusion of the more general relationship between capital and labour, such theories certainly provide the rationale for appealing to small and medium capital as well as workers and peasants in building a broad, anti-monopoly alliance (for more extended discussion of the approach to political economy underlying CME theory, see Fairley, 1980; Magaline, 1975; Theret and Wieviorka, 1977; and Valier, 1976).

That one can criticise stamocap theories on various grounds does not mean that they are incorrigibly flawed. Indeed, as demonstrated in the work of Fine and Harris on the political economy of SMC and that of Herzog on the complex, highly mediated character of state intervention on behalf of monopoly capital, the stamocap paradigm need not share the alleged properties of its theoretical object and prove parasitic, decaying, and moribund. It can also be developed in a progressive way.

The work of Fine and Harris is particularly instructive here. In proposing principles of periodisation at the level of the reproduction of the pure CMP, they provide some of the theoretical means to distinguish simple monopoly and state monopoly capitalism as specific stages of capitalism. Moreover, rather than relying on the dominance of monopolies and/or the sheer level of state intervention as descriptive indicators, they employ a series of abstract concepts referring to the forms of reproduction. Likewise, since Fine and Harris distinguish between the periodisation of the pure CMP and that of the international system, they can provide a more sophisticated account of the relationship between SMC and imperialism. Thus, although certain of their arguments (especially those concerning the role of the state in the mobilisation of counter-tendencies to the TRPF and in adapting the relations of production to the socialisation of the forces of production) coincide in several respects with those given elsewhere in advanced 'capital-theoretical' texts, the overall approach constitutes a decisive break with the Leninist(-Stalinist) problematic and also records a number of significant advances in relation to other 'capital-theoretical' studies. Moreover, in contrast to other analyses in both traditions, there is little evidence that their various arguments have been subordinated to preconceived strategic conceptions.

But the work of Fine and Harris is not without difficulties. For, although they attempt to derive the forms of the capitalist state and political class struggle corresponding to successive stages of the CMP, their analysis of political and ideological relations is heavily imbued with economism. This creates problems even for their major contribution to periodisation. While they provide various concepts necessary for an adequate periodisation of capitalism, they still encounter difficulties in establishing that the CMP is divisible into distinct *stages* rather than being characterised simply by the accentuation of certain *trends.* This occurs because their explanation for these stages is itself couched in terms of the growing trend towards socialisation of productive forces. Indeed, as their own work as well as that of CME and other theorists makes plain, there is considerable overlap between the features of simple and state monopoly capitalism at the economic level. One possible solution to this problem can be found in discontinuities at the political level. For, although the basic causal principle of socialisation may be continuous, changes in the form and content of state intervention are required to secure the dominance of the features characteristic of each stage and these changes must be accompanied by an initial restructuring of the state apparatus itself. Thus stages could perhaps be distinguished in terms of the political discontinuities involved in the restructuring of the state system associated with the transition from the dominance of the features of one stage to the dominance of those of the succeeding stage. This solution would require a more detailed account of the periodisation of the capitalist state than is offered by Fine and Harris and it also demands a more sophisticated analysis of the balance of political forces than they provide. A preliminary account of these changes, employing the categories developed by Fine and Harris for the periodisation of the CMP at the economic level, is given in the concluding chapter of the present work. Similar considerations would apply to the analysis of the various stages of imperialism and this indicates the theoretical need for concepts appropriate to the periodisation of relations among nation-states analogous to those for the capitalist state itself. In short, although it is both possible and desirable to develop their approach to the economic determinations of state monopoly capitalism, their approach to the state and state power needs to be changed fundamentally through the incorporation of concepts more suited to the *sui generis* properties and complexities of this area.

The work of Herzog initiated this process in French stamocap theory but it has remained an isolated and undeveloped theoretical-coontribution. The recent work German work of Jung on variant forms of state monopoly capitalism is also interesting and might well suggest several parallels with the growth of Thatcherism as a private variant in Britain. But both theorists still adopt a residually economistic and class reductionist analysis of political forces and still subscribe to a treatment of state power as the essential expression of state monopoly capitalism. Thus it remains to be seen how the problems of an adequate political and ideological analysis can be resolved by building upon the work of the most sophisticated stamocap theorists.

METHODOLOGICAL CRITIQUE

So far I have glossed over the exact methodological status of stamocap theory. However, as should be evident from my remarks on the specific claims of 'stamocap' theory about the nature of modern capitalism and/or the modern state, substantive criticisms are necessarily related to particular methodological assumptions. In this context it is clear that the principal (but by no means the sole) methodological approach is more indebted to the work of Lenin on imperialism than of Marx on capitalism. For 'stamocap' arguments more often proceed through empirical generalisations and/or the subsumption of particular cases under general concepts or explanatory principles than they do through a movement from abstract to concrete by way of the logical derivation and/or contingent, differential articulation by concepts, assumptions, and principles of explanation to reproduce the concrete as the complex synthesis of multiple determinations (compare the empiricist conception of historical materialism in Lenin, 1894, pp. 136—142ff, the empiricist conception of dialectical materialism in Lenin, 1908, *passim,* and the empiricist method of presentation in his principal work on imperialism, Lenin, 1917b, with the realist account of the method of political economy found in Marx, 1857, pp. 100—108, and the realist movement from

abstract to concrete as the method of presentation in *Das Kapital*).
This is not to deny that 'stamocap' theories distinguish between
abstract and concrete as well as between general and particular; nor
that they argue for the inclusion of many causal factors and recognise the existence of counter-tendencies as well as tendencies in the
dialectic of social development. It is to argue that the basic approach
adopted in much 'stamocap' work renders such distinctions and arguments nugatory and creates significant theoretical and political problems.

This approach involves the repetition of basic Marxist-Leninist
principles and the subsumption of specific cases under these principles. These include a variety of laws, tendencies, essences, and interpretive criteria pitched at various levels of generality or abstraction,
such as the laws of value, surplus-value, maximum possible profit,
and uneven development, the historical trends towards the socialisation of labour, the concentration and centralisation of production,
the relative impoverishment of the working class, and the general crisis
of capitalism, essential features of historical stages such as the five
essential features of imperialism (see above, pp. 33–34) or the fusion
of the state and monopolies into a single mechanism in the stamocap
system, and interpretive criteria such as the basic determining role of
production relations in social life, the role of class struggle as the
motor force of history, or the class and partisan nature of the science
of political economy. Now, even where such principles occur originally in the work of Marx or Engels, they no longer function theoretically as abstract principles whose effects are subject to complex
mediations and the intervention of counter-tendencies. Instead they
are transformed into essentialised principles with immediate consequences for social life and/or into generalisations which subsume particular instances. In most cases, however, these principles have been
developed during the so-called 'era of imperialism and proletarian
revolution'. They are either based on more or less careful empirical,
albeit inevitably theory-laden, observation (i.e., pseudo-induction)
and/or on more or less arbitrary theoretical arguments phrased in
terms of Marxism-Leninism (i.e., pseudo-deduction). Regardless of
their specific provenance, they are deployed in the same manner as
the transformed Marxian principles. Thus, in place of a specification
of the real causal mechanisms that are located beneath the empirically observable level of surface appearances and that generate causal
tendencies whose effects are mediated in complex ways and/or are
subject to the intervention of counter-tendencies before being actualised, they either operate wholly on the empirical level through a

reciprocal movement between the general and particular and/or penetrate beneath the surface merely to postulate essential laws or tendencies that are immediately realised on the surface and/or are subject only to inessential modifications. These methods of theory-construction and presentation are combined with a commitment to the class and partisan nature of political economy so that the development of 'stamocap' theory is subordinated to political considerations and efforts are made to draw immediate political conclusions from theoretical enquiries.

This widely prevailing methodology has several serious implications for the theoretical status of stamocap analyses. Thus, in so far as they proceed through empirical generalisations and/or essentialised laws and tendencies, they are trapped in the well-known 'double bind' or trade-off between generality and determinacy. For general statements involving a high level of determinacy (or information content) run the danger of empirical falsity in a large number of particular cases; whereas general statements with low determinacy (or informational content) tend to be meaningless. This holds true whether the general statement is lawlike (striving for the maximum profit, uneven development), an historically discernible trend (relative impoverishment of the working class, absolute ruin of the peasantry and artisanate), an essentialised concept (such as imperialism or state monopoly capitalism), or an interpretive criterion (economic determinism, class struggle). This is reflected in the frequent resort of Marxist-Leninist stamocap theory to the techniques of subsumption, i.e., the development of general principles to fix the common features or essential properties of phenomena and the subsequent treatment of particular cases as so many instantiations or illustrations of these general principles. Thus all forms of state are reduced to reactionary dictatorships of the financial oligarchy and characterised by the fusion of the state and monopolies into a single mechanism. Not only does this entail systematic neglect of the specificity of different cases with potentially disastrous political consequences (witness the policies of the Comintern towards 'social fascism' during the rise of Nazism), it also means that deviations from these common features or essential properties must be explained away. Thus, whereas conformity with the general principles is taken for granted and considered as non-problematic, deviations are dismissed as accidental, inconsequential, temporary, inessential, and so on. Alternatively they are resolved dialectically through subsumption under another general principle whose effects modify or counteract the initial principle. Thus, if it seems that the 'stamocap' state is not fused into a single mechanism with the monopoly bourgeoisie and that its policies do not unambiguously reflect the interests of monopoly capital, this is attributed to the tendential intensification of all the contradictions in capitalism and the growing mobilisation of class forces around the proletarian pole of the capital-labour antagonism. This makes it difficult to derive any unequivocal conclusions from Marxist-Leninist principles and reinforces the overall impression of indeterminacy or vacuity in much stamocap work situated in the 'monopoly-theoretical' tradition and, to a lesser extent, in the 'capital-theoretical' tradition.

It is this basic methodological approach that explains the emphasis on distinctions at the level of market relations rather than of 'capital in general' (e.g., monopoly as the negation of competition, monopoly capital vs. non-monopoly capital), the descriptive bias of key concepts (imperialism, general crisis, state monopoly capitalism), the conflation of conjunctural and structural elements in key concepts (the inclusion of the coalescence of bank and industrial capital in imperialism found in Germany rather than the general structural phenomenon of increasing mobility of money capital and private credit through the rise of markets in financial assets), an inability to offer firm criteria for historical periodisation (witness the disagreements concerning the existence of a new phase of the third stage or the emergence of a fourth stage in the general crisis and the continuing disputes as to whether stamocap is a distinct stage in imperialism or merely a tendency coeval with it), the resort to originating subjects on the surface of society in preference to the dissolution of originating subjects into their constitutive and overdetermining causal influences (the treatment of monopolies as free-willed subjects striving for the maximum possible profit or the tendency to treat the state as the instrument of a unitary monopoly bourgeoisie and/or as a unitary subject in its own right), the neglect of economic, political, and ideological forms in preferences to class reductionist accounts of their content (downgrading the value form in economic analysis in favour of 'monopoly-theoretical' explanations or ignoring the question of state form in favour of its essentialisation as class dictatorship), the failure to consider the mediations that bring about the realisation of laws and tendencies in apparently pure form as well as the mediations that result in their non-realisation or distortion due to the intervention of countervailing tendencies or analogous factors (as in the tendency of the rate of profit to fall), and so forth.

This approach is less evident in the increasing body of work in the 'capital-theoretical' tradition. A particularly clear example of this methodological shift occurs in the work of Fine and Harris but the same method of abstraction is also found in the studies of other theorists who start out from the nature of capitalist commodity production, such as Jung and Schleifstein, Katzenstein, Wygodski, and Zieschang. This is not to suggest that the 'capital logic' critique of stamocap theories is wholly correct in arguing for the strict logical derivation of the categories for an analysis of monopoly and/or state monopoly capitalism from the categories of *Das Kapital.* It is to insist that the categories for such analyses must be introduced at the appropriate moments in the movement from abstract to concrete and their articulation (whether this be logically necessary or historically contingent) established within the hierarchy of determinations and conditions of existence. Thus, before one can discuss the nature of monopoly capital, monopoly profits and/or technological rents, monopoly price formation, the forms of monopolistic competition, etc., one must first establish the nature of capital in general, valorisation and surplus-value, prices of production, the formation of the average rate of profit, etc.; only then will it prove possible to determine their points of articulation, the manner in which the more abstract and simple categories are mediated in the conditions of monopoly and/or state monopoly capitalism, and the reciprocal effects of the specific forms of the abstract laws and tendencies of capitalism on its overall reproduction. Likewise, before one can investigate the nature of the state apparatus and state functions in monopoly and/or state monopoly capitalism, one must first derive the general form of the capitalist state and its implications for the functionality of the forms of state intervention. Moreover, since it is not the case that all the categories necessary for the analysis of monopoly or state monopoly capitalism are available in Marx's work, let alone solely in those texts concerned with value analysis, it is necessary to develop new categories for this purpose in the domains of economic, political, and ideological analysis as well as to establish their differential articulation in terms of levels of abstraction and/or types of determination. This applies particularly to the development of *sui generis* political and ideological concepts for the investigation of forms of state, the nature of social forces (popular-democratic and/or class forces), the social bases of state power, the domain of international relations (approached tangentially and inadequately in the analysis of the 'general crisis of capitalism'), the production of ideological effects (especially in relation to hegemony), and problems of strategy (such as the creation of popular-democratic alliances and the conduct of an 'anti-passive' socialist revolution). In this context it should be evident that stamocap theories are sadly lacking and that much theoretical work has still to be accomplished. We return to these issues in the last chapter.

CONCLUDING REMARKS

Stamocap theory provides a rich field for enquiries into the development of theoretical knowledge. Both its pre-history and history reveal the influence of agitational and strategic considerations as well as empirical and scientific concerns; and this is reflected in the distinctive character of much stamocap theory. Thus, not only have many of its supposedly substantive propositions been conditioned more by the prevailing revolutionary strategy than the critical evaluation of actual historical developments, even the more concrete and empirical investigations tend to employ the unsatisfactory method of theoretical 'subsumption'. Indeed, since the basic assumptions, concepts, and principles of explanation are frequently vague and indeterminate, it is quite possible to subsume the most varied and contradictory phenomena under the theoretical umbrella of stamocap and thus enter a spurious claim for its validity. Nonetheless, within this broad 'subsumptionist' perspective, there are certain explanatory principles that predominate. Thus most studies adopt an evolutionist perspective inspired by the 1859 *Preface* in which capitalism is supposed to prepare the material base for its own supercession. This is coupled with the assertion that the social basis of capitalism shrinks as monopoly capital acquires a growing hold over the state machine in order to further its profit and power despite the moribund nature of the capitalist system. This indicates the real possibilities of an anti-monopoly, democratic alliance able to displace the monopoly bourgeoisie from state power. In turn this presupposes an instrumentalist conception of the state and involves a subjectivist or voluntarist understanding of revolutionary consciousness and practice: in both cases this is coupled with a class reductionist interpretation of social forces such that the state is always a class state and the revolution can only be made through class struggle organised under the leadership of the (vanguard party of the) working class. Each of these principles is controversial and should be qualified or rejected. Such a theoretical project has already been initiated within the framework of the stamocap tradition itself but is far from complete and remains open to doubt in this context. However, whilst the predominant 'monopoly-theoretical' tradition is likely to remain incurably degenerative as a theoretical paradigm (especially to the extent that a primacy of the political over the cognitive is maintained), the chances of theoretical progression within the 'capital-theoretical' perspective would seem much greater. In order to see how this process might be accelerated and how the contributions of stamocap theory could also be utilised in studies of the state, we have to consider alternative approaches to state theory. This is the task of succeeding chapters.

3

Form and Functions of the State

Whereas most 'state monopoly capitalism' theories try to describe and explain the specific features of contemporary capitalism in terms of a few basic concepts of a generalised, but somewhat indeterminate, nature, an alternative approach has stressed the need for a systematic derivation of the form and functions of the bourgeois state from the most abstract principles of political economy. Thus, in contrast to the subsumption of particular features of specific states under general concepts, such as 'the fusion of the monopolies and the state into a single mechanism', drawn largely from Leninist theories of imperialism, the so-called *'Staatsableitung'* approach refers back to the method of *Das Kapital* and attempts to comprehend the modern state through a progressive, step-by-step movement from its most abstract determinations to its diverse, contingent forms and functions in particular cases. In general its adherents have concentrated on deriving the most abstract determinations as a precondition of more detailed investigations and have employed correspondingly abstract concepts and principles drawn from the Marxist analysis of simple commodity and/or capitalist commodity production. In its purported theoretical rigour and its high level of theoretical abstraction this approach differs fundamentally from most stamocap studies (with some notable exceptions) and deserves serious consideration as a distinctive branch of state theory. In this chapter we shall therefore examine its development in Germany and Great Britain and assess its various contributions to the analysis of the modern state.

HISTORICAL AND THEORETICAL CONTEXT

The analysis of the state was rediscovered as a major theoretical problem in West Germany and West Berlin in the 1960s and 'seventies and, indeed, came to dominate discussion among German Marxists in this period. This distinctive preoccupation is attributable to the specific historical situation in West Germany. On the economic plane there had been a major expansion in the state apparatus and its activities in response to the economic crises of 1966–67 and 1974–75 and, at least in relation to the former, state intervention appeared to have resolved the crisis more or less successfully. On the political plane the 1966–67 crisis prepared the path for a social democratic government whose strong ties with the trade unions ensured working-class support for its crisis-management policies and reformist programme. The consolidation of such support for a bourgeois regime and the continued growth of the West German economy posed formidable theoretical and political problems for the various extra-parliamentary leftwing parties, groups, and tendencies. This was coupled with the development of a 'strong state' to reinforce the hegemony of social democracy with administrative, judicial, and police repression of 'extremism' and with the growth of West German hegemonial aspirations in the EEC and the wider world. On the ideological plane the extra-parliamentary left was faced with a celebration of the constitutional and democratic form of the Federal Republic and denigration of the Stalinist dictatorship in East Germany. This contrast helped to sustain the anti-communism of the working class and required a response beyond a dogmatic insistence on the essentially repressive nature of the bourgeois state. In short, while strong traditions of working-class industrial and political struggle in such countries as Italy and France have favoured a 'class-theoretical' analysis of the economy and state alike, West German Marxists were encouraged to consider them from a more determinist and 'capital-theoretical' perspective and to seek the supposed agent of revolutionary change outside the working class. However, as economic crises grew less manageable and combined with an emergent crisis of mass integration, the limits of the state derivation debate became increasingly evident and new initiatives were undertaken in the theoretical and political fields (on the historical background, see: Classen, 1979, pp. 1–6; Cobler, 1978, *passim*; Hirsch, 1980b, pp. 116–141; and Minnerup, 1976, pp. 7–44).

Originally the derivation debate was concerned with specifying the form and functions of the capitalist state and thereby showing the limits of political reformism. To all intents and purposes the debate began with a critique of 'welfare state illusions' in which Müller and Neusüss put forward the main elements of the derivationist argument. They suggested that the basis of all 'revisionism' is the twin

view that, firstly, the state is independent of production and its economic laws and responds instead to *sui generis* relations of political
force and, secondly, that the latter can be modified so that state
power can be used to eliminate the cyclical and crisis-prone course of
capitalist production, to redistribute income independently of its
method of production, and to transform capitalism step by step
(Müller and Neusüss, 1970, pp. 13–14, 18–19, 21, 26–27, 34).
Revisionists in all periods had failed to see the essential connections
between the state and production as distinct moments in the overall
movement of capital and thus failed to perceive the limits on state
action imposed by the laws of capital accumulation. In particular
they had overlooked the dual character of the commodity as exchange-value and use-value, the dual character of capitalist production as a means of valorisation of capital and as a technical labour
process, the dual character of wages as variable capital and as revenue
for the worker, etc., and the limitations these contradictory forms
impose on the activities of the state in economic management and
welfare provision. In opposition to such revisionism Müller and
Neusüss claim that one can only comprehend the nature and limits
of the state on the basis of the laws of surplus value production
(1970, pp. 23–24n, 24–25, 47–49, 61).

Thus Müller and Neusüss emphasise that commodities must first
be produced within the framework of the capital relation before they
can be distributed through the market and/or political action and
stress that the state must ensure this framework before it can begin
its redistributive activities (1970, pp. 43ff). Indeed they argue that
state intervention is not just a secondary activity aimed at modifying
the effects of a self-sufficient market but is absolutely essential to
sustain the operation of capitalist production and market relations.
For, since individual capitals compete for profit, acting in their immediate self-interest and trying to avoid all limits to such action,
some external force is required to impose the interests of capital in
general. At the same time Müller and Neusüss argue that individual
workers are unable to defend their collective interests in reproducing
their labour-power for sale: thus the state must also encourage the
organisation of the working class (albeit within the limits of reformism) to ensure continued commodity production (1970, pp. 69, 80–
81). In this context they cite Marx's discussion of factory legislation
to show the essential role of the state in securing the long-term reproduction of capital through its protection of labour-power (1970,
pp. 60–70). As the state is involved in capitalist reproduction on
both sides of the capital-labour relation and responds in this to the

fluctuations of the class struggle as mediated through the 'public sphere', it appears to be neutral and thereby sustains the 'welfare state illusions' prevalent among reformists (1970, pp. 70–72). However, although the state needs a certain measure of independence and room for manoeuvre in this context, there are definite limits to its autonomy imposed by the requirements of capital accumulation. Where the balance of forces in class struggle threatens to push the state beyond these limits, it will respond forcefully against the working class (1970, p. 72). Nonetheless Müller and Neusüss emphasise that the primary function of the capitalist state *qua* bourgeois political institution is not repression (a characteristic of *all* states) but its intervention to resolve 'social problems' on behalf of capital in general (1970, p. 77). In turn they conclude that, should the capitalist state prove unable to counteract the tendencies towards social self-destruction inherent in capitalist exploitation and competition, the 'welfare state illusion' would fade and the labour movement would be able to advance towards socialism. Just this prospect is seen in the growing inability of the state to regulate capitalist exploitation based on relative (as opposed to absolute) surplus-value and the correlative need for the working class to confront capital directly at the point of production (1970, pp. 85–90).

This seminal contribution contains all the main ingredients of the subsequent *Staatsableitung* debate. But it is also remarkable for the vehemence with which it attacks the revisionists, reformists, and Frankfurt School theorists whom Müller and Neusüss accuse of the 'welfare state illusion'. This polemical spirit is much attenuated in the subsequent *Staatsableitungdebatte* and later studies are more formal and 'academic' in tone even though they address similar issues. In particular Müller and Neusüss investigate the specificity of the bourgeois state in terms of its *form* as the illusory community of society as a whole in contradistinction to the material anarchy of production and in terms of its *function* in checking the social problems engendered through capital accumulation. They also consider the mediations between the *appearance of class neutrality* of the bourgeois state and its *essential class character* as an 'ideal collective capitalist'. Finally they discuss the inherent *limitations on state intervention* under capitalism and the prospects for the *awakening of socialist consciousness* within the working class. At the same time their work does not fully develop the potential of the derivation method. For, not only do their arguments depend as much on illustration (notably the case of factory legislation) as on formal derivation, they also put greater weight on questions of function than form. Thus Müller and Neusüss can offer only a truncated account of the mediations between the forms and movement of the economic and political spheres. This is reflected in their more or less exclusive concern with the social policies of the capitalist state and their failure to examine how its form affects the state's ability to intervene on behalf of capital. It remains to be seen how well other studies can resolve these problems through a more self-conscious use of the derivation approach.

But we must first offer a preliminary outline of what this approach involves. For, despite the proliferation of studies claiming to derive the form and/or functions of the capitalist state, there is no clear account of the nature and methods of derivation. At one extreme it has been equated with 'logical inference' in a hypothetico-deductive explanatory schema and thereby rendered indistinguishable from the methods of the positivist tradition (e.g., Kuhlen, 1979, pp. 312–321); and, at the other extreme, one study limits 'derivation' to an initial deduction of the basic form of politics (the person) from the cell form of economics (the commodity) and the subsequent elaboration of political determinations exactly homologous to those of the economic field[1] (Oberlecher, 1975, pp. 1–13 and *passim*). The majority of studies regard 'derivation' as a distinctively Marxist method of theoretical research and argumentation involving the development of concepts for political analysis from the historical materialist critique of the capitalist mode of production and/or bourgeois society; but they do not claim that all these concepts are immediately deducible from economic categories and/or already available in *Das Kapital* or the *Grundrisse*. The basic assumptions of this method seem to be threefold: that reality comprises a complex structured whole whose elements have a certain autonomy within an overall unity, that this complex structured whole can be analysed at different levels of abstraction according to a complex hierarchy of determinations, and that the results of all investigations (regardless of the order of research) must be presented as a movement from abstract to concrete so that the whole (or that sub-set of its elements actually studied) is reproduced in thought as the complex synthesis of multiple determinations. Accordingly the aim of 'derivation' is to present the complex hierarchy of necessary and sufficient conditions of possibility of a theoretical object as defined at a specific level of abstraction and/or its necessary and contingently

---

[1] An approach which produced such path-breaking concepts as 'constant' and 'variable' persons, the 'social composition of political domination', and the law of 'tendential decay in political effectiveness' (*ibid.*).

necessary consequences on a more or less inclusive basis. Finally it should be noted that the specific application of this method is over-determined through the commitment of state derivation theorists to the basic categories of Marx's critique of political economy and to the socialist transformation of bourgeois society (among the more useful discussions of derivation, see: Blanke, Jürgens, and Kastendiek, 1974, pp. 108–123; Brandes *et al.,* 1977, pp. 7–13; Classen, 1979, pp. 91–113; Flatow and Huisken, 1973, pp. 93–100, 123–124; Hennig, 1974, pp. lix–lxxvi; Holloway and Picciotto, 1978, pp. 16–31; Kuhlen, 1975, pp. 312–332; Pashukanis, 1929, pp. 67–72).

Given this approach the key theoretical issue would seem to be the appropriate starting point for the derivation of the form and functions of the state. This depends not only on the analysts' understanding of Marx's critique of political economy but also on their initial conceptualisation of politics and the state. For the choice of starting point and the adequacy of any given attempt at derivation will clearly be affected by the prior specification of what needs to be derived. We find considerable differences among the various contributors to the *Staatsableitungdebatte* in this respect as well as in regard to choice of starting point for derivation. Thus, while the explicanda involved range from 'statehood' and the 'political' through the state as 'ideal collective capitalist' and/or as *Rechtsstaat* to the interventionist state and the bourgeois democratic republic, the starting points have included antagonistic class relations in general, the circulation of commodities, the sphere of exchange relations among competing sources of revenue, the dual nature of the commodity as use-value and exchange-value, 'capital in general' vs. 'particular capitals', and the relation between capital and wage-labour. It remains to be seen to what extent such derivations are commensurable and how far their inconsistencies call into question the whole approach.

Finally we should note that, although the *Staatsableitungdebatte* originated in West Germany and West Berlin and enjoyed its most vigorous and prolific incarnation there, it has also been influential in Britain and Scandinavia. In the British case this is due mainly to the work of the Conference of Socialist Economists (above all through the advocacy of Holloway and Picciotto) in popularising the 'derivation' approach in a context of growing disquiet with the theoretical alternatives implied in the Miliband-Poulantzas debate and the conflict between fundamentalist and neo-Ricardian economists. Social democratic reformism also provided a significant foil for the state derivation debate in these countries as well as in the Federal

Republic. Conversely the debate has proved much less influential in societies with a class-theoretical tradition, strong working-class movements, and a palpable crisis in the state, such as France and Italy, and, for other reasons, due mainly to its theoreticism and seeming irrelevance to current struggles, in the United States (on the reception of form analysis, see: Abendroth-Forum, 1977, pp. 295–296, 303–304, 310; Altvater and Kallscheuer, 1979, pp. 101–114; Fay, 1978, pp. 131–136, 148; Holloway and Picciotto, 1978, pp. 3–15; Negri, 1977, *passim*).

COMMODITY CIRCULATION, LAW, AND THE STATE

One of the most important approaches in this theoretical tradition tries to derive the form of bourgeois law and/or the capitalist state from the nature of commodity circulation. This can be seen as a moment in simple commodity production or as a moment in the overall circuit of capital and there are significant differences among such derivations according to which aspect is emphasised. The most influential precursor of 'form derivation' in general and of this approach in particular was the early Soviet legal theorist, Evgeny Pashukanis, who tried to derive the specific historical form of bourgeois law and its correlative state form from the essential features of commodity circulation. The starting point for his derivation is Marx's observation in *Das Kapital* that commodities cannot themselves go to market and perform exchanges in their own right: they must be committed to circulation through the intervention of subjects who enter into voluntary contractual relations in their capacities as owners of those commodities. Thus Marx concludes that the economic relation between commodities must be complemented with a juridical relation between wilful subjects (Marx, *C1*, pp. 88–89). Pashukanis also traces the emergence of the legal subject as the bearer of rights to the emergence of the commodity as a bearer of exchange-value and argues that the logic of juridical concepts corresponds to the logic of the social relations of commodity-producing society. For it is only with the full development of such production that every person becomes man in the abstract, every subject becomes an abstract legal subject, and the legal norm assumes the pure form of abstract universal law. This occurs because the circulation of commodities not only necessitates the emergence of legal subjects corresponding to all manner of goods but also because the constant circulation of commodities facilitates a clear differentiation between the bearer of rights and the objects in which alienable rights are held. Thus, while the pre-capitalist legal subject was a concrete individual with specific customary privileges, the legal subject of bourgeois society is the universal abstract bearer of all manner of claims. The kernel of the legal subject is the commodity owner but the formal attributes of freedom and equality rooted in the economic sphere are readily generalised to other areas of civil society and the state (Pashukanis, 1929, pp. 109–133 and *passim*).

It is in this context that Pashukanis attempts to derive the form of the bourgeois state as an impersonal apparatus of public power distinct from the private sphere of civil society. He argues that the legal form of the *Rechtsstaat* characteristic of bourgeois societies is required by the nature of market relations among formally free and equal individuals. These must be mediated, supervised, and guaranteed by an abstract collective subject endowed with the authority to enforce rights in the interests of all parties to legal transactions. However, although the state authority introduces clarity and stability into the structure of law and underwrites the operation of juridical relations, the material base of the specific form of bourgeois law and the legal subject is still rooted in capitalist relations of production. In turn this implies that law and the state will both die off when their common basis in bourgeois relations of production and/or distribution is ended (Pashukanis, 1929, pp. 134–150, 63–64, 80, 94, 104, 188, and *passim*).

This pioneering attempt at a logical derivation of the necessary form of bourgeois law has been variously appropriated in recent work on law and the state under capitalism. It has also endured much criticism (e.g., Arthur, 1976; Binns, 1980; Hirst, 1979, pp. 106–122; Kinsey, 1979; Poulantzas, 1967; Redhead, 1979). But, rather than looking at the difficulties in this early text, we shall consider how it has been used in subsequent Marxist analyses. There are many such studies which follow Pashukanis in asserting an essential correspondence between the commodity form and the legal form (a good example is found in Balbus, 1977) but few that add significantly to this argument. It is with some of the latter that we are concerned in the following commentary.

Burkhard Tuschling argues that law as a specific system of social relations between individuals emerges only with the full development of capitalism. Previously law had been limited to certain categories of individuals and their relations in particular spheres but capitalism results in the legalisation of all social relations, the birth of the legal subject, the growth of a specialised legal apparatus, and the consolidation of law as an organisational principle of the total social order. The critical factor in the rise of such a legal system is not the growth of the commodity form as such but its generalisation to the exchange of labour-power with capital. Tuschling insists that it is the commodification of labour-power which permits the rule of law to be established among formally free and equal citizens as well as requiring such a legal order to justify, systematise, and regulate its exchange with capital. In short, while Pashukanis merely links the legal form to the circulation of commodities and ignores their specific qualities and origins, Tuschling emphasises that it is the capitalist organisation of the labour-market and labour process that provides the key to the legal order and concludes that law must be understood in terms of the overall articulation of production, distribution, and exchange (Tuschling, 1976, pp. 12–29; cf. *idem, 1977*, pp. 270–271).

Tuschling then considers how capitalism determines the form and function of law. He argues that law plays a crucial role in mediating the contradiction between the formal equality of the individual owners of various commodities (including labour-power) and the substantive inequality of class exploitation within capitalist production. Thus it is essential for law to abstract from substantive differences among commodity owners in mediating and guaranteeing the sphere of exchange relations. But, at the very same time as it thereby offers a formal guarantee for the appropriation and disposition of property rights via the mutual exchange of equivalents among formally free and equal commodity owners, law also underwrites the appropriation of surplus-labour without equivalent in the capitalist labour-process and provides the legal framework within which the concentration and centralisation of capital can occur at the expense of the petit bourgeoisie and less efficient capitals. It is this last function that explains why law cannot be the private concern of capitalists. For not only must it be enforced against labour and other subordinate classes but also used to uphold the expropriation of individual capitals. The administration of law must therefore be handled by an apparatus that is distinct from the various economic agents within capitalism and this task falls to the *Rechtsstaat* as an autonomous legal subject endowed with a formal monopoly of force and empowered to implement the law in all spheres of society (Tuschling, 1976, pp. 30–38, 43–58; cf. *idem, 1977*, pp. 271–278).

Indeed Tuschling argues that the capitalist state is essentially 'rechtsstaatlich' in form and that this affects how the state operates in all areas and not just in its guise as guarantor of a legal order. For the contradictions between different moments of the total circuit of

capital and between different economic agents and classes are reproduced within the legal system; and the various preconditons of
capital accumulation therefore find themselves expressed and
mediated through legal forms rather than impressing themselves
directly on the attention of the state. This implies a certain indeterminacy in its interventions relative to economic imperatives and
opens up a space for political struggle within the bourgeois form of
law. There can be no absolute guarantees that the *Rechtsstaat* will
secure the reproduction of capital. Instead the effects of its actions
on accumulation depend on how the regularities or laws of motion of
capital are reflected in the balance of political forces. The state is an
'ideal collective capitalist' only to the extent that its pursuit of currently dominant particular interests coincides with the imputed
needs of 'capital in general' (there is no real collective capitalist) and
this depends upon a complex system of mediations among the economic process, political class struggle, and the legal-political and/or
economic activities of the state. Nonetheless Tuschling implies that
the distinctive forms of law and the state in capitalist society do
favour the accumulation of capital and he continues to maintain the
fundamental and quintessential correspondence between capitalism
and the dominance of a legal order (Tuschling, 1976, pp. 47–51,
60–87, 97–113; cf. *idem*, 1977, pp. 277–287).

Blanke, Jürgens, and Kastendiek also attempt to derive the form
of the state from the sphere of commodity circulation as one moment
in the overall circuit of capital. Their initial explicandum is the necessity under capitalism for extra-economic forms of reproduction (such
as law and politics) to complement the operation of economic forces
(such as value, exchance, price, and money) (Blanke *et al.*, 1974,
pp. 74–75; *idem*, 1975, pp. 110, 130). They argue that the circulation of commodities presupposes subjects who engage in exchange;
that these subjects must severally and reciprocally recognise rights to
private ownership and to freedom and equality in exchange; that
their relations must be fixed in legal forms such as private property
and contract; that an extra-economic force (not yet, be it noted, a
state in the form of one sovereign republic among others) is required
to guarantee the operation of the law; that this force needs both to
formulate the content of legal norms (to exercise a legislative function) and to administer them (to exercise an executive and judicial
function); that the form of law and its mode of enforcement must be
adequate to the commodity form; and that this condition can be met
if legal norms are impersonal, general, and public and they are formulated and administered in a constitutional or *rechtsstaatlich* manner

(Blanke *et al.*, 1974, pp. 76–79; *idem*, 1975, pp. 122–124). Thus it is the twin task of formulating and enforcing law in conformity with the requirements of capitalist reproduction that determines the necessity of an institutional separation between the economic and political and that also conditions the form of the state as an impersonal public authority standing above private legal subjects. The result is a *'doubling'* (or duplication in different forms) of bourgeois domination into the *economic compulsion* of market forces in the process of valorisation and realisation and the *political compulsion* of subordination to an abstract, universal, public power. This 'doubling' is reflected in the separation of private law, organised around the right of private property, from public law, concerned with the maintenance of political order and the tasks of government. For Blanke *et al.* this means in turn that the basic form of politics is conflict over the creation and/or implementation of legal relations governing the private and/or public sphere of bourgeois society (Blanke *et al.*, 1974, pp. 79–81; *idem*, 1975, pp. 125–126).

After this initial derivation of the separation of the political, its basic function in reproduction, and its most adequate form, Blanke *et al.* examine how its relation with the economic is mediated through money and law. They argue that state intervention occurs through the manipulation of monetary and/or legal relations (corresponding to the two spheres of bourgeois domination) and, since these are not as such relations of production, the state is thereby limited in its power to affect capital accumulation. Hence changes in the law are limited in effectiveness because subjects identical in law might occupy different positions in the relations of production (and vice versa) and because legal subjects remain free to act contrary to the will of the state within the confines of the law. Likewise state control over money (including credit, taxation, public spending) affects economic agents as holders of money rather than as *träger* of particular economic functions; it also leaves them free to employ their net money holdings as revenue or capital for various productive or unproductive purposes (Blanke *et al.*, 1974, pp. 88–90; *idem*, 1975, pp. 129–130).

In addition to these limitations inherent in the very forms of money and law, Blanke *et al.* also discuss two further constraints upon state intervention. Firstly they note that the state responds through a range of policies oriented to different *surface* forms of the circuit of capital (such as the demand for money, labour-power, or goods). As these forms enjoy a certain autonomy and have no immediately transparent, unequivocal relation to the underlying course of capital accumulation, there can be no guarantee of the coherence of different policies nor of their effectiveness in resolving economic problems. Thus, even though there is a formal unity to such policies deriving from a common source within the state apparatus, their combined effect depends on the overall movement of capital and therefore corresponds to a logic beyond this formal unity (Blanke *et al.*, 1974, pp. 93–100; *idem*, 1974, pp. 137–138). Secondly, since the course of accumulation hinges on the balance of class forces, changes therein will also affect the state's power to intervene. Here Blanke *et al.* argue that there is a structurally fixed asymmetry between capital and labour in capacities to resist adverse state intervention and conclude that the working class is more easily forced to bear any burdens of adjustment during crises. But they also stress that rights won in proletarian struggle can hinder accumulation and argue that, in response to such struggle, the state is drawn into regulating the relations between capital and labour in the long term interests of accumulation. This is reflected in the successive institutionalisation of rights to survival as an individual wage-labourer (factory acts) and organise for better pay and conditions (unions, parties) and, latterly, of the quasi-right to employment (Keynesianism, concerted action). Yet, as the fascist interlude proved, such rights are not irreversible. Thus the working class must struggle to defend its rights as well as to gain new legal concessions (Blanke *et al.*, 1974, pp. 96–99, 100–105; *idem*, 1975, pp. 139–146).

Similar problems of legal periodisation have been discussed by the British theorist, Sol Picciotto. For, while following Pashukanis in deriving the legal form from the commodity form, he also argues that legal relations must be theorised in terms of the historical dynamic of capital accumulation. He distinguishes three stages of the legal form, corresponding to primitive accumulation, competitive capitalism, and monopoly capitalism respectively. The first stage sees the creation of individuals as economic and legal subjects, the centralisation of legitimate force in the hands of the state, and the institution of the principle of individual legal responsibility. Yet the coexistence of simple commodity circulation with primitive accumulation means that the bourgeois legal form coexists with class privileges, bribery, and overt coercion (cf. Gerstenberger, 1973, p. 221). After the consolidation of capitalist relations of production and the dominance of market forces in social reproduction, the liberal rule of law can be established and the state can restrict itself to maintaining the formal equivalence of different economic subjects. But the movement of capital continually disrupts formal as well as substantive exchange equivalence and demands state intervention to recuperate the rule of law and impose substantive equivalence (e.g., through factory legislation and social welfare). In this context the growing importance of the tendency for the rate of profit to fall (TRPF) with the consolidation of monopoly capitalism necessitates growing intervention to reorganise the whole set of bourgeois social relations. In the legal sphere this is seen in the increasing importance of administrative discretion over legal certainty, bureaucratic regulation rather than legally-mediated market forces, specific tribunals rather than courts with general legal jurisdiction, private and state insurance rather than individual responsibility and liability, socialised rights in property rather than individual private property, and so on. Thus the contradictions and tensions of capital accumulation find expression in the legal form as well as other social relations (Picciotto, 1979, pp. 170–177).

ACCUMULATION, STATE, AND STATE INTERVENTION

Whereas the analyses above derive the fundamental forms of law and state along with their functions from the sphere of circulation viewed as a moment in simple commodity and/or capitalist commodity production, other studies have started out from the sphere of capitalist production considered in itself and/or as the determinant moment in the circuit of capital as a whole. Thus they should provide a more detailed account of the state's functions in capital accumulation than those studies which merely consider how the basic function of the state in securing the juridico-political preconditions of commodity circulation is radically transformed through the commodification of labour-power. Conversely, in so far as they move directly from the political preconditons of capitalist production to the economic functions of the bourgeois state without regard to the mediation between the economic and political spheres, they run the risk of economic reductionism. Let us consider how the balance of theoretical advantage works out in these analyses.

As early and influential account was offered by Elmar Altvater in some comments on the problems involved in Keynesian demand management. His starting point is the distinction between 'capital in general' and 'particular capitals'. Thus Altvater argues that certain preconditions for the overall reproduction of the total social capital ('capital in general') cannot be secured through the actions of its constituent units ('particular capitals') because competitive pressures (or other value considerations) make it unprofitable (or impossible) for them to be so provided. This means that capital requires a special institution which is not itself subject to the constraints of valorisation facing individual capitals and which is thereby enabled to act in the interest of capital in general. It is this necessity that explains the 'particularisation' (*Besonderung*) of the state as an institution 'outside and above bourgeois society' and its crucial function in complementing and modifying the role of competition in capitalist reproduction (Altvater, 1971, pp. 98–100). Altvater then specifies four social preconditions of capitalism that cannot be secured through competition among particular capitals and must therefore be guaranteed through the actions of the state as an 'ideal collective capitalist'. These social conditions are: the implementation of the general material conditions of production (or infrastructure); the creation and enforcement of the bourgeois legal order; the regulation of the conflict between capital and wage-labour; and the promotion of the total national capital in the capitalist world market (Altvater, 1971, pp. 100–102).

In subsequent discussion Altvater concentrates largely on the first function, on the grounds that this is the principal factor determining the 'particularisation' of the state. He also adds that, while these four functions are general features of the bourgeois state, their precise scope and importance are historically determined through crises, conflicts, and struggles. For, since no single capital will voluntarily submit to objective necessities that threaten its competitive position, some external compulsion is required to stimulate the state to impose the interests of 'capital in general' on individual capitals. This need is reinforced by the fact that state intervention is not unambiguously beneficial to capital – it also entails the public expenditure of a part of the social surplus and thus presents a barrier to private accumulation (Altvater, 1971), pp. 100–108). In this context Altvater also notes that the state is not completely autonomous but is firmly integrated into the circuit of capital. It can only modify the law of value and not suspend its operation. Thus, if the state draws too heavily on the social surplus, it will threaten accumulation. And, while Keynesian techniques may prevent crises of overproduction taking the form of periodic mass unemployment and deflation, the state must consider how its expenditures affect the relations between particular capitals and/or between capital and wage-labour and must also take care that the purgative, regenerative effect of crises is secured through other means so that any tendencies towards 'stagflation' are eliminated (Altvater, 1971, pp. 76–83; cf. Altvater *et al.*, 1974a, pp. 147–148).

Likewise, following an initial derivation of the necessity and form of the bourgeois state from the sphere of commodity circulation, Läpple then proceeds to establish its functions in capitalist production. He distinguishes between short-term attempts to counteract the cyclical course of accumulation and long-term intervention to create various general conditions of (re)production. In this context Läpple focuses on the creation of general conditions of production rather than reproduction and distinguishes between *general external conditions of the CMP* (notably an appropriate legal framework and the organisation of extra-economic force) that must be secured through state action and those *general conditions of production within capitalism* (such as material or social infrastructures) whose realisation is essential for the majority of individual capitals to continue production but whose creation may or may not be secured through the state, depending on the exact historical situation. In particular he argues that, within the constraints linked to fixed capital outlays, turnover time, the non-exclusivity of certain 'public goods', the existence of 'natural monopolies', etc., the state will increase its provision of general conditions of capitalist production as the socialisation of production increases and with it the share of the total social capital needed to create these conditions (Läpple, 1973, pp. 99–101, 111, 118–121, 138–146, 166–169, 185–188, and *passim*).

A similar approach to the derivation of the form and functions of the capitalist state has been taken by a multinational trio who focus on labour-power as a unique condition of capitalist commodity production. Thus Aumeeruddy, Lautier, and Tortajada argue that the basic foundation of the capitalist state as a distinctive institution of class domination is the nature of the wage-relation. For, although labour-power is the crucial precondition of the CMP, it is reproduced as a simple commodity and enters the circuit of capital through the exchange of labour-power for revenue as a means of capitalistically unproductive consumption. There is no guarantee that labour-power will reproduce itself to satisfy the needs of capital and/or enter the labour market on terms favourable to its valorisation. Moreover, once it is subject to capitalist control within the labour process proper, there is no guarantee that wage-labour will not be destroyed through over-exploitation. Thus capital requires an extra-economic institution that can secure the individual, collective and intergenerational reproduction of a labour force suited to its needs and also ensure that conditions in the labour market favour accumulation. It is this task that is definitive of the state as an extra-economic institution because its role in securing general conditions of production does not differentiate it from those collective capitalist organisations which co-exist with the state. Reproduction of the wage relation is a complex task and requires active management of a changing conjuncture rather than pursuit of a predetermined and autonomous economic policy. Among the means that the state can employ are coercion, the wage-related individuation of the work force, education, and welfare policies. But its activities in these areas are restricted by the contradiction between the need to minimise the costs of reproduction and the need for the state to respect the formal freedom of wage-labour (see Aumeeruddy *et al.*, 1978, pp. 43–61; see also, de Brunhoff, 1976, pp. 9–32, 81–93).

A somewhat different approach has been adopted by Dieter Sauer in his derivation of the capitalist state and its functions. He located the state in terms of the contradiction between the material substance of production (its use-value) and the social form determining that production (surplus-value created in the labour process and realised through exchange) and argues that the *form* of the capitalist state is related to its separation from the exchange nexus (as a precondition of the operation of the law of value) and its *functions* are related to its role in resolving the aforesaid contradiction (especially through actions which focus on the use-value side and thus complement market-based solutions). But Sauer also stresses that such a twofold derivation must take into account how the connection between the economic and political regions thus conceived is mediated at lower levels of abstraction. The crucial mediations in his movement from the economic to the political domains concern the sphere of competition and exchange relations. For it is on this level that the 'substance-value' contradiction expresses itself in the valorisation problems of particular capitals and/or the reproduction problems of the various commodity-owners (especially wage-labourers) involved in the overall circuit of capital; and it is also on this level that the field of legal relations among exchange subjects emerges and requires mediation, regulation, and sanction in respect of the particular interests of commodity-owners ('men'), the general interests of formally free and equal members of political society ('citizens'), and the relations between the particular and general interests of these duplex, janus-faced 'men-citizens'. In this context Sauer argues that the form of the state as an apparatus institutionally separated from the exchange nexus is necessitated by the twin needs to secure the legal framework of capitalist society and to supplement market forces in overcoming the 'substance-value' contradiction. Its actions in this latter respect are directed to the material needs of valorisation and/or reproduction as these are represented in 'social problems': the state does not respond to these needs as such but to their repercussions in the political arena. Sauer also notes that state interventions are mediated through money and law; and that they are constrained by the state's reliance on accumulation for its resources and its entrapment within the contradictions of capitalism (Sauer, 1978, pp. 14–36, 68–75).

Sauer distinguishes four basic modes of state intervention: changing the formal conditions in which conflicts of interest are fought out (e.g., through industrial relations legislation), immediate interventions in support of private material production, and direct public provision of material reproduction requirements. He then discusses the effective scope and limitations of these modes of state intervention in terms of their potential repercussions on individual reproduction, competition among individual capitals, and the balance between public and private interests. In each respect it is stressed that money and law have distinct limits as means of intervention. For the abstract, general form of money and law ensures that they are inadequate means of direct control over the concrete conditions of valorisation and reproduction. Yet, if the state tries to circumvent this constraint through direct action to favour particular interests or ensure specific material preconditions, it threatens to undermine the autonomy of particular capitals and/or commodity-owners (an essential precondition for the operation of market forces) as well as to subvert the rule of law with its universal norms and formal equality. Similar problems occur within the state apparatus itself, structured as it is through its own monetary and legal forms. Thus, whereas the unity and coordination of the various branches and activities of the state apparatus depend on their common compliance with the same generalised formal principles of financial and legal accountability, their ability to intervene effectively depends on flexible response to changing conditions in the provision of resources and the conduct of policies to resolve specific 'social problems'. In this context Sauer stresses that the legally structured and conditioned sphere of political struggle over such problems and the equally *rechtsformig* organisation of the state apparatus are crucial mediations in the movement from the political to the economic. Thus 'social problems' are seen as comprising demands made by various individual commodity-owners and/or particular capitals expressing concern about the repercussions of contradictions, crises, etc., on reproduction and/or valorisation and, if they are to succeed as demands on state action and resources, linking the solution of particular problems to the realisation of general interests. Together with his analysis of monetary and legal forms and the organisation of the state apparatus, the concept of the form of 'social problems' (and the complementary notion of 'state strategies') represents an attempt to offer political mediations matching competition and exchange in the economic sphere and thus to provide a more complex, less indeterminate account of the form, organisation, functions, and limitations of the capitalist state (Sauer, 1978, pp. 70–76, 122–130, 143–180).

Similar approaches to *Staatsableitung* in terms of competition and valorisation have been developed in Britain. Thus Clarke has developed this perspective in his attack on so-called 'fractionalist' theories – which he criticises for reducing state power to a resultant of struggles among the immediate political representatives of supposedly independent fractions of capital over the redistribution of surplus-value. Instead he argues that state power must be located in terms of the valorisation of capital in general and its antagonistic relation with wage-labour. Clarke examines capital in general in terms of the various constraints imposed on the valorisation of particular capitals through their basic interdependence within the overall circuit of capital and through the averaging out of profit rates through competition. He suggests that capital in general is reproduced through the mobility of money capital (as the most elemental expression of capital in general) in search of profits above the average determined through competition: these can be found in areas where market forces have failed to secure the production of commodities necessary for the valorisation of specific capitals. If this market-mediated mechanism fails to secure the reproduction of the total social capital, state intervention will become necessary. Thus individual capitals, specific fractions of capital (as constituted through their monetary, productive, or commercial functions in the overall circuit of capital and/or their direct or indirect relation to a definite branch of production), and capitalist interest groups (as constituted through their common relation to specific economic policies pursued by the state) will mobilise to force the state to take measures intended to overcome or circumvent various barriers to their own valorisation and/or that of capital in general. The outcome of such struggles does not depend on purely political factors but is ultimately determined by the strategic importance of different capitals in the overall circuit of capital and/or the negative effects incurred through dysfunctional state interventions and expressed in monetary instability or fiscal crises. Clarke concludes that state intervention operates as a distinct 'moment' in the self-reproduction of capital and compensates for those valorisation problems unresolved through competition as its 'economic' moment (Clarke, 1978, pp. 36, 53–66; for the counter-charge of economism and essentialism, see: Solomos, 1979, pp. 143–147).

In contrast to the economic reductionist tendencies evident in the priority that Clarke gives to the state's role in valorisation and his neglect of form analysis, Holloway and Picciotto, the leading British spokesmen of the *Staatsableitung* school, prioritise the question of form and then trace its implications for the functions of the state. They derive the possibility and necessity of the capitalist state as an institutionally separate apparatus of coercion from the quintessential role of commodity exchange in mediating capitalist economic exploitation (Holloway and Picciotto, 1977, p. 79; cf. Hirsch, *seriatim*). They then argue that this 'particularisation' of the state as a distinct form of class domination provides the material basis for bourgeois political and ideological practices to fetishise the economic and political as wholly independent spheres and to maintain the separation of workers' economic and political struggles as a precondition of bourgeois domination. Yet, despite the real institutional separation of the political and economic regions and despite the ideologically inspired illusion of their total independence from each other, Holloway and Picciotto insist that the state and the sphere of commodity production are characterised by a 'separation-in-unity' as specific forms of the selfsame capital relation and are both pervaded with the contradictions involved in the antagonism between capital and labour. This means that the development of the form and functions of the bourgeois state should not be seen as having a purely political dynamic nor reduced to a simple epiphenomenon of some alleged economic base: instead they must be located in terms of an ever-renewed reorganisation of the historical complex of economic, political, and ideological conditions necessary to capital accumulation as a social relation of exploitation (Holloway and Picciotto, 1977, pp. 79–81, 84–85, 94; *idem*, 1978, pp. 14, 17–18).

In this context they discuss how the path of the capitalist state from its transitional, absolutist form through its classical liberal stage to its current interventionist stage is determined by the dialectic between the *forms* of class struggle imposed through the 'separation-in-unity' of the capital relation and the *content* of specific struggles over particular aspects of that relation. This applies both to the policies pursued in these different stages as the contradictions of the capital relation unfold and to the changing forms of the state through which such policies are effected. In addition to familiar arguments concerning the constraints implied in the exclusion of the state from the productive core of capitalism, its tax dependence, and its reliance on monetary and legal forms of intervention, Holloway and Picciotto also highlight in a novel manner the role of crises in the forcible reimposition of unity among elements that have become disjointed. Yet, as capital strives to resolve crises through attempts to overcome the barriers to accumulation rooted in the state form itself, it tends to undermine that separation of the political from the economic which is crucial to its own survival. Indeed, as the state loses its general, impartial, external form and gets directly involved in economic reproduction on behalf of particular capitalist interests, its fetishised appearance of class-neutrality declines and an important basis of bourgeois domination over the working class is thus weakened (Holloway and Picciotto, 1977, pp. 86–93).

SURFACE FORMS, COMMON INTERESTS, AND THE STATE

Whereas the studies just reviewed derive the form and/or functions of the bourgeois state from the fundamental properties of capitalist production, other studies argue that one should examine these questions at the level of the surface forms of appearance of the CMP. This claim was first adumbrated by the Marxistische Gruppe/Theoriefraktion based at Erlangen but is most generally identified with the work of Flatow and Huisken, the Projekt Klassenanalyse group (or PKA), and the Arbeitskonferenz München (a theory work-shop within the Rote Zellen movement). Let us see how this school differs from those considered so far.

Flatow and Huisken suggest that any serious attempt at derivation must seek to link the state as a phenomenon on the surface of bourgeois society with relevant surface characteristics of capitalism as a mode of production. It should not seek the essence of the state in the essence of capitalism nor derive specific state functions from the needs of capital without considering how these needs are mediated through the surface forms of the state. They locate the basic surface forms of the bourgeois state in its mediating role between particular and general interests. They then relate this role to the surface forms of specific class interests in the CMP. Here they invoke Marx's analysis of the transformation of *antagonistic class interests in valorisation* into the interests attached to different *factors of production* as sources of *revenue.* Thus the value of labour-power appears as the price of labour, surplus-value appears as profit (industrial profit and/ or interest), and surplus-profit appears as ground-rent. Moreover, while there are some respects in which these revenue categories have particular interests arising from differences in their associated factors of production, they also have three interests in common. These are an interest in the maintenance of the revenue source itself, an interest in the highest possible revenue, and an interest in the continuity of revenue. Flatow and Huisken then argue that these common interests are reflected in the three basic functions of the capitalist state: protecting property in all its forms, creating conditions in which revenue categories can raise their incomes through competition, and regulating the course of capital accumulation so that crises and business cycles are eliminated as far as possible. However, although it can be logically demonstrated that these interests are common to all revenue sources, they actually exist for specific revenue categories as particular interests and competitive forces prevent them from combining privately to secure their common interests. From this Flatow and Huisken conclude that revenue categories have a 'doubled' existence as property owners with particular interests and 'citizens' with common interests of the kind outlined. In turn this is reflected in the 'doubling' of bourgeois society into civil society and the state respectively. Thus the state should be seen as the means through which the various members of bourgeois society find their common interests in capitalist reproduction are secured alongside and sometimes in opposition to their particular interests (Flatow and Huisken, 1973, pp. 95, 99–120; cf. Marxistische Gruppe/Theoriefraktion, 1972, pp. 2–22).

In this context Flatow and Huisken argue that the general interest becomes a particular interest of the state apparatus and that it is able to pursue this interest because it has its own specialised apparatus and resources. But they also concede that the state has no privileged knowledge of the general interest and responds instead to the specific demands of particular interests. This raises the question of how such particular interests are translated into the general interest and here Flatow and Huisken seek the answer in the articulation of surface forms with the underlying movement of capitalism. Thus it is when labour as labour-power, capital as value-in-process, or land as a fundamental presupposition of capitalist production are endangered severally and/or collectively that their particular demands as a revenue source are most likely to precipitate state action which advances the general interest at the same time as it corresponds to the narrow interests of specific factors of production. From this they conclude that the functions of the state cannot be established in the abstract (nor reduced to a mere reflex of changes in majority opinion) but must instead be related to concrete problems of valorisation in definite historical conjunctures (Flatow and Huisken, 1973, pp. 123–124, 129–137).

The *Projekt Klassenanalyse* group adopt a similar approach. Their starting point is the observation that the capitalist state does not appear as a class state but as the embodiment of the 'general will' of all members of society and they conclude from this that its form must be derived from that level of the CMP on which parallel forms of false consciousness emerge. However, while Flatow and Huisken proceed from the surface of capitalist production in terms of Marx's own 'trinity formula' (which shows how the three basic classes of Victorian England appear merely as three different sources of revenue, Marx, 1894, pp. 814–831), the PKA group focuses on the relations among free and equal owners in the sphere of commodity circulation. Hence they argue that it is in simple commodity circulation, with its exchange of equivalents among formally free and equal commodity producers, that produces basis for all the juristic, political, and social appearances of bourgeois society and thereby enables the dissimulation or mystification of its essential class nature. In this context they emphasise the fundamental role of ideological reproduction (the reproduction of suitable forms of false consciousness) in the overall reproduction of bourgeois society and go on to argue that the mutual recognition of rights to property, freedom, and equality is a key precondition of economic reproduction as a whole as well as being necessary to the pursuit by individual producers of their own special interest. The PKA group expresses this idea in the claim that property, freedom, and equality comprise the 'general will' of simple commodity producers. However, since the latter are unable to realise their common interests through private means owing to conflicts among their particular interests (an argument we can express in similar terms as a contradictory 'will of all'), it is necessary for the 'general will' to be handled by a special apparatus standing outside and above the sphere of civil society. Thus bourgeois society is noted for the 'doubling' of its members into 'owners' and 'citizens', of law into private law and public law, and of society into civil society and state. However, whereas the reality of simple commodity production corresponds to its forms of appearance as a system based on freedom and equality, the same forms contradict the reality of capitalist exploitation which is certainly mediated through commodity circulation but is actually rooted in the economic compulsions and inequalities of 'wage-slavery'. Thus the possibility of an anonymous form of class domination expressed in the state as an embodiment of the 'general will' depends on complete acceptance by wage-labour of the appearance of freedom and equality in the economic sphere and on the pervasiveness of the corresponding legal forms throughout society (Projekt Klassenanalyse, 1976, pp. 81–84, 86–87, 89–90; cf. *idem*, 1973, pp. 79–126; 1974, *passim*; 1977, pp. 9–10).

In this context the PKA then discuss the form and functions of the capitalist state as the embodiment of the 'general will'. They suggest that the 'general will' is ascertained through the interplay of diverse particular interests on the field of political representation and their articulation into political programmes which justify the advancement of specific interests in terms of their integral, organic connections with the general interest. Politicians are the special agents or *träger* of this process and the PKA claim that they monopolise the representational function and seek to make themselves independent from the represented. The principal site for distilling the 'general will' in this manner is Parliament (ideally embodying the 'will of the nation' by virtue of its election through universal suffrage) and the form in which the 'general will' is executed is that of law. The latter is implemented through an executive branch financed from taxation and national debt and organised in terms of a systematic and hierarchical division of labour suited to the situational specification of general norms. The PKA also note that all economic and political relations are liable to adjudication through a specialised judicial branch in terms of their general legality and/or compatibility with constitutional prescriptions. Finally they examine the functions of the capitalist state in bourgeois social reproduction and distinguish among three broad functional orientations. These areas of intervention are: functions which arise directly from the specific form of capitalist production and its institutional separation from the political sphere (e.g., law, finance, defence); functions which concern the development of the productive forces, including labour-power, considered in abstraction from their bourgeois form (e.g., education, science, health); and, as a residual category, functions which reflect both concerns more or less equally (e.g., housing, environment, public enterprise in various areas) (see Projekt Klassenanalyse, 1976, pp. 90–94; 1977, pp. 14–17, 23, 90–92ff; cf. *idem*, 1973, pp. 94–97).

The Arbeitskonferenz München differ in important respects from the other adherents of this school. For, although the AK München also use the trinity formula and argue that the bourgeois state is required to maintain the framework in which revenue sources interact, they insist that the different revenue sources can have no common interests in a class-divided society. Instead they argue that different sources have their own distinctive interests in the existence of an extra-economic power and that these interests converge independently on the bourgeois form of state. Thus, just as competition among industrial capitals prevents them from securing certain social and material preconditions of profitable production, competition among wage-labourers and/or their conflicts with their capitalist employers involve distinct reproduction problems for the working class. Since no real general interest exists and since a power monopoly could operate against excluded interests necessary to capital accumulation, the most adequate form of state is a democracy which accords access to all those revenue sources involved in capitalist reproduction and enables them to advance their own interests. The conflicts of these revenue sources are therefore reproduced inside the state and are reflected in the policies it pursues. Thus, whereas some policies are primarily a response to the demands of capital, others are largely a response to working-class demands. The AK imply that, in so far as these demands are expressed as those of diverse revenue sources rather than those of inherently antagonistic classes, the capital relation will be maintained. At the margin of normal politics and/or where open class struggle occurs, however, the state will use force to control working class demands that threaten capital in general (see: AK München, 1974a, pp. 12–18, 32–38; and 1974b, pp. 150–165 and *passim*).

POLITICAL ECONOMY, POLITICAL SOCIOLOGY, AND CLASS DOMINATION

An alternative approach to *Staatsableitung* has been elaborated by Joachim Hirsch and involves an attempt to combine a political economy of capitalism with a political sociology of class domination. Thus, although he makes fundamental and systematic use of assumptions, concepts, and principles of explanation drawn from *Das Kapital,* he also relates the state and its functions to the overall movement of class struggles and tries to specify how the organisation of the state apparatuses and political system influence the reproduction of class domination as a whole. Hirsch argues that *all* class societies require some *relation of force* to underwrite the exploitation of one class by another: it is merely the *form* of this relation that varies from one mode of production to another. Under capitalism the relations of production and exchange must be formally free and equal and organised without the immediate threat or use of coercion. Thus

Hirsch concludes that force must be centralised in an apparatus external to production and exchange. But he also argues that it must still be made available to secure these social relations through various means (including action against particular capitals) as well as to maintain relations of class domination in other areas. However, while this particularisation of the state as a formally independent, class-neutral coercive power is *necessary* for capitalist reproduction and is made *possible* through the role of exchange in coordinating the division of labour and mediating economic exploitation, the resulting institutional separation of economic and political processes and their subordination to *sui generis* forms of organisation cast doubt on their functional complementarity in the practical realisation of bourgeois domination (Hirsch, 1973, pp. 200–204; 1974a, pp. 59–60, 63; 1974b, pp. cxxxix–cxliv; 1974c, pp. 88–89; 1976a, pp. 100, 103–108; 1976b, pp. 105–107).

In this context Hirsch initially investigated the capitalist state as an extra-economic power in terms of three general functions it could perform in capital accumulation. Firstly the state might guarantee the general external conditions of capitalist relations of production and secure those general conditions of production whose supply cannot be ensured through market forces alone. Secondly the state might engage in the administrative redistribution of revenues and/or regulate the circulation process to safeguard particular conditions of production on behalf of strategically important individual capitals and/or to sustain the reproduction of wage-labour. Thirdly the state might also promote the development of productive forces through such means as state-sponsored research and development and various forms of long-term planning and programming. Hirsch also implies that the state's role in economic reproduction (especially in relation to the second- and third-mentioned functions) becomes more important both quantitatively and qualitatively with the further historical development of capitalism and its attendant socialisation of production and growing susceptibility to the tendency of the rate of profit to fall (TRPF). Indeed, while other form-derivationists have developed similar accounts of state functions, Hirsch is distinctive among German theorists for his stress on the TRPF as the motive force behind the historical expansion of these functions. Thus, although his explanation of the tendency of the rate of profit to fall exactly follows that of Marx in *Das Kapital,* he differs noticeably in the importance he attaches to the role of the state in supplementing market forces through the mobilisation of counter-tendencies and in the way in which he relates this role to the progressive socialisation of production and the growing concentration and centralisation of capital in an expanding world market. Moreover, since the TRPF itself is not an automatic and inevitable outcome of blind economic laws but results instead from the complex interaction of competing and/or conflicting class forces, it follows that the mobilisation of counter-tendencies through the market and/or the state must also be related to the changing balance of class forces at different levels of capitalist society. In particular Hirsch argues that economic interventions should not be interpreted as purely technical in nature (as might be falsely inferred from phrases such as the 'general conditions of production') but recognised instead as being overdetermined by the need to maintain political class domination (see especially, Hirsch, 1973, pp. 208–255; 1974a, pp. 67–97; 1974b, pp. cxlix–cl; see also, 1974c, pp. 89, 93–98; 1976a, pp. 128–131, 144–146; 1976b, pp. 114–117; 1976c, pp. 135–136; 1977a, pp. 179–180; 1977b, pp. 2–3, 5–7).

An important element in Hirsch's work is his discussion of how the form of the capitalist state affects its ability to reproduce the twin system of economic exploitation and political domination. For, if the state is to act as an 'ideal collective capitalist' in performing such general 'economic' functions, it must resist the penetration of anti-capitalist forces and demands and also ensure that the collective interests of capital can be secured through its actions. In this context Hirsch considers the state as a form-determined field of class relations whose operation must satisfy three functional imperatives: to secure the process of economic reproduction, maintain the subordination of the dominated classes through coercive, concessive, and ideological means, and formulate policies able to unify the dominant fractions and classes into a relatively coherent power bloc. He also argues that state intervention is essentially reactive inasmuch as it responds to particular economic events and their political repercussions rather than trying to control fully every moment in the circuit of capital. Given these complex functional imperatives and the reactive nature of state intervention, Hirsch concludes that the state needs both a pluralistic structure and specific processing mechanisms: the former so that various class forces can press their own demands and the latter so that these demands can be made compatible with the needs of capital accumulation and political domination. Thus he views the state in terms of the specific forms it imposes on class struggle at the political level and the 'structural selectivity' inherent in the articulation of its various branches, apparatuses, and organisations. However, while these theoretical concerns persist throughout his political analyses, Hirsch throws increasing doubt on the state's ability to meet these needs. Thus, whereas his earlier work focused on the degree of class bias entailed in the 'structural selectivity' of the political system as a whole and the manner in which this allows the state to formulate and implement policies and strategies which are objectively necessary for capitalist reproduction but which might damage the immediate interests of particular capitals, his more recent work looks at the problems involved in the state's attempts to maintain both a relatively crisis-free course of capital accumulation and a constellation of class forces compatible with continued bourgeois political domination.

In discussing the class-specific 'structural selectivity' of the capitalist state Hirsch refers both to the basic structural constraints which shape the policy-making process as a complex system of decisions and 'non-decisions' and to the situational logic which predisposes the governing groups to discriminate in favour of capital. Among the basic structural constraints he emphasises: (a) the general exclusion of the state from the essentially 'private' productive core of the capitalist economy; (b) the dependence of state expenditure on revenues withdrawn from the total surplus created within the capitalist economy; (c) the supervision of ideological and/or 'mass integrative' apparatuses by the central administrative-repressive state apparatus to confine their role in ideological reproduction and/or interest mediation within manageable limits; and (d) the complex process of bureaucratic policy-making in which different fractional or class forces promote or defend their interests through bargaining, the use of vetoes, etc. He also argues that the 'governing groups' in charge of the political system (notably officials and politicians) have a vested interest in securing capital accumulation and bourgeois political domination as a basic precondition of their own reproduction as people living off politics. In particular they must take account of the demands of subordinate classes to prevent their destruction as producers of surplus labour and to ensure their continuing mass loyalty; and must also attempt to combine the competing valorisation (or analogous) interests of different fractions of capital (or other dominant classes) to secure their relative unity and cohesion as a power bloc. It is here that Hirsch stresses that measures needed to reproduce the capital relation as a valorisation process might well contradict those needed to secure bourgeois hegemony as an 'unstable equilibrium of compromise' among different class forces. He suggests that a solution to this contradiction might be sought in a tendential strengthening of the state so that it can maintain political domina-

tion without the need for economically destructive material concessions (on 'structural selectivity', see Hirsch, 1973, p. 263; 1974a,
pp. 100–101, 194; 1974c, pp. 90–93, 100–108; 1976a, pp. 135–
138; 1976b, pp. 119–121; on the situational logic of 'governing
groups', see: Hirsch, 1974a, p. 66; 1974c, pp. 118–120; 1976a,
pp. 138–141; 1976b, pp. 122–124; 1977a, pp. 166, 172, 178; on
both arguments, see also: Offe, 1972, pp. 65–106, and Offe and
Ronge, 1976, pp. 54–70; on the 'power bloc' (*Block an der Macht*)
and bourgeois hegemony, see' Hirsch, 1976a, pp. 109–110, 112,
116–123, 141; 1976b, pp. 104–105, 112–114; 1977a, pp. 166–
167, 177–178; 1978, pp. 224–226; and, on the rise of the strong
state, see: Hirsch, 1970, pp. 242–243, 265–279; 1973, pp. 264–
266; 1974a, p. 106; 1974c, pp. 125, 130–131; 1976a, pp. 145–146;
1976b, pp. 128–129; 1977a, pp. 180–181; 1978; 1980a; 1980b).

   Yet, although such structural constraints and their complementary
situational logic do produce a distinct class bias, they cannot really
guarantee that the result of party political struggles and bureaucratic
'muddling through' will go beyond a merely particularistic reproduction of conflicting fractional and class interests to secure the economic or political domination of capital as a whole (let alone to
harmonise and secure both). Accordingly Hirsch also refers to the
important role of *crises* in steering the activities of the state. He
argues that serious failures of market forces and state intervention to
reproduce those conditions needed for capital accumulation and/or
political domination threatens the 'governing groups', stimulates
demands for action, class forces, and imposes new priorities on the
state. Thus, while he continues to emphasise the role of the TRPF
(including its reflection on the political level in fiscal crises) and its
various counter-tendencies in determining the dynamic of capitalist
societies, it is the political repercussions of this tendential fall in the
rate of profit and its articulation with crises of mass integration and/
or the power bloc which constitute the principal steering mechanism
of state intervention and the reorganisation of the political system.
But Hirsch also notes that this steering mechanism is not an automatic pilot: instead it is mediated through changes in the balance of
class forces (see Hirsch, 1973, pp. 223–225, 265; 1974a, pp. 65,
75–76, 91–92, 103–104; 1974c, pp. 116–117, 126–129; 1976a,
pp. 129–130, 143–145; 1976b, pp. 116, 123, 127–128; 1977a,
pp. 178–180; 1977b; 1978, pp. 225–228; 1980a, pp. 9–53 et seq.;
1980b, pp. 127–131; on crises as a steering mechanism, see also:
Wirth, 1973, p. 38).

   These arguments can be illustrated with Hirsch's recent analyses of the crisis-induced reorganisation of mass integration in West Germany. Hirsch attributes a key role in bourgeois reproduction to certain mass integrative apparatuses whose function is to process mass needs and make their satisfaction compatible with capital accumulation and political domination. This function depends on the room available for material concessions and, in the advanced metropolitan democracies, is achieved through a reformist mode of mass integration. In West Germany this works through a social democratic cartel of integrated, *sozialpartnerschaftlich*, economistic trade unions and a bureaucratic, electoralist *Volkspartei* with the support of the ideological and repressive apparatuses. But the growing structural crises of the economy at home and on the world market and the resulting attempts at rationalisation, increased exploitation, and social modernisation has thrown the reformist mode of mass integration into crisis with the growth of strikes, protest movements, and political disaffection. In response the state has not attempted to smash the mass integrative apparatuses as such but merely to suppress protest movements operating outside them and/or potential subversives within the different mass integrative, ideological, and repressive apparatuses. This permits the reorganisation of the prevailing mode of mass integration through a more selective flow of material concessions at the expense of marginal groups, a more active policy of corporatist integration of responsible unions and parties, and a greater role for the security apparatus within the framework of bourgeois democracy (see Hirsch, 1978; 1980a; 1980b).

AN EXCURSUS ON CLAUS OFFE

Political economy and political sociology are combined in a different fashion in the work of another influential West German theorist, Claus Offe, who has contributed much, directly and indirectly, to a critique of the state in 'late capitalism'. Offe has an ambivalent and mediated relationship to orthodox Marxism. His analyses owe as much to the ideas of the Frankfurt School, radical American sociology, systems theory, and the sociology of work as they do to the orthodox Marxist tradition and it is rare for him to present his work as a direct contribution to Marxist theory. It is also worth noting that the seminal contribution to *Staatsableitung* of Müller and Neusüss was directed against the studies of Habermas and Offe as much as the revisionism of the Second International or postwar social democratic reformism. But it is also clear that Offe has always been deeply concerned with the commodity form of social relations, its political conditions of existence, its articulation with non-commodity forms, the various chronic dilemmas and acute contradictions of late capitalism, the emergent dislocations between the form and functions of the capitalist state, and the transformation of the postwar state. For this reason his analyses have also influenced Marxist state theorists in various countries and schools, most notably for our purposes through the concept of 'structural selectivity' appropriated by Hirsch and Poulantzas at certain stages in their work. Thus, in presenting this excursus on the work of Claus Offe, it is not intended to suggest that he is an explicit adherent of the form derivation school nor that he operates more generally within an exclusively Marxist framework. But his contributions are so important that it would be pedantic to exclude them from a discussion of theories concerning the form and/or functions of the capitalist state.

Offe first gained critical attention for his analysis of political authority and crisis-management in late capitalism (Offe, 1969) and has since elaborated the central ideas in this analysis in other theoretical and empirical studies. In his early work Offe criticised both conflict and integration theories of political authority, and instrumentalist and economic determinist accounts of the capitalist state, for their obvious inability to explain the specific mechanisms through which democracies secure the interests of capital as a whole in economic reproduction and political class domination (Offe, 1969, pp. 73–81; 1974, pp. 31–36). It is in this context that he introduces the concept of 'crisis-management' to account for the role of the state in economic reproduction as well as the concept of 'structural selectivity' to account for the class nature of the democratic state. In particular Offe argues that the state must be so structured internally that (a) it can develop a coherent programme corresponding to the interests of capital and not merely one that reflects the competing and contradictory interests of particular capitals and (b) it can systematically exclude the demands and interests of anti-capitalist forces and stop them from disturbing policy-making and implementation (1974, pp. 37–40). But he also notes that the capitalist state cannot effectively fulfil its essential role as an 'ideal collective capitalist' (1974, pp. 31, 35–36) unless it can conceal its institutionally-inscribed class bias behind the cloak of the general interest and democratic legitimation (*ibid.*, pp. 46–54; 1975a, pp. 25ff; 1975b, p. 127; 1976a, pp. 91–97; see also Offe and Ronge, 1975, p. 140). This means that the capitalist state must attempt to secure both capital accumulation and bourgeois legitimation and, in so far as these involve a strategic dilemma and can result in mutual antagonism, it is also obliged to compensate for any imbalance or conflict between them through appropriate administrative and/or repressive measures.

The twofold functional requirement of maintaining both accumulation and legitimation is closely connected with the complex relations between the commodity form and non-commodity forms. Thus Offe argues that the continued dominance of the commodity form which is essential to bourgeois reproduction comes increasingly to depend on the existence of social and political activities and institutions which are not themselves organised through the commodity form and its attendant principle of the exchange of equivalents. In this context he refers to two major contemporary trends. Firstly he notes that there is a continued expansion of non-productive labour which is not readily subordinated, if at all, to the principle of equivalent exchange (notably service labour in the tertiary sector of the economy, whether private or public) and, indeed, also suggests that there is a growing proportion of the population who are marginal to, or wholly excluded from, the labour market. Secondly he discusses the changing and expanding role of the state as an extra-economic institution in securing not only the general external conditons of production but also in supplying various material factors of production and/or providing welfare services outside the market-regulated economic system.

These developments pose a dilemma for capitalism. For, whereas the commodity form depends increasingly on the expansion of non-commodity forms, their very expansion threatens to undermine both accumulation and legitimation. The dominance of the exchange principle and the growth of accumulation are materially threatened by the expansion of the service sector and the state provision of 'public goods' in the mixed economy and welfare state of 'late capitalism'. This occurs through the growing politicisation of economic relations and the development of alternative criteria for the distribution of use-value and/or through the emergence of fiscal crises and the parasitic withdrawal of revenue from profitable investment by private capital. At the same time the 'decommodification' of significant areas of social life threatens the legitimacy of the political system. This can occur through the withdrawal of political support as citizens find themselves unable to exchange their commodities (including labour-power) for equivalent values or prove unwilling to accept market outcomes as legitimate and/or through the growing conflict between the formal unity of the state apparatus rooted in its rational-legal legitimation and the material diversity of its discretionary, *ad hoc,* purposive interventions oriented to specific economic and social goals. (On these crisis-tendencies, see Offe, 1973b, *passim*; 1973a, pp. 36–44, 47–53, 75–63; 1975a, pp. 9–50 and *passim*; 1976b, pp. 91–97; 1980, pp. 8–13; Offe and Ronge, 1976, pp. 140–146; see also Ronge, 1974, pp. 86–93).

The solutions suggested by Offe for these crisis-tendencies change during the course of his theoretical and empirical enquiries. At first he implied that it would be possible to avoid crises through a judicious combination of structurally selective institutional mechanisms, skilfull preventive crisis management to ensure an appropriate balance among the goals of economic stability, foreign economic and military equilibrium, and mass loyalty, and, finally, 'ideological planning' to secure popular backing for technocratically determined policies (Offe, 1969, pp. 97–105). It was his suggestions in this context that the state could avoid the escalation of economic crisis-tendencies into economic catastrophe, could displace class conflicts between capital and labour as the main driving force of social change and substitute conflicts between politically favoured and disfavoured interest groups, and could also consolidate mass support for a technocratic political system, that drew the wrath of orthodox Marxist theorists such as Müller and Neusüss (for his cutting response, see Offe, 1975c, *passim*). Whatever the precise implications of his initial contribution to political economy, his subsequent work is much less equivocal in its assessment of the crisis-tendencies of late capitalism. For, in a study that owes as much to systems theory as it does to Marxist political economy, Offe stresses that there is an emergent 'crisis of crisis-management' in the late capitalist political system. This emergent political crisis can reveal itself in three main areas: a fiscal crisis of the state, a crisis of administrative rationality, and a crisis of mass loyalty. In addition to the specific mechanisms underlying each of these three political crisis-tendencies, Offe identifies a general causal mechanism grounded in the political economy of capitalism. For the state is increasingly obliged to compensate for the failures of the market mechanisms without being able to infringe on the primacy of private production. Yet it cannot adequately compensate for these failures without undermining the dominance of the capital relation through the extension of non-commodity forms of social relation and/or undermining the fiscal, administrative, and legitimatory preconditions of its regulative functions on behalf of capital (Offe, 1973a, pp. 54–64).

In this context Offe outlines various responses to the 'crisis of crisis-management'. Initially he focused on the possibilities of the 'administrative recommodification' of economic and social life. This involves active state intervention to roll back the expanding frontiers of non-commodity forms of social relations where possible and otherwise to subordinate them firmly to the logic of equivalent exchange. Thus, if the first stage of developed capitalism involved a liberal, *laissez-faire* state combined with the maximum scope for free competition in the economic region and the second stage involved the growing socialisation and 'decommodification' of social and economic life to compensate for the failures of the market mechanism, it is possible to discern a third stage in which the state intervenes to re-establish the dominance of the market mechanism in order to limit its own crisis-tendencies as well as those of the market sector. This can be seen in three main fields of state intervention: measures to enhance the saleability of labour-power through education, retraining, regional mobility, and so on; measures to promote the marketability of capital and manufactured goods through internationalisation of capital and product markets, R and D, regional development policies, etc.; and support for market-generated and crisis-induced industrial restructuring rather than wholesale nationalisation and unconditional protection for 'lame ducks'. However, whilst these various measures may succeed in certain respects, they may also produce self-defeating effects elsewhere. Thus 'administrative recommodification' restricts the formal and substantive freedom of capital and labour and entails fiscal burdens that discourage investment. It also leads to the expansion of state-organised production facilities exempt from the commodity-form which can provide the site for political and ideological struggles against market rationality. And the transparent role of the state in the production and distribution of goods and services may also undermine 'possessive individualism' as an ideological precondition of the exchange principle (see Offe, 1973a, *passim*; 1975a, *passim*; and Offe and Ronge, 1976, *passim*).

In other work Offe focuses on the dilemmas and contradictions that occur when the state attempts to compensate for crises of administrative rationality and/or mass loyalty through the introduction of new forms of economic planning and public participation. In this context he distinguishes between two types of state activity: allocative and productive. Allocation involves the use of state resources to secure the general framework of economic activity and/or to provide general public services in accordance with general constitutional or legislative codes which reflect the prevailing balance of political forces. Production involves direct state provision or state-sponsored provision of material resources as a precondition of crisis-avoidance or crisis-management where there is no general code that can be applied and decision rules must therefore be developed in order to determine the most effective action case by case. Offe then argues that, although rational-legal bureaucratic adminstration may be appropriate to the allocative activities of the state, it is inadequate to the demands of state productive activities in so far as these are oriented to the attainment of particular objectives rather than the general application of pregiven rules. Thus bureaucracy must be replaced with new modes of policy formation and implementation: purposive action or planning based on technical rationality and/or consensus based on the democratic participation of those affected by the policies and programmes concerned. But, just as bureaucracy has certain limitations as a form of policy formation and implementation, so do purposive action and participation. Purposive action is made difficult by the absence of clear-cut, uncontroversial, and operationalisable goals, the instability of the economic and political environment, the problems encountered by the state in securing acceptance of the social and fiscal costs of effective planning, and so forth. In addition it is likely to provoke avoidance or retaliatory measures from particular capitals when it harms their particular interests. But democratic participation is likely in turn to generate demands that are inconsistent with capital accumulation and will politicise the process of administration. In short, whatever the form of policy-making and implementation adopted in the capitalist state, it could prove ineffective from the viewpoint of capital accumulation and legitimation (Offe, 1975a, pp. 9–50 and *passim*; Offe, 1975b, *passim*; Ronge, 1974, *passim*).

Thus, although he started out by arguing that the internal structure of the capitalist state guaranteed the domination of capital, Offe soon arrived at the conclusion that the form of the capitalist state is deeply problematic for accumulation and legitimation alike. This theme is pursued in his recent work with reference to the increasing difficulties that confront the competitive party system and the Keynesian welfare state in securing the conditions for accumulation and legitimation (e.g., Offe, 1980, *passim*; 1981b, *passim*; 1981c, *passim*) and with the likely contradictions that would follow from the introduction of functional representation or 'neo-corporatism' and/or more far-reaching forms of technocratic decision-making (e.g., Offe, 1980, pp. 9–11; 1981a, pp. 136–141; 1981c, pp. 13–15; and Offe and Wiesenthal, 1978, pp. 70–80). In this sense these studies confirm the argument he advanced earlier: that the basic problem of the capitalist state does not concern the specific policies to be pursued in solving the difficulties thrown up by the process of accumulation but actually resides in the prior creation and institutionalisation of general forms of policy-making and implementation that can reconcile its internal mode of operation with the successful performance of its functions on behalf of capital (Offe, 1975b, pp. 140 and 144). This means that, far from providing a guarantee of the class character of the state as an 'ideal collective capitalist', the 'structural selectivity' of the state is potentially inimical to the interests of capital without thereby necessarily favouring the subordated classes or new social movements (cf. Offe, 1978, pp. 28ff).

STATEHOOD, WORLD MARKET, AND HISTORICAL CONSTITUTION

The preceding theories are often formalistic and/or ahistorical in their derivation of the nature and functions of the capitalist state and, indeed, in the case of theories operating at the level of surface forms, have clear voluntarist implications in developing something akin to a 'social contract' theory of the state. In contrast to such purely logical derivations of the necessary institutional form of the state in a fully developed capitalist society (i.e., its 'formal constitution'), other state theorists have argued for the need to examine the historical constitution of the state during the transition from precapitalist to capitalist society. Moreover, whereas the existence of a plurality of nation-states in the capitalist world system is systematically neglected in deriving the formal constitution of the capitalist state at the level of the pure CMP, these theorists also argue that this plurality must be considered as a constitutive feature of the historical development of the capitalist state in an expanding world market and must be considered from the outset of any attempt at derivation. Let us see how such views are developed in the work of West German and British state theorists.

In a critique of other theories Heide Gerstenberger argued that the form of the capitalist state had been derived from the fully developed capital relation — yet the state is not simply the result of a bourgeois society but is also its presupposition. Throughout Europe the growth of bourgeois state functions preceded the emergence of the formal structure of the capitalist state (e.g., constitutionalism and universal suffrage). This means that the historical constitution of the bourgeois state as an administrative apparatus performing functions necessary for accumulation is not identical with its formal constitution as a *Rechtsstaat* imposing particular forms on social relations in bourgeois society. In this context Gerstenberger focuses on the role of the absolutist state persuing mercantilist policies as an important factor in the development of capitalism and in the rise of the bourgeois form of state. She argues that the development of the administrative structure of the capitalist state is historically rooted in the need for the absolutist state to supplement the activities of merchant capital in conquering foreign markets and in promoting national economic growth. The ability of the state to pursue these interests depended on the creation of a standing army and navy independent of the feudal aristocracy, the development of an orderly monetary system and an efficient system for managing the national debt, the introduction of a modern tax system and an effective bureaucratic apparatus to administer it, and the development of 'political arithmetic' and protectionist economic policies. It was in the context of this material constitution of a modern administrative apparatus that the formal constitution of the bourgeois state as a *Rechtsstaat* occurred with a greater or lesser lag according to various historical circumstances. This involved the exclusion of direct force from social relations and the consolidation of the bourgeois rights of freedom and equality vis-à-vis the absolutist monarchy. At first this process is confined to the sphere of circulation and the state still deploys force to influence the valorisation of particular capitals and to ensure the availability of free wage-labour. But, once the general framework for the self-reproduction of capital through market forces has been secured and the commodification of labour-power is completed, then the establishment of the bourgeois *Rechtsstaat* can also be fully secured (see Gerstenberger, 1973b, pp. 207, 211–225; cf. *idem*, 1972, pp. 134–139; and, for an account of the coincidence of material and formal constitution in the growth of the U.S. state, see *idem*, 1973a, pp. 90–188; Hirsch follows Gerstenberger in distinguishing between material and formal constitution but also argues that the centralisation of the means of political coercion depends in turn on the development of the productive forces, monetary relations, trade, etc. stimulated through the emergence of capitalist relations of production within feudal society, see Hirsch, 1976a, pp. 131–134).

Hochberger develops these arguments more fully in distinguishing two aspects of the capitalist state: its administrative apparatus and its juridico-political form of interaction. He derives the form of interaction (*Verkehrsform*) from simple commodity circulation between formally free and equal individuals; conversely the administrative apparatus is constituted historically in the course of the primitive accumulation of capital. In contrast to Gerstenberger, who explains historical constitution in terms of the mercantilist policies of the absolutist state in relation to the world market, Hochberger focuses on the administrative implications of creating a free wage-labour force for the home market out of artisans and peasants through state intervention and is less concerned with absolutism as such. In this context Hochberger notes that the administrative apparatus is the institutional expression of the use of coercion as an *economic* force to separate the direct producers from access to means of subsistence and/or from control over the means of production and he argues that the juridico-political form of interaction evolves as a result of various class struggles within the framework of this apparatus and is finally established after the complete commodification of wage-labour. He illustrates this approach with reference to Marx's own analysis of the recurrent political cycle of democratisation alternating with authoritarian regimes in nineteenth-century France as the bourgeoisie attempted to employ state power to promote the primitive accumulation of capital against the resistance of the subordinate classes and he concludes that the formal constitution of the French bourgeois state was not completed until early in the twentieth century when a majority of the working population had been proletarianised (Hochberger, 1974, pp. 174–177, 185–187, 190–201).

Both these studies insist that the historical constitution of the bourgeois state must be related to the development of the capitalist world market. Claudia von Braunmühl takes this approach further. She argues that the world market was the necessary base for primitive accumulation and has since become an increasingly significant base for the organisation of production as well as the circulation of commodity and money capital. The development of this world market is certainly mediated through competition among capitals but it is more than the sum of individual (or, indeed, national) capitals to the extent that it comprises the level of capital in general and its laws of motion. In the competitive struggle for profits in the world market particular capitals will use any available means to promote their interests: this includes the appropriation of existing state apparatuses and their reorganisation to secure the conditions necessary for valorisation and realisation. Initially this leads to the crystallisation of multiple centres of accumulation organised around nation-states and thereafter these nation-states are involved in the contradictory economic cross-currents of internationalisation and nationalisation of the circuit(s) of capital. Accordingly Braunmühl concludes that it is only in the context of the developing world market that one can analyse the growth of the nation-state and its specific functions in capital accumulation (see Braunmühl, 1978, pp. 162–177; cf. *idem*, 1973, pp. 12–13, 32–35, 42–45, 50–52, 64–65, 68–69, 90–91; and *idem*, 1974, pp. 35–51).

Similar arguments have been developed in Britain by Colin Barker. He insists that an analysis of the bourgeois form of state must start from capital in general at the level of the world market. Thus, just as capitalism comprises a world system of competing capitals in the economic sphere, in the political sphere it comprises an international community of nation-states. Likewise, just as capital in general forms a contradictory unity of anarchy (competition among particular capitals) and despotism (control exercised within each individual capital), so the international political community entails a contradictory unity of despotism (sovereignty within each nation-state) and anarchy (competition among nation-states). The actual historical constitution of these nation-states is irrelevant to Barker's argument. What matters is that each separate nation-state represents the fusion of a particular segment of world capital and other classes into a nation formed in opposition to other nations and in competition with them. Accordingly the capitalist state should not be seen as a purely despotic organ of domination over subordinate classes within the nation but should also be considered as a means of intra-capitalist competition on the world market. Barker also notes here that the state will be subject to the contradictions created through the tendential internationalisation of capital and the counter-tendential formation of a national capital organised around an extensive system of political interventions with productive state capital at its core. In conclusion he discusses the limitations on state intervention at the national level due to the fact that the laws of motion or capital operate through the world market and cannot be suspended on the command of one nation-state (see Barker, 1978a, pp. 120–124, and 1978b, pp. 24–37; for a useful critique, see Williams, 1979, pp. 67–70).

In developing such arguments about the historical constitution of a plurality of nation-states within the context of an aboriginal world market these studies highlight the important fact that the capitalist state develops on the basis of the pre-capitalist state. Yet many other attempts at 'Staatsableitung' appear to assume that, in establishing the particularisation of the bourgeois form of state, they are deriving the necessity of the state as such. Yet this is to confuse the form of the state corresponding to a particular mode of production with the need for some form of extra-economic coercion in any class-divided society regardless of its specific form of appropriation of surplus-labour. In this context some theorists have emphasised the analytical priority of deriving the general need for a political form of social re-production in class-divided societies before attempting to derive its particular form and/or necessary functional capacities at the level of particular modes of production. This procedure is implied in Hirsch's distinction between the basic reasons for the existence of class co-ercion (*Existenzgrund*) and the factors determining the changing forms of that coercion (see Hirsch, 1976a, pp. 103–106; cf. 1976b, pp. 104–107) but is theorised more explicitly in the work of Schütte and Classen in terms of a distinction between statehood (*Staatlich-keit*) or 'state as form' ('*Staat als Form*'), on the one hand, and, on the other hand, specific state forms (*Staatsformen*) corresponding to distinct modes of production. They also distinguish among specific types of regime (Staatstypen or Herrschaftsformen) in terms of the precise institutional structures and functions of a given state form in actual societies. Let us see how they derive the basic necessity of statehood or the 'state as form'.

Schütte and Classen both follow Engels in explaining the need for the state in terms of the division of society into antagonistic classes but their derivations are far from identical. Thus, whereas Classen proceeds from the formal necessity for the state to control the per-manent threat of open class conflict between propertied and pro-pertyless and to regulate the conflicts among the propertied them-selves, Schütte starts from the historical constitution of the state with the original alienation of political functions in the social div-ision of labour from communal control. Moreover, whereas Classen then considers the general form of the state as a relation of class domination and emphasises that it must combine the use of repres-sion with ideological and integrative activities, it is the changing pat-terns of articulation between the economic and political forms of social reproduction in class societies that interest Schütte. In this context Schütte distinguishes between the *substantive doubling* of reproduction in class-divided societies into economic and political processes and its *formal doubling* within bourgeois societies into the institutional forms of society and state. The substantive doubling of reproduction is traced to the separation of coercive functions from communal control owing to their takeover by an emergent exploiting class and/or their usurpation by an independent officialdom as occur-red in Oriental despotism. The formal doubling of reproduction must await the emergence of a mode of production mediated through formally free and equal exchange and thus no longer dependent on the immediate use of extra-economic compulsion in the appropriation of surplus-labour. Here Schütte points to certain elements of a formal doubling in Greek and Roman antiquity but argues that it cannot be completely realised until the commodification of labour-power is achieved. In contrast Classen argues that bourgeois society, despite its apparent foundation in the freedom and equality of exchange relations among its members, needs a state because it is still based on class exploitation. For, should the tendentially self-reproducing mechanisms of the market and/or the forms of false consciousness rooted in commodity circulation break down and reveal the fundamental antagonism between capital and wage-labour, then coercion will be required to maintain bourgeois rule. Only when the necessity of the state as a relation of coercion has been established, argues Classen, can one ask why it takes the form of an impersonal public authority. His own answer to the question is pitched in terms of the need for the bourgeois state to transcend the level of competing capitals and secure the interests of capital in general (see Schütte, 1977a, pp. 541–543, and *idem*, 1977b, pp. 14–30; Classen, 1979, pp. 51–63 and 249–262; and, for another account of the prefiguration of the formal doubling of state and society in antiquity, Müller, 1975).

SUBSTANTIVE CRITIQUE

There is clearly wide variation in the approaches adopted in this debate concerning the most appropriate starting point for deriving the form(s) and/or function(s) of the capitalist state. Moreover, while some have remained relatively undeveloped and, in certain cases, have even been disavowed by their original proponents, others have experienced considerable sophistication and elaboration. This further complicates the task of criticism and suggests the need to concentrate on the most advanced representatives of each approach. Thus my comments do not follow the exact order of presentation above but proceed instead according to how problematic the theories see the functioning of the capitalist state. For, although all the theories considered above deal with the necessary and/or contingent functions of the state, not all are equally concerned with the extent and manner in which its basic form and organisation renders these functions contradictory and ineffective. Accordingly theories that problematise the functioning of the state are discussed only after those that takes its functionality more or less for granted.

This latter approach is most apparent in the work of Altvater, Aumeeruddy *et al.*, and Clarke. Thus Altvater confined himself to some problems of state intervention rather than aiming at a full-blown derivation of both form and functions; and he tends to take the existence of the state as an ideal collective capitalist for granted and merely lists four functions which the state must fulfil in this role. Likewise, although respectively they privilege one function (maintaining the wage-relation) and discuss functions in a generalised manner, Aumeeruddy *et al.* and Clarke also treat its functionality as broadly unproblematic. All three studies locate the limitations on the state's functions in the nature of capital in general as a valorisation process rather than in the form of the state itself. Nor is there any attempt to specify this form beyond positing the particularisation of the state as a distinct moment in the self-reproduction of capital (as a whole or as variable capital) or to explain how the state is able to act as an ideal collective capitalist beyond a purely gestural and inadequate invocation of class struggle as the means of imposing the collective interests of capital. Läpple has attempted to advance on this approach in several respects. Thus, as well as offering a more rigorous account of the so-called general conditons of production and introducing an historical postulate about the worsening contradiction between the material preconditions and the valorisation requirements of capital accumulation, he also locates the functions of the state in terms of its form as a *Rechtsstaat* and considers how this imposes legal limits on valorisation and also causes *sui generis* legitimation problems as the state is forced to break these limits to sustain accumulation (Läpple, 1975b, pp. 114–134, 144–158). A further advance is recorded by Sauer in his attempt to avoid economism through introducing the mediating categories of 'social problems' and 'state strategies' as well as those of competition and exchange and in his emphasis on the form-determined limitations of state intervention. Particularly interesting is his argument that economic deficits must be represented as social problems and that particular interests must be articulated with the general interest. But, despite these innovations, Sauer has not developed the concepts needed to break radically with the residual economism evident in his continuing assumption that social problems are ultimately economic in origin and the class reductionism evident in his account of social forces.

Paradoxically it is the work of Altvater himself that has broken most sharply with the reductionist implications of his early essay on state intervention. In subsequent studies of the West German and

Italian states he introduces various arguments that radically qualify his initial position. Thus, not only does he now include the form of the state (as nation-state, tax-state, and democratic state) and its means of intervention (law, money) among the limits on its functional capacities (Altvater *et al.,* 1976, pp. 100–113), he also argues that class struggles can restrict the state's room for manoeuvre on behalf of capital and rejects the view that all state measures can be derived from an objectively necessary 'logic of capital' (*ibid.,* pp. 110–111, 113). Moreover, while his work on the German state is concerned with the differential effects of fascism, the 'CDU-Staat' of Adenauer, and the social democratic regime, he also cites recent studies in arguing that the Italian state has been so deformed through the pressure of individual capitals and the operation of Christian democratic clientilism that it cannot function effectively as an ideal collective capitalist (Altvater *et al.,* 1974a, pp. 55–149; cf. Altvater *et al.,* 1974b, pp. 5–23; and, on the Italian state, Altvater, 1976, pp. 74–75ff, and Genth and Altvater, 1976, pp. 87–89). The latter conclusion suggests that the particularisation of the state is far from a structurally pre-given feature of capitalist societies but rather a feature that must be constantly reproduced in and through political practice (cf. Holloway and Picciotto, 1977, pp. 80–81, 97). Indeed Genth and Altvater themselves argue that analyses of the bourgeois state must go beyond economism and 'Ableiterei' to study the historically specific forms and content of 'societalisation' (i.e., modes of articulating social relations to create a relative unity in a social formation) and the role in such 'societalisation' of the political, cultural, and moral leadership exercised by the bourgeoisie through various political and cultural centres (Genth and Altvater, 1976, pp. 94–97; cf. Altvater and Kallscheuer, 1979, pp. 103–104). And, in this context, they suggest that diverse class and popular-democratic struggles in Italy have precipitated a crisis of hegemony and a veritable societal crisis and conclude that the working class must respond with its own hegemonial strategy embracing other classes and non-class subjects (Genth and Altvater, 1976, pp. 93–108; cf. Altvater and Kallscheuer, 1979, pp. 105, 125–127). This shift in theoretical strategy has obviously been influenced by the work of Gramsci and the political experiences of the PCI but, in contrast to much neo-Gramscian theorising, it remains firmly attached to value-analysis of the economy and tries to combine Gramscian political concepts with form-determination in its analyses of the state.

The approach to *Staatsableitung* through *'Oberfläche'* or surface forms seems far removed from the approach represented by the early work of Altvater. For, whereas the productivist perspective seems to ignore the specific form of the capitalist state in favour of its functionality for capital, surface form theories emphasise the problem of form. And, whereas the productivist perspective tries to derive state functions from the most abstract levels of the movement of capital, surface form theories emphasise its immediate forms of appearance. Yet, despite this seeming polarisation between the two approaches, there is a fundamental coincidence and theoretical complicity between them. For, whereas the early Altvater argues that the state must act as though it were an ideal collective capitalist and immediately thereafter introduces its four key functions, surface form theorists argue that the state appears as the representative of the common interests and/or general will of those in capitalist society and then proceed to argue that valorisation and/or reproduction problems ultimately determine which particular interests are represented as being in the general interest. Indeed it is only through the latter argument that surface form theorists could avoid the charge of tautology or circularity in suggesting that the state administers general interests and that general interests are precisely those administered by the state. For they have no proof that the state enjoys privileged knowledge of the general interest and also argue that the pluralistic interplay of political forces alone is insufficient to determine the general interest. In this context it is difficult to see how surface form theorists could then avoid the alternative charge that the concept of the state as representative of the 'general interest' is superfluous or redundant in explaining the development of its functions on behalf of capital and/or that they are operating with the inadequate method of 'subsumption' rather than derivation in equating all state functions with the general interest or its three instances. Hence both the productivist and surface form approaches take the functionality of the state for granted and essentialise its form as an adequate expression of this functionality. (The charge of tautology has been levelled by Blanke, Jurgens, and Kastendiek, 1974, p. 200; and that of redundancy by Reichelt, 1974a, pp. 44–45, who also develops other lines of attack.)

In fact it would seem that surface form theorists have conflated the separate problems of explaining the development of state functions and explaining the legitimacy of the state. Even in relation to the latter problem, however, this approach is inadequate. Not only does it overlook the crucial distinction between the historical and the formal constitution of the capitalist state and its implications for the development of the bourgeois democratic republic as the institutional embodiment of the general will, it also tends to ignore the brute fact that the modern state does not always have a bourgeois democratic form. Furthermore, to the extent that they do realise this and have not merely hypostatised false consciousness as an essential trait of the capitalist state, surface form theorists fall back on the equally essentialist view that the state is basically an organ of repression and will use force to maintain bourgeois domination whenever false consciousness is dissolved. This inability to explain either the form or the functions of the state does not mean that these theories are completely without merit. For they do at least include the need for appropriate forms of ideological awareness among the various preconditions of capitalist reproduction and thereby reject the view that false consciousness is an automatic, epiphenomenal effect of exchange relations and is somehow reducible to commodity fetishism. Unfortunately this is vitiated by the failure to develop appropriate concepts for examining the differential articulation of particular and general interests and the reduction of these interests to the issue of economic reproduction for different revenue categories.

So far I have argued that neither the productivist approach with its focus on the most abstract determinations of the CMP nor the surface forms approach with its concern for the necessary forms of appearance of the CMP is adequate to the analysis of the capitalist state. For both approaches are marred irredeemably by essentialism and functionalism due to their reduction of the form of the state to an essential expression of certain functional needs in the self-reproduction of capitalism. In one case, these are the valorisation needs of competing capitals, in the other, it is the need to reproduce appropriate phenomenal forms. To what extent are these problems avoided by approaches which start at intermediate levels of abstraction and argue that there can be no form-determined guarantees concerning the functionality of the state in capitalist reproduction?

It was noted above that commodity circulation has a role in the circuit of capital as well as in simple commodity production. Yet it is often suggested that studies begining from commodity circulation cannot explain the specificity of the bourgeois state and legal order. These arguments ignore the fact that labour-power enters the circuit of capital as a simple commodity (cf. Aumeeruddy *et al.,* 1978) and that law and money mediate the exchange of labour-power against capital as well as the circulation of capitalist commodities. They also presuppose that such legal and state forms have an immutable bourgeois essence and cannot exist outside the pure CMP. Yet it is most important to distinguish between these forms and their changing functions in different contexts. Thus, while it might be argued that law and the state only attain their full development with their institutional separation from the economic region and the associated legal mediation of exploitation through the exchange of wage-labour with capital, this does not mean that they have no pre-history, cannot survive beyond capitalism, and cannot have non-capitalist functions. It is worth recalling here the distinction between the material and formal constitution of the capitalist state and extending it to the legal sphere. The distinction drawn by Tuschling between the cell-form of law (the legal subject as bearer of rights) and the legal order typical of bourgeois societies (the individual legal subject, private property, freedom and equality, rule of law, state monopoly over force) could also be used to refine the material-formal couplet and to establish the specificity of the bourgeois forms of law and the state (cf. Tuschling, 1976, pp. 93–94; 1977, p. 278). We should also note how legal and state functions are overdetermined by the commodification of labour-power and its substantive inversion of the formal freedom and equality of legal relations in the economic and political spheres (cf. Blanke *et al.*, 1974, pp. 110–111, 125–129; Picciotto, 1979, p. 170; Tuschling, 1976, pp. 20–39; *idem*, 1977, p. 270). In short, though the starting point for these analyses of the capitalist state is commodity circulation, it does not follow that they are unable to theorise its form and functions in relation to capitalist production and the circuit of capital as a whole.

Besides allowing for the commodification of labour-power and taking account of the overall movement of capital, this approach has progressed beyond the early Pashukanis in other ways. This is most evident in its concern with the role of law in the mystification of class relations and the individuation of social forces and with the limitations of the legal form as a means of state intervention. In focusing on the abstract, universal legal subject, however, it suffers from a certain formalism. For it neglects the differential effectivity of different categories of legal subject and/or different modes of legal reasoning and it also ignores the problem of their articulation with non-legal subjects and/or non-legal discourses. Likewise, in noting how the bourgeois state and law abstract from class relations in constituting the state as an impersonal public power and establishing the abstract, universal legal subject, it also fails to consider how the state is constituted as a class power and how the content of law is adapted to the needs of capital. For to argue that the simple maintenance of the *rechtsstaatlich* political form and the rule of law are sufficient guarantees of bourgeois reproduction would be to essentialise these forms and to imply that, once the necessary juridico-political framework has been established, economic forces alone can ensure the expanded reproduction of capital. While the disorganisation of subordinate classes may prove beneficial to capital, it is certainly crucial for the bourgeoisie to develop some cohesion in its capacity as the dominant class. Indeed Pashukanis himself notes that the unity of private and public law is historically constituted, largely formal, inherently contradictory, and particularly unstable (Pashukanis, 1929, pp. 47, 60, 96, 101–106, 137–138, 167, 176–177); and these problems are just as characteristic of other aspects of the state apparatus and state power. Thus Blanke *et al.* observe that the various policies pursued by the state have only a formal unity (1974, p. 138; 1975, p. 94), Tuschling notes that the mediation of economic imperatives through legal forms entails a certain indeterminacy in policies and their effects (1976, pp. 100–111), and Picciotto points to the 'porosity' of bourgeois law and the scope this offers for the exercise of economic and social power in determining juridical outcomes (1979, p. 175). In this context gestural references to the role of class struggle in filling out these indeterminacies are particularly inadequate because these very theories insist that *rechtsstaatlich* and legal forms disorganise class struggles. Nor does the ritual invocation of class struggle suffice to explain how the interests of capital in general can be secured through these forms. Even if this failing could be overlooked in relation to the purely liberal moment of the state as the passive guarantor of the external conditions of production, it is unpardonable in relation to active state intervention to secure other conditions of economic and/or social reproduction. In short, despite the merits of these theories in focusing on the forms of law and the state and problematising their functionality in terms of limitations inherent in the forms themselves, they have failed to complement this form-analysis with an analysis of social forces that can explain the development of the liberal and interventionist moments of the state and the relationship between them.

Finally these theories often appear to reduce the capitalist state to the *Rechtsstaat* and to equate politics with conflicts about legal norms and rights. That this is unsatisfactory has been well established by other state theorists. Thus Hirsch argues that the state constantly breaches the organisational principles of the rule of law through its resort to executive measures to secure the specific material conditions required for capital accumulation. It is also prepared to use coercion outside the framework of law to secure bourgeois rule whenever the proletariat threatens the foundations of the capitalist order. Freedom, equality, and the rule of law are only one side of bourgeois rule: its other side is *raison d'état,* class bias, and open violence. Both facets are essential to the reproduction of bourgeois society and neither should be neglected (Hirsch, 1978, pp. 64–65). Similar views are expressed by Ulrich Preuss in his attempt to elaborate a Marxist constitutional theory in opposition to liberal theories of law and the constitution. He argues that the restriction of state power exclusively to the rule of law is only conceivable on the basis of production relations which are not only mediated through exchange but also non-antagonistic, i.e., on the basis of simple commodity production. In such cases there is a harmonious coordination of labour and property and the creation of value is directly concerned with the satisfaction of needs. This means that general laws can govern exchange relations and protect property rights without adverse effects on the overall process of reproduction. But the subordination of living to dead labour under capitalism and the dominance of 'exchange-value' considerations over substantive needs means that the bourgeois state must also resort to extra-legal and exceptional concrete measures and policies which are directed to the satisfaction of the concrete needs of concrete individuals in concrete situations. Thus the rule of law (the sphere of bourgeois legality) must be complemented with activities whose discrete, exceptional, and purposive nature must be justified in terms of their particular effects on the reproduction of capitalism (Preuss, 1973, pp. 7–105). So, although Blanke *et al.* suggest that the actions of the state are constrained by its need to respect the law (1974, p. 90; 1975, p. 130), it is actually necessary to consider the state as a contradictory functional unity of legality and illegality without essentialising either moment. For it is no more aacceptable to reduce actual states to their juridical, *rechtsstaatlich* form than it is to adopt the Leninist stance that the state is essentially an organ of class repression. Instead one needs an adequate analysis of the complex mediations between these two moments as well as the conditions in which one or other is dominant in particular capitalist states.

The most prolific West German state theorist, Joachim Hirsch, adopts an approach different from those criticised above. He emphasises the non-identity of economic and political domination and examines its implications for class struggle over accumulation and legitimacy. Thus, whereas form analyses typically concentrate on deriving the most adequate form of the capitalist state and/or specifying the limitations inherent in its forms of intervention, Hirsch appears less concerned with the specific form of the state beyond its particularisation and focuses instead on the limitations inherent in its very separation from the economic region. This does not mean that he ignores the problems of the bourgeois state as a form of the capital relation and/or particular types of bourgeois state and political regime. Indeed Hirsch discusses these issues in considerable detail and has increasingly concentrated on changing modes of mass integration as a definitive aspect of the latter. But in tackling these issues he proceeds beyond the immediate terrain of form derivation and introduces new categories into the analysis. I deal with the methodological implications of his work in the following section and concentrate here on its substantive theoretical import.

In outlining the economic functions of the state Hirsch presents a list similar to those of other state theorists but he places particular weight on its roles in developing the productive forces and, above all, in mobilising counter-tendencies to the TRPF. However, while there can be little quarrel with Hirsch's typology of economic functions, the manner in which he explains their development is more troublesome. For example, although the TRPF certainly condenses many different factors in the movement of capital and is certainly incomprehensible in isolation from the movement of class struggle, it is not the sole source of crises and contradictions to which the state must respond and it is misleading to place so much weight on it in a general account of state intervention. Moreover, as Hirsch himself stresses, it is the *political* repercussions of crisis to which the state responds. In this respect the concept of economic crisis (let alone those particular forms of crisis provoked by the TRPF) might seem superfluous in explaining state intervention. For it is the balance of political forces that immediately determines such intervention and economic movements are thus reflected only indirectly in state intervention. This is true in a double sense. Not only is economic policy-making subject to political mediation in its economic moment, in its political moment it is overdetermined by *sui generis* considerations of political domination. This means that there can be no necessary and inevitable correspondence between particular forms of economic crisis and particular policies and programmes pursued by the state. In turn this means that economic movements must enter into state theory through their representation in the political discourses of different social forces and/or through their *ex post* constraints on particular policies and programmes. This requires a careful specification of the movement of capital as a point of reference for political action and/ or as a key principle of explanation for the limitations of such action. That this has been recognised more or less explicitly in Hirsch's own theoretical development demonstrates its importance for the state derivation debate.

A further contribution is found in his emphasis on the problems of securing cohesion in state policy and coordinating the long-run economic and political interests of capital. Hirsch recognises more clearly than other form analysts the difficult task confronting the bourgeoisie in avoiding a merely particularistic reproduction of specific interests in state policy at the expense of the interests of capital in general and, indeed, suggests that these latter interests are at least contingently, if not inherently, self-contradictory. He also stresses that the state has no privileged knowledge of bourgeois interests and that its support for capital in general cannot be taken for granted. Hirsch seeks the solution to these problems in two rather different directions whose relations he never satisfactorily resolves: the internal organisation of the state and the constitution of a hegemonic power bloc. The arguments concerning structural selectivity merely specify certain negative limits on state intervention (exclusion from production, tax-dependence) which cannot ensure that the collective interests of capital are pursued within these limits or, alternatively, allude to positive organisational practices (central supervision, bureaucratic bargaining) whose impact on these interests cannot be taken for granted. The situational logic of the 'governing groups' is open to similar criticism. Accordingly Hirsch is forced back to the apparently economistic principle of crisis as a steering mechanism. But even here he admits that crises do not operate as an automatic pilot but depend for their effects on the balance of forces. In this context there can be no guarantee that this balance will always favour capitalism rather than a transition to socialism or, indeed, the 'mutual ruin of the contending classes' (Marx and Engels, 1848, p. 482). The solution to this theoretical indeterminacy might be found in developing the concept of hegemony as political, intellectual, and moral leadership and linking it with the analysis of different modes of mass integration. This is the other approach adopted by Hirsch and it makes the unity of state policies and the overall cohesion of society depend on contingent social practices rather than on in-built structural guarantees. However, although Hirsch has developed the concept of modes of mass integration in some detail in relation to the West German state, the notion of hegemony remains undeveloped relative to the explanatory burden he places on it. The differential articulation of hegemony over the power bloc and over the masses is likewise unexplored. Nonetheless, whilst much work remains to be accomplished here, the basic framework is already sketched out in the recent studies of Hirsch.

Claus Offe has also developed a cogent argument in support of the view that the form of the capitalist state problematises its functions on behalf of capital. As noted earlier his initial position was essentialist in so far as it ascribed the class character of the state to its 'structurally selective' internal organisation. I have already rehearsed the theoretical objections to this hardline position (along with the objections to the approach via the 'situational logic' of the governing groups which is also found in Offe's work) in criticising its use by Joachim Hirsch. In his more recent work, however, Offe breaks decisively with essentialism. Indeed he demonstrates far more clearly than any of the declared adherents of form derivation the full extent to which the form of the capitalist state calls into question its functionality for capital. Thus, not only does he discuss the relatively abstract problem of maintaining the privatisation of market relations as a sphere free from state control and the cognate problem of maintaining the particularisation or relative autonomy of the state as an extra-economic instance able to secure the general framework for accumulation, he also discusses this problem in terms of the specific dilemmas and contradictions entailed in more concrete forms of 'policy production'. The difficulties in his recent work stem, somewhat paradoxically, from just this contribution. For, if there are so many form-determined obstacles in the path of capital, how are accumulation and legitimation ever possible? In looking for an answer Offe is led back to the constraint theories he earlier rejected along with simple instrumentalism. Thus he now places particular emphasis on the veto powers enjoyed by capital on account of the institutional separation of the economic and political – powers which cannot be adequately mastered by the state nor adequately countered by labour through the organisation of trade unions or their political integration within a system of political neo-corporatism (see especially Offe, 1978, pp. 31–32, 36; 1981a, pp. 146–153; 1981c, pp. 10–15; and Offe and Wiesenthal, 1978, pp. 70–80). In addition Offe has returned to the central role of competition between mass political parties in making democratic participation compatible with continued accumulation and legitimation (1981c, *passim*; cf. *idem*, 1969, pp. 81–85, 100–108). Both mechanisms are important. But an adequate examination of the foundation of capitalist power and domination in the *'institutionalised right of capital withdrawal'* (Offe, 1978, p. 32) would require a more complex and concrete analysis of the circuit of capital than Offe is able to provide with his emphasis on the sphere of market relations rather than production relations. Likewise the emphasis on the role of mass parties is salutary but is best developed in connection with the nature of class hegemony and modes of mass integration. Only in these ways can we reach a sound understanding of state power as a form-determined condensation of the balance of political forces and understand the difficulties that Offe himself outlines in effecting a democratic transition to socialism (1978, *passim*).

Finally let us turn to the studies that discuss historical constitution, world markets, and statehood. The distinction between historical and formal constitution is important and suggests that the reproduction of the state as apparatus and form is far from an automatic effect of the CMP. Whether or not the specific functions so far identified as crucial for historical constitution are the decisive ones is surely an historical problem itself and needs examining in each case. The theoretical utility of this distinction is also evident in the analogous couplet of state apparatus-state form developed within the CSE. The London-Edinburgh Weekend Return Group argues that it is essential to distinguish between two senses of 'state': the state apparatus as an institutional ensemble with no immediate class relevance and the state as a form of social relations which structures class relations in a selective manner. This implies a degree of indeterminacy in the institutional separation of the state from the economic region and suggests the need for specific practices to complete the *embourgeoisement* of the state. Indeed the group argues that there is always a tendency for a break to develop between the state apparatus and the way it tries to mould social relations in the interests of capital. In turn this suggests that it is possible simultaneously to work in and against the state to the extent that its employees resist and counteract any attempts to impose bourgeois forms (London-Edinburgh Weekend Return Group, 1979, pp. 37–38, and 1980, pp. 58–61; cf. Holloway, 1979, pp. 24–25). In short, as well as struggles outside the state and/or over its effects on civil society, an important role in bourgeois reproduction is played by struggles within the state apparatus. Recognition of this fact is an important contribution to state theory.

It is also necessary to locate historical constitution in terms of the world market. But one must be careful not to identify the latter with the entire globe or to ignore the articulation of the CMP with other modes of production and/or forms of social and private labour in this process. It is likewise important to periodise this development in terms of the internationalisation of commodity, money, and productive capital (cf. Fine and Harris, 1979, pp. 146–154) and to consider the role of nation states in the interplay between internationalisation and its counter-tendencies as mediated through class and/or popular-democratic struggles. A significant criticism of derivations that abstract from the world market and focus implicitly on the nation state or national capital is that their arguments indicate the need for a single, global state. For, if the movement of value is insufficient to secure all the conditions necessary for the reproduction of capital in general, a world state would be required to complement market forces with extra-economic compulsion. This suggests that the concept of the capitalist state must not be equated with the form of the sovereign nation-state but should be identified initially with the separation or 'doubling' of bourgeois reproduction into economic and political processes (cf. Blanke *et al.*, 1974, pp. 115–122; 1975, pp. 68–81). One can then investigate how the political process is organised on the global level and to what extent it is possible for capital to compensate for the absence of a unitary world state. In this context the importance of an hegemonic force (whether it be a nation-state, national capital, or international fraction) over the plurality of nation-states cannot be underestimated; witness the obvious contrast between the periods of *pax Britannica* in the latter half of the nineteenth century and *pax Americana* from Bretton Woods to the late 1960s and the turbulent period spanning the two world wars and, most recently, the crisis-torn 'seventies and early 'eighties. Thus, while those who insist upon the analytical priority of the world market in studying the capitalist state have made an important critical point, this does not mean that it is necessary to reject *tout court* the most sophisticated form analyses.

The notion of statehood is important in two senses. For not only is it necessary to accept that the bourgeois state is not the original form of the state, but it is also important to recognise that some aspects of the state cannot be derived from the analysis of value alone. These arguments indicate a possible means of linking class-theoretical and capital-theoretical analyses of the bourgeois state in a two-stage derivation. Thus one could first establish a general class-theoretical account of the state as form and then examine the implications of the specific forms of appropriation of surplus-labour for the substantive and/or formal doubling of economic and political processes and for the forms of class struggle. These arguments also suggest the possibility of extending the analysis of statehood to discuss elements not included within class and/or form analysis. Thus the popular-democratic moment of the state, involving the potential contradiction between people and officialdom and hitherto analysed mainly by anarchist and liberal state-theorists, could be considered in its articulation with the class moment and in its overdetermination through particular modes of production (cf. Jessop, 1980b, *passim*; and see the concluding remarks in chapter 5). In raising these possibilities, however, it has already proved necessary to move beyond the immediate terrain of form derivation theories and to consider how they can be combined with other theoretical perspectives. This suggests that it is time to consider the methodological implications of form analysis.

METHODOLOGICAL CRITIQUE

The *Ableitungsdebatte* is methodologically self-conscious in a way that is alien to the stamocap approach considered as a whole. Indeed form analysis is inspired in part through dissatisfaction with the basic method and/or reformist implications of stamocap theories and it tries to return to the methodological and substantive theoretical concerns of Marx (e.g., Altvater, 1971, p. 99; Ebbighausen and Winkelmann, 1974, pp. 27–35 and *passim*; Gerstenberger, 1972, pp. 134–135; *idem*, 1976, pp. 84–86; Müller and Neusüss, 1970, pp. 15–16; Tristram, 1974, pp. 108–123; Wirth, 1972, pp. 12–14, 18–19; *idem*, 1973, pp. 298–312). However, while form derivation might seem methodologically superior to the subsumptionism of the 'monopoly-theoretical' tradition in stamocap theory, it is itself subject to various unresolved methodological problems and theoretical difficulties. Let us consider them.

A basic presupposition of form analysis is that reality comprises a complex structured whole whose elements have a certain autonomy within an overall unity. Thus the economic and the political are considered as different but complementary moments in the reproduction of the social whole constituted by capitalism and they are also characterised by a distinctive 'separation-in-unity'. This view bears some similarities to the Althusserian structuralist school in its rejection of crude economic reductionism and its insistence on analysing the connections between the economic and political moments of the CMP. Thus the Althusserians argue that a mode of production (and, by extension, a social formation) is a complex structured whole, comprises several relatively autonomous regions which nonetheless condition each other, is characterised by the dominance of one region (economic, juridico-political, or ideological) over the other regions, and is subject to economic determination in the last instance in so far as the mode of reproduction of the relations of production assigns the dominant role to one or other of these regions (see Althusser, 1965, pp. 151–218; Althusser *et al.*, 1968; Poulantzas,

PPSC, pp. 12–33; and, for subsequent self-criticism, Althusser, 1976; and Balibar, 1975, pp. 203–246). But there are two major differences between the form derivation and Althusserian structuralist approaches to capital as an ensemble of social relations. In considering these differences we can better understand the nature and limits of these related traditions.

Firstly, whereas most form analyses tend to rely on theories of fetishism to account for the subjective moment of social relations and otherwise concentrate on the articulation between the economic and the political, the Althusserians have stressed the discursive interpellation of subjects as the crucial mechanism of ideological practice and traced its implications for economic and political struggles. In this context 'interpellation' embraces all the diverse mechanisms through which biological individuals and collective agents are discursively recruited to specific positions in social relations and endowed with a corresponding sense of self-identity. Theories of interpellation and fetishism agree in rejecting the argument that individuals are pre-given, unitary, free-willed subjects but they disagree fundamentally about the processes through which individuals acquire subjectivity. Thus, while theories of fetishism tend to treat consciousness as an epiphenomenon of relations of production and/or as a complex ideological effect determined in the last instance by the economic and serving simultaneously to support and mystify economic relations, theories of interpellation stress that there are distinct mechanisms of subjectivation which have their own conditions of existence and fields of operation and which can constitute a distinct terrain of ideological class struggle with major repercussions on the economic and political regions. This emphasis is salutary and marks an important advance on theories of fetishism. In particular the latter operate economistically through establishing commodity fetishism as the model for other regions and also adopt a subsumptionist approach in reducing all forms of ideological domination to fetishism. Furthermore, where attempts have been made to go beyond theories of fetishism, there is a depressing tendency to substitute an analysis of the opposition between general and particular interests without regard to their complex mediations and immediately discursive character. In contrast theories of interpellation are able to relate the definition of interests to specific discursive mechanisms and to consider how particular and general interests are articulated through the exercise of hegemony.

Secondly, whereas the Althusserians are rather perfunctory in their treatment of economic determination in the last instance (although this is a principle to which they subscribe) and typically focus on the specific mechanisms of the juridico-political and ideological regions as if they were fully autonomous from the economic, the form derivation theorists give analytic and causal priority to economic categories in deriving the form and functions of the capitalist state and legal order. This contrast is worth noting because Holloway and Picciotto claim that form derivation theories actually start from the historical materialist categories of the capital relation as a whole rather than from economic categories taken in isolation (Holloway and Picciotto, 1977, pp. 78, 82, 85–86; *idem,* 1978, pp. 3–4, 10, 14–15, 17–18, 26). If this means simply that the capital relation encompasses more than economic relations and is irreducible to an epiphenomenal base-superstructure relationship, it is perfectly acceptable; it is unacceptable, however, if it implies that the capital relation is an essentially unitary ensemble of social relations with analytic and causal priority over its elements. Indeed, while Marx certainly criticised bourgeois economics for focusing on the surface forms of economic relations and treating them as relations between things (*pace* Holloway and Picciotto), his critique of political economy did not involve the substitution of historical materialist categories (whatever these might be) for economic categories *tout court* but rather the development of an epistemologically realist, multi-level account moving from the abstract to the concrete and aiming to explain the form of the capitalist economy, its conditions of existence, its laws of motion, and its social effects. In this context Marx indicated that the anatomy of civil society and the state could be deciphered from 'the specific *economic* form, in which unpaid surplus-labour is pumped out of the direct producers' (Marx, *C3,* p. 791, emphasis added). This is certainly the approach adopted by other form derivationists and, indeed, Holloway and Picciotto themselves also derive the 'doubling' of the capital relation into economic and political forms from the nature of commodity exchange and its overdetermination by the commodification of labour-power (Holloway and Picciotto, 1977, pp. 78–79). In short, at the same time as respecting the necessity for political conditions of existence of the economic and recognising the intervention of the political into the economic region, it is also necessary to respect their differences and to take as starting point the form of appropriation of surplus-labour. This is the strength of the form derivation approach in comparison with the 'politicist' tendencies of Althusserianism and neo-Gramscian approaches (see chapter 4) and it should not be confused by talk about *sui generis* historical materialist categories.

In this context what meaning should we attribute to the concept of 'separation-in-unity'? Its diacritical function is clear. It tries to distinguish the form derivation approach from crude economic reductionism in which the form and functions of the state are held to correspond inevitably and automatically with the needs of capital and from the twin deviation of 'politicism' with its assumption of the complete autonomy of the political region and the state. But it nonetheless runs the risk of conflating economic and political relations as production relations and thereby reducing the political to its (relatively autonomous) role in bourgeois reproduction. And it also runs the risk of essentialising the moment of unity rather than separation so that the latter becomes a subordinate, functionally necessary element in the reproduction of this unity. Such essentialism would ultimately render the particularisation or separation of the state illusory and present its apparent autonomy as a ruse of capital. This would avoid economism only at the expense of reducing the state to the needs of the self-reproduction of capital seen as a relation that is simultaneously economic *and* political. Why should one assume that the combination of economic and political practices together can assure the reproduction of capital when the economic alone are insufficient? Indeed, as Holloway and Picciotto themselves argue, this unity is far from automatic and essential: it must be reproduced through specific class practices. But, if one accepts that the so-called 'separation-in-unity' is a problematic and contingent result of specific practices of 'societalisation', it cannot be privileged theoretically and invoked without explanation or mediation to account for the form of state and its functions in capitalism. Indeed it is a further strength of the form derivation approach that it proceeds beyond mere 'capital logic' to establish that the particularisation of the state renders its functionality on behalf of capital deeply problematic. In this context the concept of 'separation-in-unity' cannot serve as an unconditional principle of explanation for bourgeois reproduction but only as a point of reference for assessing the effects of societalisation practices.

This critique leads to another problem with form derivation, that is, the relation between logical derivation and historical explanation. Once one denies that history is simply an effect of the logically necessary self-realisation of capital and concedes that class struggle (however defined and mediated) makes a difference, what sense is there in attempting to derive the form and functions of the state from the categories of capital as an ensemble of social relations? An adequate answer must specify the relation between capitalism and class struggle and also examine the nature of historical explanation.

The capital relation cannot be considered in isolation from class struggle. For accumulation is conditional on the continued ability of capital itself to secure *through struggle* the many different conditions necessary for the creation and appropriation of surplus-value on an ever-expanding scale. This means that its laws of motion are not natural and inevitable but depend for their realisation on the balance of forces in the conflict between capital and labour. Thus one should not artificially separate the logic of capital from its historical conditioning through class struggle nor oppose a determinate, eternal logic of capital to an indeterminate, contingent historical process. For the 'logic of capital' is a theoretical abstraction which expresses the average movement and regularities of capital accumulation resulting from the activities of individual capitals (including their relation to wage-labour) and assuming that individual capitals act capitalistically. In discussing the laws of motion of capital one must abstract from historical particularities and this introduces a certain indeterminacy into the analysis (which can be closed, for example, with the assumption that individual capitals are simply *träger* of the capital relation); in discussing specific conjunctures one re-introduces certain historical particularities and reduces indeterminacy through historical specification rather than assumption. Thus, while Marx abstracts from individual capitals to examine capital in general and treats them simply as *träger* in examining competition, more concrete analyses can consider the differential interpellation and modes of calculation of particular capitals and assess their impact on the realisation of laws of motion and the incidence of competitive forces on different capitals. Likewise Marx abstracts from the role of wage-labour in discussing capital in general and competition among capitals (focusing on crisis tendencies such as the TRPF which can be analysed at the level of capital in general and/or on wage-labour as variable capital exploited more or less efficiently by individual capitals relative to the socially necessary labour time established through competition); more concrete analyses can examine the specific form and content of working-class struggles as well as how crisis tendencies are overdetermined by specific failures on the part of capital to maintain its domination over wage-labour. In short, it has to be recognised that, *the more abstract the level of analysis, the more indeterminate it becomes*; and that, whereas abstract analyses cope with this indeterminacy through reference to the average and/or through assumption, concrete analyses eliminate this indeterminacy through specifying historically what had been indeterminate. Finally it should be noted that there is a complex hierarchy of levels of historical abstraction. For abstract concepts such as 'commodity', 'capital', 'wage-labour', 'state', and 'legal subject' are historical in the same manner as more concrete concepts such as 'car', 'bank', 'dustman', 'military dictatorship', and 'joint stock company' and differ only in terms of the relative indeterminacy of their historical conditions of existence.

—Furthermore, while the 'capital logic' approach tends to conflate form and content in its attempts to derive the nature and functions of the capitalist state from the CMP, the more sophisticated versions of form analysis distinguish several stages in derivation and attempt to determine form at a given level of abstraction whilst treating content as indeterminate. This is exactly what is entailed in arguing that the form of the capitalist state problematises its functionality. Thus, while it is possible to derive the appropriate form of the capitalist state from the analysis of the specific form in which surplus-labour is appropriated and, indeed, to periodise state form through an analysis of the periodisation of the economic form, it is not possible to derive specific functions and their effects at the same theoretical level. At most one could derive certain abstract functions which the state should perform as conditions of existence of capital accumulation in a given conjuncture. In short the derivation of content involves moving beyond the field of determinations that establish form and, *a fortiori*, so does an account of the dialectic between form and content. For, just as the appropriate form of the state must be established and reproduced through specific practices, specific practices are also involved in its functioning and these may not coincide with those required fr the reproduction of form. There is a major ambiguity here in form analysis. Sometimes the aim is to establish the appropriate form and/or functions of the capitalist state to show the theoretical possibility of the CMP (given that the movement of value alone cannot ensure its reproduction) and then to invoke them as an abstract principle of explanation of such reproduction (on the assumption that the state is a *träger* of the capital relation); sometimes the appropriate form and/or functions of the state act as a point of reference for problematising and evaluating the effectiveness of constitutive and/or functionally-oriented practices in securing bourgeois reproduction. However, while the 'capital logic' approach resolves this ambiguity by transforming the assumption that the state is a *träger* into an essentialist principle of explanation so that logical correspondence is conflated with causal necessity, the more sophisticated versions of form analysis distinguish between logical correspondence and causal necessity and resort to further determinations to account for the historical realisation of state forms and functions.

Finally, by way of summary, we can say that there is no funda-mental and absolute opposition between logic and history or between determinacy and indeterminacy. The logic of capital is the expression of the historical movement of particular class struggles and can be specified at different levels of abstraction. The relative indeterminacy of this logic at high levels of abstraction can be progressively elimina-ted through its concretisation and/or complexification. Such an approach need not involve the essentialisation of capital in general or its state form through the argument that there is a determinate, al-beit abstract, essence and that deviations therefrom at more con-crete, complex levels are inessential. On the contrary it implies that the appearance of a 'pure' course of accumulation or 'pure' capitalist state is as much the product of overdetermination as the existence of, say, progressive 'de-industrialisation' or a state that results in 'the mutual ruin of the contending classes'. In this context it must be stressed that determinacy and contingency are not properties of the real world but are properties of theoretical systems. Theories can be more or less determinate or contingent. Thus a completely deter-minate system is one in which it is possible to predict the values of all the theoretically defined variables at any point in time from a knowledge of the laws of that system and of the values of those vari-ables at some other time. A theory can be determinate only in rela-lation to a specific set of variables or properties (which, in the limit case of a totally closed theoretical system, comprises every variable). It is therefore logically improper to assert that a theory is determinate without also stating the properties in respect of which it is deter-minate. On the other hand, a theory is contingent (or indeterminate) in so far as it is impossible to predict the values of certain variables from those of other variables in the system (sometimes including the values of the independent variables at another time) and the laws governing that system. This suggests that contingency can be elimina-ted through the specification of additional or auxiliary determina-tions drawn from the same theoretical system and/or from other theoretical systems. In this way the theoretical object can be repro-duced as the complex synthesis of multiple determinations and is made fully determinate at its chosen level of abstraction and com-plexity.

These remarks lead to a third problem area with form derivation. If we want to establish a fully determinate account of the capitalist state, what should the starting point for an analysis be? For different studies start from different categories in the capital relation and a large part of the *Staatsableitungdebatte* involves an incestuous process of mutual criticism for having chosen the wrong starting point. This is associated with a tendency to absolutise the question of the starting point and to suggest that there is some unique point from which one could derive all the categories necessary to determine the form and functions of the capitalist state. It is more appropriate to recognise that the state, as a 'real-concrete' object, is the complex synthesis of many determinations (Marx, 1857, p. 101). In this sense a fully determinate account of the state should have a number of different starting points and should combine different form analyses rather than privilege one — provided that they are individually satisfactory and collectively commensurable. It is the merit of the theorists of 'statehood' to have seen that derivation must proceed in stages and this argument needs extension to the entire field of state derivation. In short, since the form of the state is complex and its functions likewise, its derivation must also be complex.

In this context it is important to refute the view that derivation is simply a process of unfolding the logical implications of an initial conceptual starting point as if the latter contained *in nuce* all other determinations. Such an approach is both essentialist and idealist in character (cf. Blanke *et al.*, 1974, pp. 115–117; *idem*, 1975, p. 72). But, if the process of derivation is not reducible to the simple logical deduction of more concrete categories from a single abstract starting point, how are categories of varying degrees of abstraction-concretion actually articulated? For there is a fine line to be drawn between the method of articulation and theoretical eclecticism. This is one source of difficulty in locating Offe's contributions to state theory. For, although he correctly draws on various principles of explanation in his work on the form and functions of the capitalist state, he does not attempt to establish their general commensurability nor their precise points of articulation in his analyses. This involves some indeterminacy in Offe's earlier work in so far as he attempts to combine Marxist categories and principles of explanation with others drawn from systems theory and the sociology of organisations. For this weakens the strength of his arguments about the political character of crisis tendencies in late capitalism and the problematic relationship between the commodity form and the state form. These difficulties are largely remedied in Offe's later work. This is theoretically more unified and demonstrates in some detail the benefits of a heterodox use of articulation in developing Marxist theory. However, since Clause Offe does not relate his work explicitly to the *Staatsableitung* school and is more heterodox in his approach than the open advocates of form derivation, it is important to consider the views of the latter on the nature of their method of theory construction.

The proponents of *Ableitung* are none too precise here. Rather than a detailed specification of the derivation process we find a series of loose statements suggesting that it involves some kind of conceptually informed development of categories for the analysis of the state starting from the nature of the capital relation. Hidden here is a systematic ambiguity concerning *degrees of abstraction-concretion in one plane of analysis* (e.g., commodity, capital, organic composition, TRPF, price of production, and so forth in the plane of value-analysis) and *different planes of analysis* (e.g., the value-analysis of capitalist production as opposed to its analysis as a technical labour process, the analysis of capital accumulation in use- and exchange-value terms as opposed to the analysis of political domination). Even in the plane of value analysis the movement from abstract to concrete requires the introduction of categories not already contained in higher level concepts (e.g., labour-power as a unique commodity, competition among individual capitals as opposed to the assumption of a unitary capital in general, price of production, luxury goods, fictitious capital, ground-rent, and so forth). The recognition that there are other planes of analysis with their own *sui generis* degrees of abstraction-concretion complicates this process still further. Thus Braunmühl *et al.* argue that derivation must set out from general categories developed in *Das Kapital* but must then proceed to develop *sui generis* political categories according to the method of movement from abstract to concrete (1973, p. 7); Heide Gerstenberger claims that form derivation needs to be complemented with the introduction of factors whose analysis Marxists have hitherto left exclusively to political science, such as bureaucracy, constitutional structures, and typical modes of class struggle (1976a, p. 158); Hirsch argues that the general derivation of form cannot go beyond trivialities and concludes that the theoretical investigation of the state must proceed beyond value and capital in general to embrace the whole of the social, political, and national conditions of production of a social formation (1974a, pp. 66, 74–75, 82–83); and Holloway and Picciotto admit that form analysis needs to be supplemented through the analysis of the specific historical struggles through which the dialectic of form and content in the political sphere is mediated (1978, pp. 30–31). But none of these theorists specify how this supplementation is to be achieved. It is nonetheless significant that various form derivation theorists have since introduced arguments and concepts pertaining to the movement beyond value analysis in order to encompass categories appropriate to political class struggles and/or ideological relations. In many cases this has involved reference to the political writings of Marx as opposed to his abstract critique of political economy. In other cases we find a resort to the Gramscian concept of 'hegemony' (in addition to various studies cited above, see Classen, 1978, pp. 61–63, 264–266). And we can also find new categories introduced, such as 'mode of mass integration' (Hirsch, 1976a, 1976b, 1977a, 1977b, 1978, 1980), 'mode of domination' (London-Edinburgh Weekend Return Group, 1979, 1980), 'corporatism' (Kastendiek, 1980), which provide a framework within which to consider the articulation between economic and political domination. But these approaches remain indeterminate in so far as the points of articulation between value analysis and other categories remain unspecified.

In short, despite their methodological self-awareness and stress on a careful adherence to the methods of Marx, the proponents of form derivation have failed to provide a fully coherent account of the nature of derivation. It is not a simple logical process of unfolding more concrete concepts from an abstract starting point along a single (albeit ramified) plane of analysis. Instead it involves the differential articulation of concepts of varying degrees of abstraction situated in different planes of analysis to reproduce the concrete as the complex synthesis of multiple determinations. That this is implied in the methods of research and the method of presentation of the most advanced versions of form analysis is reasonably clear; it should also be evident that it has been misunderstood through the general insistence of form analysts that they are following Marx in *Das Kapital* and the *Grundrisse* without realising that the method of presentation might well remain the same while the changed nature of the object of enquiry requires movement beyond value-analysis. Moreover, since most form analyses had only a limited theoretical goal (typically confined to a derivation of the form and/or functions of the state as conditions of possibility of the CMP), they did not need to move much beyond the sphere of value-analysis. But the state is a 'real-concrete' object irreducible to its value-analytic moment and needs a more complex method of analysis. The restriction of form theories to value-analytic categories runs the risk of reducing the state and/or social formation to a simple spatialisation of the pure CMP (thereby abstracting from the world market) and a simple concretisation of the pure CMP (thereby ignoring its articulation with other economic forms and its overdetermination through non-class relations). In short they run the risk of reduction and subsumption. Thus form derivation is only one element in a much broader, more inclusive theoretical project — an analysis of the state as a 'real-concrete' object.

CONCLUDING REMARKS

We have now examined the arguments proposed by a variety of form derivation theorists from a substantive and methodological viewpoint. It should be evident that there is much of real theoretical worth in this approach and it is unwise to be too readily dismissive of form analysis because of its high level of abstraction (Fay, 1978), its reductionist tendencies (Jessop, 1977), or its intensive preoccupation with a philosophical problem of its own making (Therborn, 1978, p. 30). It is correct to accuse different theorists of attempting to absolutise their respective starting points but wrong to overlook how *collectively* they have advanced our understanding of the capitalist state. Henceforth studies that ignore the implications of form for the analysis of content can be criticised with some justification. Let us review the approach.

The form analysis approach marked a significant theoretical advance over Marxist-Lenninist and class-theoretical studies through their proof that the state cannot be conceived as a mere political instrument set up and controlled by capital. Its proponents have clearly established that the capitalist state is an essential element in bourgeois reproduction. It is a political force complementing the economic force of competition and must intervene against capital as well as the working class. This illustrates the error of viewing the state as a simple instrument of capital. These studies also reveal some of the problems involved in political reformism: for they argue that the state, precisely because it is an essential element in the overall process of capital accumulation, necessarily reflects and reproduces its basic contradictions. Moreover, while these arguments could be criticised in their 'capital logic' variant for suggesting that the form and effects of the political are fully determined at the economic level, other studies note that the form of the state problematises its functionality and that state policies are overdetermined through a class struggle whose content (as opposed to its economic form) is not completely determined through the capital relation. Indeed, far from claiming that the capitalist state can secure all the needs of capital at one time, more sophisticated theorists argue that it is impossible to secure these needs other than tendentially and, perhaps, sequentially.

Its very emphasis on historical specificity and class struggle, however, reveals the limitations of form analysis. For it lacks certain concepts necessary for historical analysis and also works with an unduly restricted view of class struggle. In particular it needs new categories to cope with classes outside the CMP, with non-class forces and social relations, and with political and ideological practices. Value analysis can provide neither the concepts to analyse the economic formation as a whole (since this involves the articulation of the CMP with other modes of production and/or forms of labour) nor those required for class struggle (whose content is not fully determined in value terms) and its articulation with non-class forces (which lie beyond the economic sphere). Within the derivation approach there is a partial, emergent consensus that such categories as 'hegemony', 'power bloc', 'mode of mass integration', 'mode of domination', and so on, could serve these purposes. We must therefore consider approaches for which these categories are central and assess how far their apparent promise is realised.

4

Hegemony, Force, and State Power

Once we focus on state power at the level of the social formation rather than the form of the state apparatus at the level of the mode of production, it is essential to introduce a much more complex system of concepts able to organise our analyses of the social bases of state power and the nature of political crises. Indeed, as was noted in the discussions of stamocap and 'form-derivation' theories, there is growing recognition of a need to break with the cruder forms of state theory and develop more sophisticated analyses of the capitalist state and its role in social reproduction. It is here that the studies of Gramsci and the 'neo-Gramscian' school are most relevant. For these theorists have investigated the dialectic of coercion and consent, the specificity of political and state crises, the institutional mediation of ideological practices and their social effectivity, the nature of popular-democratic antagonisms as well as class struggles, and the problems of revolutionary strategy in advanced capitalism. Before discussing the leading representatives of the 'neo-Gramscian' approach to state theory, however, I deal with the work of Gramsci himself.

GRAMSCI AND STATE POWER

Gramsci shares with Lenin and Trotsky the distinction of being one of the three most significant and influential Marxist theorists of the imperialist epoch as well as being directly active in revolutionary communist politics (on Gramsci's life and politics, see Cammett, 1967; Davidson, 1977; Fiori, 1970; Hoare and Nowell Smith, 1971; Joll, 1977; Pozzolini, 1970; Spriano, 1979; and Williams, 1975). But, whereas the views of Lenin and Trotsky were decisively shaped by the revolutionary process in backward Russia, Gramsci was concerned above all with the conditions for a successful revolution in more advanced capitalist societies. It is with his views on this issue (especially as developed in the prison writings of 1929–1936) that we are concerned here rather than with his earlier role in the Turin factory council movement and the formation of the Italian CP or his major contributions to Marxist epistemology and philosophy. For it is in his theories of state power and ideology that Gramsci's originality and continuing influence are most deeply rooted.

However, although the theoretical and political stature of Gramsci is not in doubt, disagreement abounds concerning the exact meaning of his concepts and their interrelations. This is especially true of the prison notebooks. For the interpretation of these fragmentary and unsystematic writings is inordinately complicated by their exploratory and provisional character; radically new ideas are being elaborated in frameworks that are often inappropriate and/or obsolescent as well as through a series of concrete, historical investigations rather than through the more abstract, formalised methods of derivation adopted by Marx in *Das Kapital.* These studies are certainly not the occasion for Gramsci to present a coherent, polished series of general conclusions about political class domination in the imperialist epoch.

It is therefore particularly important to present some guidelines for locating Gramsci's work in its historical and theoretical context. First, since Gramsci was principally concerned with questions of political strategy, one should recall the events and circumstances with which he was concerned. Above all these include the defeat of the Italian factory council movement in 1920, the successful seizure of state power in the Russian revolution, the problems of socialist construction in the Soviet Union, the crisis of the liberal state and the growth of fascism with special reference to Italy, the factional and strategic problems of the PCI and the Comintern, the impact of the economic crisis of 1929–1932 on the political situation in Europe and America, and, lastly, the manifold implications of technological change for social relations in capitalism. Secondly, in responding to such events and circumstances, Gramsci was particularly anxious to confront the widespread and multifarious influence of economism within the labour movement. To this tendency he counterposed an analysis of the crucial influence of the political and ideological moments and developed a novel approach to the traditional problem of the relations between base and superstructure. Third, since Gramsci's political theory is linked to definite problems of revolutionary strategy (and despite the tendency for the imprisoned Gramsci to define these problems in global and epochal terms), it elaborates concepts and principles that are relevant to political practice in determinate conjunctures in specific nation-states. Thus

Gramsci is less bothered with defining abstract laws of motion for the economy or with the general role of the state as an 'ideal collective capitalist' in a pure mode of production than with specifying the complex relations among a plurality of social forces involved in the exercise of state power in a given social formation. Finally, given the variety of interpretations of Gramsci's work, it is worth stating a general methodological rule for the study of Marxist political theory. Namely, when a theorist presents a whole series of concepts and principles of explanation concerned with a particular problem, they must be considered as a connected and reciprocally qualifying system rather than treated in isolation or in a unilateral fashion. This rule has already been stressed in considering the studies of Marx and Engels on the state and it is also highly relevant for an analysis of Gramsci's theoretical approach (cf. Gramsci, 1971, pp. 382–383, where he presents a similar canon of interpretation himself).

Gramsci's resolute rejection of all forms of economism does not mean that he regarded the specific qualities of the capitalist mode of production as unimportant. For, although he made no major original contribution to Marxist economic theory (unless we include his attempt to break with economism itself), Gramsci always accepted its fundamental principles and integrated them into his political studies. Thus he insisted that capitalism was a contradictory and historically limited system of production based on capitalist exploitation of wage-labour, that capitalism prepared the material conditions for a transition to socialism, and that only the working class can lead a revolution to eliminate oppression and exploitation (Gramsci, 1977, pp. 86, 89, 156, 176, 260–262; 1978, pp. 287–289; 1971, pp. 402–403). He also oriented his revolutionary strategy in terms of the conditions associated with the growing concentration and centralisation of industrial capital, the tendential elimination of free competition through monopolies and trusts, the increasing weight of the banks and finance capital, the international consolidation of imperialism, and the general crisis of capitalism (Gramsci, 1977, pp. 69–70, 83, 128, 155, 165–166, 168, 175–176, 257, 262, 297, 301–304; 1978, pp. 255, 271, 291, 405–406; 1971, pp. 279–294, 310–316). Such concerns are by no means extraordinary, of course, as we saw in our analysis of the origins of stamocap theory. They were quite orthodox planks in the Marxist-Leninist platform of the Third International and its affiliated Italian Communist Party and, indeed, provide the measure of Gramsci's originality in developing theories of the state, state power, and ideology radically different from those dominant within the Comintern and orthodox postwar Communist analyses.

For Gramsci also emphasises that one cannot reduce questions of political practice to those concerned with the mode of production or fundamental economic relations. The overall structure of a society and its involvement in the imperialist system certainly do affect the form of state, the course and outcome of political crises, the possibilities of establishing hegemony over other social forces, and the likelihood of a successful transition to socialism (Gramsci, 1977, pp. 48, 70, 106, 128, 162, 305; 1978, p. 404; 1971, pp. 116, 117, 161–162). But such effects are neither unconditional nor unilateral. They are always subject to the mediation of political forces and ideological practices whose specific form and impact are relatively autonomous (Gramsci, 1977, pp. 48–50, 73–74; 1978, pp. 70, 408–409; 1971, pp. 106, 162, 165–167, 175–179, 185, 222, 366, 407–408). Thus Gramsci argues that the most favourable conjunctures for proletarian revolution do not necessarily occur in those countries where capitalism is most advanced but may emerge instead where certain structural weaknesses in the fabric of the capitalist system make it least able to resist an attack by the working class and its allies (1978, p. 345). Likewise, although economic crises may cause the state to tremble and/or objectively weaken it, they cannot in themselves create revolutionary crises or produce great historical events (Gramsci, 1971, pp. 184, 199, 233, 235, 238). Instead the impact of economic crises depends on the strength of the institutions of civil society as well as political institutions and on the resulting balance of social forces (Gramsci, 1971, pp. 230–239, 243, 257–270). This leads Gramsci to focus on the constitution of the political and ideological 'superstructures' and the ways in which the relations of political forces decisively shape the ability of capital to reproduce its class domination. He also emphasises that political relations are decisively influenced by ideological practices – which he endows with their own institutional foundations, social supports, and important repercussions (see below). This means that a revolutionary movement cannot restrict itself to economic struggles but must combine them with political and ideological struggles for the ultimate goal of seizing state power, socialising capitalism, and creating a new social order.

It is in this context that Gramsci's analyses of state power are most significant. Even his early writings reject simple instrumental or epiphenomenal views of the state. For he depicts the state as a class force which has a vital role in the organisation of class domination, in securing the long-run interests of the bourgeoisie as well as its unification, in facilitating concessions to the subordinate classes, and in securing the active consent of the governed (in parliamentary democracies) or effecting their demobilisation (in more despotic forms of state) (Gramsci, 1977, pp. 39–42, 73–74; 1978, pp. 32–33, 129–131, 267–269, 346–349). This means that the working class must build its own organs of political unity and state power – initially seen as factory councils, subsequently in terms of the leading role of the revolutionary party. The aim of the party is to organise the working class, to form organic links with the masses and disarticulate the democratic basis of the bourgeois state in the consent of the governed, to paralyse the functions of legal government over the masses and to move on to positive activity, to establish the most effective form of class dictatorship – one based on the conscious and spontaneous acceptance of authority seen as indispensable to the attainment of common aims (Gramsci, 1977, pp. 66, 142–146, 167–172, 191–192, 334–339; 1978, pp. 11, 32–34, 71–73, 287–288, 313–319, 354–375, 431).

These ideas are extended and deepened in various ways following the fascist conquest of power. Thus, although Gramsci still views the state as an organisation of class domination which plays a crucial role in the unification of the ruling classes, he now emphasises that this unity is fundamentally rooted in the organic relations between the state (or 'political society') and 'civil society' (Gramsci, 1971, pp. 12, 52, 160, 235–239, 242–245, 262–264). Conversely the tendential unification of the subordinate classes is interrupted continually through their integration into a plurality of economic-corporate groups with limited aspirations and demands and their alignment with 'blocs' associated with the dominant groups (Gramsci, 1977, pp. 41–43, 46; 1978, pp. 79–81, 267, 307, 331, 449–452, 454–462; 1971, pp. 57–64, 74, 77–82, 94–96, 100–102, 155–156, 160–162, 182). In short the key to Gramsci's new approach is found in his emphasis on the organic relations between the governmental apparatus and civil society. Rather than treating specific institutions and apparatuses as technical instruments of government, he relates them to their social bases and stresses the ways in which their functions and effects are influenced by their links to the economic system and civil society (Gramsci, 1977, pp. 135–137, 145, 334–336, 372–374; 1978, pp. 73, 79–81, 256, 261, 318, 346–349; 1971, pp. 83, 115, 189, 211–217, 220–221, 222–223, 249, 269–270, 272–274, 285). This emphasis stems from Gramsci's concern with the maintenance of class domination through a variable combination of coercion and consent. For, if one focuses on the exercise of state power rather than the internal organisation of the state apparatus, the overall effects of state intervention will depend on the totality of social relations in a given society. Accordingly Gramsci examines the roots of state power within the economy (e.g., hegemony in the factory, Gramsci, 1971, p. 285) and civil society (e.g., Fordism, Americanism, education, intellectuals) as well as within the state apparatus itself. Further, since Gramsci refuses to reduce political practice to an automatic effect of class belonging or to identify all political subjects as class subjects, he also examines how political support is established and/or undermined through economic, political, and ideological practices that go beyond the field of class relations to include the whole field of social relations (Gramsci, 1971, pp. 294–305, 316–318, 322–343, 348–357, 365–366, 377, 397–398, 419–421).

It is in this context that we must locate Gramsci's attempts to define the state and his concern with coercion and consent. For, given his emphasis on the relational nature of state power, the distinction between state apparatus and state power might seem redundant. Thus, as opposed to the reductionist-essentialist problem of how class dictatorship is unambiguously and necessarily inscribed within the state apparatus or the instrumentalist problem of how the dominant class manipulates an inherently class-neutral state apparatus, Gramsci focuses instead on the modalities of class domination within the social formation as a whole. Thus he once defined the state as 'the entire complex of practical and theoretical activities with which the ruling class not only justifies and maintains its dominance but manages to win the active consent of those over whom it rules' (Gramsci, 1971, p. 244). On several occasions he employs a formula to the effect that 'State = political society + civil society' (Gramsci, 1971, pp. 239, 261, 263); and he also once asserted that, 'in actual reality, civil society and the State are the same thing' (Gramsci, 1971, p. 160). Provided one interprets such definitions in relation to the exercise of state power (rather than as an attempt to establish the boundaries of the state apparatus itself), Gramsci's supposed inconsistencies and/or antinomies do not seem very significant (for an emphasis on his antinomies, see Anderson, 1977). This is not to deny that Gramsci noted the differential effects of specific forms of regime (e.g., parliamentarism) on the class struggle. But it is to insist that he gave historical primacy to the class struggle over the institutional structure of the state apparatus. Thus it is much more important to examine how Gramsci analyses the modalities of state power and the periodisation of forms of state than to consider his various definitions of the state.

Gramsci identified two modes of class domination – force and hegemony. *Force* involves the use of a coercive apparatus to bring the mass of people into conformity and compliance with the requirements of a specific mode of production (1971, p. 56n). In this sense force is clearly associated in capitalist societies with the state – which is traditionally seen by Marxists as a specialised repressive apparatus. But Gramsci refuses any simplistic identification of force and the state in his approach to class domination. The reasons for this are rooted not only in the activities of armed bands such as the *fascisti* and in the need for revolutionary violence against the state; but also in Gramsci's analyses of the complex relations between the police and military and their social bases in civil society and of the importance of ideological factors in determining the relations of political-military force (Gramsci, 1977, pp. 181, 190, 341–342, 354, 361, 372–374; 1978, pp. 44, 54, 59, 63, 152, 260, 350; 1971, pp. 175–185, 196, 214, 229, 231–232, 266). Conversely *hegemony* involves the successful mobilisation and reproduction of the 'active consent' of dominated groups by the ruling class through their exercise of intellectual, moral, and political leadership. This should not be understood in terms of mere indoctrination or false consciousness – whether seen as the reflex of an economic base or as an arbitrary set of mystifying ideas. For the maintenance of hegemony involves taking systematic account of popular interests and demands, shifting position and making compromises on secondary issues to maintain support and alliances in an inherently unstable and fragile system of political relations (without, however, sacrificing essential interests), and organising this support for the attainment of national goals which serve the fundamental long-run interests of the dominant group (1971, pp. 12, 52–53, 61, 78–79, 80n, 161, 182, 195, 253, and *passim*). Moreover, in addition to this element of political leadership in Gramsci's analysis of bourgeois hegemony – an element already emphasised in his strategy of proletarian leadership of the peasantry in the continuing struggle for socialist revolution in Italy (1978, pp. 11, 104, 253–254, 288, 368, 431–432, 443), Gramsci also stresses the element of intellectual and moral leadership involved in the constitution and reproduction of a collective will, a 'national-popular' outlook, a common world-view which is adequate to the needs of social and economic reproduction. This intellectual and moral leadership is constituted through ethical-political and ideological practices that operate on *and through* the prevailing system of beliefs, values, common-sense assumptions, and social attitudes to organise popular culture in its broadest sense and adapt it to the needs of the dominant mode of production (Gramsci, 1971, pp. 12,

60–61, 103–104, 130–133, 137, 181–182, 196–197, 258, 271, 279–318, 325–327, 330–331, 340–341, 381–382, 396–397). Finally it should be noted that, just as the moment of force is institutionalised in a system of coercive apparatuses, so hegemony is crystallised and mediated through a complex system of ideological (or hegemonic) apparatuses located throughout the social formation. But the practice of hegemony is nonetheless concentrated in the sphere of civil society or so-called 'private' organisations, such as the Church, trade unions, schools, the mass media, or political parties (Gramsci, 1971, pp. 10–12, 15, 56n, 155, 210, 243, 261, 267) and in the activities of intellectuals whose function – which is itself conducted in and through ideology rather than being simply manipulative – is to elaborate ideologies, to educate the people, to organise and unify social forces, and to secure the hegemony of the dominant group (Gramsci, 1971, pp. 5–23, 60–61, 270–272, 418–419, and *passim*).

Not only does Gramsci elaborate these modes of securing political class domination but he also examines their differential articulation. In particular he argues that the weight of hegemony and the hegemonic apparatuses is considerably greater in the advanced capitalist systems of Europe and North America (especially where hegemony is expansive in nature rather than involving 'transformism' or 'passive revolution') than it was in the backward conditions of Tsarist Russia. This difference is linked with differences in the appropriate revolutionary strategy. For the weakness of the institutions of civil society and the tenuous hegemony of the ruling groups in Russia fused with the dissolution of the moment of force in an erstwhile repressive state to permit a rapid and violent destruction of state power (Gramsci, 1977, pp. 50–53; 1978, pp. 199–200, 408–409; 1971, pp. 238, 243). In contrast, following the consolidation of imperialism in the 1870s and the development of parliamentary democracies with their massive complexes of institutions and organisations in civil society alongside the flexibility inscribed within such governmental systems (Gramsci, 1971, pp. 179, 242–243), the moment of hegemony has acquired decisive weight in securing class domination and is particularly significant in enabling the ruling class(es) to respond effectively to economic crises and/or other threats (such as a military failure) to the authority of government (Gramsci, 1971, pp. 184–185, 210–211, 235, 238). This implies the need for a different revolutionary strategy – the steady disaggregation of the social bases of ruling class hegemony and the consolidation of intellectual and moral leadership. In this way the ruling class will be isolated and demoralised prior to the political-military resolution of the struggle for state power. Thus, while the Tsarist state could be smashed largely through a 'war of manouevre' organised by the Bolshevik Party and based on an alliance between the proletariat and peasantry (although this did not obviate the necessity for a 'war of position' to sustain that alliance after the dictatorship of the proletariat was established and the economic foundations for a socialist society were constructed) (1978, pp. 414–416, 431–432), a successful revolution in advanced capitalist systems presupposes a protracted 'war of position' to alter the relations of forces and prepare for a transition to socialism before the political-military conquest of political society (Gramsci, 1971, pp. 52–53, 57, 57n, 181–183, 185, 199–200, 237–238, 239, 243, 267).

In developing these views Gramsci nowhere suggests that state power in a capitalist society is necessarily bourgeois in character nor that there is any guarantee that bourgeois domination can always be reproduced through an appropriate mixture of coercion and consent. Indeed, far from adopting such essentialist ideas, Gramsci emphasises the obstacles in the path of the bourgeois 'integral state' (in which force is combined with hegemony) and stresses the fragility of the 'unstable equilibria of compromise' on which such hegemony is premised (Gramsci, 1971, p. 182 and *passim*). Thus the accession of fascism is attributed to the historical weakness of the Italian state. This is traced to the failure of the Italian bourgeoisie to establish 'intellectual, moral, and political leadership' over the whole nation through Jacobin-style agrarian reform and the concomitant failure to give the Risorgimento a national-popular dimension and thus secure a solid class basis independent of the big landowners (Gramsci, 1978, pp. 79, 343–354, 449–452; 1971, pp. 55–89). The political conditions necessary for an effective liberal parliamentary state producing government with permanently organised, active consent were thus absent. Instead of an 'expansive hegemony' the Italian state was characterised by a 'transformist' social base, i.e., one dependent on the continuing absorption into the ruling class of the intellectual and political leaders of subordinate groups and on the resulting decapitation and disorganisation of those groups (Gramsci, 1978, pp. 79–80, 346, 348–349; 1971, pp. 58n, 80n, 97–98, 109, 128n, 227). In this sense 'transformism' involves a 'war of position' conducted by the ruling class against subordinate groups. It is also discussed in terms of 'passive revolution', i.e., a reorganisation of economic, political, and ideological relations, often in response to a crisis, that maintains the passivity of subordinate groups and the separation of leaders and led (Gramsci, 1971, pp. 58n, 59, 59n, 105–120).

In developing these concepts Gramsci is concerned not only with providing criteria of historical interpretation but also with specifying communist strategy in different circumstances — including the transition to socialism. In the latter context he concludes that a transition period involves an 'economic-corporate' phase in which the dominant class employs state power to secure the economic foundations of its hegemony through promoting the economic interests of subaltern classes and thereby consolidating their support. It is this argument that informs Gramsci's discussion of the New Economic Policy in the Soviet Union (Gramsci, 1978, pp. 430—432). The 'economic-corporate' phase then provides the basis for developing an 'integral state' in which the principal modality of state power is the exercise of hegemony based on the active consent of a people who have undergone a radical 're-education' through the revolutionary process and the activities of the party in its capacity as a collective intellectual and moral leader as well as political organ (Gramsci, 1971, pp. 133, 370, 404, 340—341, 350, 381). With the consolidation of an integral state based on such 'expansive hegemony', 'political society' begins to wither away — assuming the role of a nightwatchman as more and more of social life is organised through the institutions and associations of a free and democratic civil society (Gramsci, 1971, pp. 257—263).

In presenting this review of Gramsci's politics, I do not claim to have given a complete account of his theoretical work and political activities. But it should be clear that Gramsci's originality lies in the radical reappraisal of the nature of the state apparatus and state power implied in his various analyses of hegemony. Although the latter concept had long figured in communist views concerning the leading (or hegemonic) role of the proletariat in mass revolutionary struggle, Gramsci also applied it to the political practice of the bourgeoisie and extended it to include intellectual and moral leadership as well as political leadership. This entailed a shift away from seeing the state as an essentially coercive apparatus to focusing on the relative weight of coercion, fraud-corruption, and active consent (Gramsci, 1971, p. 80n). This theoretical break also implies a concern with the hegemonic apparatuses of state power and the role of intellectuals in organising the hegemony of the dominant class and forming an 'historic bloc' in which there is an adequate, mutually supportive relation between base and superstructure. Gramsci's discussion of these issues is constantly concerned with the lability of the relations of forces that shape state power and condition the emergence and resolution of political and ideological crises and he therefore develops a complex range of concepts for the analysis of these relations and crises. At the same time he is concerned with the periodisation of the state (linking the decisive weight of hegemony to the imperialist epoch and to strong links in the imperialist chain) and the forms, social bases, and effects of different types of regime. Thus, although he contributed little to the analysis of the pure capitalist mode of production (especially its economic moment), Gramsci made a major, indeed decisive, contribution to the analysis of state power at the level of the social formation. It is with the reception and the subsequent development of his work that we are concerned in the following pages.

GRAMSCI'S POSTWAR RECEPTION

The theoretical break with orthodox Marxism achieved in the *Prison Notebooks* did not receive immediate recognition. For, not only did the prison writings remain wholly unpublished until 1947, but they were also subject to censorship when publihed (to produce the distorted image of Gramsci as a loyal Stalinist) and even then appeared in piecemeal fashion. This was associated with the restriction of discussion concerning Gramsci's work to his relationship to the Italian progressive cultural tradition and the extent to which Gramsci remained theoretically and politically faithful to the Marxist-Leninist tradition. The whole debate was heavily imbued with, and overdetermined by, narrow political considerations and involved attempts at the exclusive appropriation of Gramsci's thought and prestige by different factions, tendencies, and parties (cf. Davidson, 1972, pp. 448–461; Mancini and Galli, 1968, pp. 325–338; Mouffe and Sassoon, 1977, pp. 32–36; Mouffe, 1979a, pp. 1–15). In the aftermath of the 'de-Stalinisation' of 1956, however, just as there was a shift in the orthodox communist analysis of postwar capitalism and a fresh look at stamocap theory, there was also a shift in the theoretical and political interpretation of Gramsci's work. This shift was initiated above all by Togliatti (1958). It involved a serious concern with Gramsci as a theorist of the political moment in the context of imperialism, the defeat of the revolutionary movement in the West, the rise of fascism, the economic crisis of 1929, the growth of the interventionist state, and the appropriate revolutionary strategy in these conditions (see especially, in addition to Togliatti, 1958, Ragionieri, 1967, pp. 101–146; Buci-Glucksmann, 1975, *passim*; de Giovanni, 1977, pp. 259–288; Sassoon, 1978, pp. 9–38; and *idem,* 1980, *passim*). In this area Gramsci has increasingly been interpreted as the theorist of revolution in the West and interest has increasingly been focused on the concepts of civil society, hegemony, war of position, passive revolution, intellectuals, and so on. Moreover, while the discussion of Gramsci among Italian theorists was initially somewhat parochial as well as polemical and contributed little to the theoretical advance of Marxist political analyses, the debates around Gramsci's work on the nature of the state, state power, and ideology have precipitated some significant theoretical insights that go beyond the progress recorded by Gramsci himself. This is most evident in the work of theorists who argue that Gramsci managed to avoid not only economic determinism but also class reductionism more generally and/or who insist on the importance of Gramsci's interest in literature and comparative linguistics and thereby relate his arguments to recent developments in discourse theory and the analysis of ideology (see below). In tandem with these currents there has also been growing interest in Gramsci's contribution to Marxist philosophy as well as the analysis of politics and ideology. Here we find an emphasis on Gramsci's attempt to break with positivism as well as economism and to develop a new approach to philosophy as a mediating link between theory and politics (cf. Mouffe and Sassoon, 1977, pp. 51–59). Of particular importance in this context is the work of the so-called 'Bari school' (or 'école Barisienne') and its resort to Gramsci in developing Marxism as a 'science of politics' in opposition to the residual economism of the Comintern as well as the blatant economism of the Second International (representative of this school is the work of Badaloni, Cerroni, Colletti, de Giovanni, Luporini, and Vacca). In the following review, however, I am less concerned with conflicting interpretations of Gramsci himself than with the attempt to develop Gramsci's state theory and analyses of ideology in new directions. Thus, rather than looking at Italian theorists, who have generally been more concerned with the interpretation and appropriation of Gramsci as such, we begin with the work of Nicos Poulantzas, who went beyond such issues to develop an influential and broad-ranging political theory based on a distinctive reading of Gramsci's work on hegemony. I shall then give a brief account of the 'discourse-theoretical' approach to hegemony and end with some general comments of the implications of the neo-Gramscian school.

THEORETICAL DEVELOPMENT OF POULANTZAS

Poulantzas is the single most influential Marxist political theorist of the postwar period and, up to his premature death in 1979 he produced a significant body of work on the capitalist state, social classes, and socialist strategy. It is impossible to discuss all aspects of his work here and I focus on his contribution to Marxist state theory (for a more extended analysis, see Jessop, 1982). Given his reputation as a structuralist and the marked tendency (at least among English-speaking critics) to locate his work within the structuralist-instrumentalist problematic, it might seem perverse and idiosyncratic to discuss Poulantzas in terms of the neo-Gramscian approach. But, if we ignore his earliest studies of law and the juridical system with their strongly Sartrean overtones (e.g., 1965a, 1965b, 1966, 1967a) and his obvious flirtation with Althusserian structuralism in his first major work on the capitalist state (*PPSC*) and its residues in his subsequent analyses (see below), it is apparent that his principal sources of inspiration among twentieth-century Marxists are Gramsci and Lenin and that Gramsci is the more influential in many respects. This blunt assertion can be substantiated through a brief review of his theoretical development.

Poulantzas first embarked on a critical analysis of the capitalist state in an essay on the nature and role of hegemony as the distinctive organisational principle of this type of state (1965c). He argues that there is a radical difference between the state in pre-capitalist formations and the state in capitalist societies and that this derives from differences in the modes of production. The 'natural ties' of direct producers to a hierarchically organised community and the mixed economic-political character of class exploitation precludes democratic forms of politics in pre-capitalist societies and requires the use of coercion to impose the immediate private interests of the dominant class (*ibid.*, pp. 870–876). The institutional separation of economics from politics in the CMP means that the former is dominated by surplus-value and exchange as the direct aim and motive of production and also permits a distinctive, *sui generis* mode of political domination. For, in so far as this separation involves more than the development of a specialised coercive organ distinct from the people and actually involves the exclusion of extra-economic coercion from the sphere of production, it enables the state to operate as a universalising instance which can promote the interests of the dominant class through the exercise of hegemony (*ibid.*, pp. 880–882). This leads Poulantzas to note that, whereas the pre-capitalist state acts in an 'economic-corporate' manner through marginal, mechanical compromises and distributes state power in a zero-sum fashion, the capitalist state must offer guarantees to the subordinate classes and impose short-term sacrifices on the dominant class to secure its long-term political goals (*ibid.*, pp. 882–884). The crucial importance of the state as a universalising instance through which the dominant class represents its interests as those of the nation as a whole clearly gives great weight to the role of intellectuals and ideological class struggle in organising and leading the dominant and dominated classes alike (*ibid.*, pp. 885–890).

Poulantzas then considers how hegemony operates not only to secure the active consent of the dominated classes but also to unify dominant class fractions and/or classes into a coherent power bloc. He follows Gramsci in arguing that political class domination in capitalism rests on a distinctive combination of active consent articulated with constitutionalised forms of coercion. But he also extends Gramsci's work to argue that the economic fractioning of the bourgeoisie can be overcome only through a state which displays its own internal (class) unity and institutional autonomy vis-à-vis the dominant class fractions. The existence of a relatively unified power bloc cannot be explained in terms of the imposition of the economic-corporate interests of the dominant fraction on other fractions and classes (as suggested in the work of stamocap theorists) nor could it be secured through a state which comprised a disparate ensemble of dislocated powers and counter-powers and so lacked any ability to organise and lead a bourgeois power bloc (*ibid.*, pp. 1050–1058). In short Poulantzas insists that the capitalist state must be understood as an institutional ensemble which has a major function in organising hegemony within the power bloc as well as in the mobilisation of active consent vis-à-vis the dominated classes and thus society as a whole (*ibid.*, pp. 1061–1066).

It should be clear that Poulantzas is indebted to the pioneering work of Gramsci in this essay and that many of his key ideas pre-date his appropriation of Althusserian structuralism. Indeed, not only does he consider the role of hegemony in relation to the dominated classes, he also applies it creatively to the organisation-direction of a power bloc. Likewise, whereas Gramsci tends to see the integral state (i.e., hegemony armoured by coercion) as characteristic of the imperialist era and relates its development to the expansion of civil society (in the sense of ideological apparatuses), Poulantzas derives the crucial role of hegemony from the institutional matrix of capitalism as a whole and relates it to the separation between the public sphere of politics and the private sphere of civil society (considered as the site of economic relations). But both theorists stress the important role of intellectual/ideological as well as political practices in constituting hegemony. All these analyses will be taken up and developed in further work by Poulantzas and combined therein with elements of structuralism.

Two important transitional studies in this respect are a critique of Marxist political theory in Britain and a review of Althusser's *For Marx*. In the former Poulantzas insists on the utility of Gramsci's concepts (such as hegemony, power bloc, etc.) when placed in a non-historicist, non-subjectivist problematic (cf. Althusser) and proceeds to criticise the twin failings of the quasi-Lukacsian interpretation of Gramsci that he discerns in the work of Anderson and Nairn from the *New Left Review* (1966a, especially pp. 1699–1701). In the latter Poulantzas affirms the importance of Althusser's epistemological break in modern Marxist theory but also notes certain difficulties in his approach to economic determination in the last instance (1966b, especially pp. 1971–1982). In both studies Poulantzas begins to juxtapose, combine, and synthesise Gramscian and Althusserian analyses and thereby introduces a tension into his own work that will become more significant with time.

It is in *Political Power and Social Classes* (1968) that Poulantzas presents his first extended analysis of the capitalist state. It bears the obvious imprint of both Gramscian and Althusserian perspectives – emphasising the Gramscian elements in the analysis of (political) class struggle as the motor force of history, emphasing the Althusserian elements in the analysis of the institutional matrix of capitalism and the global reproduction of the social formation, and, to the extent that Poulantzas attempts to reconcile these elements, emphasising the primacy of the structures over the class struggle. This stress upon the primacy of objective structures reached its highpoint in the first intervention by Poulantzas in his debate with Miliband and it is this controversy that has dominated the English-speaking reception of his work (see Poulantzas, 1969). But, although these tensions remain in more recent studies, there has been a progressive elimination of structuralist formalism and 'super-determinism' and a shift to the primacy of class struggle over structure.

Throughout his work Poulantzas emphasised the need to develop 'regional' theories of the state corresponding to particular modes of production (1965c, p. 878; *PPSC*, pp. 12, 16–17, 29; *SPS*, pp. 14–20). He himself concentrated on the theoretically typical form of the capitalist state (representative democracy) and two of its exceptional forms (fascism and military dictatorship). At first he examined the capitalist state in isolation from the economic region of the CMP – he focused on its organisational role in reproducing political domination and largely ignored more direct state involvement in organising capitalist economic exploitation (see *PPSC, passim*). But even here Poulantzas often talked of the role of juridico-political ideology and legal institutions in maintaining the 'isolation effect' among dominated classes at the economic level (i.e., the competitive individuation of producers that prevents them experiencing production relations as class relations) (*PPSC*, pp. 130–137, 139–140, 143, 148, 151, 188, 213–214, 275–276, 291–293, 353) as well as examining its repercussions for the constitution and operation of liberal democracy as the institutional locus of the public unity of privatised, individuated, competing citizens (*PPSC*, pp. 123–125, 133–134, 136–137, 140–141, 188–189, 214–216, 276–279, 281, 288–289, 291, 353). Later Poulantzas shifted attention from the normal capitalist state considered apart from the periodisation of the CMP towards both exceptional and normal states in its so-called 'monopoly-imperialist' stage. This stage is supposed to be associated with the rise to dominance within the matrix of the CMP of the political level in place of the economic (*PPSC*, pp. 55–56, 91, 150, 211, 345; 1971, pp. 20–21, 74–75, 303, 313; 1974, pp. 42, 45, 81, 100–101, 165–168; and *SPS*, pp. 166–168). Paradoxically this is reflected in Poulantzas's growing concern with economic intervention and the consequential reorganisation of the capitalist state. Thus, while his analysis of *Fascism and Dictatorship* (1970) focused on the key political functions of an exceptional form of the interventionist state during the consolidation of monopoly capitalist domination within the CMP, *Classes in Contemporary Capitalism* (1974) considers the economic functions of the interventionist state in various phases of the 'monopoly-imperialist' stage as well as its political functions. This analysis was extended in the final work on state theory (*SPS*) to take account of further growth in economic intervention and its implications.

In tandem with this increasing concern with economic intervention and its limitations, Poulantzas also showed increasing interest in the reproduction of the class struggle within the state apparatus and its implications for revolutionary strategy. For, while *Political Power and Social Classes* tended to endow the capitalist state with a structurally determined, objective function in maintaining cohesion and to presuppose its essential class unity, the analysis of the crisis form of state in *Fascism and Dictatorship* and the enquiry into the collapse of the military dictatorships of Southern Europe presented in the *Crisis of the Dictatorships* (1975, 1976b) have led Poulantzas to emphasise more strongly the primacy of the class struggle over structures and to stress the fissured, contradictory nature of the capitalist state. This shift of emphasis is reaffirmed in *State, Power, Socialism* and, for the first time, is related to the problems of the transition to socialism. In the space available here it is impossible to summarise, let alone critically dissect, all the concepts, assumptions, principles of explanation, and arguments in his work. So neither his concrete historical analyses of exceptional regimes nor his work on class formation are discussed here and I focus instead on the basic ideas underlying Poulantzas's contributions to a theory of the capitalist state.

THE STATE, SOCIAL CLASSES, AND POWER

In the 'Introduction' to his first major text Poulantzas locates his approach in terms of the Althusserian problematic and describes it as an attempt to produce theoretically a complex hierarchy of concepts for the analysis of the political superstructure of the state in the CMP, i.e., to produce a regional theory of the state in a particular mode of production (1968, pp. 11, 16–17). He argues that this cannot be achieved through a simple logical derivation of progressively more concrete concepts from the most abstract concepts nor through the mere subsumption of more concrete concepts and the most abstract as so many particular instances of the latter (1968, p. 13). Instead it requires a complex work of theoretical elaboration in which concepts are precisely located in relation to the process of thought from the most 'abstract-formal' level to the 'concrete-real' and in relation to the specific object of thought (e.g., the particular region of the CMP) on which they bear (1968, p. 13; cf. pp. 145–146). In this context Poulantzas suggests that a scientific study of the capitalist type of state involves a threefold theoretical elaboration: the development of the historical materialist *general theory* of modes of production, class-divided social formations, states, and politics viewed in isolation from specific modes of production, the development of a *particular theory* of the CMP in order to determine the exact place and function of the state and politics in the theoretically typical matrix of its economic, political, and ideological levels, and, to the extent that the capitalist state enjoys a specific institutional autonomy within the CMP enabling it to be a *sui generis* object of thought, the development of a *regional theory* of the capitalist state and politics (1968, pp. 12, 16–18, 142). But he does not discuss the problems of constructing concepts on these different levels and/or planes of abstraction nor that of articulating them to produce a concrete analysis of specific societies – at best we are provided with the answers implied in Poulantzas's order of exposition.

Thus, rather than developing all the elements of the general theory and the particular theory of the CMP, he merely invokes the general theory of modes of production extracted from Marx's *Capital* by Althusser *et al.* in *Reading Capital* and argues that *Capital* itself presents the particular theory of the CMP and the regional theory of its economic level. This leaves him free to concentrate on the general theory of the state, social classes, and power and the regional theory of the state within the CMP. Even here there is no attempt systematically to construct the concepts but instead they are gradually introduced on the basis of his reading of the political writings of Marx, Engels, Lenin, and Gramsci. This method of argument and presentation has definite effects on Poulantzas's work and we shall refer to these in subsequent substantive and methodological criticism.

Poulantzas argues that the political region is concerned with the institutionalised power of the state as a particular structural ensemble and that political practice has as its specific object the maintenance or transformation of the 'present moment' (or conjuncture) through control over state power. In presenting this general argument he abstracts from particular modes of production and thus from the differential forms of labour process ('real appropriation' or 'possession') and appropriation of surplus labour ('property relation' or 'economic ownership') and their corresponding matrices of economic, political, and ideological regions. This gives his general theory of the state and politics a 'class-theoretical' and functionalist cast. Thus Poulantzas argues that the state is defined by its general function as the factor of cohesion or unity in a class-divided social formation rather than by specific institutions: the precise place of the state, its particular form, its institutional structure, and its boundaries depend on the nature of the (dominant) mode of production and social formation. This does not mean that actual states can perform no functions beyond maintaining cohesion — merely that this is the general, constitutive function of all states, that other functions vary according to the (dominant) mode of production and social formation, and that any such functions are overdetermined by the general function. At the same time Poulantzas analyses the state in 'class-theoretical' rather than 'capital-theoretical' (or analogous) terms: for a general theory must abstract from particular modes of production and is obliged to adopt a 'class-theoretical' approach. In this context he argues that the state reflects and condenses all the contradictions in a class-divided social formation, that political practices are always class practices, and that state power is always the power of a definite class to whose interests the state corresponds.

This does not mean that the state should be seen as a mere instrument of the dominant class. Rather it implies that, to the extent that the state successfully performs its general function in managing class contradictions and thereby securing cohesion, it maintains the political conditions necessary for the reproduction of the (dominant) mode of production (cf. 1968, pp. 54, 137). Moreover, in arguing that the state can be understood neither as a simple instrument or 'thing' nor as a sovereign, free-willed subject, Poulantzas suggests that it is best seen as a form-determined field of social relations in which the regional structure of the political has definite effects on the political class struggle (1968, p. 103; 1974, pp. 26, 98; 1976a, p. 74; 1976c, pp. 38–39; 1978, pp. 128–129, 158). At this point, however, we reach the limits of the general theory of the state. To progress further Poulantzas must move from a functionalist, 'class-theoretical' account to a form-determined, 'capital-theoretical' analysis. It remains to be seen how this is achieved. (For the general theory, see Poulantzas, 1968, pp. 37, 40–54, 99–100, 115–117; also, 1969, pp. 68, 73–77; 1970, pp. 303, 304; 1974, pp. 24–28, 78, 98, 156, 164, 169; 1976a, pp. 72–74, 79–81; 1976c, pp. 31–32, 38–39; 1978, pp. 14–17, 19–21, 38–44.)

In considering the particular theory of the CMP, Poulantzas first contrasts the relations of production in capitalist and pre-capitalist modes of exploitation. He argues that the latter were characterised by the immediate access of the direct producers to the means of production and their ability to set these to work without the intervention of the exploiting class of owners; and that this meant that the owners had to employ extra-economic compulsion to control the use of the means of production and to appropriate surplus-labour. In contrast the CMP involves the separation or dispossession of the direct producers (as individuals and as a collective labourer) from the means of production and the effective coincidence (or 'homology') of the twin economic powers of possession (control over the labour process) and ownership (control over the goals of production and the appropriation of surplus-labour) in the hands of the exploiting class. Exploitation now takes the form of exchange owing to the embodiment of surplus-labour in commodities and compulsion is not required within the relations of production − instead it is confined to maintaining the 'external' conditions of such exploitation (see 1968, pp. 27, 28, 29–32, 126–127, 129, 227–228; 1974, pp. 19, 32, 63, 94, 116; 1976c, pp. 32–33; 1978, pp. 18–19, 26, 35; cf. 1965c, pp. 870–876). Thus the CMP involves a distinctive autonomy of the economic and political regions. For the economic region is now freed from direct political control – it operates through distinct economic apparatuses (enterprises) and under the dominance of *sui generis* economic laws (mediated via market forces and ultimately determined by the circuit of productive capital). Likewise the political region is able to monopolise and constitutionalise the use of coercion and to specialise for the first time in the global political function of maintaining cohesion rather than being directly implicated in the organisation of the labour process and the appropriation of surplus-labour (1968, pp. 21, 29, 32, 46, 48n, 127, 129, 143n, 226–227; 1970, p. 304; 1974, pp. 32, 64, 92, 94, 96; 1978, pp. 18, 50–51, 53, 82; cf. 1965c, pp. 879–880). But this institutional separation and functional specialisation do not mean that the economic and political regions have become completely autonomous and self-sufficient. For the economic region has definite political conditions of existence and the political region performs economic functions under the dominance of its global cohesive function. Nonetheless it is still possible to develop a theory of the political region of capitalism without resorting to crude economic reductionism of a 'capital logic' kind. Indeed, as the capitalist state represents the global political interests of the power bloc rather than the immediate economic interests of its various class (fraction) constituents, one must start from *sui generis* political concepts rather than the economic categories of capital accumulation (1968, pp. 17, 50–51, 53–56, 130–131, 190, 282; 1970, pp. 20–21, 311, 313; 1974, pp. 21, 81, 99–101, 165–168; 1976a, pp. 78–79; 1978, pp. 17–19, 38, 168–169; and, for a critique of 'capital logic', see: 1978, pp. 51–52).

In this context Poulantzas argues that the capitalist state must be related to the structural matrix of the CMP *and* to the field of class relations. Moreover, although the structural matrix receives priority in his order of exposition (since classes are seen as an effect of this matrix in the field of social relations), it is class relations that are accorded the principal role as the motor force of history. Thus, while the place of the capitalist state in the CMP, its unique organisational form as a national-popular representative state, its precise boundaries, and its specific functions in capitalist reproduction depend on the distinctive matrix of the CMP and its transformation according to the stages and phases of capital accumulation, they are modified within these basic structural limits by the changing conjunctures of class struggle in the various regions of capitalist society and their overdetermination by the political class struggle in its global sense (see Poulantzas, 1968, pp. 38, 57, 63–64, 99, 125–137, 143, 148–151, 157, 309; 1970, pp. 16, 24, 40–42, 53, 70, 310–311; 1974, pp. 27–28, 97–98, 156, 161n; 1976a, pp. 71–72, 74; 1976b, pp. 21, 82, 90–92; 1976c, pp. 32–33, 37; 1978, pp. 123–124, 204). Thus, having derived the distinctive institutional separation of the political region and its functional specialisation as the factor of cohesion from the matrix of the CMP, Poulantzas proceeds to examine the nature of the capitalist state in terms of its distinctive relation to the field of class struggles. His starting point is not found among the economic categories of the capital relation but comes instead from the political region itself. For Poulantzas first introduces the concept of the 'isolation effect' and then traces its implications for the form and functions of the capitalist state. This approach differs fundamentally from *Staatsableitung* and we must now consider it in greater detail.

ON PRIVATE INDIVIDUATION AND PUBLIC UNITY

Poulantzas ascribes a crucial role to the capitalist state in the structural matrix of the CMP in securing the specific external conditions of existence of the economic region as well as its general precondition of social cohesion. He also argues that the state has specific effects on the economic and political class struggles. In this section we shall ignore state intervention in the relations of production (see below, pp. 173–177) and concentrate instead on its role in the class struggle. Here Poulantzas notes that the specific autonomy of the different regions in the CMP entails a distinctive separation of the different fields of the class struggle and poses definite problems of class unity for dominant and dominated classes alike. This structural effect is reinforced by the 'isolation effect' created through specific juridico-political and ideological practices mediated through the state. Together these effects condition the complex terrain of class struggles in capitalist societies and permit the development of the capitalist type of state as a state characterised by hegemonic class leadership (1968, pp. 89, 91–92, 130–141, 190–191).

Poulantzas argues that the juridico-political region has a crucial effect on the field of class struggle. For it interpellates the agents of production as individual juridical subjects rather than as members of antagonistic classes (on the meaning of interpellation, see above p. 000). Thus economic agents do not experience capitalist relations as class relations but as relations of competition among mutually isolated individuals and/or fragmented groups of workers and capitalists. This 'isolation effect' extends to the entire field of economic relations in capitalist societies and permeates classes belonging to other modes of production located therein (1968, pp. 130–131, 213–214, 275–276, 310; 1978, pp. 63–67, 69–70, 86–88). The same effect is evident in the field of political class struggle. For law and juridico-political ideology duplicate the 'fracturing' of the 'private' sphere in the interpellation of the people as mutually isolated, individual 'citizens' and/or political categories. But Poulantzas also argues that the 'isolation effect' in the private sphere and the realm of citizenship is coupled with something we might term the 'unifying effect' of the capitalist state. For this presents itself as the strictly political (i.e., non-economic), public unity of the people-nation considered as the abstract sum of formally free and equal legal subjects. Moreover, not only does the state embody the public unity of private individuals through the operation of its various representative institutions (suffrage, parties, legislative assemblies, etc.), through its distinctive centralising bureaucratic-hierarchical framework it also organises and regulates the relations among diverse individual subjects and social categories in order to maintain cohesion (1968, pp. 125, 133–134, 188–189, 215–216, 276–277, 279, 288, 291, 348, 349–350; 1978, pp. 49, 58, 63–65, 86–88). This means that the capitalist state is related to socio-economic relations as refracted through the 'isolation effect', i.e., class relations are constitutively absent from the organisation of the capitalist state and its actions aim to secure cohesion and unity among individuated citizens (1968, pp. 133, 188, 213, 223, 279, 310). In turn this means that the organisation and internal functioning of the state can assume the form of a rational-legal administration. Thus the bureaucracy can appear as an impersonal, neutral institution embodying the general interest and can operate according to a hierarchically structured, centrally coordinated system of formal, general, universal, and codified rational-legal norms. Indeed the very possibility of a formally rational administration depends not only on the economically grounded monopoly of force enjoyed by the state but also on the absence of open political class domination from its organisation (1968, pp. 216, 226–227, 332, 347–350; 1974, p. 186; 1978, pp. 59, 65, 76–77, 80–82, 88–89, 91).

Nonetheless, although the individuals of civil society are formally free and equal and the state is the formally sovereign and 'class-less' embodiment of their unity, the manner in which this cohesion and unity are realised is necessarily overdetermined by the need to reproduce class domination. Thus Poulantzas argues that, while the capitalist state must prevent any political organisation of the dominated classes that would threaten to end their economic isolation and/or social fracturing, it has to work continually on the dominant class fractions and/or classes to cancel their economic isolation and secure the unity of the power bloc and its hegemony over the dominated classes (1968, pp. 136–137, 140–141, 188–189, 284–285, 287–289; 1974, pp. 97–98, 157–158; 1978, pp. 127, 140–141). This dual political task is achieved through the organisation of a unified power bloc under the leadership of a specific class (fraction) and the successful presentation of its global political interests as those of the people-nation as a whole. In turn this involves the continual negotiation of interests in an 'unstable equilibrium of compromise' and requires real (albeit limited) material concessions to the economic-corporate interests of the dominated classes (1968, pp. 137, 190–191; 1970, pp. 71–72, 313; 1974, pp. 91–93, 97–98, 163–164; 1976b, pp. 47–48, 79–81, 83, 102–103; 1976c, p. 37; 1978, pp. 30–31, 133, 140–141, 184–185).

In discussing the dual constitution of hegemony Poulantzas refers to a wide range of institutional effects and political and ideological practices. Among its basic conditions of possibility are the separation of the political region from the economic (endowing the state with the relative autonomy it requires to mediate the management of contradictions and secure cohesion) and the 'isolation effect' (enabling the hegemonic class or class fraction to articulate its interests with those of an individuated, fractured people-nation). Within this context Poulantzas then focuses on the effects of the specific institutional structures and their so-called 'structural selectivity' in securing the unity of the dominant classes and fractions in the power bloc under the hegemony of a specific class (fraction). Thus, whereas his early studies focused on the differential presence of competing dominant class or fractional forces in the various branches and power centres of the state and their unification through the dominance of the legislative branch (typical of competitive capitalism) or of the executive branch as organised in turn under the dominance of a specific power centre (typical of monopoly capitalism), his subsequent work extends this analysis of the unity of the power bloc and the concomitant unity of state power to include the differential presence of class forces in the so-called ideological state apparatuses (or ISAs) as well as the branches of the state apparatus proper (also referred to as the 'repressive state apparatus' or 'RSA') and to give far greater weight to the 'polycentrism' of the executive branch itself as a terrain of class and fractional struggles ultimately unified through the central role of one power centre within a complex hierarchy of power centres (cf. 1968, pp. 303–307; 1969, pp. 74–77; 1970, pp. 299–309, 311–312, 318, 325, 327; 1974, pp. 98, 163–164, 186–187; 1976a, p. 75; 1976b, pp. 49–50, 82, 100–101, 103; 1976c, pp. 39–42; 1978, pp. 132–137). In this context Poulantzas stresses that the mediation of the contradictions within the power bloc depends not only on the formal institutional structure of the state (e.g., the centralism and/or hierarchical organisation of the RSA and its regimentation of the ISAs) but also on specific political practices (classified, paradoxically, as a process of 'structural selectivity') such as short-circuiting decision-making processes, selective filtering of policy implementation, partial 'non-decision-making', displacing functions between power centres, and reversing the predominant repressive or ideological roles of different state apparatuses (1970, pp. 329–330, 334; 1974, p. 164; 1976a, p. 75; 1976c, p. 40; 1978, p. 134). He also notes that these practices involve not only members of the dominant classes and fractions themselves but also their representatives on the 'political scene' (the field of party competition and parliamentary politics), their 'ideological watchdogs' and 'organic intellectuals', and the heads of the state apparatus whose function as formally impartial representatives of the public or national interest is necessarily qualified by their *de facto* polarisation around different class and fractional interests within the power bloc (1968, pp. 216, 246–252, 315, 320–321, 336–340, 336n; 1969, pp. 73–74; 1970, pp. 73–75, 77–78, 102–103, 125–127; 1974, pp. 183–189; 1976b, pp. 33, 50, 102–103, 120; 1976c, pp. 46–47; 1978, pp. 61, 135–136, 154, 156, 159).

Somewhat different considerations are advanced in relation to the constitution of hegemony over the dominated classes and popular masses. Poulantzas has consistently emphasised the importance of genuine class *alliances* extending beyond the power bloc in the economic, political, or ideological fields and has also stressed the role of *support* from subordinate classes based on ideological illusions concerning the nature of state power rather than on real political sacrifices on the part of the power bloc and its allies (1968, pp. 216, 240–245, 285–286, 288, 297; 1970, pp. 112, 243, 327, 330; 1974, pp. 78–79, 290–294, 296–298, 333–335; 1976b, p. 103; 1976c, p. 43; 1978, p. 142). Conversely he has argued that state power (at least in the theoretically typical forms of capitalist state) corresponds unequivocally to the interests of the power bloc and that the working class cannot advance its fundamental interests (presumably in a transition to socialism) and/or secure its own hegemony through the capitalist state (1968, pp. 100, 256–257, 288; 1974, p. 164; 1976a, p. 72; 1976b, p. 103; 1978, p. 143). Yet, while the dominated classes cannot establish their own state power simply through the capture of the existing state apparatus and must develop their own class unity in and through the struggle for a new form of state, they are present in the capitalist state in a disunified, fragmented manner and can advance their particular, isolated, 'economic-corporate' interests through this state to the extent that such advances also sustain bourgeois hegemony. Indeed Poulantzas notes that the bourgeoisie typically deploys several ideological state apparatuses specially designed to inculcate bourgeois ideology into the working class and through which, in certain cases, working-class struggle is channelled with pertinent effects on state policy. In this context he cites trade unions and social democratic parties and argues that they must pursue working-class interests as a condition of reproducing bourgeois hegemony (1970, pp. 101, 127n, 144, 151–155, 172, 196, 308; 1974, p. 277; 1976a, p. 69; 1976b, pp. 55–56, 83; 1978, pp. 142, 144; see also, 1968, pp. 251, 285). This is reflected in the nature of the dominant ideology. For, in rejecting a class reductionist view of ideologies (if not, *pace* Laclau, 1977, pp. 92–99, of ideological elements), Poulantzas denies that the dominant ideology is an exclusive creation of the dominant class and has a pre-given, unitary content determined outside ideological class struggle. Instead it includes elements of petit bourgeois and working-class ideologies as a condition of successfully 'cementing' social cohesion in a class-divided society. It is dominant because it corresponds to the interests of the dominant class in a struggle for hegemony in the context of the 'isolation effect' and the concrete relation of political forces in a given social formation (1966b, pp. 67, 70; 1968, pp. 200–210, 214; 1970, pp. 106, 165–167, 306; 1974, pp. 287–288, 289–290). In turn this is reflected in the permeation of (elements of) the dominant ideology into the ideologies of the subordinate classes so that the dominant ideology even comes to structure the very forms of popular resistance to the power bloc (1968, pp. 183–184, 195, 213, 221–223, 310–312, 356–357; 1970, pp. 144–147; 1978, pp. 86, 87–89, 236).

Poulantzas also relates hegemony to the form of the state. Indeed, while arguing that hegemony is a phenomenon of the field of political (and ideological) class practices he also insists that these must be located in terms of the structure of the state. For, whereas a given form of state imposes limits on the composition of the power bloc and the nature of the hegemonic class or fraction, changes in either will require reorganisation of the state. Thus Poulantzas argues that the liberal (or non-interventionist) state is the best possible shell for securing the political domination of competitive capital and suggests that monopoly capital must replace it with an interventionist state (and, later, an 'authoritarian statist' form) to secure the best shell for its political domination (1968, pp. 150–151, 234, 242, 248, 314; 1970, pp. 21, 27, 28–29, 72–73, 75, 95, 311; 1974, pp. 45, 98, 101–103, 158; 1978, p. 123, 166–167, 172, 203–204). Within these limits, however, it is quite possible for different fractions of capital to enjoy hegemony and thereby influence the specific course of development of capitalism in a given social formation (1974, pp. 92–93). For, in addition to its constitutive fractioning according to the stages of the CMP, capital is also divided into fractions according to its place in the circuit of capital on a national and international scale. Thus, not only does Poulantzas follow Marx and Engels in suggesting that hegemony in the liberal state can be exercised by the industrial, commercial, banking, or agricultural fractions of capital, he also argues that it can be exercised by the industrial or banking fractions of monopoly capital in the interventionist state and, in other contexts, refers to shifts in hegemony between US-oriented and EEC-oriented fractions of monopoly capital (1968, pp. 232–240, 302, 302n, 306–307, 314; 1970, pp. 94–95, 116; 1974, pp. 74–75, 76, 92–93, 96, 109, 130–131, 132–133, 136; 1976b, 28–31, 33, 47; 1978, pp. 128, 133, 212).

ON 'NORMAL' AND 'EXCEPTIONAL' FORMS

The significance of these views on political class struggles and hegemony emerges particularly well in the analyses Poulantzas offers of 'normal' and 'exceptional' states. The most general distinction between these forms of state is found in the claim that the former corresponds to conjunctures in which bourgeois hegemony is stable and secure and the latter corresponds to a crisis of hegemony (1968, p. 293; 1970, pp. 11, 57–59, 72, 298, 313; 1976b, pp. 92–93). Thus, while the moment of consent dominates that of constitutionalised violence in 'normal' states, the 'exceptional' state involves the increased use of physical repression and an 'open war' against dominated classes (1968, p. 226; 1970, pp. 152, 316, 318, 330; 1976b, pp. 9, 92, 129). This is reflected in the fact that, whereas representative democratic institutions with universal suffrage and competing political parties characterise the 'normal' state, 'exceptional' states suspend the electoral principle (with the possible exception of plebiscites and/or referenda) and eliminate the plural party system (1968, pp. 123, 230, 246–247; 1970, pp. 324–327; 1976b, pp. 49, 91, 114). Moreover, while the ideological state apparatuses in the 'normal' state are typically private and so enjoy a significant degree of autonomy from its control, those in the 'exceptional' state are subordinated to the repressive state apparatus, in part to legitimate the increased coercion, in part to overcome the ideological crisis accompanying the crisis of hegemony (1970, pp. 314–318; 1976b, pp. 113–114). This control is matched by an increase in bureaucratism in the organisation and internal functioning of the state apparatus (1968, pp. 333, 334–340, 344–349; 1970, pp. 327–328, 330; 1974, pp. 274–276; 1978, pp. 58–60) and by a decline in the separation of powers among its branches tied to the infiltration of subordinate branches by the dominant branch and/or the expansion of parallel power networks and transmission belts cutting across and linking different branches (1970, pp. 315–316, 328–329; 1976b, pp. 50, 100–101). This is evident in the contrast between the rule of law and its concomitant constitutional limits to, and legal regulation of, the transfer of power in the 'normal' state and the 'exceptional' resort to arbitrariness (at least in the sphere of public law) in order to reorganise the field of hegemony (1968, pp. 226–227, 311; 1970, pp. 320–324; 1978, pp. 87–92, but contrast, 1978, pp. 76, 85). In short, if the 'normal' state depends on the stable operation of representative democratic institutions under the hegemony of the dominant class(es), the 'exceptional' state eliminates democratic institutions and the autonomous organisations of dominated classes and relies instead upon coercion together with certain material concessions and an ideological offensive to secure the rule of capital.

Poulantzas argues that representative democratic institutions facilitate the organic circulation and reorganisation of hegemony based on 'unstable equilibria of compromise' within the power bloc as well as between this bloc and the popular masses. It thereby inhibits major ruptures or breaks in the global reproduction of bourgeois society. In contrast the 'exceptional' state develops in order to reorganise the power bloc and its relations with the people in response to a political and ideological crisis that cannot be resolved through normal democratic means. But it also tends to 'congeal' the balance of forces prevailing at the time of its constitution and thus prove inflexible in the face of new disturbances and contradictions (1976b, pp. 30, 38, 48–50, 90–92, 93, 106, 124). At best this form of state can retain a certain degree of manoeuvrability to the extent that it builds a political apparatus to concentrate and channel mass support (e.g., the fascist party and trade unions), duplicates transmission belts and parallel power networks to facilitate rapid changes in the distribution of power in response to 'black parliamentarism' (to use Gramsci's term, with its analogy to the role of 'black markets') of the behind-the-scenes struggles among competing interests or group, and instils an ideology that permeates the dominated class(es) as well as the dominant class(es) and thus acts as the 'cement' of the social formation (1968, pp. 105–106, 128–129, 251–256, 329–330, 331; 1976b, pp. 71, 83–85, 124). At worst, such regimes are isolated from the masses, lack any specialised politico-ideological apparatuses to channel and control mass support, display a rigid parcellisation of state power among 'clans', 'camarillas', and 'fiefs', and lack an ideology able to cement the state apparatuses together into a unified bloc. This results in a muddle of inconsistent policies towards the masses in an effort to neutralise their opposition and in purely mechanical compromises, tactical alliances, and settling of accounts among 'economic-corporate' interests in the power bloc (1976b, pp. 49–50, 55–57, 76, 79–80, 83–84, 94, 120–121, 124–126; cf. 1965c, pp. 882–884, 1050–1058; 1970, pp. 330, 345). In turn this intensifies the internal contradictions of the state apparatus and its inflexibility in the face of economic and/or political crises (1976b, pp. 91, 93–94, 112–113, 120, 125–126). The two cases are illustrated by fascist states and military dictatorships respectively and, although Poulantzas has not discussed it to the same extent, Bonapartism would appear to be an intermediate case. For, while Bonapartism lacks a mass party comparable to fascism (1970, pp. 87, 113) and, indeed, is associated with a decline in the representational role of parties on the political scene in favour of executive predominance (1968, pp. 320, 358–359), it does consolidate a mass base through the mobilisation of petit bourgeois political support and develop a distinctive ideology articulating this support to the interests of the power bloc (1968, pp. 79, 107–108, 180, 243–244, 258–260, 283, 286). Moreover, although it is not a 'normal' form of state and corresponds to a crisis of hegemony and a representational crisis (*ibid.,* pp. 302, 320), Bonapartism still displays a marked degree of centralism organised around the unifying role of bureaucracy (*ibid.,* pp. 158–259, 261, 282–283, 357–358). It should still be noted, however, that, despite important differences among these 'exceptional' forms of state, none can secure the flexible, organic regulation of social forces and the circulation of hegemony that is possible under bourgeois democracies (1976b, p. 124). And, for this reason, just as the transition from a 'normal' to an 'exceptional' state coincides with political crises rather than developing by a continuous, linear route, so the transition from an 'exceptional' to a 'normal' form will also involve a series of breaks and crises rather than a simple process of self-transformation (*ibid.,* pp. 90–91, 93–94, 95, 97, 124).

'AUTHORITARIAN STATISM'

These analyses of 'exceptional' states also influenced Poulantzas in his more recent discussions of the 'normal' state. He suggests that the new form of capitalist state is 'authoritarian statism' and defines its basic developmental tendency as 'intensified state control over every sphere of socio-economic life combined with radical decline of the institutions of political democracy and with draconian and multi-form curtailment of so-called 'formal' liberties' (1978, pp. 203–204). More particularly he argues that the principal elements of authoritarian statism and its implications for representative democracy comprise: firstly, a transfer of power from the legislature to the executive and the concentration of power within the latter; secondly, an accelerated fusion between the three branches of the state – legislature, executive, and judiciary – accompanied by a decline in the rule of law; thirdly, the functional decline of political parties as the privileged interlocutors of the administration and the leading forces in organising hegemony; and, finally, the growth of parallel power networks cross-cutting the formal organisation of the state and exercising a decisive share in its activities (1979a, p. 132; cf. 1976c, pp. 55–57; 1978, pp. 217–231). These changes correspond to a peculiar sharpening of the generic elements of political crisis and state crisis articulated with the economic crisis supposedly characteristic of the entire current phase of capitalism. They may also be reinforced by the 'state-in-crisis' (when crises are 'of' the state rather than 'in' the state) as exemplified in France, Portugal, Greece, Spain, and Italy (1978, pp. 206, 214; 1979a, pp. 128, 131). This means that 'authoritarian statism' must be seen as a normal form of the capitalist state (and thus as still essentially democratic in character) rather than as an exceptional form (which, Poulantzas argues, is always temporary and conjuncturally determined rather than a permanent, structural feature of an entire phase of capitalism) (1978, pp. 208–209; cf. 1979a, p. 239). Nonetheless, owing to the permanent instability of bourgeois hegemony in the leading capitalist societies and the generic elements of political and state crisis, certain exceptional features are closely articulated with the dominant normal features of this new state form. In particular there emerges a reserve repressive para-state apparatus, parallel to the main organs of the state and serving in a pre-emptive capacity to police popular struggles and other threats to bourgeois hegemony (1976c, p. 56; 1978, pp. 186–187, 210, 212; 1979a, pp. 129–130). More generally the various exceptional elements characteristic of all forms of state are now crystallised and orchestrated into a permanent structure running parallel to the official state. This duplication of the state seems to be a structural feature of authoritarian statism and involves a constant symbiosis and functional intersecting of the two structures under the control of the commanding heights of the state apparatus and the dominant party (1978, pp. 208, 210, 245; 1979a, p. 132).

In discussing 'authoritarian statism' Poulantzas focuses upon the 'irresistible rise of the state administration'. He relates this mainly to the growing economic role of the state as this is modified through the political situation. For state intervention means that law can no longer be confined to general, formal, and universal norms whose enactment is the preserve of parliament as the embodiment of the general will of the people-nation. Instead, legal norms are subject to ever more elaborate specification by the administration in respect to particular conjunctures, situations, and interests and even their initial formulation has passed almost entirely from parliament to the administration (1978, pp. 218–219). This shift towards particularistic regulation at the expense of the rule of law reflects not only the imperatives of detailed economic intervention but also the problems of the permanent instability of monopoly hegemony within the power bloc and over the people. Thus, in addition to its economic effects, the decline of law is also evident in the increasing concern for pre-emptive policing of the potentially disloyal and deviant rather than the judicial punishment of clearly defined offences against the law (1978, pp. 219–220). These changes encourage the fusion of the three branches of the state – legislature, executive, and judiciary – which enjoyed at least a formal separation in the liberal constitutional state (1968, pp. 303–307, 310–315; 1974, p. 173; 1976c, pp. 55–56; 1978, pp. 222–225, 227–228; 1979, p. 132). Thus, while the institution of parliament has become a mere 'registration chamber' with very limited powers, the state bureaucracy is becoming the leading actor as well as the principal site in the elaboration of state policy under the aegis of the political executive. Real power is rapidly becoming concentrated and centralised at the summits of the governmental and administrative system and, indeed, is increasingly focused in the office of president/prime minister at the apex of the various administrative structures with the resultant appearance of a personalistic presidential/prime ministerial system (1968, pp. 311–314; 1978, pp. 221–222, 224, 227–228, 233, 238). At the same time there are important changes in the party system and the role of political parties. Most significant here are the loosening of the ties of representation between the parties of power and the power bloc (which finds it difficult to organise its hegemony through parties in parliament and concentrates instead on the administration) and of those between the parties and the popular masses (with such representation increasingly mediated through the lobby system on a reformist, economic-corporative level) (1968, pp. 313, 313–314n, 320; 1974, p. 171; 1978, pp. 221–223). Rather than fulfilling their traditional functions in the elaboration of policy through compromise and alliances around a party programme and in the legitimation of state power through electoral competition for a national-popular mandate, these parties have evolved into transmission belts for executive decisions (1978, p. 229). In turn the principal channels of political legitimation have been redirected through plebiscitary and manipulative techniques relying on the mass media and dominated by the executive (*ibid.*). The decline of parliamentary institutions, the rule of law, and political parties in the current phase of the CMP entails a radical decline in representative democracy and its political liberties and the concomitant extension of authoritarian control over all spheres of social relations (*ibid.*, pp. 230–231).

Nonetheless, while the state bureaucracy has become the principal agent in the elaboration of state policy in the interests of a power bloc dominated by monopoly capital, its activities continually run up against limits inherent in its material organisation and/or its internal reproduction of conflicts and contradictions among different classes, fractions, and social categories. This poses the problem of how the state administration is to be unified and homogenised to ensure its effective operation on behalf of monopoly capital. In exceptional states this is accomplished through a political apparatus (such as the fascist party, the army, the political police) which is distinct from the administration; in the theoretically normal case of representative democracy it is accomplished through the organic functioning of a plural party system located at a certain distance from the central administrative apparatus (1978, pp. 231, 232–233; cf. 1968, pp. 318–320, 335–337, 345–346, 348, 353–355; 1970, pp. 316–317, 332, 340–341, 353; 1976b, pp. 33, 104–107). But how can this be realised in the case of 'authoritarian statism'? Poulantzas suggests the need for a dominant mass party which can function as a parallel network and ensure the strict political subordination of the entire administration to the summits of the executive. This 'state party' acts as a political commissar at the heart of the administration and develops a growing material and ideological community of interest with key civil servants (1978, pp. 233–236). At the same time this party must transmit the state ideology to the popular masses and reinforce the plebiscitary legitimation of authoritarian statism (*ibid.,* pp. 236–237). Although authoritarian statism tendentially needs a single, highly unified and structured dominant mass party and is most likely to achieve this when there is a long period without alternation in government, this need can also be satisfied through a single inter-party 'centre' dominating the alternating parties of power in a plural party system (*ibid.,* pp. 232, 235–236).

Yet, despite the consolidation of authoritarian statism within the metropolitan capitalist states, there is a further sharpening of the generic elements of political crisis and state crisis. This is visible in the partial polarisation of the increasingly politicised permanent administration to the left rather than to the side of the dominant 'state party' (especially among lesser officials with their close ties to the new petit bourgeoisie and their front-line role in confrontations with the popular masses), the relative rigidity of the relationship of forces within the administration compared with the flexible reorganisation of forces possible through an organic plural party system, and, lastly, the various forms of mass struggles precipitated by the new forms of state intervention (*ibid.,* pp. 240–247). In short, while authoritarian statism involves a definite strengthening of state power at the expense of representative democracy, it also involves a definite weakening of its effectiveness in securing the conditions for bourgeois hegemony. This presents both opportunities and dangers to the left in its struggle for a democratic transition to socialism (*ibid.,* pp. 241, 263–265).

THE DISPLACEMENT OF DOMINANCE TO THE POLITICAL

Initially Poulantzas argued that capitalism involved a distinctive institutional separation of the economic and political regions and then added that the economic was not only determinant in the last instance (as it was in all modes of production) but also dominant (in the sense that the labour process and the appropriation of surplus labour were mediated through exchange relations rather than extra-economic force). This does not mean that the state does not intervene in the economy but implies instead that its role is confined to maintaining the 'external' conditions of capital accumulation. Thus Poulantzas noted how law sanctions relations of production and exploitation through their juridical representation as rights attached to private property, organises the sphere of circulation through contractual and commercial law, and regulates state intervention in the economic region (1970, pp. 322, 324; cf. 1968, pp. 53, 56, 163, 214, 228; 1974, p. 100; 1978, pp. 39, 191). He also argued that the juridico-political region has important effects on economic class struggle through the 'isolation effect'. For the legal order interpellates the agents of production as individual juridical subjects rather than as members of antagonistic classes: this means that economic agents do not experience capitalist relations as class relations but as relations of competition among mutually isolated individuals and/or fragmented groups of workers and capitalists (1968, pp. 130–131, 213–214, 275–276, 310; 1978, pp. 63–67, 69–70, 86–88). This effect already poses problems concerning the 'externality' of the economic and political regions and, indeed, in later self-criticism, Poulantzas admits that he tended to view these regions as distinct and mutually impermeable and was consequently unable to grasp the nature or role of economic 'interventions' by the state (1976a, p. 18; cf. 1974, pp. 100–101, 167–168; 1978, pp. 17–19, 26–27, 166–167). These problems are compounded by the frequently advanced claim that the growth of monopoly capitalism involves a displacement of dominance from the economic to the political region without, however, changing the basic matrix of the CMP (1968, pp. 55–56, 91, 150, 211, 345; 1970, pp. 20–21, 74–75, 303, 313; 1974, pp. 42, 45, 81, 100–101, 165–168; 1978, pp. 166–168). At most Poulantzas concedes that this involves a transformation in the form of separation of the economic and political regions of the CMP and stresses that the growth of economic intervention still depends on the separation of the two regions (1974, p. 168; 1978, pp. 166–167, 190). The various arguments concerning this 'displacement' are so crucial to Poulantzas's overall periodisation of the capitalist state as well as to his account of the CMP itself that we must now consider them in such detail as is possible.

Let us begin by recalling two arguments. Firstly Poulantzas says that the typical matrix of the CMP emerges with the 'real subsumption' of wage-labour under capitalist control. This occurs with the rise of large-scale industry or machinofacture (rather than simple cooperation based on manufacturing) and is associated with the determination of the overall circuit of capital by the cycle of productive capital (as opposed to that of commercial or commodity capital in the transitional period of manufacture) (1968, pp. 32, 127, 159; 1974, p. 96; cf. Marx, 1867, pp. 312–315, 478). Secondly Poulantzas argues that the basis of all capitalist exploitation in the pure CMP is the creation and appropriation of surplus-value (1968, pp. 32, 129; 1970, p. 304; 1974, pp. 19, 53, 63, 92, 95–96, 116, 132, 211–213, 221; 1978, pp. 17, 18).

In this context Poulantzas follows Marx in distinguishing two forms of appropriation of surplus-value: absolute (based on extending the working day and/or intensifying effort) and relative (based on increasing productivity for a given duration and intensity of labour) (cf. Marx, *C1*, pp. 173–500). Poulantzas then uses this distinction to demarcate two stages of the CMP: competitive or liberal capitalism (based on absolute surplus-value or 'extensive exploitation') and monopoly capitalism or imperialism (based on relative surplus-value or 'intensive exploitation' and associated with the importance of the tendency of the rate of profit to fall (TRPF). In the competitive stage the state intervenes to secure the general 'external' conditions of capitalist exploitation; in the monopoly stage it intervenes in the valorisation process itself — especially to promote the intensive exploitation of labour-power and to mobilise counter-tendencies to the TRPF (1968, pp. 55–56, 345; 1970, pp. 20, 40–41, 95, 98, 192, 220–221, 302–303, 313; 1974, pp. 42, 62–63, 99–102, 107, 111–112, 116–118, 125, 135, 165–168, 172n; 1976c, pp. 35–36; 1978, pp. 166–168, 173–177, 212). Thus the state moves from a role more or less limited to securing the general political and ideological conditions of capital accumulation (permitting the reproduction of labour-power through the *wage form* as well as enabling individual capitalists to control valorisation) to a role in which the state is heavily involved in the reproduction of labour-power (education, training, health, housing, transport, collective services, etc.) and in the process of valorisation (scientific research, technological innovation, industrial restructuring, monetary and fiscal measures to integrate the production cycle and the sphere of circulation-consumption, promoting the devalorisation of a portion of the total social capital to raise the average rate of profit, etc.) (1974, pp. 63, 117–118, 125n, 166–167, 171, 172n; 1978, pp. 174, 179, 184, 187). Included among the latter functions is the state's role in the socialisation of the relations of production to match the socialisation of the productive forces (described as such in two early texts, later redefined as a closure of the gap between increasingly integrated international economic possession and powers of economic ownership which are still relatively dispersed: contrast 1968, p. 272, and 1970, p. 313, with 1974, pp. 58–60, 118–120, 121–127, 141, 147, 166, and 1978, pp. 176–178). Moreover, whereas economic relations — in the sense of market forces as the principal mediation of the law of value — were dominant in competitive capitalism and the state's economic functions were subordinated to its strictly political role as the factor of social cohesion, in monopoly capitalism it is the economic functions of the state that are superordinate and incompressible while central areas of valorisation have also been transferred from the market into the field of state intervention (1968, pp. 55–56; 1970, p. 303; 1978, pp. 167–169). In turn this is associated with the re-organisation, extension, and consolidation of the economic state apparatus(es) so that its economic role is no longer masked by the dominance of repressive or ideological functions of a global political character (masked even for Poulantzas himself, 1974, p. 99) and so that it emerges as a privileged centre for the fraction of monopoly capital which exercises hegemony within the power bloc and thus plays a crucial role in the unity-centralisation of state power (1970, p. 304; 1974, p. 99; 1978, pp. 33, 137, 170–172, 195). In short, on the understanding that the cycle of productive capital has become crucially dependent on state intervention and that the state's global political role has been subordinated to its new economic functions, Poulantzas concludes that there has been a displacement of dominance in the matrix of the CMP from the economic (or market forces) to the political (or state intervention) in the overall reproduction of the capital relation.

In presenting these views, Poulantzas continues to stress the fact that economic intervention must be related to class struggle. This holds not only for the economic class struggle at the heart of the valorisation process within the cycle of productive capital but also for the political and ideological class struggle concerning the general conditions of class domination (1968, pp. 44–56; 1974, pp. 21, 24–25, 27, 32, 81, 97–99, 107, 167–168; 1978, pp. 35, 163, 185–189). In particular Poulantzas rejects the view that the economic role of the state is somehow technical and class-neutral and insists that it is determined in and through class struggle. Contradictions among the dominant classes and fractions in the power bloc and between the dominant and dominated classes are necessarily reproduced within the economic activities of the state – both in relation to their short-term economic impact and to their repercussions for hegemony within the power bloc and/or over the popular masses. This helps to explain the incoherence of economic policies and the translation of economic crises into political and ideological crises. It is also relevant in understanding how economic policies contribute to the maintenance of hegemony through the forms of individuation and social fracturing which they impose on class relations as well as through the material concessions they involve for the dominated classes (1970, pp. 86–88, 95, 98, 134–135, 167, 191–197, 257, 180–284; 1974, pp. 75, 144–146, 148, 154–155, 163–164, 169–174; 1978, pp. 132–137, 143–144, 172, 179, 182–189).

Poulantzas also argues that its dominant economic role introduces certain rigidity into the state. It can no longer avoid the adverse ffects of intervention through refusing to intervene – inaction vould itself precipitate economic problems because of the resulting 'ailure to secure crucial political preconditions of capital accumu- ation in the current stage of capitalism. Thus economic functions 'ollow a logic of their own which may run counter to the need to ecure hegemony for monopoly capital. The subordination of these ictivities to the interests of monopoly capital casts doubt on the .tate's claim to embody the national-popular interest; and its reliance on *ad hoc,* discretionary intervention casts doubt on the legitimacy of the state's actions to the extent that they are still justified through egality or the rule of law. Poulantzas suggests that this is resolved in part through a shift in the dominant ideology from juridico-political to technocratic values and norms but still concludes that the current itage of capitalism entails a generic problem of hegemony within the power bloc and over the masses (1968, pp. 211–213, 215, 221, 310–314, 315; 1970, pp. 252, 254, 327; 1974, pp. 169–174, 238– 239; 1976b, pp. 120, 130; 1976c, pp. 49–54; 1978, pp. 55, 57, 169–170, 191, 205, 213–214, 218–219, 221, 245).

Finally Poulantzas analyses the limits to state intervention in the economic region. He locates these in three areas: the separation between the economic and political regions in the CMP, the institu- tional form of the state, and the effects of class struggle. He argues that, although the state cannot avoid intervening in the economy, it is also excluded from the productive core of the circuit of capital: it is therefore reduced to a predominantly reactive role – coping with the effects of capitalism without being able to act decisively on their causes. This exclusion also means that the availability of resources to the state depends on the fluctuating profitability of capital and this, in turn, makes it difficult to plan revenues and can precipitate fiscal crises. The incoherence of its policies is also attributed to the admin- istrative inertia, 'muddling through', bureaucratic ponderousness, and countervailing veto powers of the state apparatus itself. These factors are reinforced by the class struggles within the power bloc and between the power bloc and the dominated classes that are neces- sarily reproduced on the terrain of the state (1974, pp. 168–174; 1978, pp. 190–194).

ON THE TRANSITION TO SOCIALISM

The views of Poulantzas on political strategy have changed *pari passu* with his changing views on the nature of the capitalist state. Initially he advocated a Leninist strategy in which the working class should be mobilised in a counter-state organisation external to the capitalist state and under the leadership of a revolutionary vanguard political party. Since the capitalist state was the unambiguous and unequivocal institutional expression of bourgeois political domination, it would be impossible for the working class to utilise this state form to effect a transition to socialism. Indeed Poulantzas stresses that the working class cannot, *pace* Gramsci, attain hegemony before it has seized state power (1968, pp. 108, 204, 275, 287–288, 299). These views were elaborated somewhat in Poulantzas's reflections on Comintern strategy and tactics towards fascism and their residues in contemporary communist theories of state monopoly capitalism and the anti-monopoly alliance. In criticising the errors of the Comintern Poulantzas suggests that a successful communist revolution (or, indeed, defence of working-class gains in capitalist societies) requires the primacy of political class struggle over economic class struggle, the consistent pursuit of a mass line, and a commitment to proletarian internationalism. In turn this would involve the development of workers' councils as the site of mass struggle (with economic demands subordinated to political class struggle), the development of a united front of the working class at the rank-and-file level, and the development of a popular front with the poor peasantry and petit bourgeoisie. Poulantzas also argues that contemporary communist parties tend to separate economic and political class struggles, to neglect a mass line and rely on electoral pacts to mobilise intermediate classes through their own organisations, to give priority to the popular front (wrongly defined to embrace non-monopoly capital as well as the intermediate classes) over the development of a united front, and to overemphasise the national side of the communist programme (1970, pp. 18, 40, 44, 46, 140, 143, 164–165, 214–216, 223, 225, 228–231). This commitment to a mass line involving alliances with intermediate classes is also central to Poulantzas's reflections on classes in contemporary capitalism. He argues that the communist party must seek to polarise the petit bourgeoisie around the working class and unify the 'people' under the leadership of the working class against the power bloc. This will not occur simply because the petit bourgeoisie is becoming proletarianised through its objective place in relations of production – it depends on winning the petit bourgeois fractions away from support for bourgeois organisations to support for working-class organisations through active and protracted representation of their specific interests. This involves more than short-term, mechanical 'compromises' and 'concessions' to the petit bourgeoisie – it requires a long-term strategy that recognises the differences among the classes and fractions in the alliance, that attempts gradually to resolve the 'contradictions among the people' and to unify them, and that attempts to modify the class positions (or demands) of potential allies so that they come to share the objectives of the working class in the transition to socialism (1974, pp. 9–10, 24, 155, 331–335).

These arguments are significantly altered in Poulantzas's later work under the impact of his continuing reflections on the military dictatorship in his native Greece and the changing nature of the state in advanced capitalism. In particular he denied the continuing validity of the Leninist dual power strategy to the extent that it was premised on a rupture between the capitalist state as a monolithic apparatus and a centralised popular power parallel and external to this official state. There appear to be three main reasons for this change of argument: the reorganisation and expansion of the state so that it now penetrates all areas of social life, the condensation of class contradictions inside the state so that it is possible for any rupture(s) to pass through the state, and the historical fact that the military dictatorships collapsed without the development of such a dual power situation. Poulantzas concluded that a new strategy is required in the current stage of capitalism. This involves the close articulation and coordination of class struggle *within* the official state apparatus aimed at intensifying its internal contradictions, polarising significant sections of its personnel around a transition to socialism, and provoking ruptures among the various power centres, branches, and apparatuses of the integral state; and class struggle *at a distance* from the official state apparatus aimed at changing the balance of forces within the state, building organs of direct rank-and-file democracy, and unifying the popular masses in opposition to the power bloc. The collapse of the military dictatorships occurred largely because of internal contradictions within the power bloc that were intensified through popular struggles at a distance from the core of the state; the failure of a revolutionary mass party to coordinate and centralise these popular struggles under working-class hegemony was the chief reason why the dictatorships were replaced by bourgeois democratic regimes. In this context Poulantzas emphasises that the state is not a mere instrument to be captured by the working class in a frontal assault or through infiltration and encirclement – it has an institutional form that circumscribes changes in the balance of forces and enables the bourgeoisie to recaperate state power if the working class does not establish the institutional conditions for the exercise of its own power. It is for this reason that a successful transition towards democratic socialism requires action within the state, action to transform the state, and action at a distance from the state (1976b, pp. 76, 86–87, 142, 144–149, 151–152; 1977, pp. 3–5; cf. his preliminary reflections on the Greek military dictatorships, 1967b, *passim*).

The necessity for a close articulation of popular struggles within and without the state is reaffirmed in Poulantzas's final remarks about the capitalist state and the transition to socialism. But certain new elements are also introduced. Firstly he emphasises the need to preserve and extend the institutions and liberties of representative democracy alongside the developing organs of direct rank-and-file democracy. For not only does historical experience suggest that the abolition of supposedly 'bourgeois' parliamentary democracy inevitably leads to the suppression of direct democracy by the vanguard party due to the elimination of so-called 'formal' liberties and a plural party system, but there is also a clear danger that direct democracy would soon degenerate into a disunified, economic-corporate system unless there was a parliamentary forum in which different interests could be organised and unified around the socialist project (1977, pp. 6–8; 1978, pp. 256–263). Secondly Poulantzas appears to reject the need for a single mass revolutionary party to act as the vanguard in the transition to socialism. This rejection is linked to the view that representative democracy involves a plurality of parties and to a reappraisal of the vanguard party itself. In this context Poulantzas suggests that communist parties are in crisis because of their commitments to the primacy of the working class and to the primacy of struggles in the enterprise; this means that they have underestimated new social movements (such as feminism, regionalism, ecological movements, student unrest, etc.) that are 'pluriclassiste' and/or located outside the place of production. He concludes that parties must be actively present in the new social movements without becoming merely populist and that these movements must find a place in the parties without losing their own (non-class) specificity. In turn this implies that a certain irreducible tension between working-class parties and social movements is a necessary condition of the dynamic of transition to democratic socialism (1978, pp. 263–264; 1979b, pp. 181–183; 1979c, pp. 200–201). Finally, in apparent contrast to his early commitment to so-called proletarian internationalism and his criticism of an overemphasis on the national side of communist policy, Poulantzas adopted a commitment to national roads to socialism and argued that attempts to short-circuit national realities would be insane (1976d, p. 6; 1978, pp. 97, 115, 118–119).

A CRITIQUE OF POULANTZAS

The starting point for Poulantzas's analyses is the institutional separation of the juridico-political region from the economy in the CMP and the theoretical opportunity this offers for a separate account of this region in capitalist societies. Indeed Poulantzas argues that, characterised as it is by hegemonic class leadership and the representation of the political interests of the dominant class(es), it is through appropriate *political* concepts that the capitalist state must be investigated (1968, p. 190; 1978, pp. 51–52). Moreover, even though Poulantzas later paid more attention to the economic role of the state, his analyses of the limitations of such intervention still focus largely on political factors. This approach obviously poses problems about the role of economic determination in his account of the juridico-political region – especially as he originally suggested that the economic region of the CMP was not only determinant but also dominant. Indeed, as Poulantzas himself once argued in his review of Althusser's *For Marx*, structuralist views on 'economic determination in the last instance' combined with an insistence on the 'relative autonomy' of different regions can easily lead to an 'overpoliticisation' of the class struggle and an 'overdominance' of the political level in general (1966b, pp. 1974–1079). In Poulantzas's theoretical system, moreover, this 'politicist' tendency is reinforced by two other elements. For Poulantzas also argues that the constitutive function of the state is to maintain the global cohesion of a class-divided social formation and that the capitalist state is the first to specialise in this function through its structurally-determined capacity to secure hegemonic class leadership. In short the attempt to combine Althusserian and Gramscian perspectives within the context of a general theory of the state as an organ of political domination has aggravated the 'politicist' potential inherent in each perspective considered in isolation.

These tendencies towards *'overpoliticisation'* are reflected in many aspects of Poulantzas's work. Thus, despite his initial advocacy of economic determination in the last instance, this seems to function merely as the warrant for privileging political determination in the first instance. At most Poulantzas discusses economic determinations in terms of contradictions in the field of economic class struggle and their repercussions on the struggle for hegemony (1970, pp. 89–96, 114–123; 1974, pp. 109–155; 1978, pp. 140, 171–172, 192–193); otherwise he refers only to the limitations imposed by the exclusion of the state from the productive core of the capitalist economy

(1974, p. 168n; 1978, pp. 166, 191–192). There is no attempt to consider how the basic forms of the capital relation impose distinctive structural constraints on the functioning of the state apparatus and the exercise of state power (on which, see chapter 3). Instead of exploring the complex interrelations between economic and political factors in determining the nature of the state apparatus and state power Poulantzas actually adopts a political problematic involving both structuralist and Gramscian moments. On the one hand he examines how political class domination is inscribed within the basic institutional forms of the capitalist state; and, on the other hand, he considers how the dominant class(es) and/or fractions establish their hegemony through specific political and ideological practices. The so-called 'isolation effect' mediates these two moments in so far as it provides the matrix both for the institutional articulation of the state and for the practices concerned with hegemony. However, although the structuralist and Gramscian moments are mediated in this way, there are serious theoretical difficulties with each moment and with their articulation through the 'isolation effect'. These difficulties can be seen in the various attempts that Poulantzas makes to explain the relative autonomy and class unity of the state apparatus, the constitution of hegemony in the power bloc and over the dominated classes, and the role of class and non-class forces in political struggle. Let us deal with each of these problem areas in turn.

Poulantzas introduces the notion of relative autonomy to perform a precise function in his analysis of the capitalist state. It refers to that form and degree of institutional autonomy relative to the dominant classes and fractions necessary to organise their hegemony. In this sense it is starkly differentiated from two other possible forms of relative autonomy: that facilitating a revolution from above during the transition from feudalism to capitalism (1968, pp. 271–273) and that due to an equilibrium among social forces allowing the state to arbitrate among them (*ibid.*, pp. 262, 286–287, 289–290n, 302; cf. 1970, p. 86). Initially Poulantzas explained the relative autonomy of the state in the first sense in terms of the particular place of the political region in the structural matrix of the CMP. For he argued that it is based on the institutionalised unity of the state as the instance concerned to maintain the unity of the various levels of the CMP; and he adds that this unity or autonomy itself is possible only because of the institutional separation of the state from the economic region and the concomitant separation of political and economic class struggle (1968, pp. 256–257). However, while Poulantzas certainly does place relative autonomy is a structuralist framework (cf. Laclau, 1975, p. 98), he also locates it in terms of the field of (political) class struggle (Poulantzas, 1976a, p. 77). In this context he tries to show that the specific forms and degree of relative autonomy depend on the precise conjuncture of the class struggle (1968, pp. 257, 262, 282–286, 317–321; 1970, pp. 85–86, 313; 1974, p. 98; 1976a, p. 72; 1976b, p. 92; 1976c, pp. 37, 42–43; 1978, pp. 128–129ff). Thus Poulantzas actually adopts two approaches to the relative autonomy of the state: structuralist and conjunctural.

This introduces a fundamental contradiction into his analysis. For Poulantzas maintains that, while the policies of the capitalist state are prodigiously contradictory and incoherent in the short-term, in the long-term they can only correspond to the political interests of the bourgeoisie (1968, pp. 284–285, 286; 1974, pp. 163–164; 1976a, p. 72; 1978, pp. 132–139). This argument poses increasing problems for Poulantzas as his theoretical position progressively shifts away from the structuralist metaphysic to an insistence on the primacy of class struggle over structural causation – a shift reflected in his increasing assertions that class struggles are reproduced within the heart of the state apparatus and in his growing recognition of the tendency towards disunity in the state apparatus.

How does Poulantzas resolve this contradiction in his discussion of relative autonomy? It seems that he abandoned the commitment to a structuralist interpretation of structural effects as reflecting the functional imperatives of the self-reproduction of the social whole; and substituted an account which sees structural effects as specific, form-determined effects of political institutions on class struggles. Thus he suggests that the long-term political interest of the bourgeoisie emerges as the resultant of a multiplicity of diversified micro-policies reflecting in turn the class struggles and contradictions inscribed in a specific manner within the state itself (1974, pp. 161–164; 1978, pp. 134–136). Thus his solution apparently depends on the metaphor of a parallelogram of forces and/or on a structural selectivity inherent in the institutional form of the state as such. But how can this 'macroscopic necessity' emerge out of such 'microscopic diversity'? Either Poulantzas's solution is void because it cannot move from an infinity of contradictory policies to an unambiguous, final result or else it is tautological because he merely postulates the resultant that his theoretical approach demands (cf. Althusser's critique of Engels's views on economic determination in the last instance; Althusser, 1965, pp. 118–125). Furthermore, if Poulantzas had been able to show that the relative autonomy of the state guaranteed bourgeois political domination, this would have had serious consequences for his overall analysis. For it would clearly undermine his argument concerning the possibility of crises of that very hegemony which its relative autonomy is supposed to secure and/or entail a teleological account of exceptional states in which they would emerge in order to reconstitute bourgeois hegemony (e.g., 1976b, p. 98). Alternatively it would mean that his explanation would be pitched at such a high level of abstraction that the concept of relative autonomy becomes redundant. For since there are only two fundamental classes in capitalist societies (the petit bourgeoisie having no long-term political interests of its own and being unable to exercise state power) and hence only two possible effects of state power (reproduction of the CMP or a transition to socialism), all outcomes short of a transition would count as the long-run maintenance of capitalism (cf. 1970, p. 243; 1974, pp. 297, 334; 1976b, p. 103). On this interpretation of his argument the notion of relative autonomy is redundant because any form of state in capitalist society would have the same effect *sub specie aeternatis*. Moreover, if Poulantzas really intended such an argument, he could not also advocate operating inside as well as outside the state to produce a decisive break or rupture in its functioning on behalf of capital. In short there are fundamental difficulties in his account of relative autonomy.

These problems are reproduced in Poulantzas's analysis of the unity of state power. Indeed, as we noted above, he originally established a circular relation between the relative autonomy of the state apparatus and the class unity of state power (1968, pp. 256–257, 282–283, 288–289). In later studies Poulantzas tends to undermine his arguments about the class unity as well as relative autonomy of the capitalist type of state. Thus, whereas he originally considered the class unity of state power in terms of the structurally determined role of the state as the factor of unity in a capitalist formation and explained it in terms of the institutional framework of political democracy that allows a sovereign state to present itself as the representative of the general interest of the people-nation as well as organising a unitary power bloc under the hegemony of a specific class fraction (1968, pp. 276–289, 300–305, 353–354), subsequent works render this notion of class unity more and more problematic as, firstly, Poulantzas introduces the concept of a plurality of relatively independent ideological state apparatuses alongside a single state repressive apparatus with a vigorous internal unity (1969, p. 77; 1970, pp. 305–308), secondly, he concedes the possibility that contradictions within branches of the repressive state apparatus and within different ideological state apparatuses can acquire a principal rather than merely secondary role in the functioning of the state and, presumably, undermine the internal unity normally based on the dominance of whichever branch of the RSA is the privileged centre of the hegemonic fraction (1970, pp. 328–330, 334; 1974, pp. 163– 164, 817; 1976b, pp. 33, 49–50, 82–84, 86–87, 94, 97, 103–104, 112–113, 124–125), thirdly, he considers the relative autonomy of the capitalist state as the sum of relative autonomies commanded by different branches, apparatuses, or networks vis-à-vis others of their kind and the class unity of its power as the resultant of a multiplicity of diversified, mutually contradictory macro-policies (1976b, p. 75; 1978, pp. 135–139), and, finally, he abandons the argument that, whereas the classes and fractions of the power bloc can have privileged seats of power within the state apparatus, the dominated classes can have only diffuse centres of resistance, and instead suggests that the dominated classes can eventually secure real centres of power in the capitalist state itself (contrast 1978, pp. 142–143 and pp. 258–289). This gradual shift in position reflects Poulantzas's progressive abandonment of structuralist formalism in the analysis of class practices but it is still combined with a continuing formal insistence on the relative autonomy of the state apparatuses as a whole and on the class unity of state power exercised in and through these apparatuses. This insistence is formal because it is relegated to the celebrated last instance, the long-run, the conclusion of the process, etc., and, as has often been remarked, the lonely hour of the last instance never comes, the long-run is merely the aggregate of a series of short-runs, and the process is never concluded but ever-renewed. But Poulantzas continues to insist on these principles in order to distinguish his analyses from instrumentalist approaches and/or those that propose a gradual, non-ruptural, piecemeal conquest of state power. However, while these twin principles were necessary for a *structuralist* critique of such positions, the latter are more effectively attacked from a different vantage point. The structuralist residues remaining in Poulantzas's analyses undermine rather than strengthen such attacks and also contradict the premises of his own revolutionary strategy with its stress on the primacy of class struggle over any structures.

In explaining the constitution of bourgeois hegemony Poulantzas encounters similar theoretical difficulties. For although he argues that hegemony is not a property of the state as a structural ensemble but is constituted on the terrain of class practices (1968, pp. 137– 138, 140, 224; 1976a, p. 149), he sometimes discusses hegemony as the necessary, objective, and teleologically-determined effect of the relative autonomy of the state and sometimes gives primacy to the contingencies of political class struggle. In both cases it is the political level that is given crucial weight either in the guise of the structural principle of relative autonomy or else in that of the overdetermining role of political class struggle. This ambiguity can be seen in two contrasting approaches to defining hegemony. Thus Poulantzas sometimes identifies the hegemonic fraction in terms of the net balance of political advantages stemming from a particular form of state and/or regime and concludes that this form corresponds to the interests of the hegemonic fraction (e.g., 1966b, p. 70; 1968, pp. 284–285, 297, 299, 300–301, 305; 1970, pp. 85–86, 88; 1974, pp. 47, 97–98, 164; 1976b, p. 92; 1978, pp. 125–127, 141). But on other occasions he identifies the hegemonic fraction in terms of specific political and ideological practices which establish its long-term economic and political interests as those of the entire power bloc and/or people-nation as a whole and thereby 'polarise' class positions around these interests in an 'unstable equilibrium of compromise' negotiated under its leadership and protection (e.g., 1968, pp. 140–141, 239–240, 283, 297, 319; 1970, pp. 72–73, 100–101, 123–125, 248; 1974, pp. 24, 98, 144, 146, 333–335; 1976a, p. 72; 1976b, pp. 30, 44, 46, 60, 136; 1978, p. 137). Thus Poulantzas sometimes relates hegemony to the *structural determination* of political class domination rooted in the objective coordinates of state form and sometimes to the field of political *class position* with its notions of strategy, alliances, etc. (see 1974, p. 15).

Unfurtunately Poulantzas himself does not attempt to reconcile these contrasting approaches to hegemony and we must now see whether this is at all possible. Perhaps the most plausible starting point is Poulantzas's efforts to avoid an instrumentalist position at the same time as insisting on the importance of class struggle. Thus, if it is correct to argue that the bourgeoisie is constitutively unable to act as a unitary class subject because of its internal fractioning and mutually contradictory interests, the state must be seen as a crucial factor in organising and maintaining bourgeois unity and, *a fortiori,* the hegemony of one fraction within the power bloc. Interpreted in an Althusserian perspective this translates into the structuralist notion of relative autonomy and thence to the conflation of hegemony with a structurally-inscribed political domination. In this context the hegemonic fraction is merely the dominant element in the dominant bloc (1968, p. 237) and the concept of class struggle, although it is still employed, appears to become redundant. However, as Poulantzas progressively abandons structuralism and comes to see state power as a form-determined condensation of social relations, it becomes easier to reconcile these apparantly contradictory approaches to hegemony. For it can be seen as subject to a double delimitation through (a) specific class practices in the global field of class practices within (b) limits established by the structural effects of a given state form and/or regime (cf. Poulantzas, 1968, pp. 94–97). This means that a given state form and/or regime involves a structural privilege for a specific fraction in the contest for bourgeois hegemony without guaranteeing its success (e.g., the interventionist state and monopoly capital) and that there is genuine scope within these structural limits for some marginal variation in long-run hegemony (e.g., banking or industrial monopoly capital in the interventionist state) and greater variation in the short-run (e.g., periods of unstable hegemony, dissociations between hegemony within the power bloc and that over the people-nation, crises of hegemony, etc.).

This argument would explain a number of apparent difficulties in Poulantzas's various accounts of hegemony. It would explain why he can talk of the organic circulation of hegemony within democratic regimes: for, in addition to the more abstract level of structural determination, it is also necessary to take account of more concrete struggles aimed at polarising class positions around particular strategies or 'hegemonic projects'. It would also explain the structural resistance ('relative autonomy') the state offers to the successful realisation of strategies organised under the leadership of structurally disprivileged fractions or classes (e.g., democratisation under working-class hegemony in the erstwhile military dictatorships, 1976b, pp. 136, 141–144, 157–158). At the same time it would explain why Poulantzas can talk of working-class hegemony in the democratisation process and/or the transition to socialism and still insist that the working class cannot win hegemony before the conquest of state power with its attendant 'smashing' of the capitalist state. For, while the working class could establish its hegemony over the popular masses at the level of class positions and/or exacerbate any disunity among the fractions of the power bloc on the terrain of the capitalist state, it could not secure hegemony at the level of structural determination until it has consolidated a new form of state that corresponds to its long-run, global political interests. In short, if one interprets Poulantzas sympathetically, the inconsistencies in his account of hegemony appear presentational rather than fundamental. But this interpretation clearly depends on rejecting the structuralist problematic in favour of form-determined and class-theoretical analyses.

Even if we accept this sympathetic interpretation of Poulantzas's work, however, his account of hegemony is still liable to criticism. For, despite his insistence on the constitutive absence of class from the bourgeois state and his argument that its relation to civil society is refracted through the individuation and differential fragmentation of social agents, he overlooks the implications of the 'isolation effect' for the creation of hegemony in favour of a class reductionist account of political forces and ideologies. Rather than exploring the contingent relation between political forces and/or ideologies and the requirements of capital accumulation in particular conjunctures, Poulantzas often ascribes a necessary class belonging to political parties and other apparatuses and/or to specific ideologies and also neglects the role of non-class (e.g., gender, ethnic, youth) movements in the struggle for intellectual, moral, and political leadership. Indeed it is symptomatic that Poulantzas himself defines hegemony in terms of structurally-determined political class domination and/or in terms of a polarisation of *class* positions around an 'unstable equilibrium of compromise' under the leadership of a particular *class* fraction. However, if one accepts his claims about the 'isolation effect' in the constitution of civil society and the capitalist state, then the influence of non-class forces and non-class ideologies must assume a central place in political analysis. These difficulties are already apparent in the ambiguities surrounding the 'class belonging' of such agents of hegemonic struggle as politicians, the military, officials, and 'ideological watchdogs' as well as that of the internal ideologies of specific branches of the state apparatus with their distinctive modes of refraction of bourgeois and/or petit bourgeois ideology (cf. 1968, pp. 332, 347–348, 355, 357; 1970, p. 243; 1976b, pp. 107, 112–117, 120–121, 123, 125). These difficulties become acute once Poulantzas recognises the importance of various new social movements based on non-class divisions, located outside the sphere of production, and with a 'pluriclassiste' affiliation (cf. 1978, pp. 43, 211, 246–247; 1979b, pp. 181–183; 1979c, pp. 200–201). Given his belated recognition of these forces and his premature death it is impossible to know how Poulantzas might have modified his theoretical position on hegemony to take account of these non-class forces and ideologies. Accordingly we must conclude that his class reductionism and structuralist tendencies prevented him from developing the concepts necessary for a more detailed investigation of hegemony.

Another range of problems occurs in Poulantzas's provocative account of 'normal' and 'exceptional' forms of the capitalist state.

For not only is the crucial concept of 'hegemony' underdeveloped relative to the explanatory burden placed upon it, but the arguments for the benefits of 'normal' forms are largely asserted and depend for proof on the contra-indications of 'exceptional' regimes. These difficulties are accentuated in Poulantzas's discussion of 'authoritarian statism'. Thus, not only does he present this as a hybrid form comprising both normal and exceptional elements (presumably articulated under the dominance of the normal elements), he also insists that authoritarian statism leads to a decline in representative democracy (the allegedly normal form of bourgeois state) without specifying how it substitutes new forms of democratic participation and so maintains the democratic framework. All the evidence he adduces points to a long-term decline of democracy and not its internal transformation. This is probably related to his neglect of new forms of representation (such as 'liberal corporatism' based on function within the division of labour) in favour of an eclectic account of the decline of their traditional, parliamentary form and the growth of authoritarian state control over the people. Moreover, while his own methodological and theoretical principles require Poulantzas to demonstrate how the development of 'authoritarian statism' entails a *break* or *rupture* in the political process (since it involves a transition to a new state form), he admits that it results instead from the *accentuation of tendencies* coeval with monopoly capitalism and hence also characteristic of the interventionist state. The self-same continuity with the preceding phase of capitalism is evident in his explanation of this new state form in terms of the increasing economic role of the state and/or the permanent instability of the hegemony of monopoly capital. In short, even if we accept the basically descriptive account of 'authoritarian statism' as a normal form, it remains unclear how far Poulantzas can offer a distinctive explanation for its emergence and future dynamic.

Indeed his whole approach to periodising capitalism and its state raises interesting questions about its relation to stamocap theory. For although Poulantzas is a vehement and unrelenting critic of the orthodox PCF theory of state monopoly capitalism for its economism, instrumentalism, and reformism (1968, pp. 273, 273n; 1970, pp. 83, 97; 1974, pp. 48, 82, 102–108, 117, 139–140, 157–164, 169–170, 183, 197–198, 303–304; 1976a, p. 81; 1978, pp. 19, 52, 128, 172–173, 183), some convergence seems to have occurred between Poulantzas's views and more sophisticated stamocap theories. This is evident in several areas. His most recent work emphasises that the state's current economic role does not derive from a unilinear accumulation of functions but involves a number of breaks with the preceding phase of monopoly capitalism which are more significant overall than the break of that phase with competitive capitalism (1976d, p. 3; 1978, p. 166; 1979c, p. 200). He argues that whole areas of the valorisation of capital and the reproduction of labour-power are now directly inserted into the state and that this insertion occurs principally to the advantage of monopoly capital (1974, pp. 46, 62, 81, 102, 125, 134, 148–150, 155, 158, 168, 172; 1978, pp. 136, 191, 225). He suggests that monopoly capital has not only subsumed non-monopoly capital under its economic domination but is also the sole member of the power bloc capable of imposing its hegemony; and, indeed, notes that non-monopoly capital has lost the capacity to act as an autonomous social force (1974, pp. 148–149, 160n, 160–161, 168). In this context Poulantzas also argues that the dominance of the economic functions of the state threatens to undermine the hegemony of monopoly capital and so widens the space for compromises between the 'people' and non-monopoly capital as well as for popular alliances embracing the petit bourgeoisie (*ibid.*, pp. 155, 333–335; 1978, p. 211). In turn this leads monopoly capital to dismantle traditional democratic forms and to construct authoritarian forms in the attempt to compensate for this permanent, generic crisis of hegemony (1978, *passim*). This remarkable convergence does not mean, of course, that Poulantzas also shares the economism, instrumentalism, and reformism of orthodox stamocap theory. On the contrary it would almost seem that, the more Poulantzas developed his distinctive views on political and ideological hegemony, the relative autonomy of the state as a structural ensemble, and the importance of revolutionary struggle within, against, and outside the state, the more easily he could embrace certain substantive arguments from stamocap theories. For their articulation with his own views means that they will lose their economistic, instrumentalist, and reformist overtones and acquire new theoretical and political implications.

Despite these criticisms it must be emphasised that Poulantzas developed one of the richest and most complex theoretical systems in contemporary Marxism. In focusing on the political determinations of the state apparatus and state power in capitalist societies he broke with economism and returned to the distinctive political ideas of Marx, Engels, Lenin, and Gramsci. Even a cursory glance at his work reveals the crucial significance of a complex body of *sui generis* concepts for the analysis of political class struggle: power bloc, hegemonic fraction, ruling class, class in charge of the state, class alliances, party ententes, supporting classes, political scene, etc. Moreover although he appears to have seized somewhat inadvisedly on Althusserian structuralism as the initial theoretical warrant for developing a regional political theory and although there are still a number of structuralist residues in his most recent work, the primary thrust of his analysis was increasingly directed towards the political class struggle. In this context terms which originally had patent structuralist connotations (such as relative autonomy) slowly came to acquire new meaning as they were articulated with the argument that the state should be seen as a social relation. Essentially this means that state power is a form-determined condensation of class relations and must be investigated in terms of the complex inter-action between the so-called 'institutional materiality' of the state apparatus (its form) and the balance of forces involved in political action as the overdetermining level of class struggle (social relations). In this context the concept of hegemony remained at the heart of Poulantzas's analyses. Indeed, not only does hegemony function as the fundamental criterion of interpretation or point of reference in his studies of the capitalist state, it also becomes an essential element in his own revolutionary strategy aimed at democratic socialism rather than the 'passive revolution' of an 'authoritarian statism' in either Western or Eastern guise. This growing commitment to a left Eurocommunist outlook is perhaps the final proof of Poulantzas' debts to Gramsci.

A 'DISCOURSE-THEORETICAL' APPROACH

Although I have devoted the bulk of this chapter to the analyses of Poulantzas, it would be quite wrong to suggest that he was alone in developing Gramsci's work on hegemony and its implications for Marxist theories of the capitalist state. However, whereas Poulantzas tried to integrate the analysis of hegemony into an abstract regional theory of the political and to consider its structural determination as well as its constitution in and through class struggle, most of the other neo-Gramscian theorists follow their mentor in developing more concrete, historically specific, conjunctural analyses in which almost exclusive attention is paid to the class struggle and/or the changing balance of social forces. Some of these studies are very fruitful and provide new insight into specific conjunctures (e.g., Abraham, 1981; Bew, Gibbon and Patterson, 1979; Buci-Glucksmann and Therborn, 1981; Gray, 1977; Hall *et al.,* 1978; Hirsch, 1980; Middlemas, 1979; Nairn, 1978) but it is clearly beyond the scope of this chapter to review specific historical studies (witness my neglect of Poulantzas's work on fascism and military dictatorships). But there are also a few studies that aim to develop an alternative account of hegemony in more abstract terms and establish it as a crucial concept in a regional theory of the ideological with often global territorial ambitions. In this context one can cite the attempts to develop discourse analyses of cultural production and the formation of agents with specific subjectivities: these attempts generally reveal a greater debt to the works of Althusser, Lacan, Derrida and Foucault than to Gramsci and will not be further considered here (but see, for example, Adlam *et al.,* 1977; Althusser, 1971; Coward and Ellis, 1977; Hall *et al.,* 1980; Hirst, 1979; Macherey, 1978, Pêcheux, 1975; Woods, 1977). Rather than reviewing such tangential attempts to specify the meaning of hegemony in terms of discourse theories, I concentrate on the individual and collaborative work of Ernesto Laclau and Chantal Mouffe. They focus on ideologies and ideological class struggle rather than the state and politics as such but also relate these to the development of political hegemony and the struggle for state power. Since this is an area seriously neglected by Poulantzas, it is well worth comment here.

In complementary articles Mouffe and Laclau have attacked economism in the analysis of politics and ideology. This critique is stated most clearly by Chantal Mouffe in her review of the concept of hegemony in Gramsci's *Prison Notebooks.* She outlines three phases in the movement from economism to anti-economism in political and ideological analysis: the pure and classic form of economism comprised a base-superstructure model coupled with the claim that all economic, political, and ideological subjects were at bottom class subjects (e.g., the Second International); the second phase breaks with epiphenomenalism in endowing the political and ideological levels with their own effectivity but remains economist in tracing the origins of political and ideological practices to wilful class subjects whose actions are determined by the evolution of a class consciousness appropriate to their economic position (e.g., Korsch, Lukacs); the third phase breaks with this class reductionist view of the *a priori,* originating subject and treats ideological practice as a process which constitutes subjects who are neither pre-given at the level of economic relations nor, once constituted in and through ideologies, endowed with a necessary class belonging (e.g., Gramsci, Togliatti) (see Mouffe, 1979, pp. 169–178; cf. Laclau, 1977, pp. 141–142n, 158–159, 163–164; Laclau, 1980b, pp. 252–255; Laclau and Mouffe, 1981, *passim*).

In this context Mouffe discerns in Gramsci's prison studies an anti-epiphenomenalist, anti-class reductionist account of ideology — admittedly only in the practical state rather than fully theorised — on the following grounds. Firstly she argues that Gramsci rejects the view that all political forces are essentially class subjects and suggests instead that political forces are constituted as inter-class (or, better, 'pluriclassiste') collective wills in and through ideological struggle. Secondly Gramsci rejects the view that there are pure class ideologies corresponding in a paradigmatic manner to different classes and argues instead that there is a pluralistic universe of ideological elements which different classes can selectively articulate in different ways to produce their own class ideologies. This implies that ideologies are transformed through a reworking of existing ideological elements rather than through the total displacement of one paradigmatic class ideology through another than is exclusive and non-overlapping in content. This also means that hegemony is not achieved through the imposition of one paradigmatic class ideology on other classes to form a class alliance — it involves the articulation of elements from different ideological discourses around a specific hegemonic principle to create a relatively unified but syncretic ideological system. Thirdly Gramsci insists that there are important ideological elements which have no necessary class connotations and belong instead to the field of the 'national-popular'. Indeed Gramsci treats these 'national-popular' elements as the site *par excellence* of ideological class struggle: the two fundamental classes compete to articulate these elements into their own class discourse so that it becomes a 'popular religion' or organic expression of the national interest with the active consent of the people. The agents of this ideological struggle are intellectuals and it is mediated through an ensemble of hegemonic apparatuses. In developing such perspectives Gramsci emphasises that political leadership and the mobilisation of the 'collective will' are quite crucially linked to 'intellectual and moral reform'. Finally, if there are no paradigmatic class ideologies and we are faced instead with a plurality of ideological elements whose class connotation (especially in the case of 'national-popular' elements) depends on their insertion into a specific ideological ensemble, how does Gramsci establish the class character of different ideological systems? Here Mouffe undertakes a symptomatic reading of Gramsci's notebooks and suggests that the class unity of the common world-view created through such political, intellectual, and moral leadership derives from its articulation around a value system whose realisation depends on the key role played by the fundamental class at the economic level. It is this value system which constitutes the 'hegemonic principle' permeating the common world-view and endowing it with a distinctive class nature (see: Mouffe, 1979, pp. 178–195; for a parallel presentation of Togliatti, see Laclau, 1980b, pp. 253–258; Laclau himself uses these arguments in his critique of Poulantzas but differs from Mouffe in locating the unifying principle of class ideologies in the particular concept of subjectivity which condenses other ideological subjects, e.g., the idea of 'race' in Nazism, 1977, pp. 101–103, 120–121).

Now while Mouffe and Laclau had together prepared the ground for a definite break with economism and class reductionism in the analysis of ideologies, there are still significant residual elements of class reductionism in their initial studies. Firstly, although they concede that there are no paradigmatic class ideological ensembles and ascribe to at least some ideological elements a (necessary?) 'national-popular' or 'popular-democratic' belonging, it is unclear whether at least some other ideological elements have a necessary class belonging (above all the hegemonic principle) or whether class connotations are invariably contingent on the insertion of class-neutral elements into an ensemble whose class character depends on its effects in specific conjunctures. Thus Mouffe argues both that ideological elements have no necessary class belonging and that they derive their class character from their articulation with a hegemonic principle (which is presumably an ideological element) that is always provided by a fundamental class (1979, pp. 194, 200). Likewise Laclau insists that ideological elements taken in isolation have no necessary class belonging yet he is equally emphatic that Marxism-Leninism is an abstract and necessary condition for the full development of working-class hegemony (Laclau, 1977, pp. 99, 110–111n). Secondly, although they recognise that there are *sui generis* 'popular-democratic' or 'national-popular' ideological elements, they deny that these can be constituted into pure non-class ideological ensembles and insist that these elements are always overdetermined through the class struggle. In this sense both Mouffe and Laclau privilege the economic region as a principle of explanation in the ideological region: Mouffe refers explicitly to the role of economic determination in the last instance (1979, pp. 171–172, 199–200) and Laclau considers that class antagonism between the fundamental classes is inscribed in the nature of the mode of production whereas 'popular-democratic' antagonisms are treated as contingent on the social formation as a whole and comprise the field of ideological class struggle *par excellence* (1977, pp. 106–109, 158–160). Thirdly, although they reject the assumption that all political subjects are class subjects in appearance and even in essence, they still claim that only the two fundamental clases in the dominant mode of production can win hegemony (Mouffe, 1979, pp. 183, 193–194, 197; Laclau, 1977, pp. 114, 163–164, 167). This would be less worrying if they interpreted it in terms of the *effects* of ideological struggles rather than in terms of class *agency*: but the basic thrust of their argument at this stage is that it is through the struggle between these two fundamental classes to articulate their interests to the 'people' that ideologies are transformed. This implies that at least some political and ideological subjects are reducible to class subjects. Thus, although Laclau admits that there is no necessary identity between economic classes and empirically observable political and ideological groups, he must ascribe a class belonging to at least some of them in order to assert that the agents of ideological transformation are the fundamental classes (1977, pp. 163–164, 174, 195–196; cf. Mouffe, 1979, pp. 193, 198). Ultimately this reduces popular-democratic forces to the *objects* of the two fundamental class *subjects* and denies popular-democratic forces any long-term autonomy or effectivity outside class struggle. In short, despite the important advances which Laclau and Mouffe recorded in their initial studies of hegemony, their work shifts uncomfortably between anti-reductionist and class reductionist notions.

In subsequent studies Laclau and Mouffe attempt to overcome such problems and are now developing a general theory of the discursive constitution of hegemony. They argue that all social relations derive their social character from their discursive constitution: that is, all social practice constitutes itself as such in so far as it produces meaning (Laclau, 1980a, p. 87). This approach has important theoretical implications for the relations between 'levels' and for the analysis of social subjectivity. Firstly, since the discursive is considered to be coextensive with the social and all social relations are thought of as constituted in and through discourse, Laclau and Mouffe reject orthodox Marxist views of 'base-superstructure' relations in which the so-called material base is seen as extra-discursive and the superstructure alone treated as discursive. Thus, even if one wished to retain the metaphor of 'base' and 'superstructure' or the topographical image of 'regions', their interrelations must be considered in terms of the articulation of discursive practices. In turn this implies that the unity of a social formation depends on the contingent articulation among these discursive practices rather than deriving from a necessary correspondence between base and superstructure. In this sense Laclau and Mouffe re-interpret Gramsci's notion of 'historic bloc' in discourse-theoretical terms (see p. 151 above). Secondly this approach implies that the subjects through whom social relations are mediated and reproduced are also constituted in and through discourse. One can no longer privilege class subjects over popular-democratic forces nor treat class struggle as necessarily more influential than popular-democratic struggles. Class antagonism is not inscribed in the relations of production considered as an extra-discursive structure but derives instead from the particular discursive identification (or 'interpellation') of class subjects. This suggests that class struggle is first of all a struggle about the constitution of class subjects before it is a struggle between class subjects (cf. Przeworski, 1977, pp. 371–373). It follows from this that the field of political intervention is extremely broad. For the class struggle is no longer confined to the articulation of pre-given classes to popular-democratic or national-popular forces but extends to include the very constitution of class forces themselves. This must surely have crucial implications for the analysis of hegemony as well as for the struggle for such 'political, intellectual, and moral leadership'. (On certain of these implications, see: Laclau, 1980a, p. 87; similar arguments are developed in Jessop, 1980b, pp. 63–72.)

What does this mean for the analysis of hegemony? The struggle for hegemony is re-interpreted in terms of intervention to articulate different discursive elements into more or less discrete ideological ensembles which serve the interests of a fundamental class. Elements can be articulated to form different discourses (sic) because they have common nuclei of meaning which are not fully determinate in denotation and can be connotatively linked to other elements to produce the specific meanings they reveal in different discursive ensembles. Thus ideas such as 'people', 'motherhood', 'competition', 'equality', and 'citizenship' acquire different connotations according to their articulation with other elements to form a specific discourse. This means that a successful ideological struggle should adopt the mode of 'interruption' rather than 'interpretation'. Whereas interpretation assigns to different elements a necessary belonging to a closed ideological ensemble and thus excludes the possibility of meaningful debate between mutually opposed and antagonistic discourses, interruption involves an 'inter-discursive' approach which attempts to absorb or appropriate elements from the interlocutor's discourse in an open process of perusasion and debate on the terrain of the common nucleus of meanings (cf. Silverman and Torode, 1980, pp. 4–19 and *passim,* on interruption vs. interpretation, and Pêcheux, 1975, on inter-discourse).

It is impossible to give a single model of these inter-discursive practices outside of specific conjunctures but Laclau and Mouffe do refer to two basic modes of hegemonic articulation. In the case of a discourse of *difference* hegemony depends on the neutralisation of ideologically constituted antagonisms through their re-interpretation as differences within a national-popular collective will (e.g., when class antagonisms allegedly inscribed within the relations of production are transformed into positive-sum differences among economic agents performing complementary functions in the division of labour). This involves the pluralisation of differences which must be negotiated and compromised within a broad consensual framework established through the dominant discourse concerning the parameters of the 'national-popular' collective will. Examples of such a discourse of difference include the 'One Nation' discourse of Disraeli and the 'transformist' politics of Giolitti. An alternative form of hegemonic discourse involves the constitution of a system of equivalences among different positions and subjects in either (a) a common polarity which is juxtaposed in an irreducible dualism to another pole and defined as superior to it or (b) a common antagonism to an internal and/or external enemy which must be defeated as a condition of advancement of each particular position or subject. This involves the polarisation of the different positions or subjects constituted in and through discourse and the interpellation of the two poles as either contrary and unequal or as contradictory and antagonistic. Examples of such a discourse of equivalence would include the irreduble dualist discourses of *apartheid* or patriarchy and the ruptural populist discourses of Chartism in England, Jacobinism in France, Fascism in Italy, and Maoism in China.

Both modes of discourse contain dangers to the dominant class. Thus, although a discourse of difference transforms negatively-charged contradictions into positively differentiated contrarieties and creates the ideological conditions necessary for the integration of different subjectivities into a system of democratic politics, the dominant class can go too far in absorbing and legitimating the demands of those in subordinate positions so that the dominated class(es) can impose their own discourse within the state apparatus during crises which undermine the neutralising capacities of the dominant class. This can be seen in the appropriation of democratic discourse into a socialist discourse as monopoly capital finds it increasingly difficult to maintain liberal democratic traditions and institutions. Likewise, although the dominant class can assimilate the 'people' in a discourse of equivalence to its own hegemonic project (particularly during periods of crisis), it runs the risk that populist forces will develop the anti-status quo, anti-capitalist elements in populist discourse to the point of a radical break with the interests of the dominant class. This can be seen in the threats posed by the Nazi left drawing on socialist traditions as well as the Italian fascist left drawing on the Mazzinian, Garilbaldian, and syndicalist traditions. Moreover, whereas the basic tendencies of the discourse of difference are integrative in so far as it disarticulates the organisation of the various subordinate positionalities into a single 'people' interpellated as the dynamic pole of controntation with the power bloc, the discourse of equivalence is more readily 'turned' to radical, ruptural goals through the articulation of the 'people' to a revolutionary project rather than to a populism of the right (Laclau, 1977, pp. 121–122, 162–163; 1980a, pp. 90–93; 1980b, pp. 255–258; Laclau and Mouffe, 1980, pp. 20–22).

Although these arguments are still in the process of development (see Laclau and Mouffe, 1982), their principal implications are clear. Firstly, not only does a discourse-theoretical approach involve a rejection of the more or less complex forms of economism entailed in the capital-theoretical analysis of the state, it also involves a rejection of the *a priori* privileging of classes as social forces found in class-theoretical analyses. Instead of these positions we find an insistence that the economic region is itself constituted discursively, that social unity derives from the articulation between different discursive practices rather than from some logically necessary correspondence between an extra-discursive base and a discursive superstructure, and that class as well as non-class forces are constituted in and through discourse rather than being inscribed in extra-discursive systems of social relations and functioning as their subjective *träger* or supports. Secondly, if all the various 'levels' or 'regions' of a social formation are constituted in and through discourse and are liable to transformation through forces which are likewise constituted, we must replace the notion of the causal primacy of the economy so long maintained among Marxists with a 'primacy of the political' (Laclau and Mouffe, 1981, p. 22) or, better, a 'primacy of the discursive'. This means that the economy is as much the field of struggle as the political and ideological regions and that its so-called 'laws of motion' are not governed by an extra-discursive 'capital logic' (or its equivalent in other modes of production). Instead the movement of the economy must be explained in terms of the hegemonic articulation existing in a given society (*ibid.*). Thirdly, since any given society is characterised by a vast plurality of subjects and there is no reason to privilege class subjects, hegemony must be seen in terms of the dis-

cursive articulation of different subjects. Thus, if the dominant class
or the working class are to contest the role of 'political, intellectual,
and moral leadership', this must depend on their respective abilities
to develop a political project recognised by other subjects as essential
to the realisation of their own interests and to develop an 'organic
ideology' which can serve as a shared ideological frame of reference
in terms of which a plurality of subjects can redefine and negotiate
alliances to advance that project. The centrality of a fundamental
class (bourgeois or proletarian) in a hegemonic project can only be
the result of efforts to interpellate and unify that class around the
struggle for 'political, intellectual, and moral leadership': there are no
theoretical guarantees or extra-discursive necessities that a fundamental class will inevitably occupy such a position of leadership nor
that other subjects will accept such leadership (cf. Laclau and Mouffe,
1981, pp. 21–22). Finally, since hegemony is achieved through the
discursive articulation of different subjects who are themselves constituted in and through discourse, we can interpret hegemony as a
'discourse of discourses' (to coin a phrase) and focus on the various
discursive mechanisms available to different political forces in the
struggle to articulate subjects around a specific project.

  In evaluating this approach to hegemony we must first clarify
some deep-seated ambiguities concerning discourse. Laclau and
Mouffe stress that discourse is not simply the 'text', not just 'langue'
and 'parole', not just ideological elements: it is 'the ensemble of
phenomena in and through which social production of meaning takes
place' (Laclau, 1980a, p. 87). This seems to mean that discourse is a
complex practice rooted in the complex articulation of extra-discursive conditions (such as the means of production in economic discourse) and specific modes of interpellation and calculation (such as
the constitution of the formally free wage-labourer and the rules of
double-entry book-keeping) under the dominance of the discursive
(so that the extra-discursive conditions are effective only through the
discursive) and against a background of other discourses which affect
its conditions both of production and reception (such as legal discourse as a precondition of commodity production and fashion discourse as an influence on the marketability of commodities) (cf.
Gramsci, 1971, p. 377, on the unity between material forces as
content and ideologies as form). However, although there is an explicit recognition that discourse involves more than 'text', it is 'text'
that is placed at the centre of their work. There is little recognition
in practice that extra-discursive conditions are effective not only
through their prior mediation through discourse but also through

post hoc empirical necessities; nor that discourse in its more inclusive sense can generate unintended structural effects or emergent properties which limit the effects of such discourse. Thus, while we may well wish to reject technological determinism as a theoretical perspective in Marxist discourse, we cannot deny the role of technical determinations in the economic, politico-military, or ideological fields. Likewise, if we wish to comprehend the 'laws of motion' of the capitalist economy or the operation of electoral systems in parliamentary democracies, we must go beyond an analysis of particular economic or political discourses to consider their interaction to generate effects which may not be intelligible within any one of these discourses. Indeed, when we refer to the effects of 'market forces' or to the importance of the 'balance of politico-military forces', we refer to emergent properties of systems of interaction which are not reducible to any one of the discourses which help to constitute those systems. In this context it is regettable that the discourse-theoretical approach of Laclau and Mouffe slides all too easily from a general conception of discourse as the production of social meaning to a particular focus upon ideological discourse to the exclusion of economic, legal, military, administrative, and other discourses and then emphasises the 'discourse of discourses' involved in the production of hegemony itself. For this slippage forces them back to the 'text' and seems to reduce hegemony to an effect of various interpellative mechanisms considered in isolation from their conditions of production or reception. Thus, although there is no doubt that the success of Disraeli's 'One Nation' strategy or that of Giolitti's *'trasformismo'* depended in part on a discourse of difference, it is unfortunate that Laclau and Mouffe ignore their additional dependence on specific forms of political representation and government intervention, specific forms of political organisation, specific degrees of economic manoeuvre, specific forms of political repression, and so on. In short, if a discourse-theoretical analysis is to avoid the charge of 'logocentrism' or 'textual reductionism', it must consider both the discursive and extra-discursive moments of discourse and do so not only in relation to the 'discourse of discourses' (hegemony) but also in relation to other fields of discursive practice.

A second range of problems with this approach concerns the crucial distinction between 'political hegemony' and 'organic ideology'. There is no doubt that political leadership is won or lost in the context of 'intellectual and moral reform'. But there is a danger that 'political hegemony' and 'organic ideology' are conflated. Whilst the development of an appropriate ideological cement is the field *par excellence* of the creation of shared meanings, 'common' sense, etc., political leadership works on these meanings in various ways to generate particular projects or national-popular programmes that require specific resources, policy initiatives, forms of mobilisation, etc. One cannot reduce Fascism or Nazism as hegemonic projects to the role of 'corporativism' and 'race' as hegemonic principles: they also involved quite specific programmes of political action designed to advance specific class and 'national-popular' objectives. In addition to 'intellectual and moral reform' it was necessary for the fascist movements to reorganise the Italian and German state apparatus as a precondition of implementing their projects of national regeneration. In this context the notion of the 'structural determination' of hegemony implicit in the work of Poulantzas is useful in so far as it points to the structural constraints on the ability to win a position of class hegemony. Moreover, given the difficulties in identifying the class character of the hegemonic principle that unifies an 'organic ideology', it would seem particularly fruitful to attempt to decipher this issue at the level of a specific political project. Thus, in so far as a specific project of hegemony makes the advancement of the demands of allied or subordinate subjects conditional on the realisation of the long-term interests of a fundamental class, it is reasonable to ascribe that project a specific class character. Even this solution involves a certain ambiguity. For hegemony could be seen in terms of political leadership on the terrain of class position without reference to the effects of the hegemonic project or it could be extended to include the requirement that the hegemonic project actually advances the long-term interests of the hegemonic class (fraction). In the former sense there seems no good reason to deny the possibility of populist hegemonic projects in which political leadership is exercised by a non-fundamental class or a non-class force (e.g., Jacobinism); in the latter sense such a project is inconceivable except as a merely transitory phenomenon (cf. Laclau, 1977, p. 175) and, indeed, many projects with an apparently clear 'fundamental class' character in terms of leadership might well fail to advance the long-term interests of that class (e.g., embarking on a disastrous war, cf. Gramsci, 1971, p. 210). In any case we can surely agree that the class character of a hegemonic project does not depend upon the class origins of its organic intellectuals nor on any supposed *a priori* class belonging of its constituent elements. Moreover, if we want to decipher the complexities and contradictions involved in such hegemonic projects as liberal social imperialism, the 'Keynesian-welfare state', fascism, or Thatcherism, it should be obvious that we must consider not only questions of leadership but also those of the effects of a project.

Finally a discourse-theoretical approach along these lines raises a number of issues concerning the nature and limits of hegemony. Although Laclau and Mouffe note that there are specific conditions of production and reception of discursive practices, there is no attempt to theorise these conditions beyond the assertion that they should be considered as other discourses (Laclau, 1980a, p. 87). The conditions of reception are almost wholly ignored. Yet, as Gramsci himself was careful to observe, there is a world of difference between historically organic ideologies and ideologies that are arbitrary, rationalistic, or 'willed' (Gramsci, 1971, pp. 376–377). Moreover, however plausible a given hegemonic project may appear in terms of its intended articulation of class and non-class subjects and demands, it will only become 'directive' to the extent that strategically significant forces support it and likely sources of resistance are neutralised. An 'interruptive' mode of discursive intervention in an 'interdiscursively' constituted ideological space may well be a necessary condition for the successful deconstruction and re-articulation of hegemonic projects: it is far from a sufficient condition. We still need to explore the social conditions that determine the 'openness' of subjects to specific projects and/or make them structurally 'available' for mobilisation. Moreover, although these conditions may well have a discursive moment, they will also have an extra-discursive moment (e.g., the way in which working-class solidarity is sustained not only discursively but also through the spatial organisation of working-class communities). We should also note how hegemonic projects are typically promoted through a combination of means that includes not only persuasion and moral compulsion but also material inducements and bodily repression. This implies that we must consider discourses of repression and resistance to repression and discourses of material concessions and willingness to make material sacrifices as well as those discourses which depend on rational and democratic debate among the organic intellectuals of competing projects. In this respect Laclau and Mouffe tend to ignore the fact that Gramsci viewed state power as 'hegemony armoured by coercion' and also noted how hegemonic capacities depended on the flow of material concessions. This neglect means that their novel account of hegemony must be adjudged partial and incomplete.

METHODOLOGICAL CRITIQUE OF NEO-GRAMSCIANISM

The neo-Gramscian studies considered above adhere closely to the method of articulation. This is evident not only in Poulantzas's total rejection of subsumption and logical derivation as appropriate methods of theory construction (*PPSC*, p. 13) but also in the argument of Laclau and Mouffe that articulation is the organisational principle of social relations as a whole and not of ideological discourse considered alone (Laclau, 1980a, p. 87; Laclau and Mouffe, 1981, pp. 17–22). In turn this reflects the Althusserian structuralist formalisation of Lenin's views on the 'overdetermined' conjuncture as well as Gramsci's own attempts to break with the economist notion of necessary correspondence and to replace it with the concept of a contingent, socially constituted 'historical bloc'. Clearly, if we reject the economist approach with its reduction of the social formation to a base-superstructure system and also reject the subjectivist doctrine that social formations are a product of agents endowed with reason, autonomy, and free will, it is necessary to develop an alternative account of the relative unity and cohesion of social formations (the so-called 'society effect') and to suggest an alternative approach to the analysis of social subjectivity and the role of social action in social reproduction. In this respect Laclau and Mouffe appear to have advanced further than even the mature Poulantzas. For, although Poulantzas attributed the relative unity and cohesion of a social formation to the activities of the state as a vehicle of hegemonic class leadership, he did not provide an adequate account of social subjectivity and typically relapsed into a class reductionist position. In contrast Laclau and Mouffe tackle both issues in 'discourse-theoretical' terms – subjects are interpellated in and through discourse and social formations are unified in so far as there is a hegemonic 'discourse of discourses' able to mobilise and 'direct' the energies of diverse subjects so that they form a 'collective will'.

These theorists are not alone in opposing reductionist accounts of politics and ideology and it will be helpful to contrast their approach with an alternative solution advanced by Barry Hindess and Paul Hirst. The latter have developed a sustained critique of the recurrent Marxist conception of the structured whole endowed with causal priority over its elements so that there is a necessary correspondence among them – in the sense that each secures the conditions of existence of the others and thus of the self-reproduction of the whole. For, although there is room in this conception for the 'relative autonomy' and the 'reciprocal effectivity' of different elements within the whole and it thus records a major theoretical advance on simple reductionism with its completely autonomous base and ineffective epiphenomena, it nonetheless imposes a spurious unity on these elements and establishes arbitrary limits on their articulation through

its overriding commitment to the causal primacy of the self-reproducing complex whole. In particular Hindess and Hirst argue that,
whilst one can legitimately specify the conditions of existence of a
given theoretical object (e.g., capitalist relations of production), it is
quite illegitimate to conclude that these conditions are necessarily
and automatically realised. For such a conclusion would in practice
deny that the means to their realisation have a real measure of
autonomy in social reproduction and would instead imply that any
variation in these means (institutions, practices) and their impact is
determined heteronomously by the requirement that certain conditions of existence be met. This critique is applied not only to the
relations among various regions of a social formation but also to the
link between class location and political behaviour. In the latter
respect it is held that there is no necessary correspondence between
classes as sets of economic agents and the forces present on the
political scene. For Hindess and Hirst argue that classes as such are
never present as political forces, that class interests are not objectively (i.e., non-discursively) predetermined through abstract relations
of production but depend on particular forms of conjuncturally-
oriented calculation whose nature is determined at least in part
beyond the economic region, that the relationship between political
forces and the realisation of class interests cannot be construed as
one of direct representation but is mediated through the forms of
representation as well as varying with the mode of political calculation, and, lastly, that many political forces are concerned only
tangentially with class issues and are rooted in non-class relations
such as gender or race. In short we find here a sustained critique of
economism and class reductionism and a spirited advocacy of an open
and complex account of the nature of social formations and their
multiple determinations (see especially: Cutler *et al.,* 1977, pp. 167–
328; *idem,* 1978, pp. 233–293; Hindess, 1977, pp. 95–107; Hindess,
1980, pp. 117–123; Hirst, 1977, pp. 125–154; Hirst, 1979a, *passim;*
Hirst, 1979b, pp. 1–21 and *passim*).

Moreover, not only do Hindess and Hirst reject the view that there
is a necessary unity to a social formation and thus a necessary correspondence among its different regions or levels, they also emphasise
that there can be no privileged point of reference for all practices and
that there can be no single principle of explanation or causal model
for all events. Instead they insist on the heterogeneity of social relations, the multiplicity of points of reference and their discursive
rather than extra-discursive character, and the variability of causal
relations and principles of explanation (e.g., Hirst, 1979, pp. 1–21).

This underpins their claim that one cannot substitute the thesis of a 'necessary non-correspondence' for that of 'necessary correspondence'. For both theses presuppose that the social formation comprises various instances unified into a totality. They reject the notion of a totality and its attendant problems of the relations among the economic, political, and ideological regions in terms of a necessary hierarchy of determinations (including determination in the last instance by the economic), relative autonomies, reciprocal effectivities, and so forth (cf. Cutler *et al.*, 1977, pp. 178–179, 226–228). In short, rather than retaining the idea that there are distinct, unitary regions but denying their necessary correspondence in favour of their mutual independence, Hindess and Hirst reject the initial assumption of distinct, unitary regions and *a fortiori* the view that they could be involved in a relationship of 'necessary non-correspondence' (Hirst, 1979, p. 18). They argue that all talk of relations of correspondence or non-correspondence is unacceptable because there are no unitary entities among which such relations could obtain. Instead it is proposed to investigate the conditions of existence of specific practices and institutions without any commitment to a totalising perspective or any *a priori* judgement or hypostasis concerning the causal connections among these conditions and the object of enquiry (cf. Cutler *et al.*, 1977, pp. 226–230). Such an approach clearly excludes all resort to the methods of subsumption or logical derivation and points instead to the need for an analysis of the contingent articulation among discursively constituted theoretical objects.

Unfortunately, while Hindess and Hirst engage in the most rigorous and uncompromising of critiques, it is much less clear how they would analyse the relations among different elements of a social formation. They themselves provide only a serial listing of these elements and argue that these elements do not combine to produce a 'society effect', that is, do not function as a definite and relatively coherent social unity or whole (Cutler *et al.*, 1977, pp. 230–231; Hindess and Hirst, 1977, pp. 49–57). In particular, while one may well support their rejection of the principle of economic determination in the last instance and/or the idea of holistic functionalism which endows causal priority to the whole over its parts, it is far from clear how the distinction between 'conditions of existence' and the 'forms' through which they may (or, alternatively, may not) be secured is meant to function in their method of theoretical enquiry. Thus Hindess and Hirst reject the rationalist method with its attempts to deduce the specific forms through which general conditions of existence are secured from the relations of production themselves (i.e., derivation) and are equally opposed to the empiricist method in which such forms are empirically given to theory by particular circumstances lying beyond the realm of theoretical determination whereas the conditions of existence can be so determined (i.e., subsumption) (Cutler *et al.,* 1977, pp. 219–220). But this still leaves open the problem of how one can connect an abstract, high level theoretical specification of conditions of existence with a concrete, low level empirical datum about the wide variation in the forms through which these conditions are realised. Let us consider how Hindess and Hirst tackle this problem.

It seems that they wish to identify a particular theoretical object in terms of a specific theoretical discourse (rather than depart from an extra-discursively constituted and pre-given 'real-concrete' considered as a whole), to establish at least some of its conditions of existence (presumably this is accomplished through the method of hypothetical retroduction rather than through a hypostatising process of deduction), and then to examine empirically how such conditions are secured (if at all) in particular conjunctures (which requires that one respects the differential effectivity of particular forms if the charge of subsumption is to be avoided) (on the concept of 'retroduction', see: Sayer, 1979, pp. 105–141; and on the concept of 'hypostasis' as opposed to 'hypothesis', see della Volpe, 1969, pp. 161–209). In adopting this procedure Hindess and Hirst neglect two important aspects of the method of articulation. Firstly they fail to distinguish different levels of abstraction in theoretical discourse. This means that they encounter spurious difficulties in closing the gap between abstract conditions of existence and empirical variation in the forms through which these conditions are secured. Instead we could try to establish a hierarchy of conditions of existence corresponding to the hierarchy of levels of abstraction at which the theoretical object can be specified: the more concrete the specification of the explicandum, the more determinate will be the forms through which they can be realised. This method is implicit in Poulantzas's account of the forms of state corresponding to class-divided societies, capitalist societies, monopoly capitalist societies, and so forth. Secondly Hindess and Hirst neglect the conditionality of 'conditions of existence' and thus overemphasise their independence from the institution or practice whose existence they help to secure. But there is no good *a priori* reason to assume that, say, economically relevant conditions of existence and the institutions and practices conditioned by the economic must be mutually exclusive categories. Indeed, if we examine Hindess and Hirst's own serial

listing of the conditons of existence of capitalist relations of production, we find that it includes a determinate form of legal system and
specific forms of state and politics. Yet the reproduction of law,
state, and politics presumably has among its conditions of existence
specific forms of revenue articulated with capitalist relations of production (e.g., the analyses of the 'tax-state' developed in the form
derivation debate). It should be clear that such an argument need not
re-introduce the thesis of economic determination in the final instance
but it does raise the question of economic determination in a pertinent manner. It is in these terms that we can introduce the issue of
the articulation of heterogeneous elements to constitute a relatively
unified social formation capable of reproduction, the limits on
covariation involved in the mutual presupposition and/or codeter-
mination of these elements, and the relative importance of various
elements in the overall determination of social cohesion. Such an
approach need not involve any rejection of Hindess and Hirst's commitment to the heterogeneity of social relations, the multiplicity of
theoretically possible points of reference for establishing conditions
of existence, and the variability of causal relations. Indeed it would
seem to offer a more complete account of what the method of
articulation actually involves.

Following this theoretical detour we can now return to the
methods employed in the works reviewed above. It is clear that in his
earlier studies Poulantzas sometimes did adopt the reductionist position criticised by Hindess and Hirst. In discussing social reproduction
he did tend to treat the state as a factor of cohesion whose relative
autonomy and effectivity were inscribed in the global structure of
the CMP; and he also viewed political forces as the representatives on
the political scene of classes inscribed in the matrix of the self-same
CMP. In his later studies, however, Poulantzas modified this approach. He came to reject the structuralism of the Althusserian
school and began to treat the state as a complex, non-unitary institutional ensemble whose role in social reproduction depended on the
balance of forces. In addition to his long-standing argument that the
economic region is fractionated and subject to the 'isolation effect'
and his equally long-standing emphasis on the heterogeneity of ideological elements and the socially constructed nature of class ideologies,
Poulantzas gradually embraced the view that there was no necessary
unity to the state apparatus and that such unity as emerged was the
result of specific class practices. He thereby arrived at a 'relational
theory' in which state power is investigated as a (partially) form-
determined condensation of political forces. Moreover, in contrast

with the implicit denial of Hindess and Hirst that one can investigate conditions of existence and the forms in which they are secured at different levels of abstraction, Poulantzas explicitly tackled such an investigation at various levels. Thus, the greater the degree of abstraction, the greater the weight he allotted to determination through *form*; and, the greater the degree of concretisation, the greater the emphasis on specific social forces. Moreover, whereas most contributions to the form derivation debate were ignorant or oblivious of the distinction between levels and planes of abstraction, Poulantzas initially took such pains to emphasise the *sui generis* characteristics of the political region that he laid himself open to a charge of 'politicism'. In subsequent studies he was more careful to consider the complex articulation of economic, political, and ideological determinations and to offer specific conjunctural explanations of the various phenomena he investigated. This development culminated in Poulantzas's belated recognition that socialist strategy required the articulation of the class struggle with *sui generis* social movements rooted in non-class relations. But even his earliest studies stressed the crucial theoretical role of the double articulation of levels and planes of abstraction in order to provide a complete account of 'real-concrete' phenomena and so present them as the 'complex synthesis of multiple determinations'.

In certain respects Laclau and Mouffe subscribe more closely than did Poulantzas to the approach advocated by Hindess and Hirst. While Poulantzas came to grips with discourse theory only in his most recent work and seems to have been seriously influenced only by Foucault (cf. Poulantzas, *SPS*, pp. 66–70, 146–153; and 1979b, pp. 14–15), the others have all been engaged with discourse theory for some time and it holds a strong influence on all of them. In addition all four theorists are vehement in their opposition not only to economism but also to class reductionism and their work can only be fully appreciated in this context. Despite these theoretical affinities, however, Laclau and Mouffe reject one principle allegedly supported by Hindess and Hirst. For, if the latter have sometimes given the impression that they wish to oppose the reductionist principle of 'necessary correspondence' with the anti-reductionist principle of 'necessary non-correspondence' (although, as we have seen above, they reject both principles), the former criticise the principle of 'necessary non-correspondence' on the grounds that it excludes any theoretical possibility of investigating the relative unity of a social formation. Their own solution to this problem of 'non-necessary correspondence' (to coin a phrase) is to argue that it stems from specific forms of discursive articulation – which they summarise in the portmanteau concept of 'hegemony'. Provided that one reads this notion of 'contingent correspondence' in a non-totalising manner, i.e., as applying to specified elements of a social formation rather than the entire system, it would seem to offer an appropriate answer to the hoary question of social order. In this sense the concept of 'articulation' in discourse theory provides a valuable paradigm for the explanation of the contingent relations among phenomena located in different planes of abstraction. It remains to be seen whether Laclau and Mouffe can avoid the dangers of 'textual reductionism' in developing this approach.

CONCLUDING REMARKS

We have considered both the contribution of Antonio Gramsci to an anti-reductionist, relational theory of the state and state power and its subsequent development in two novel directions. It is hoped that the substantive theoretical advances achieved by the (neo-)Gramscian school have emerged in the course of this discussion. In brief the most important advances comprise: the notion of the 'integral state' considered as 'hegemony armoured by coercion', an emphasis on the social bases of state power in civil society as well as in political society, the anti-reductionist notion of the 'historical bloc' as a *contingent*, socially constructed form of correspondence among the economic, political, and ideological regions of a social formation, and the anti-reductionist emphasis on the specificity of the 'national-popular' and 'popular-democratic' in contradistinction to class demands and struggles. In addition Poulantzas has attempted to delineate the structural determination of 'hegemony armoured by coercion' through his focus on state forms as an ensemble of social relations with a definite effectivity on the balance of social forces and has also elaborated the distinction between 'normal' and 'exceptional' forms of state. In turn Laclau and Mouffe have extended the work of Gramsci through a concern with the discursive mechanisms through which hegemony can be achieved and have thereby provided some defence against the charge that the conceptual instrumentarium of neo-Gramscian studies merely comprises a set of pigeon-holes to which different facts can be allotted in a purely *ad hoc,* empiricist manner.

In developing these contributions, however, certain theoretical costs have been incurred. In particular the (neo-)Gramscian focus on 'political, intellectual, and moral leadership' has been associated with a corresponding neglect of economic contradictions and constraints. In the case of Poulantzas this results in a tendency towards 'politicism' in so far as he combines the Gramscian concept of hegemony with the Althusserian concept of the relative autonomy of the state. In the case of Laclau and Mouffe it results in a tendency towards 'logocentrism' or 'textual reductionism' in so far as they have focused on the discursive moment *par excellence* in studying hegemony as an overarching 'discourse of discourses' in the field of ideological struggle. Nonetheless, precisely because both Poulantzas and Laclau and Mouffe have adopted the method of articulation (which, it should be emphasised, is not universally true of the neo-Gramscian school), it is possible to recuperate their contributions without adopting in addition their 'politicist' or 'textual reductionist' tendencies. Some indications of how this can be achieved are offered in the final chapter.

5

Towards a Theoretical Account of the State

The three most important postwar European approaches to a Marxist theory of the capitalist state have now been reviewed and it is time to draw some general conclusions. These approaches have been tackled from two different viewpoints: firstly, as bodies of substantive theory concerned with particular issues in Marxist political analysis; and, secondly, as products of distinctive methods of research and presentation. It should be clear that there is little consensus concerning either the particular theoretical object(s) to be investigated or the manner in which they are to be examined. It should also be clear that I do not consider that these approaches are all equally productive. Accordingly in this chapter I offer some general guidelines for constructing an adequate theoretical account of the state and outline the methods that should be employed to this end.

AGAINST A GENERAL THEORY

We ought first to exorcise the spectre haunting Marxist state theory – the prospect of a general theory of the state. The schools considered above have developed different approaches to the production of a Marxist account of the state but all lay some claim to providing a valid overall perspective. But this claim can be understood in several different ways. If it is interpreted as suggesting that one can develop a fully determinate theory of the state, it must be rejected. For, while any attempt to analyse the world must assume that it is determinate and determined, it does not follow that a single theory can comprehend the totality of its determinations without resorting to reductionism of one kind or another. The various abortive efforts to develop a general theory of the state get their impetus from conflating the determinacy of the real world with determinacy as a

211

property of a given theoretical system, thereby aiming to explain the former in terms of the latter. The comments above suggest that we can distinguish three basic methods whereby attempts are made to construct general theories: reductionism, empiricism, and subsumption. For purported general theories commit at least one of the following errors: invoking one plane or axis of theoretical determination to explain everything about the state and politics; mistaking a more or less complete synchronic description and/or historiographic account of an actual event for an adequate explanation of that event; and subsuming a particular description and/or history of this kind under a general principle of explanation as one of its many instantiations. All three approahces can be found in the field of Marxist theory and they must be rejected severally and collectively as an adequate basis for theoretical investigations of the state and politics.

Against such approaches it must be stressed that state theory is not concerned to produce 'raw' descriptions or genealogies, however detailed, of particular events – except as a very preliminary step in the movement from the 'real-concrete' to the 'concrete-in-thought'. Nor is it interested in abstract speculation about the essence of politics or the *a priori* class nature of the state. Instead it attempts to explain the 'contingent necessity' of specific conjunctures and their outcomes in terms of their various determinants. The concept of 'contingent necessity' with its apparent *contradictio in adjecto* highlights the fact that, while the combination or interaction of different causal chains produces a determinate outcome (necessity), there is no single theory that can predict or determine the manner in which such causal chains converge and/or interact (contingency). Thus Marx writes in the 1857 *Introduction* that the goal of scientific analysis is to reproduce the 'real-concrete' as a 'concrete-in-thought', that is, as a complex synthesis of many different determinations (1857, pp. 100–101). This presupposes the analysis of determinations which can be combined to give a coherent, consistent account of the concrete situation.

A correct application of this method enables one to avoid three errors in theoretical analysis. The first is to equate the 'real-concrete' with the level of appearances and thus to overlook the more abstract determinations (powers, tendencies, counter-tendencies, etc.) that enter into its formation. The second is to reduce the 'real-concrete' to the abstract (in extreme cases to just one of its abstract determinations) and thus to overlook the mediations that connect the abstract to the level of appearances. In addition the basic distinction between 'abstract' and 'concrete' excludes the method of subsumption with its foundation in the distinction between 'general' and 'particular'.

In short, if we are to avoid the empiricism that derives from an exclusive emphasis on appearances, the reductionism that derives from an exclusive emphasis on one or more abstract determinations, and the subsumptionism of the 'particular' vs. the 'general', we must engage in an analysis of the many determinations that are combined in a concrete conjuncture and show how they are interrelated as necessary and/or sufficient conditions in a contingent structure of causation. This entails both movement from the abstract to the concrete within a single plane of analysis (e.g., from capital-in-general to particular capitals) and the combination of determinations drawn from different planes of analysis (e.g., popular-democratic antagonisms rooted in the relations of political domination vs. class antagonisms rooted in the relations of economic exploitation). Such an approach excludes all pretence to the construction of a general theory and aims at producing the theoretical tools with which particular conjunctures can be examined.

ON THE METHOD OF ARTICULATION

In this context we can now present some general comments on the method of articulation as a technique of theory construction. The remarks so far should have indicated that this method is premised on a realist account of science. For the notion of the 'real-concrete' as the complex synthesis of multiple determinations implies that the 'real-concrete' is stratified into various layers and regions which require different concepts, assumptions, and principles of explanation. This does not mean that currently existing theories necessarily correspond to the structure of the real world and can fully comprehend it. Indeed, as I argue below, there is no immediate access to the real world. Thus all theory construction and evaluation is mediated through specific conceptual systems and techniques of empirical enquiry. This means in turn that it is necessary to specify the particular ontological and epistemological views and the particular conventions for empirical testing adopted in a given enquiry and to maintain a critical stance towards them. What do these arguments imply for state theories?

It must first be emphasised that, regardless of the chosen level of abstraction, all analysis has a theoretical or discursive dimension. There are no raw facts external to thought and thus free from theoretical presuppositions. It is for this reason that I bracketed the

Marxian notion of 'real-concrete' in quotation marks to suggest its problematic epistemological status. For the concept of 'real-concrete' actually indicates a particular characterisation of the real and should not be juxtaposed to the 'concrete-in-thought' as if the former were a theory-free representation of the real world as it actually exists beyond the gaze of the scientist. Not only does this hold for the natural world (which exists outside thought but may be transformed through social practices) but also for the social world (which is constituted in and through discourse but also involves extra-discursive elements). In all cases we must define the phenomena to be included in the 'real-concrete' before they can be appropriated and reproduced as a 'concrete-in-thought'. Thus, although an adequate explanation of social phenomena must sooner or later refer to the discourse(s) of the agents involved, the characterisation of these discourses is never theoretically innocent and they can no more be treated as unproblematic than the extra-discursive elements involved. In no case does movement occur from a theory-free 'real-concrete' to a theory-laden 'concrete-in-thought': the method of articulation always occurs on the domain of theoretical discourse. Let us consider the implications of this claim for assessing the adequacy of explanations in theories of the state.

Given the theoretical status of all steps in the method of articulation, it is essential that they can be related in a consistent and coherent manner. Accordingly an explanation will be considered adequate if, at the level of abstraction and the degree of complexity in terms of which the problem is defined, it establishes a set of conditions that are together necessary and/or sufficient to produce the effects specified in the explanendum. This implies that a particular scientific enquiry need not start afresh from the real world in all its complexity (which would entail an empiricist understanding of the 'real-concrete' rather than a stress on its theoretical status) but can establish its explanendum at various levels of abstraction and different degrees of complexity. In turn this means the adequacy of an explanation must be assessed in relation to the particular explanendum rather than to the totality of social relations. From this it follows that one cannot criticise a given explanation for failing to explain phenomena that are beyond its specific explanendum either in terms of greater concreteness and/or in terms of greater complexity. Indeed, as I noted in relation to the *Staatsableitungdebatte,* the principle of the overdetermination of the 'real-concrete' (i.e., its 'contingent necessity') implies its underdetermination at more abstract and simple levels of analysis. But this does not mean that any adequate explanation is as good as any other at a given level of abstraction or complexity. For, if the explanendum in question is redefined or elaborated through concretisation (lowering the level of abstraction) and/or through what might be called 'complexification' (adding determinations from other planes of analysis), it should be possible to extend or expand the corresponding explanation without making the overall argument inconsistent. Thus an explanation will be considered inadequate if it cannot be extended to a lower level of abstraction without contradiction. This suggests two strategies for explanation. Either an explanation must recognise its indeterminacy vis-à-vis lower levels of abstraction and leave certain issues unresolved at its chosen level of operation; or it must make certain assumptions that permit a determinate explanation without pre-empting subsequent concretisation. The former strategy can be seen in the argument that form problematises function; the latter can be seen in the assumption of an average rate of profit or the assumption that individual capitals act simply as *träger* of the capital relation (see above, pp. 134–135). This criterion also implies that explanations adequate to one plane of analysis should be commensurable with those adequate to the explanation of other planes. In the case of incommensurability, however, any rules for preferring one of these explanations over others must be conventional. There are no formal rules able to guarantee a correct choice as to which explanation should be retained and which rejected; and any substantive rules will depend on the specific theoretical framework(s) within which the investigator is working.

Hitherto I have talked rather loosely about degrees of abstraction-concretion in one plane of analysis and about different analytic planes as if these were both wholly unproblematic notions. In general terms these distinctions are entailed in any realist account of scientific enquiry. For, while the realist approach assumes that the real world is stratified into different domains or regions which reveal distinctive, *sui generis* emergent properties and thus require the development of different scientific disciplines to consider their respective conditions of existence, it also argues that each domain comprises not only a level of appearances or phenomenal forms but also an underlying level or levels at which are located the mechanisms that generate the surface phenomena of that domain. The former assumption entails the necessity of different planes of analysis, the latter implies the necessity of different levels of abstraction in each plane. At a minimum we need to distinguish among three levels of abstraction: the 'empirical' (with the twin qualifications that the empirically observable is technically and discursively conditioned and that empirical observation can in some sense be false or erroneous), the 'actual' (the level of specific 'agents' and 'events' on the surface of a domain), and the 'real' (the level of the specific mechanisms which generate actual agents and events). While the independent existence of the 'actual' is a condition of intelligibility of empirical observation, that of the 'real' is a condition of intelligibility of the operation of known laws in open systems as well as of experimentation in closed systems (in drawing these distinctions I rely on Bhaskar, 1978, pp. 12–20ff). Beyond this minimum set of three levels of abstraction, the actual number to be distinguished will depend, firstly, on the depth of stratification of the 'real' and the various mediations between specific mechanisms and 'actual' events and, secondly, on the discursive structure and conventions adopted in the order of presentation of a given theory or explanation. There is certainly no reason to assume that each plane of analysis must have the same number of levels of abstraction-concretion as the realm of value considered by Marx in *Das Kapital.* Depth and complexity will both vary across events. In turn this will be relevant to the number of levels of abstraction and the range of analytic factors to be discussed. In this context it is the precise specification of the explanendum that will determine the formal adequacy of an explanation and its substantive adequacy will depend on the particular rules or conventions established for testing that explanation.

In general the greater is the degree of abstraction, the more indeterminate is the 'real' mechanism with reference to the 'actual' and the more formal is the specification of its mediations. Thus Marx's account of the tendency of the rate of profit to fall initially abstracts from the mobilisation of counter-tendencies (which are typically located at lower levels of abstraction), ignores the so-called 'transformation problem' involved in the movement from values to prices, and invokes the 'class struggle' as a formal mediation whose substantive specification must await more concrete analysis. Likewise the assumption that individual capitalists act as the '*träger*' of the capital relation is a purely formal mediation in the realisation of the law of value and more concrete analyses must consider the differential interpellation and modes of calculation of particular capitals in assessing how they function in the realisation of that law and how competitive forces influence different capitals. Apparently similar problems occur in an account of how the state acts as if it were an 'ideal collective capitalist', that is, as a political '*träger*' of the capital relation. But, although this mode of explanation can account *at its chosen level of abstraction* for the possibility of the CMP in terms of the state's role in securing its general external conditions of existence, *it cannot be extended* to lower levels of abstraction without contradicting its initial assumption that it is the state's function that determines its form and without recognising that the very form of the state problematises its functionality for capitalism. Conversely, once we concede that theoretical objects can be studied at different levels of abstraction, it is possible to solve the purported problem of the gap between abstract conditions of existence and the actual forms in which they are realised. Thus, the more concrete the explanendum, the more concrete are its conditions of existence and the more determinate the forms in which they can be realised. Lastly we should note that explanations adequate to different planes of analysis should be commensurable. For example, although a class reductionist account of the state may seem adequate to an explanendum couched in class-theoretical terms, extension of the explanendum to include non-class relations will reveal the inadequacy of such an account not only in relation to the extended explanendum but also the initial problem. This point emerges particularly clearly in the (neo-) Gramscian account of political *class* domination in terms of hegemony as 'political, intellectual, and moral leadership' oriented to the 'national-popular' as well as the 'economic-corporate'. This suggests that a genuinely adequate account of a class-theoretical explanendum will not itself be phrased in class-reductionist terms even though it must contain class-*relevant* concepts, assumptions, and principles of explanation.

Finally we should consider exactly what is involved in the retroductive movement from the 'real-concrete' to abstract and simple determinations and thence to the 'concrete-in-thought'. The concept of 'retroduction' has a diacritical function as well as a positive significance. For it differentiates the logic of discovery and techniques of research in the method of articulation from those employed in other approaches to theory construction. Thus retroduction involves neither induction from a number of empirically observable regularities to a law-like empirical generalisation nor does it involve logical inference or deduction from specific major and minor premises to an outcome entailed therein. Instead it involves a process of rational inference from some problematic aspect of the 'real-concrete' or some theoretically constituted anomaly back to one or more mechanisms that could possibly generate this problematic or anomalous explanendum together with the conditions in which such mechanisms could actually produce the effects in question. Thus retroduction involves the production of a *hypothesis* concerning the conditons of possibility of a given phenomenon or explanendum in terms of a real mechanism and its mediations. Such mechanisms could include the law of value, the tendency of the rate of profit to fall and the mobilisation of counter-tendencies, the particularisation of the state, the logic of electoral competition or coalition formation, the mechanism of the interpellation of subjects, and the semiotics of the discursive production of meaning. However, since these mechanisms are potential or tendential and may not always be actualised and, if actualised, may not always produce the same events, it is also necessary to specify the conditions (including countervailing mechanisms as well as facilitating conditions) under which they produce their 'contingently necessary' (or 'overdetermined') effects. It is for this reason that I stressed above that it is just as necessary to explain the actualisation of a 'pure' course of accumulation or a 'pure' capitalist state as it is to account for the existence of progressive 'de-industrialisation' or a state whose activities promote the 'mutual ruin of the contending classes'. In this context we can note that levels of abstraction will be reflected in the retroductive specification of a hierarchy of conditions of possibility — the more abstract levels being compatible with more possible outcomes at the same time as being indeterminate with reference to the actual result, the more concrete levels defining progressively more restrictive limits on the actual result as they overdetermine the more abstract conditions of possibility. Similar considerations apply to the 'complexification' of an explanation to correspond to a complex explanendum so that the introduction of additional planes of analysis further delimits possible outcomes of a given mechanism or set of mechanisms.

It should be apparent that retroduction involves the formation of *hypotheses* which require a critical evaluation. There are three interrelated moments in such a critique: formal, substantive, and empirical. However, since we shall be discussing the substantive aspects of state theory in subsequent sections and since substantive criteria for other bodies of theory are irrelevant here, we will concentrate on the formal and empirical aspects of evaluating hypotheses.

In formal terms we have already emphasised that a sound hypothesis must exhaust the explanendum, that is, must specify the 'contingently necessary' conditions which taken together fully account for the existence of the explanendum at the level of abstraction and the degree of complexity in terms of which it is defined. The hypothesis should also be capable of extension to lower levels of abstraction and/or greater degrees of complexity as appropriate. In addition the 'contingently necessary' conditions it specifies must be independent of the phenomena to be explained, that is, the hypothesis should not be tautological and should not comprise merely an empirical general- isation. Related to this criterion is the stipulation that the hypothesis should not comprise a hypothetico-deductive system whose premises (as well as its conclusion) are confined to the actual. Lastly we should note that the various elements forming an hypothesis should be logically consistent, and in so far as they are drawn from different planes of analysis, compatible.

While these formal criteria can be deployed to assess the formal adequacy of an explanation or hypothesis, attempts should also be made to assess its empirical adequacy. However, because there is no unmediated access to the real world, knowledge is always an effect of a complex interaction between theories, techniques of investigation, and reality itself. Indeed, precisely because all knowledge is genera- ted through a complex, overdetermined process of enquiry, it is im- possible to assess how much each of these determinants contributes to the formation of the so-called 'facts' and thus how 'accurately' they represent the real world as it is assumed to exist independently of its intellectual and material signification. Since hypotheses cannot be tested through a direct confrontation with the real world, empiri- cal evaluation involves comparing the propositions from the hypoth- esis with evidence in the form of propositions produced through specific empirical techniques and procedures. In the natural sciences this can often be accomplished through experimentation in control- led conditions: in the social sciences we must resort to historical and comparative analyses and/or to practical interventions in basically open systems. In all cases it should be emphasised that such empirical testing is subject to conventional, theoretically constituted criteria of falsification. Thus, although a certain consistency between the two sets of propositions can be taken as *prima facie* support for the empirical adequacy of the hypothesis under investigation, such sup- port is far from irrefutable and incontrovertible. For the consistency could be spurious, random, circumstantial, or the effect of some other mechanism. Likewise, while inconsistency may offer *prima facie* falsification of the empirical adequacy of the hypothesis, it does not imply that the theory being tested is necessarily inadequate or erroneous. Rather it raises the problem of how to repair the in- consistency through further theoretical work. If it cannot be traced for the moment to the theories and/or the techniques involved in the production of the evidence, it is necessary to consider whether the inconsistency can be resolved within the terms of the theory or theories being tested through the modification or recombination of different elements. If this cannot be done, attempts should be made to replace the theory or theories with an alternative that *can* resolve these contradictions or else *dis*solve them through a redefinition of the initial explanenda. (In this discussion of retroduction, hypothesis formation and empirical testing we have drawn extensively on Bhaskar, 1978, and Sayer, 1979, and, to a lesser extent, on della Volpe, 1969, and Laclau, 1975.)

In these general comments on the method of articulation I have deliberately avoided any commitment to particular substantive propositions. Theoretical analysis is a continuing process involving the ever-renewed transformation of existing theories, concepts, techniques, and evidence and it is important not to foreclose subsequent discussion of substantive issues in an overview of epistemological and methodological questions. Of course the latter are also liable to transformation. But we need to suspend disbelief on these matters while developing substantive theory and it was therefore necessary to establish some epistemological and methodological canons for the following sections. In particular I have emphasised that substantive theories should be able to comprehend the 'real-concrete' as a complex synthesis of multiple determinations. And I have argued that this means the method of articulation is the most fitting basis for theory construction and presentation as long as it is combined with a commitment to empirical evaluation as well as formal and substantive criticism. It is through the combination of these different forms of criticism that theoretical progress occurs within the limits and opportunities which are determined by the current theoretical 'raw materials', investigative techniques, and social relations of theoretical activity and are overdetermined by the general economic, political, and ideological conjuncture. This said, let us now consider some more substantive issues.

WHAT IS TO BE THEORISED?

We can now turn to the question of the substantive criteria relevant to an evaluation of Marxist state theory. Here we must note that there is no reason to expect a purely Marxist approach to exhaust the analysis of the state. For, while Marxism as a theoretical approach is concerned with the analysis of relations of production, their various conditions of existence, and their effects on other social relations, the state is located on the terrain of the social formation and this comprises more than economic relations and their conditions of existence. This is not to suggest that one cannot examine the economic conditions of existence of the state nor the manner in which the state as a whole influences the reproduction of economic relations. It is to suggest that an analysis of the state, its various conditions of existence, and its effects on other social relations will include much more than the issue of economic relations and class forces. Nonetheless I can offer some criteria which should be satisfied by an adequate Marxist approach and to which could be added further criteria to ensure a more rounded theoretical investigation.

Accordingly a Marxist analysis of the state in capitalist societies will be considered adequate to the extent that (a) it is founded on the specific qualities of capitalism as a mode of production and also allows for the effects of the articulation of the CMP with other relations of social and/or private labour, (b) it attributes a central role in the process of capital accumulation to interaction among class forces, (c) it establishes the relations between the political and economic features of society without reducing one to the other or treating them as totally independent and autonomous, (d) it allows for historical and national differences in the forms and functions of the state in capitalist social formations, and (e) it allows not only for the influence of class forces rooted in and/or relevant to non-capitalist production relations but also for that of non-class forces (cf. Jessop, 1977, p. 353). The justification for putting these substantive criteria forward should already be apparent from our critique of the three major postwar schools of Marxist state theory. In suggesting the most suitable ways of satisfying these criteria we shall in any case provide a commentary on their rationale. So let us now present some guidelines for the construction of an adequate Marxist account of the state in capitalist societies.

Firstly, the state is a set of institutions that cannot, *qua* institutional ensemble, exercise power.

Secondly, political forces do not exist independently of the state: they are shaped in part through its forms of representation, its internal structure, and its forms of intervention.

Thirdly, state power is a complex social relation that reflects the changing balance of social forces in a determinate conjuncture.

Fourthly, state power is capitalist to the extent that it creates, maintains, or restores the conditions required for capital accumulation in a given situation and it is non-capitalist to the extent that these conditions are not realised.

The first guideline involves an institutional definition of the state and entails no guarantees about its capitalist nature. For, if the state is not to be constituted *a priori* as capitalist or viewed as a simple instrument, it is necessary to define it in terms that involve only contingent references (if any) to the capitalist mode of production and/or the economically dominant class. In short, while it may well be necessary to refer to the specific qualities of the CMP and the relations between capital and wage-labour in discussing the state in capitalist societies, it is important to avoid any relation of logical entailment such that the existence of the CMP necessarily implies the capitalist character of the state apparatus and/or state power. Thus it should be emphasised that, while capitalist relations of production may be a basic condition of existence of the so-called 'particularisation' or structural differentiation of the state form, it does not follow that the state form is therefore essentially capitalist nor that it will necessarily serve in turn to reproduce capitalist relations of production. This is especially important to emphasise because the state is located on the terrain of the social formation rather than the pure CMP and is also the site of non-class relations as well as class relations.

The most appropriate way of avoiding these problems is to adopt an institutional definition of the state. In this context it is acceptable to define its institutional boundaries in terms of the legal distinction between 'public' and 'private' provided that one does not treat the state as an originating subject endowed with an essential unity nor neglect the role of private institutions and forces in securing political domination. For much of the controversy about the state makes sense only on the false assumption that the state has a definite unity because it is a subject or because it performs a specific, pre-given function or functions in capitalist reproduction. But there are no valid grounds for presupposing the essential class unity of the state and various arguments suggest that it is necessarily fragmented and fissured. The state comprises a plurality of institutions (or apparatuses) and their unity, if any, far from being pregiven, must be constituted politically. Indeed, not only has this been emphasised in (neo-)Gramscian analyses of hegemony (above all in the later work of Poulantzas), it is also stressed in some studies in 'form derivation' in so far as they treat the institutional separation of state and economy as problematic and conditional on the imposition through struggle of various fetishised forms of action. More generally it should be noted that this suggestion, precisely because it involves no arguments about the necessary form and functions of the state, can accommodate changes in these variables and their articulation without recourse to reductionist or essentialist arguments. Indeed, once we proceed from abstract arguments about the institutional separation of the economic and political under capitalism to more concrete and complex analyses of these regions, concern with the exact institutional forms of political representation and state intervention is crucial.

The strength of this first guideline can be demonstrated most easily by considering the implications of rejecting it. Thus to treat the state as a real (as opposed to formal, legal) subject with a pre-given unity is to exclude from view political struggles within and between state apparatuses as well as the effects of its institutional structure on the constitution and conduct of political struggles beyond the state. Likewise to endow the state with an essential unity or inevitable bourgeois character is to engage in crude reductionism and to suggest that the only valid form of socialist political struggle is one concerned to smash the existing state apparatus. Moreover, if one adopts such an essentialist position or simply argues that all institutions of class domination (or, *pace* the early Poulantzas, all institutions securing social cohesion in a class-divided society) should be included in one's definition of the state, it becomes impossible to differentiate between democratic and non-democratic forms of domination and to discuss the effects of changes in the overall insti-tutional boundaries of the state. All states in capitalist societies would be reduced to the indifferent status of 'dictatorships of the bourgeoisie' and there would be no reason to prefer one or another state form or form of regime. (This said, it must be admitted that the legal distinction between 'public' and 'private' is in one sense 'tain-ted': for it is a distinction internal to bourgeois law and it develops most fully only with the dominance of the liberal, *laissez-faire* stage of capitalism. Nonetheless its effects are not reducible to its condi-tions of existence – any more than the conditions of existence of capitalist relations of production thereby become essentially bour-geois in nature. Where this juridical approach to a definition is con-sidered inappropriate, it might be possible to define the state in terms of its monopoly over coercion. But even here the same prob-lem occurs at one remove: for this monopoly is itself typically constitutionalised and provides one of the grounds for differentiating the 'public' from the 'private'. In addition there is no guarantee that the state can successfully maintain this monopoly in all circum-stances. In any event the arguments in favour of some form of insti-tutional definition as an initial point of reference for a study of the state should become clearer as we consider our other guidelines.)

The second guideline must be interpreted in association with our emphasis on an institutional definition of the state. Together they exclude an instrumentalist approach. For, although the state should not be seen as a subject capable of exercising power, it does have unequal and asymmetrical effects on the ability of different social forces to realise their interests through political action. This means that the state is not and cannot be a neutral instrument. It does not exclude the view that the state (or, more precisely, its various institutional means and resources) can be *used*: this, after all, is the very rationale behind the struggle for state power. But the structures of political representation and state intervention involve differential access to the state apparatuses and differential opportunities to realise specific effects in the course of state intervention. It is for this reason that a principal aim of class struggle must be the reorganisation of the state apparatuses in order to redefine their accessibility and/or their instrumentality for various class forces. This argument is reinforced through a consideration of the way in which political forces are themselves constituted at least in part through the institutional structure of the state and the effects of state intervention. *Prima facie* support for this approach is provided by a brief reflection on the growth of corporatism at the expense of parliamentarism, struggles over electoral reform, laws on secondary picketing, the role of legislation and state policy-making in the interpellation of particular subjects and the constitution of their interests, and so forth. This means that classes should not be seen as already-constituted political forces which exist outside and independently of the state and which are able to manipulate it as a simple, passive instrument. For, although classes as objective categories of economic agents are defined at the level of the relations of production, their political weight depends on the forms of organisation and means of intervention through which their economic (and other) class interests are expressed. In this sense one can say, following Przeworski, that political class struggle is first of all a struggle to constitute classes as political forces before it is a struggle between classes (see Preworski, 1977, pp. 371–373 and, in addition, pp. 242–244 below). In this context the nature of the state is an important variable. Similar considerations apply to other political forces besides capital and wage-labour – whether primarily class forces or non-class forces (see below). Thus the state should be investigated as a system of political domination whose structure has a definite effect on class struggle through its role in determining the balance of forces and the forms of political action.

The third guideline implies a firm rejection of all attempts to distinguish between 'state power' and 'class power' (whether as descriptive concepts or principles of explanation) in so far as they establish this distinction by constituting the state itself as a power subject

and/or deny the continuing class struggle within the state as well as
beyond it. This is not to argue that state power is reducible to class
power nor is it to deny the influence of political categories such as
the military, bureaucrats, or parliamentary deputies. It is to argue
that any attempt to differentiate among types of power should be
made in terms of their institutional mediation and/or their social
bases. In this sense we could distinguish state power from economic
power in terms of its *sui generis* institutional mediation or distinguish
'bureaucratic despotism' from the 'bourgeois democratic republic' in
terms of their respective social bases. A *fortiori* we could also distinguish among forms of state power in terms of the specific branches
of the state system through which they are mediated as well as
among different forms of democratic republic according to their
specific configurations of social support. In denying the validity of
the distinction between 'state power' and 'class power' in these terms
we are not denying that the role of the state as a system of political
class domination may sometimes be secondary to its role as a system
of official domination over 'popular-democratic' forces. For this
latter distinction does not involve the illegitimate assumption that
the state is a power subject but merely treats it as an institutional
complex conditioning and conditioned by the balance of forces. Nor
do we deny that non-class forces initially located beyond the state
(i.e., social categories based on the terrain of civil society as opposed
to political categories and economic classes) can be involved in the
exercise of state power and be affected by state intervention. For
this merely indicates the complexity of the state apparatus and state
power. Instead our third guideline is intended to stress that state
power is a form-determined, institutionally mediated effect of the
balance among all forces in a given situation.

This implies that state power is an explicandum, not a principle of
explanation. That is, rather than explaining specific events in terms
of an immediate, unexplicated exercise of state power, it is necessary to problematise the effects of state intervention and examine
their specific institutional mediation and social bases. It also means
that power must be seen in conjunctural, relational terms rather than
as a fixed sum of resources which can be appropriated by one social
force to the exclusion of others. In short our third guideline is intended to redirect studies of state power away from simple instrumentalist or subjectivist views of the state to a complex investigation
of state power as a form-determined condensation of social forces in
struggle.

The fourth guideline implies a radical displacement of analytical focus from the search for guarantees that the state apparatus and its functions are necessarily capitalist in all aspects to a concern with the many and varied contingent effects of state power on accumulation in determinate conjunctures. These effects depend on a wide range of factors and cannot be reduced to a simple realisation of purported needs of capital. Indeed, since the conditions of existence of capital accumulation are neither unitary nor mutually consistent and since the course of capital accumulation is relatively open, it is imperative to specify which particular conditions contingently necessary for a given course of accumulation are being secured in what respects, over which time period, and to what extent. The very complexity and contradictoriness of these conditions of existence and the range of potentially viable paths of accumulation invalidate all attempts to suggest that the state in capitalist societies is unequivocally and universally beneficial to capital.

The guideline suggests that capital accumulation should have a dual theoretical function in an analysis of the state in capitalist societies: it is both a point of reference and a principle of explanation. We should not conflate the two nor stress one to the exclusion of the other. To treat capital accumulation solely as a principle of explanation would reduce the state to a more or less complex effect of the self-realisation of capital: to treat it solely as a point of reference would endow the state with absolute autonomy vis-à-vis the movement of capital. Instead we should examine how the particular institutional form of the state and the character of state intervention affect its ability to secure various conditions of existence of capital accumulation considered as a point of reference as well as how the nature and course of capital accumulation as form and process conditions the state apparatus and circumscribes (without fully determining) the effects of state intervention. In other words, in so far as we are dealing with the form and extent of realisation of the conditions of existence of capital accumulation, capital accumulation acts initially as a point of reference; and, in so far as we are dealing with the economic conditions of existence of the state apparatus and the economic laws delimiting the effectiveness of state intervention, capital accumulation can be considered as a complex of causal mechanisms and thus as a principle of explanation.

Such an approach permits the analysis of the dialectic between the economic and political at the same time as it allows one to establish their 'relative autonomy' in accordance with the third criterion for an adequate Marxist analysis of the state (see p. 221 above). In this context it should be noted that 'relative autonomy' is either an ab-

stract, formal concept serving merely a diacritical function in demarcating our preferred approach from simple reductionism and/or
the absolute autonomisation of different regions or else it is a concrete, descriptive concept whose content varies across conjunctures.
It cannot function as a principle of explanation in its own right but is
itself an explicandum in the same way as concepts such as 'state
power'. For, although many theorists invoke its 'relative autonomy'
to explain the alleged functionality of the state for bourgeois reproduction, such an approach merely ascribes a 'relative autonomy' to
the state in order the better to guarantee its subordination to the
imperatives of capital accumulation and bourgeois political domination. The institutional separation of the state is an important element
in its 'relative autonomy' but, far from assuring its functionality, this
separation actually problematises the capacity of the state to secure
the conditions necessary to bourgeois reproduction. The 'relative
autonomy' of actual states is the complex resultant of their form(s)
of separation from the economic region and civil society (in the sense
of the site of 'private', non-economic relations), their *sui generis*
institutional structure, their social bases of support and resistance,
and the effectiveness of their policies in relation to bourgeois reproduction (or some other point of reference). To neglect this complex
overdetermination of state power in favour of the essentialisation of
'relative autonomy' as an abstract principle of explanation is to
neglect the deeply problematic functionality of the state apparatus
and state power.

It is also important to recognise that the manner in which the
dialectic between the economic and political is analysed will vary
with the problem under discussion. The more concrete and complex
the explanendum and hence the more specific the conditions of
existence to be examined, the more we must move beyond the invocation of general laws, tendencies, and counter-tendencies and the
more detailed we must be about their mediations. However useful
the concept of the 'TRPF' or that of the 'contradiction between the
socialisation of the productive forces and the private character of the
relations of production' may be in abstract analyses of the economic
region and the role of the state, they are too indeterminate for an
adequate explanation of actual economic and political events and it
is essential to study their overdetermination in different conjunctures. Failure to consider this overdetermination in more concrete
and complex situations can easily lead to a slippage from the method
of articulation to that of subsumption and to a treatment of the state
as essentially rather than contingently capitalist in character.

Although our comments on the fourth guideline have been addressed to the role of the state in bourgeois reproduction they are also applicable to its role in the reproduction of other social relations. Thus similar considerations would obtain in an analysis of the dialectical interaction between patriarchal domination and the form and functions of the state or an examination of the state as a site of bureaucratic despotism rather than class domination. Indeed all four of the guidelines presented above can be adopted with appropriate changes in considering other points of reference in terms of their political conditions of existence and/or their role in determining the nature and effectiveness of the state. In this respect I am in full agreement with Hindess and Hirst concerning the multiplicity of possible points of reference in social analysis and hence in refusing to privilege the reproduction of the dominant mode of production as *the* point of reference. Similarly I insist on the multiplicity of possible causal mechanisms or principles of explanation and refuse to privilege economic determinations in the first, intermediate, or last instance. This is not to deny the validity of the Marxist approach to political economy nor to suggest that the ending of economic exploitation is not a primary goal of socialist political struggle. It is to argue that the Marxist approach is not a self-sufficient totalising perspective and that economic exploitation cannot be the unique point of reference in social analysis. My own approach to state theory is intended to provide the means to integrate Marxist perspectives with other points of reference and principles of explanation so that concrete, complex phenomena can be adequately theorised and explained. It is for this reason that I must reject economism and class reductionism and recognise that the weight of economic determinations and class forces in an explanens must change with the nature of the explanendum. Let us now see how this approach can be developed further in the light of the above-mentioned substantive criteria.

POLITICAL REPRESENTATION AND STATE INTERVENTION

I have argued that the state is best seen initially as an institutional ensemble and it is now time to elaborate this argument. In general terms we can say that the state is an institutional ensemble of forms of representation, internal organisation, and intervention. This implies that state forms and regime types can be distinguished in terms of the differential articulation of political representation, internal organisation, and state intervention. This approach has several advantages. It provides a means to examine the linkages among the state, economy, and civil society in terms of the form-determined mediation of demands and support as well as the state's form-determined role in maintaining political domination, capital accumulation, and private, non-economic forms of domination. This will prove particularly useful in examining the social bases of support for and resistance to the state. It also enables us to examine the effects of incongruence between forms of representation and intervention and/or their inadequate linkage within the state apparatus itself (e.g., the crisis of liberal parliamentarism accompanying the growth of state economic intervention). It emphasises the hybrid character of the state and thus points to the need to assess the hierarchy among different forms of representation and intervention and the role played by the internal organisation of the state in reproducing the pattern of domination and subordination among these forms. This will prove useful in considering problems of periodisation as well as in comparing 'normal' and 'exceptional' forms of state. It points to the areas where crises can occur in the state form: representation, internal unity, intervention, and the relations among these elements. Finally, in treating the state as an institutional ensemble in this way, we are also considering it as a 'structurally selective' system of political domination which conditions the formation of political forces and their ability to achieve specific effects through the state.

These forms can be analysed at different levels of abstraction and complexity. At the most abstract and simple level of a Marxist analysis we can consider how the institutional separation of the economic and the political implies the possibility of divorcing political representation in formal terms from questions of economic ownership at the same time as it implies the indirect and mediated character of state intervention in the circuit of capital. Some of the abstract constraints and/or opportunities this entails have already been well rehearsed in the analyses of the 'Staatsableitungdebatte' and in the work of Nicos Poulantzas. More determinate analyses must specify the particular forms of representation and intervention and consider their articulation with changing balances of social force. In this context some preliminary distinctions can be introduced which may help to order subsequent analyses without suggesting that they are exhaustive or definitive. Let us begin with some forms of representation and then consider types of economic intervention.

Without claiming that they include all possible forms of representation it is nonetheless useful to distinguish among five systems relevant to a discussion of state intervention. *Clientilism* may be characterised as a form of representation based on the exchange of political support in return for the allocation of politically-mediated resources and involving a hierarchical relationship between dependent client(s) and superordinate patron(s). *Corporatism* involves political representation on the basis of function within the division of labour and is characterised by the formal equivalence of 'corporations' whose members perform substantively different functions. *Parliamentarism* may be defined as a form of representation based on the indirect participation of individual 'citizens' in policy-making through their exercise of voting and accompanying rights in relation to an elected legislature and/or political executive; it is associated with formal equality among individual 'citizens' and the formal freedoms necessary for its operation provide the basis for the development of pluralism as well as party organisation. *Pluralism* is a form of representation based on institutionalised channels of access to the state apparatuses for political forces representing interests and/or causes rooted in civil society (as opposed to function in the division of labour) and recognised as legitimate by relevant branches of the state. *Raison d'état* is a limit case of intervention without formal channels of representation but it is not incompatible with informal channels of representation nor with attempts to legitimate such intervention in terms of the national or public interest (cf. the remarks in Jessop, 1979, pp. 193–201; and *idem*, 1980b, pp. 59–63).

These forms have definite (but not fully determinate) effects on the accessibility of the state to different political forces and also influence the way in which political forces themselves are constituted. Thus, whereas parliamentarism encourages the political fragmentation of economic categories and promotes the interpellation of those who belong to economic classes as individual citizens (cf. Poulantzas on the 'isolation effect'), corporatism encourages the organisation of economic classes into functionally heterogeneous, interdependent, and formally equivalent groupings for whom collaboration and concertation are mutually advantageous and discourages their organisation as polarised, antagonistic, mutually contradictory classes (cf. 'surface form' theorists on 'revenue categories'). Again, whereas clientilism and pluralism promote the particularistic reproduction of specific 'economic-corporate' and 'civil-corporate' interests and thereby help to sustain a pattern of non-hegemonic, 'transformist' politics, parliamentarism provides a medium through which political parties can seek to mobilise political support behind an appropriate hegemonic project and thereby contribute to the consolidation of hegemony. A final example of the political effects of different forms of representation can be found in the way in which the growth of corporatism displaces the dominant field of representation to the advantage of vested economic interests at the expense of forces seeking representation through electoral channels. It is difficult to be more precise about the implications of forms of representation since they also depend on the forces in contention and the links between representation and intervention.

In this context it is important to stress that an adequate account of the state must go beyond the forms of representation and intervention to include the internal organisation of the state apparatus itself. For otherwise the state will appear simply as a 'black box' inside which external demands and support are translated into specific policies that are then directed outwards. This 'black box' view is misleading not only because representation occurs within all parts of the state system but also because intervention can be directed inwards as well as outwards. At the same time it must be emphasised that the state is not exhausted by the forms of representation and intervention that link it to the economy and civil society: it also involves *sui generis* forms of organisation concerned with the reproduction of the state apparatus itself as a system of political domination. This requires not only the mobilisation of resources for the continued operation of the state (such as finance, personnel, means of administration) but also the formal and substantive coordination of its different branches and activities. The unity of the state apparatus – both as an institutional ensemble and as an organ of class domination – is a continuing problem.

The formal unity of the state as an institutional ensemble is typically related to the growth of bureaucratisation. This involves not only the formation of a special category of career officials separated from ownership of the means of administration but also their subordination to formal rules of legal and financial accountability within a hierarchical chain of command linking different levels and branches of the state. However this formal unity depends in turn on the unity of the political executive at the top of the chain of command and can also be circumscribed or undermined through the resistance or non-compliance of officials at different levels or branches of the bureaucratic system. Moreover, although bureaucratic forms are appropriate to the execution of general laws or policies in accordance with the rule of law, they are less suited to *ad hoc,* discretionary forms of intervention (see below). In this sense the transition from liberal through simple monopoly to state monopoly capitalism exacerbates the contradiction between the bureaucratic preconditions for the formal unity of the state system and the substantive efficacy of policies oriented to accumulation. This can be seen in the expansion of quasi-non-governmental organisations (or 'quangos') charged with substantive support and facilitation of economic and social activities and/or with imperative or concertative direction of these activities and given much greater freedom of manoeuvre than the ministries and departments which remain formally within the bureaucratic chain of command. This expansion poses major problems even in defining the formal boundaries of the state as an institutional ensemble (on the British case, for example, see Hood *et al.*, 1978) and also threatens the substantive unity of the state through its potential for clientilistic degeneration and the pursuit of particular 'economic-corporate' demands. This suggests the need for the bureaucratic mechanism to be complemented through an overarching political executive and/or cross-cutting networks that can coordinate the activities of different parts of the state. But the substantive unity of the political executive and/or networks of this kind depends in turn on their commitment to a 'hegemonic project' able to harmonise particular interests with a specific set of 'national-popular' goals (see below).

In this context it is important to note how the articulation of the various branches and departments of the state system (including bodies such as 'quangos') contributes to the structural determination of class hegemony. For, in addition to the general periodisation of state forms and its implications for the long-term hegemony of competitive, monopoly, or state monopoly fractions, it is also necessary to consider how the relative dominance of particular departments or ministries can underwrite the hegemony of a given class fraction. Thus the dominant role of the Treasury-Bank of England nexus in Britain is an important element in the structural determination of the hegemony of banking capital; and that of the Ministry of International Trade and Industry plays a similar role on behalf of industrial capital in Japan. This structural dominance needs to be combined with the successful propagation of an 'hegemonic project' for the structurally privileged fraction to become truly hegemonic but, in the absence of this, state structures can nonetheless undermine the pursuit of a project favourable to another class or class fraction. This can be seen in Labour's failure to pursue its project of industrial modernisation and economic planning during its 1964–70 administration. For, although the incoming Labour government established a new planning ministry favourable to industrial capital in the Department of Economic Affairs and undertook other initiatives to promote industrial reorganisation, the Treasury and Bank of England remained dominant and used their fiscal, expenditure, and monetary powers to turn the economic crisis to the advantage of banking capital (for a more detailed account, including reference to other causal factors, see Jessop, 1980a, pp. 38–47 and *passim*). In turn this implies that a long-term shift in hegemony requires not only a new 'hegemonic project' but also the reorganisation of the state system as a whole.

The internal structure of the state is also crucial in considering 'normal' and 'exceptional' regimes. For, whereas normal states can be categorised in terms of the relative dominance of different channels of democratic representation (clientilist, corporatist, parliamentary, and pluralist), exceptional states can be distinguished in terms of the relative dominance of different parts of the state system (such as the military, bureaucracy, political police, fascist party, and so forth). This is not to suggest that one can ignore the relative dominance of different parts of the apparatus of administration and intervention in normal states nor to suggest that exceptional states function without any channels of representation. It is to emphasise that normal and exceptional states can only be differentiated through a rigorous analysis of their institutional structure as well as their social bases.

The third aspect of institutional structure to be considered here is the nature of state intervention. For, just as there are different forms of representation, there are also different types of intervention. In the field of political economy we can distinguish among the following basic forms. In the case of *formal facilitation* the state maintains the general external conditions of capitalist production: these include a formally rational monetary system, a formally rational legal system, and a formally rational system of administration. To perform this facilitative role alone implies that capitalist production itself operates in a self-expanding, self-equilibrating manner through the profit-and-loss system resulting from laissez-faire and free competition. To the extent that this is not the case, some other form(s) of intervention will be required. In the case of *substantive facilitation* the state reproduces certain general conditions of production within capitalism, i.e., conditions whose provision is essential for the majority of individual capitals to continue production. The most general condition of this kind is labour-power since it is not produced in the enterprise itself but is bought into the labour process as a simple, non-capitalist commodity in exchange for wages (cf. Aumeeruddy *et al.*, 1978, and de Brunhoff, 1976). In addition it may prove necessary for the state to supply means of production which have a general significance for capital, e.g., infrastructure, energy supplies, transport, basic research and development, economic statistics. In the case of *formal support* the state alters the general external conditions of production in a particularistic manner and/or establishes external conditions favourable to particular capitals. This can be accomplished through the introduction of substantively rational criteria into the legal framework, through modifications in the financial costs of specific economic activities, and through particularistic administrative measures. It should be noted that the state intervenes indirectly in offering formal support, i.e., through the mediation of law, money, and administrative measures; and that it is left to market forces to determine whether these changes are exploited by economic agents who remain formally free and autonomous. Among these measures could be included changes in competition policy, company law, investment allowances, regional employment premia, and the conditions of access to corporatist decision-making bodies. In contrast *substantive support* involves the direct allocation of particular conditions of production to particular economic agents rather than leaving it to the autonomous choice of market forces which agents, if any, benefit from state action. Measures of this kind could include licences, monopolies, state credit, state sponsorship, and so forth. Although the core activities in these types of support are distinct, there is some ambiguity at the margins.

Finally, in the case of *direction,* the state overrides the formal freedom of economic agents and directs that they either act or refrain from acting in particular ways. Here the state no longer relies merely on facilitating or supporting market forces but intervenes to support, counteract, or modify them through restrictions on the formal autonomy and freedom of these agents. It should be noted that such restrictions on formal autonomy may promote the substantive rationality of capitalism through recognition of the substantive interdependence among economic agents and promotion of their collective interest at the cost of their particular interests. In some cases direction may be associated with the socialisation of the relations of production to match the socialisation of productive forces and thus promote rather than undermine accumulation. It should also be noted that 'direction' need not be secured through 'imperative coordination' from above: it can also be mediated through the operation of corporatist forms of concertation in which capital and/ or labour cooperate with each other and with branches of the state apparatus. (For similar typologies of intervention, see Offe, 1975b, and Winkler, 1977.)

These types of intervention can now be linked to three points of reference: the circuit of capital, periodisation, and forms of political representation. But it is first necessary to correct any impression that this typology implies the necessary functionality of the state. For it is intended only to provide criteria with which to assess the manner and extent to which particular states maintain, restore, or undermine the preconditions of capital accumulation. In so far as a given state fails to secure the general external conditions of production, to provide basic general conditions of production, to support the activities of particular capitals in key sectors, and to impose or concert the degree of direction necessary at a specific stage of socialisation, then economic crises can be anticipated. It will then be subject to various pressures to respond to such crises – pressures which may involve demands for more government intervention, new kinds of intervention, or even disengagement and resort to private, market-generated solutions. In this context it is important to recall the argument advanced by Joachim Hirsch that the state responds to the political repercussions of crisis and not to the economic crisis (or crises) as such. It is for this reason that an adequate account of state intervention must consider state power as a form-determined condensation of the balance of forces in struggle. In any event it is vital to reject any attempt to establish the functionality of the state on behalf of capital on *a priori,* essentialist grounds. The extent to which a state actually succeeds in maintaining, restoring, or strengthening the various conditions necessary for accumulation must always be established in each conjuncture.

In this context the most appropriate course of theoretical analysis is to link the effects of state intervention to the circuit of capital. This provides the theoretical means to discuss both the effectivity and preconditions of capital accumulation at different levels of abstraction and also permits the analysis to be modified to take account of various forms of this circuit and different forms of state integration into it. Moreover, because the concept of the circuit of capital also reveals the complex relations between production, distribution, and exchange, it provides a superior theoretical means to analyse crises and their resolution. Finally it provides the means to analyse the articulation of the CMP with other modes of production and/or forms of private and/or social labour through their location in the circuit of capital as a whole.

In its most simple and abstract form the circuit can be examined in terms of the transformation of money capital into commodities and thence into money revenue embodying surplus-value (or, in the conventional Marxist notation, M-C'-M') and the general external conditions of existence of this transformation. It can then be considered in more concrete and complex terms to take account of the specificity of the commodity of labour-power, the different fractions of capital (banking, industrial, commercial, merchant), the different forms of the circuit (laissez-faire, simple monopoly, state monopoly), the forms of its internationalisation, its various tendencies and counter-tendencies, the withdrawal of revenue from the circuit in the form of taxation, and so forth. The more specific the definition of the circuit and hence the more specific its articulation with the state, the more determinate become the explanations of events. Thus, although one can analyse the linkages between the circuit M-C'-M' and the 'present' state considered as a rational abstraction, the analysis will necessarily be highly indeterminate. One can specify certain conditions of existence of M-C'-M' that cannot be secured through the circuit itself (e.g., legal forms, legal tender, the reproduction of labour power, etc.) but it does not follow that all these can and/or must be secured through political action undertaken through a state apparatus. As the analysis becomes more concrete and complex the role of the state can be considered not only from the viewpoint of formal and/or substantive facilitation but also in terms of particular measures in the area of formal and substantive support for particular capitals (including variable capital or wage-labour) and the sphere of substantive direction. This permits a more detailed account of the interaction between forms of state intervention and the overall circuit of capital.

Thus the circuit of state monopoly capital requires, inter alia, a flexible taxation system and a market in state credit as preconditions of Keynesian techniques of demand management oriented to the realisation of surplus-value and/or of post-Keynesian attempts to make state credit function directly as capital. But such intervention is influenced in turn by the circuit itself. The market in state credit depends on the activities of autonomous financial institutions as well as on the state and they may calculate their opportunities for profit in ways contrary to the requirements of effective state intervention. Keynesian techniques are also limited because they affect the circuit of capital only via the sphere of circulation (through their impact on economic agents as holders of money which they remain free to use as revenue and/or as capital) and because these techniques cannot satisfactorily modify the global circuit of capital into which such economic agents are linked. If the state tries to circumvent these limits by using state credit directly as capital it will encounter problems of valorisation as well as realisation and will also confront difficulties in reconciling its role as a 'real individual capitalist' with its role as an 'ideal collective capitalist'. Conversely, if the state attempts to avoid these problems through the allocation of state credit to particular private capitals in the form of formal and/or substantive support, it becomes dependent once again on economic agents outside its direct control. In short, although the circuit of state monopoly capital requires specific forms of political intervention, the institutional separation of the state casts doubt on its functionality.

After this brief illustration of the connections between the circuit of capital and state intervention we can now consider the question of periodisation in more general terms. In this context the work of Fine and Harris provides an important point of reference. In abstract, simple terms it is apparent that the period of *laissez-faire* capitalism is tied to formal facilitation: the state secures the formal framework of capital accumulation and leaves the substantive development of the economy to the operation of market forces. This is not inconsistent with the operation of concertation at the micro (or plant) and meso (or industrial) levels to the extent that this is the private concern of formally autonomous economic agents. Indeed, even where the state itself adopts a *laissez-faire* approach to economic development in the simple monopoly as well as liberal stages of the CMP, private concertation becomes a significant vehicle of economic direction at the meso- as well as micro-level. This is evident in the growth of cartels, trusts, syndicates, etc., organised on vertical and/or horizontal lines; in the development of concertational links between the banks and industry not only in investment banking but also in industrial restructuring; and in the rise of bilateral consultation between employers' associations and trade unions. Moreover, with the increasing socialisation of the forces of production, the growing capital-intensity of production and the growing importance of technological innovation in improving labour productivity, the lengthening turnover time of certain key branches of production, and the emergence of cyclical crises associated with dislocations in the private credit system and the relative exhaustion of major technological revolutions, the stage of simple monopoly capitalism also witnesses the growth of substantive facilitation as well as formal and/or substantive support for capital accumulation. Under state monopoly capitalism there is a further shift in the forms of state intervention with growing importance attached to the role of direction mediated through concertation and/or imposed from above. In particular it is no longer always in the power of individual capitals acting alone or in concert at the meso-level to mobilise the resources necessary to ensure capital accumulation and it is necessary for the state to supplement the activities of 'real collective capitalists' at the meso-level with macro-level facilitation, support, and direction. It is in this context that we must situate not only the growing importance of nationalisation, state credit, and taxation but also the development of new forms of representation through which state direction of the economy is mediated.

Indeed it should be emphasised that changing forms of articulation between the circuit of capital and state intervention should ideally be accompanied by changes in forms of representation. For the effectivity of different forms of intervention depends not only on the technical adequacy of the available policy instruments but also on their articulation with strategies which can secure the support and/or minimise the resistance of those affected. The laws of motion of capitalism are not natural and inevitable: they depend for their realisation on the balance of forces in the complex relation between capital and labour. It follows that a reorganisation of this balance may become a prerequisite of restoring the conditions necessary for the creation and appropriation of surplus-value on an expanding scale. Changes in the articulation of different state apparatuses, in the forms of political representation, in the character of state intervention, and in political strategies and alliances could prove important in this respect. In turn this suggests that crises of accumulation can occur through the structural dislocation of forms of intervention and representation as well as through adverse changes in the balance of forces where these forms are at least formally complementary. The failure to develop corporatist forms to facilitate macro-level concertation of state direction of economic and social reproduction in state monopoly capitalism is merely one example of this (see Jessop, 1980a, pp. 38–54, 82). More generally we should emphasise that structural crises in the state and/or crises in the balance of political forces can precipitate or aggravate economic crises and reject any suggestion that economic crises have purely economic roots and are themselves the unilateral cause of state and political crises.

In this context we can explore the *formal* complementarity between intervention and representation. Liberal capitalism is characterised by a clear-cut institutional differentiation between the economic and political spheres so that the economy operates within the limits of market rationality and the state ideally adopts a *laissez-faire* stance apart from its role in formal facilitation. A constitutional *Rechtsstaat* or at most a liberal parliamentary regime would be appropriate here. This would entail the division of representation between political conflict over the formal framework of economic activities (*Ordnungspolitik*) and economic bargaining in markets and the work-place concerning the terms of exchange and the conditions of work. Such a system permits stable, calculable administration according to the rule of law while changes occur in the balance of political forces and, through its articulation with an elected parliament, provides the means to change the formal framework of economic activities and to enact general legislative measures to control the worst effects of market rationality. The development of private meso-level concertation and the growth of formal and substantive state support under simple monopoly capitalism involve breaks with free competition in the economic region and with the liberal rule of law in the political region. For this reason it is best associated with the supplementation of liberal parliamentarism with corporatist forms of representation. The latter are particularly crucial when intervention concerns issues that cannot be readily effected without the cooperation of capital and/or labour; and/or that cannot be readily accomplished through rational-legal administrative means. For corporatism provides the channel through which capital and/or labour can be directly involved in the formulation of economic policies rather than relying on the haphazard territorial aggregation of individual citizens' votes and the vagaries of party competition; and also provides the means through which they can be involved in the implementation of policies which are increasingly *ad hoc* and discriminatory in character.

The emergence of state monopoly capitalism intensifies the need for the reorganisation of the forms of economic and political representation to match the changing forms of articulation between the two regions. These changes can be seen in a number of areas: the significant role of state credit, taxation, and nationalisation; the expansion of the state's directive functions in all areas to match the growing substantive interdependence of formally autonomous enterprises, branches, and national economies; the growing importance of the economic role of the state as compared with its strictly political functions in securing law and order and defending its territorial integrity; and the relative decline of rational-legal administration according to the rule of law in favour of *ad hoc*, selective, and discriminatory action oriented to specific economic objectives. All these changes reinforce the advantages of a system of political representation based on function in the division of labour rather than one mediated through electoral competition and inter-party conflicts. It is worth recalling here that economic intervention is not just technical in character but also requires suitable political support. Corporatism can function in both respects. For it organises classes into functionally heterogeneous, formally equivalent communities represented through 'corporations' and requires their compromise and cooperation as a condition of effective intervention. In turn this means that the corporations must accept the legitimacy of the existing economic order and confine themselves to demands compatible with its expansion. However, just as parliamentarism is not unequivocally beneficial to capital accumulation and bourgeois political domination, corporatism also poses problems in so far as it introduces class conflict into the heart of the state apparatus and cannot guarantee that unions will not resort to industrial action to influence or circumvent corporatist policies nor that particular capitals will not seek a competitive advantage through selective compliance with such policies and/or through major economic activities abroad to escape corporatist control. Thus, although macro-level concertation embracing capital, labour, and the state and its coordination with meso- and micro-level concertation becomes desirable with state monopoly capitalism, even its full introduction (which encounters major obstacles everywhere) would involve crucial problems both in itself and in reconciling its operation with that of parliamentary (and other) forms of political representation.

Such problems are not limited to state monopoly capitalism. For all state systems are 'hybrid' in form and face problems in harmonising their different constituent elements. In part this 'hybridity' reflects the combination of different forms of the circuit of capital (liberal, simple monopoly, state monopoly) and their linkage with non-capitalist economic forms but it is also influenced through the existence of private, non-economic relations requiring political mediation as well as through the 'economic-corporate' activities of political categories within the state. In all cases it should be emphasised that the formal correspondence among economic and political forms, if any, is the result of specific social practices: it is not guaranteed through economic determination in the first, intermediate, or final instance. Nonetheless the degree of correspondence or dislocation does have definite effects on economic reproduction and the role of the state apparatus. Thus we must consider how different forms of representation and intervention are articulated and how different modes of articulation affect the operation of the state.

By way of illustration we can return to the relations of corporatism and parliamentarism under state monopoly capitalism. Both forms involve *sui generis* problems. Thus liberal parliamentarism poses difficulties in the electoral mediation of hegemony, the unification of a power bloc, the possible anti-bourgeois domination of parliament, the potential failure of governmental control over the administrative apparatuses, the threat to a stable *Ordnungspolitik* posed by adversary politics and the electoral cycle, the technical incompetence of politicians in economic programming, and so forth. Corporatism also poses problems. These include securing effective coordination across micro-, meso- and macro-level concertation, limiting the extent to which class conflict and competition undermine concerted action, avoiding the clientilist degeneration of corporatist policy-making and implementation, preventing the displacement of class conflict from union-employer relations to the relations between union members and incorporated union leaders, circumventing the effects of representational crises on corporatist self-administration, coping with the unincorporated sectors, and so forth. In addition there are significant problems facing the successful combination of these disparate forms. Here we can mention their contrasting and potentially contradictory bases of representation and support (citizenship and its associated rights of political participation vs. function in the division of labour), principles of decision-making (simple majority or even simple plurality vs. unanimity or perhaps concurrent majority), principles of legitimation (parliamentary sovereignty tied to an electoral mandate vs. economic sovereignty coupled with industrial self-government), criteria of substantive rationality (social cohesion and territorial integrity vs. economic performance in an international economy), time-span of decision-making (electoral cycle vs. long-term economic programming), and so forth. Such problems would be further complicated through the existence of other forms of representation (e.g., clientilism, pluralism) and the need to harmonise economic and non-economic interventions. But it should be emphasised that the extent to which a 'hybrid' state of this kind can successfully create, maintain, or restore the conditions for capital accumulation depends not only on these institutional factors but also on the balance of forces represented through such forms and on the economic constraints confronting the state.

SOCIAL BASES AND RESISTANCES

So far I have concentrated on rather abstract issues concerning the institutional mediation of representation and intervention and have only hinted at a second aspect — relations of force or the balance of power. This can be considered from two closely related aspects: how is support mobilised behind particular policies, programmes, and hegemonic projects and how is resistance organised and/or overcome in pursuing such policies, programmes, and projects? In both cases it should be recalled that the various social forces on the political scene are not pre-given and unchanging. For they are constituted in part through the forms of representation and intervention and are themselves objects of political transformation. Let us consider this in more detail before discussing the social bases of the state and the nature of resistance.

It is a commonplace nowadays in Marxist theory that class determination (i.e., location in the relations of production) entails little for class position (i.e., stance adopted in class struggle). This suggests that relations of production are not the objective basis for class formation in the sense of constituting singular and mutually exclusive 'classes-in-themselves' which necessarily develop sooner or later into 'classes-for-themselves'. Instead we must recognise that the specific interpretations of these relations offered in various class schemata and ideologies (including denials that classes exist or that, if they exist, they involve irreconcilable antagonisms) are integral but independent elements in the formation of class forces. This is not to argue that the relations of production have no impact on class formation and merely serve as a point of reference in the constitution of class forces. For they also involve differential patterns of association and interaction and impose definite limits on the success of particular class projects, strategies, and tactics. But they are typically compatible with various configurations of class forces and it is important to recognise how class formation is influenced by *sui generis* practices concerned with the organisation and reorganisation of these forces (cf. Przeworski, 1977, pp. 367ff).

Once we concede that there are many different sites of struggle and that class forces must be constituted through specific practices, there seems little point in adopting a class reductionist view in political analysis. Since class forces in the economic, political, and ideological spheres may not coincide with their class determination through the relations of production, it is essential to specify how particular class forces are interpellated and organised. This applies as much to an open antagonism between polarised, class-conscious proletarian and bourgeois forces as it does to muted conflicts or co-operation among a plurality of 'class-oblivious' forces. This suggests that we must operate with two distinct but related notions of 'class forces' and 'class struggle'. At the level of 'class position' we can legitimately define 'class forces' as forces interpellated and organised as such ('classes-for-themselves') and differentiate them from 'non-class forces' interpellated and organised in non-class terms; at the level of 'structural determination' we can equally legitimately define 'class forces' as forces whose actions, whether or not class-conscious in character, have pertinent effects on class relations ('class-relevant forces'). Again, whereas 'class struggle' can legitimately be restricted at the level of 'class position' to cases of open war and/or war of position between 'classes-for-themselves' to the exclusion of relations among 'class-oblivious' forces, this does not rule out another sense of class struggle in terms of the differential impact of 'class-relevant' forces on the reproduction of class domination. In making these proposals we are clearly rejecting the idea that 'class struggle' can be unproblematic on either level and arguing instead that 'class forces' and 'class struggle' must first be explained before they can be used to account for specific situations, actions, and events.

The indeterminacy of class forces in relation to class location provides the space for the practices involved in securing hegemony. The latter involves the interpellation and organisation of different 'class-relevant' forces under the political, intellectual, and moral leadership of a given class (fraction) or, more precisely, its political, intellectual, and moral spokesmen. In this sense one can say that the exercise of hegemony assigns a 'class-relevance' to non-class forces and that acceptance of an 'hegemonic project' facilitates the relative unity of diverse social forces within a social formation. The key to the exercise of such leadership is the development of a specific 'hegemonic project' which can resolve the abstract problem of conflicts between particular interests and the general interest. This involves the mobilisation of support behind a concrete, national-popular programme of action which asserts a general interest in the pursuit of objectives that explicitly or implicitly advance the long-term interests of the hegemonic class (fraction) and which privileges particular 'economic-corporate' interests compatible with this programme whilst derogating the pursuit of other particular interests that are inconsistent with it. Normally hegemony also involves the sacrifice of certain short-term interests of the hegemonic class (fraction) and a flow of material concessions to other class and fractional forces. It is therefore conditioned and limited by the capital accumulation process. These 'hegemonic projects' need to be adapted to the stage of capitalism (liberal, simple monopoly, state monopoly), to the international context facing particular national capitals, to the specific balance of forces at home, and to the margin of manoeuvre entailed in the productive potential of the economy. Among such projects we may include 'social imperialism' (the extension of the international dominance of a national capital in such a way as to secure significant economic, political, and ideological benefits for subordinate groups), 'Keynesian-welfare statism' (aimed at overcoming stagnationist tendencies through macro-level demand management which also secures full employment and/or meets popular aspirations for social welfare) and, most recently, 'social democratic corporatism' (aimed at overcoming stagflationary tendencies through an active and concerted *Strukturpolitik* which also grants the demands of subordinate groups for participation and offers the prospects of renewed economic expansion). In all these cases the elaboration of 'hegemonic projects' requires specific forms of representation to allow the articulation of interests in an 'unstable equilibrium of compromise' among different social forces as well as specific forms of intervention suitable for creating the various economic, political, and ideological conditions in which a project can be realised.

In this context it is useful to distinguish between 'one nation' and 'two nations' projects. Thus 'one nation' strategies aim at an expansive hegemony in which the support of the entire population is mobilised through material concessions and symbolic rewards (as in 'social imperialism' or the 'Keynesian-welfare state' projects). In contrast 'two nations' strategies aim at a more limited hegemony concerned to mobilise the support of strategically significant sectors of the population and to pass the costs of the project to other sectors (as in fascism and monetarism). During periods of economic crisis and limited scope for material concessions, the prospects for a 'one nation' strategy are restricted (unless it involves an equitable sharing of sacrifice) and 'two nations' strategies are more likely to be pursued. Where the balance of forces permits, moreover, such strategies may also be pursued during periods of expansion. In both cases it should be noted that 'two nations' projects require containment and even repression of the 'other nation' at the same time as they involve selective access and concessions for the more 'favoured nation'. This is associated with attempts to reorganise the bases of political support to reflect a vertical, antagonistic cleavage between the 'productive' and the 'parasitic' in economic terms and/or the 'loyal' and the 'disloyal' in political terms and/or the 'civilised' and the 'uncivilised' in terms of civil society (e.g., the discourses of Thatcherism, Stalinism, and apartheid respectively). In short, whereas a 'one nation' strategy involves a pluralistic discourse of difference addressed to groups performing diverse economic functions, expressing different political views, and displaying various life-styles, a 'two nations' strategy is underpinned by a dichotomous discourse of antagonism (cf. Laclau, 1980a). Such contrasting interpellative strategies must nonetheless be coupled with appropriate forms of organisation, representation, and intervention if they are to provide an adequate social base for exercising state power.

In discussing these strategies attention must be paid not only to political forces rooted in the economy and civil society but also to the role of forces grounded in the state apparatus itself. An 'hegemonic project' plays a crucial role in limiting conflicts within and among the various branches of the state apparatus and providing an ideological and material base for their relative unity and cohesion in reproducing the system of political domination. The pervasive problem of articulating certain 'particular interests' to a 'general interest' favourable to capital and discouraging the assertion of other 'particular interests' occurs within the state apparatus as well as in the economic region and civil society and it affects not only the 'representation' of economic and civilian interests inside the state but also the *sui generis* interests of political categories such as bureaucrats, the police, deputies, and judges. Indeed the problem of avoiding a merely particularistic reproduction of competing and contradictory 'economic-corporate' interests and securing some coordination and cohesion of the state apparatus becomes more pressing with the expansion of that apparatus and the extension of its activities beyond formal facilitation to include a wide range of supportive and directive activities. Thus the role of political categories in supporting or resisting the implementation of an 'hegemonic project' on their own behalf and/or in the name of other social forces grows in importance with the expansion of the state apparatus and state intervention. It is in this context that Poulantzas's discussion of the 'state party' should be located and related to the role of other forces involved in the organisation of hegemony.

The organisation of hegemony involves not only the mobilisation of support through the coupling of particular interests to the general interest postulated in a given 'hegemonic project' but also requires the management of resistances which counterpose particular interests to the general interest and/or propose an alternative 'hegemonic project'. The (neo-)Gramscian formula of 'hegemony armoured by coercion' stresses this aspect but is misleading in so far as it implies that resistance is only handled through repression. Thus, in addition to noting that a pluralistic discourse of difference provides some legitimacy for certain forms of resistance and that the weight of various particular interests is continually re-negotiated in the 'unstable equilibrium of compromise' that underpins hegemony, we should also consider how the reorganisation of forms of representation and intervention can modify the effectiveness of resistance through its repercussions on the constitution of political forces and the re-routing of state intervention. For example it might be possible to weaken the resistance of a particularistic, fragmented union move-ment to Keynesian forms of economic management through its in-volvement in corporatist forms of macro-level concertation (requiring greater cohesion and centralisation of the union movement) or through a more laissez-faire, facilitative state role in economic management with the result that the need for union cooperation is attenuated in favour of greater reliance on market disciplines and strong managerial control. This is not to suggest that coercion is un-important in handling resistance (especially where the latter takes violent forms itself) but it is to insist that one considers how repres-sive and non-repressive responses are articulated.

This implies that an adequate account of the state requires atten-tion not only to its forms of representation and intervention but also to its characteristic social bases of support and resistance. Two points deserve special emphasis here. Once we abandon class reductionism and concede the diversity of social forces, it is essential to specify the actual constellation of forces mobilised in support for and/or resist-ance to particular 'hegemonic projects' rather than endow them with a necessary class belonging. This is especially important when con-sidering 'exceptional' regimes which suppress certain forms of class organisation but cannot thereby eliminate the need for support from strategically significant economic forces. For, whilst an 'exceptional' regime may try to annihilate certain organisational forms of class resistance (such as unions, parties, and press), it cannot afford to physically annihilate productive labour-power. This means that 'exceptional' regimes must seek to consolidate working-class support through ideological, integrative, and concessive 'carrots' as well as through exemplary punishment, organisational suppression, and the suspension or reorganisation of those channels of representation most accessible to dissident forces. Secondly, although institutional-ised forms of political representation (such as clientelism, parliamen-tarism, corporatism, and pluralism) play a major role in securing and reorganising the social bases of support for 'normal' state forms, this should not lead to neglect of other means of representation and other channels (such as Gramsci's 'force, fraud, and corruption') useful for the consolidation of support. Conversely, although 'excep-

tional' state forms typically suspend or nullify the effective operation of formal democratic institutions and rely on more restricted
forms of representation and/or on the 'black parliamentarism' of
informal representation through branches of the state apparatus, it is
still necessary to consider how formally undemocratic institutions
and informal channels serve to consolidate support and disorganise
resistance rather than assume that they have no effects. It is only
through an analysis of the complex articulation of forms of representation and intervention and the various social forces active on
the political scene that we can understand the complex nature and
dynamics of political domination.

OFFICIALDOM vs. PEOPLE

Hitherto I have concentrated on the state apparatus as a system of
political class domination and have considered state power largely as
a form-determined condensation of the balance of class forces. But I
have also hinted that the state can be examined in relation to other
axes of determination and have noted that the class aspects of the
state will be overdetermined by various kinds of non-class relations.
The latter comprise private, non-economic relations grounded in civil
society and 'public' relations among political categories. In this
section we shall expand these hints and allusions through a brief
sketch of the state as a site of 'officialdom-people' relations and its
implications for class hegemony and popular-democratic struggle.

To establish the theoretical space for an analysis of this kind we
must first consider the nature of social classes and the state in more
detail. In opposition to the view that classes can only be defined in
terms of the totality of economic, political, and ideological relations
in a pure mode of production or even a complex social formation, we
argue that classes must be defined at the level of economic relations
and that 'civilian' and 'public' relations are relevant only in so far as
they serve as conditions of existence of economic reproduction and/
or are themselves affected by economic relations. Thus the relations
among political categories are not *per se* class relations but they may
well be class-relevant relations and/or be overdetermined by class
relations. Indeed, just as the institutional separation of the economic
and political regions implies the relative autonomy of state apparatuses and state power from economic apparatuses and economic
power, it also implies the relative autonomy of relations among
political categories from relations among economic classes. There is
certainly no obvious or immediate isomorphism or coincidence

between class relations and relations among political categories: thus the state intervenes against particular capitals and individual members of the dominant economic class as well as against members of subordinate classes and state functionaries themselves do not necessarily belong to the dominant economic class. This means that the precise articulation between class and political relations will depend on the overall structure of the social formation and the prevailing balance of forces in the exercise of state power.

In this context it is essential to examine the internal organisations of the state apparatus (e.g., bureaucracy, administrative law, financial controls), the complex relations between the state and the forces liable to state intervention, and the complex relations between the state and those non-functionaries involved in policy-making and/or implementation. If we focus on the relations among political categories it is possible to establish a 'people-officialdom' axis of determination parallel to the class axis emphasised so far in our analyses. In these terms we can say that 'bureaucratic despotism' exists where state functionaries are dominant within the 'people-officialdom' relation and that 'democratic government' exists where the targets of state intervention comprise the dominant force in 'people-officialdom' relations. In both cases dominance should be understood in the sense of a form-determined condensation of political forces and not merely as a relation among individual wills. Thus a 'pure theory' of democracy should focus on the forms of representation and accountability and on the organisation and interpellation of the political forces whose relations are mediated through these forms. It should also be noted that between the extremes of 'bureaucratic despotism' and 'democratic government' will be a series of intermediate cases ranging from the dominance of one branch or fraction of the state apparatus (e.g., military, bureaucracy, political police) to the dominance of one sector or fraction of the 'people' (e.g., whites, men, those meeting restricted suffrage qualifications). Finally it will be necessary to introduce the overdetermination of such relations through class relations and trace its implications. Adopting such a procedure reveals a major ambiguity in the conceptual couplet of 'normal' and 'exceptional' regimes. For orthodox Marxist analyses have ignored the possibility that a 'normal' state could be characterised by the dominance of a unified, autonomous 'people' rather than one unified heteronomously under the hegemony of a specific class (fraction) and have only occasionally recognised how the enhanced relative independence of the 'exceptional state' permits its degeneration from 'class dictatorship' to 'bureaucratic despotism'. In other words, to the extent that Marxist theories have been class reductionist in approach, they have failed to provide an adequate account of democratic and non-democratic regimes. Let us see how this defect might be remedied.

Whilst class relations are determined in the first instance by the relations of production in the economic region, relations among political categories depend directly on the form and operation of the state. In this context the 'people' comprise those agents who are subject to state intervention and 'officialdom' comprises the agents of intervention. The exact composition of the 'people' will depend on the form and range of state intervention (since it is this that establishes the pertinence of categories such as taxpayer, criminal, citizen, conscript, licensee, pupil, pensioner, and supplementary benefit claimant); and it would be quite wrong to conclude that the 'people' is limited to individual agents to the exclusion of collective agents — let alone to these individual agents solely in their capacity as electors. This poses the problem of the relation among different sites of 'popular' struggle and thus of the relative unity of the 'people' as a political force. It is this heterogeneity and pluralisation of the 'people' that Poulantzas identified as the juridico-political 'isolation effect' and to which he attributed a key role in opening the space for the politics of hegemony. It must also be stressed that the unity of 'officialdom' can no more be taken for granted than that of the state apparatus and that different public agencies and agents can respond in contrasting ways to 'popular' demands and interests as well as to various class demands and interests. Indeed, although the institutional separation of the state from the economic region and civil society is a precondition of various 'popular' struggles, the incidence and extent of such struggles also depends upon the precise interpellation of the respective public duties of officialdom and the people. In this sense 'popular-democratic' struggle should extend beyond questions of the forms of representation and accountability and the organisation and unification of various 'popular' forces to include the definition and dissemination of shared standards of official conduct and civic duties. In the absence of such standards there is an evident danger of replacing 'bureaucratic despotism' with 'authoritarian populism' rather than 'popular-democratic' government.

'Popular-democratic' struggle can therefore be said to cover three areas of political action. Firstly it involves questions of the formal scope and institutional mechanisms of representation and accountability and the formal definition of those entitled to participate in the democratic process. In this area there is considerable room for particular 'popular-democratic' struggles in capitalist societies but there are also significant structural obstacles to a general (albeit still formal) democratisation. For the institutional separation of the state from the economic region and civil society ensures that certain key areas remain beyond the scope of formal democratic political control; and, inside the state itself, further obstacles arise from the separation of powers and/or the insulation from popular control of branches and departments crucial in economic reproduction and the exercise of repression. In this context it should also be noted that, as the extent and forms of state intervention shift with the passage from *laissez-faire* through simple monopoly to state monopoly capitalism, there is a corresponding shift in the areas most central for successful 'popular-democratic' struggle as individual citizenship and parliamentarism become less significant in comparison with membership of 'corporations' and functional representation. Secondly 'popular-democratic' struggle involves questions of the substantive conditions in which popular control can be effectively exercised. This is a key issue in differentiating between 'pure democracy' and 'class democracy', i.e., between cases where the 'people' are autonomously or heteronomously unified. Where the 'people' is highly fragmented and massified through the 'isolation effect' and is unified, if at all, only through an 'hegemonic project' which couples national-popular objectives with the pursuit of the interests of capital, then any resulting democratic regime will be limited and class-biased. To move beyond such a 'bourgeois democratic republic' would require the democratisation of the economic region and civil society so that class-determined and class-relevant inequalities in political communication and organisation can be eliminated. Such reforms would not mean that the 'people' became autonomous in the sense of a free-willed, unitary, originating subject but only that its objectives and relative unity will no longer be determined in a class-biased milieu: the role of political, intellectual, and moral *leadership* will not thereby be eliminated any more than the need for compromise and negotiation about popular-democratic objectives. Thirdly 'popular-democratic' struggle involves the interpellation of the 'people' as well as 'officialdom' in the democratic rules of the game. Formal democratic institutions do not (and cannot) guarantee that politics will be conducted in a substantively democratic manner and could well provide the means to institute populist, authoritarian government rather than popular-democratic rule. A genuine system of democracy requires not only formal democratic institutions but also a commitment to temper particularistic demands in the light of broad popular-democratic objectives.

The preceding arguments have underlined the close linkage between class relations and relations among political categories. But they should also have suggested the space that exists for the dissociation of class and popular struggles on the field of political practices as well as for the structural dislocation of the form and function of the state relative to the requirements of economic reproduction. In the field of political practices a wide range of particular 'popular(-democratic)' struggles can occur in isolation from the class struggle. Indeed, although the spheres of state/civil society relations and state/subject relations constitute the field *par excellence* for such 'popular (-democratic)' struggles (which may nonetheless have a latent class relevance), it is also possible for the sphere of state/economy relations to be interpreted in these terms – especially with the increasing importance of state direction of economic activities and the concomitant need for new forms of political representation. In this sense we can argue that state economic intervention has both a class and a popular-democratic moment and also note that it could serve bourgeois class interests to divert opposition to such intervention from its class to its popular-democratic moment. Nonetheless it must be stressed that, whatever the prospects for the dissociation of particular 'popular' or 'popular-democratic' struggles in specific domains from the field of class struggle, a general movement on these lines cannot escape the acquisition of a class pertinence in the long run owing to the limits to democratisation inherent in capitalism. This can be illustrated from the response to a structural dislocation between state power and economic reproduction. Where 'officialdom-people' relations constitute the principal contradiction in a society and class antagonisms assume a secondary role, a broad-based 'popular front' can develop in isolation from any hegemonic class project. Once the introduction or restoration of democratic rule is achieved or nearly achieved, however, class relations acquire greater significance. This is particularly clear in the development of 'popular front' opposition to 'exceptional' regimes that have degenerated into 'bureaucratic despotisms' of one kind or another (see, for example, Poulantzas, 1976b, *passim*). Even in less extreme cases, moreover, similar patterns can be seen (e.g., the coupling of anti-statist currents to Thatcherism rather than democratic socialism). In short, despite the prospects for 'pure' democratic movements of a limited kind in the long term and of a general kind in the short term, it is impossible to escape class overdetermination entirely. Lest this be interpreted as a residual class reductionism, it should also be noted that 'pure' class movements will be overdetermined through 'officialdom-people' relations. It follows that we must theorise and struggle on both fronts in tackling the state.

Thus, although Marxists have concentrated on the state as a site of class domination, an adequate account must also consider it as a site of 'officialdom-people' relations. Such issues as the relative autonomy of the state vis-à-vis the dominant economic class, the nature of hegemony as 'national-popular' leadership, the dynamics of 'exceptional' regimes, and the relations between socialism and democracy, can all be illuminated through the complex articulation between class and popular relations and forces. We must also consider non-class antagonisms and forces in their own right if the fully complexity of the state is to be understood. The concepts adumbrated above should prove useful in this respect.

A 'RELATIONAL' ORIENTATION

The various guidelines suggested above imply a 'relational' approach to the analysis of the state apparatus and state power. Indeed the very concepts of 'articulation', 'contingent necessity', and 'over-determination' suggest that the focus of analysis should be the relations among relations. For the complex synthesis of multiple determinations which produces actual events cannot be reduced to a single principle of explanation and must be interpreted instead as the resultant of the interaction of various causal chains. It is the 'relational' character of the method of articulation that makes many key concepts in state theory appear to be formal and empty at abstract, simple levels of analysis. Thus such major notions as 'structural constraint', 'power', 'interests', 'relative autonomy', and 'balance of force' can be fully determined only through an analysis of the relations among different relations comprising the social formation. Failure to recognise this leads to a reductionist or subsumptionist account of such notions and/or to attempts to specify them in empiricist terms. Let us consider how a 'relational' approach differs from these in some key theoretical areas.

One of the most difficult problems in social analysis have recurred in attempts to differentiate between structure and practice, structure and conjuncture, or structure and process. Among the elements of a solution to this problem is a recognition that structure must be defined relationally. Thus we can distinguish between the 'structural' and the 'conjunctural' moments of a given conjuncture or situation.

The 'structural' moment can be defined as those elements in a social formation that cannot be altered by a given agent (or set of agents) during a given time period: it may include practices as well as their emergent properties and material preconditions and it may be more or less enduring beyond the time period in question. The 'conjunctural' moment can be defined as those elements in a social formation that can be altered by a given agent (or set of agents) during a given time period. This approach has several important implications. It implies that the same element can function as a 'structural constraint' for one agent (or set of agents) at the same time as it appears as a 'conjunctural element' open to transformation by another agent (or set of agents). In this context we could compare the potential power of different agents in terms of the relative importance of 'structural constraints' and 'conjunctural opportunities' in specific situations. It implies that the same element can act as a 'structural constraint' for one agent (or set of agents) and provide a 'conjunctural opportunity' for the same agent(s) in association with another agent (or set thereof). This highlights the importance of strategic and/or tactical alliances in the struggle to transform situations. It implies that a short-term structural constraint can become a conjunctural element in the longer term. Indeed the distinction between 'war of position' and 'war of manoeuvre' is premised on this time lag. A 'war of manoeuvre' takes place on a given structural terrain (which can vary for different participants according to the particular constraints affecting them) and involves a test of the currently prevailing balance of forces in struggle. But it is the differential transformation of this terrain itself and its effects on the balance of forces that constitutes the object of struggle in a 'war of position'.

A 'relational' approach also enables us to locate the problematic concept of 'power'. We have already argued that power should not be seen as a pre-given quantum or property of particular agents that is allocated in a zero-sum fashion and have suggested that it should be viewed instead as a complex social relation reflecting the balance of forces in a given situation. Power can be defined as the production of effects within the limits set by the 'structural constraints' confronting different agents. It results from the 'contingently necessary' interaction of their conduct in a given situation and must be related to the conduct of all relevant actors in that situation. This does not imply that agents are morally responsible for these effects by virtue of being free-willed, originating subjects but it does mean that agents cannot be seen simply as the *träger* of self-reproducing structures. We can identify the exercise of power in terms of the impossibility of

predicting these effects from a knowledge of the 'structural constraints' in isolation from knowledge about particular agents so that
the actual effects can meaningfully be said to depend in part on their
actions or inaction. This insistence that the exercise of power involves the production of effects that 'would not otherwise occur' is
quite compatible with an account of the agents involved as non-
unitary subjects constituted in and through discourse. For all that is
required to sustain this conception of power is the notion of agents
who can discursively interpret their situation and decide upon a
course of (in)action. In this context the idea that individual and/or
collective subjects can be non-unitary, 'interdiscursive' agents of
interpretation, calculation, and intervention is an important element
in sustaining an adequate account of power. Such an account would
be simultaneously anti-structuralist (anti-*träger*) and anti-voluntarist
(opposed to the assumption of a unitary, rational, free-willed, autonomous subject). In this sense it would help to explain the indeterminacy of events at the level of structural constraints. (It should also
be noted that 'interdiscursivity' is a crucial precondition of effective
ideological intervention.) At the same time a 'relational approach'
implies that the exercise of power is overdetermined at the level of
social action in so far as it depends on the interaction of all relevant
agents in the power relation. This makes it difficult to attribute the
outcome of an interaction unequivocally to one agent among all
those involved in a power relation except in the limiting case of a
purely subject-object relation. More generally we must focus on the
conjoint reproduction and/or transformation of social relations
through the interaction of different agents and attempt to specify
their various contributions to the overall outcome within the limits
set through the structural constraints severally and/or collectively
facing such agents.

This means that power as such is not an appropriate concept for
the explanation of social relations. For, in so far as it does not simply
denote the production of effects in general within the limits imposed
by structural constraints, it identifies a field of determined effects
which constitute an *explanandum* rather than *explanans* and so cannot have any independent status in causal analysis. In this sense
power is a formal concept empty of content and incapable of explaining how particular effects are produced or it is rendered redundant through the elaboration of substantive chains of determination
that are 'contingently necessary' to the production of the effects
under investigation. Neglect of this point tends to produce purported
explanations of social relations in terms of an exercise of power

whose sole theoretical and evidential support involves reference to the self-same relationship or else leads to the introduction of power to 'explain' those aspects of a social relation that cannot be attributed to other types of determination. Such circular reasoning and residual categories would be quite bad enough if power could indeed be employed as an explanatory principle but, since it cannot be so used, it is doubly serious because it leads to fruitless attempts to specify how power as such can be invoked to explain particular events.

Thus power can have only a limited and descriptive role in social analysis. It is a concept that is conventionally used to identify a production of significant effects through the actions of specific agents in a given set of circumstances. It is limited to the extent that such an account abstracts from these circumstances to attribute the significant effects to the actions in question. It thereby encourages the assumption that such actions were freely chosen as well as the decisive causal factor in the relation. Yet the exercise of power is not the unconditional outcome of a mechanical clash of wills but has definite social and material conditions of existence and is circumscribed through its links with other determinations in a social formation. This is why politics can be justly described as 'the art of the possible'. The analysis of these limits and constraints is therefore logically prior to the study of the actions of the agents involved in a power relation. Moreover, unless one regards such actions as random within the 'structural constraints' confronting these agents or else considers them as the result of an otherwise unconstrained free will, it is also necessary to investigate how the attributes, capacities, and modes of calculation of these agents further limit the possibilities of action and thereby help to determine the resulting power relation. An adequate analysis should therefore construct an historical account of the specific combination of social forces, actions, structural constraints, etc., that is necessary and/or sufficient to produce the effects in question.

This discussion implies that what is conventionally called 'power' is a complex, overdetermined phenomenon. At best the concept of 'power' can be retained to identify the production of significant effects (i.e., significant or pertinent at the level of abstraction and degree of complexity in terms of which the explanandum is defined) through the interaction of specific social forces within the limits implied in the prevailing set of structural constraints. The contingency of power in comparison with the determinacy of structure is theoretical rather than actual. All it implies is that the conduct of the agents in question and, *a fortiori,* its effects in a given set of circumstances cannot be predicted from knowledge of the circumstances themselves. It does not mean that power is indeterminate in terms of factors peculiar to the agents themselves and/or indeterminate in terms of the pattern of their interaction. In this sense the analysis of power is closely connected with the analysis of the organisation, modes of calculation, resources, strategies, tactics, etc. of different agents (unions, parties, departments of state, pressure groups, police, etc.) and the relations among these agents (including the differential composition of the 'structural constraints' and 'conjunctural opportunities' that they confront) which determines the overall balance of forces. In discussing this balance of forces regard must be paid not only to the range (in terms of pertinent areas of influence as well as their various determinations) and determinacy (or certainty of the effects in question) of potential influence but also to the net costs and benefits of different courses of (inter)action. It is only through the latter calculation that we can assess the extent to which the exercise of power creates, maintains, or restores the conditions of capital accumulation or helps to secure the conditions of existence of some other point of reference.

It is in this context that we can locate the concept of 'interest'. For the analysis of interests must be undertaken in a relational context concerned with comparative advantage rather than some notion of absolute interests posited in isolation from specific conjunctures. A situation, action, or event can be said to be in an agent's interest if it secures a greater net increase (or smaller net decrease) in the realisation of that agent's conditions of existence than do any feasible alternatives in a given conjuncture. This implies that an agent's interests must be assessed in relation to the structural constraints and conjunctural opportunities obtaining in a given period. It implies that it could be to the advantage of an agent to sacrifice certain benefits in order to secure more important benefits in other areas (e.g., to sacrifice certain short-term 'economic-corporate' benefits within limits compatible with continued economic reproduction in order to secure support for an 'hegemonic project' necessary to long-term reproduction). It implies that agents can face conflicts of interest such that a given situation, action, or event undermines at least some conditions of existence in at least some respects at the same time as it advances these and/or other preconditions in other respects. This has been recognised in several contributions to state theory in terms of the contingent opposition or contradiction between the economic interests of capital in accumulation and its political interests in legitimation but it should be specified in greater detail to allow for the diversity of interests in relation to various conditions of existence and their conjunctural overdetermination. This means that we must always specify which aspects of an agent's interests are being (dis) advantaged rather than engage in blanket assertions about such matters (cf. our earlier comments on the contingently capitalist character of state power). Moreover, in so far as an agent is involved in different relational systems and/or has been interpellated with different subjectivities or identities, there may be conflicts among the conditions of existence relevant to these systems and/or subjectivities with the result that the agent has no unitary and non-contradictory set of interests capable of realisation.

The 'relational' approach to interests thus implies that they can only be assessed in terms of the alternative outcomes in particular situations for specific subjects interpellated in a particular manner. The net balance of advantages for a given agent can change in parallel with variations in conjunctural opportunities and structural constraints and the same conjuncture can have different implications for interests if the manner in which the agent is interpellated is changed. Indeed a key area of ideological struggle consists in the redefinition and/or recombination of subjectivities and hence the interests that agents may have in various situations. Thus such struggle could focus on the interpellation of workers as wage-earners or as exploited proletarians, the weight to be attached to class as opposed to gender subjectivities in the case of male and female workers, or the recombination of class and popular-democratic subjectivities to form a new political alliance around a new 'hegemonic project'. In turn this implies that class struggle is not only a struggle to form class forces but also a struggle to define the reference points for the calculation of class interests; and, once given such class forces and their interests, the so-called 'class struggle' is constituted through the interaction among these forces and their differential impact on class interests. This argument should help to clarify the manner in which a given 'hegemonic project' privileges certain particular interests compatible with its conception of the general interest and derogates other competing or contradictory particular interests.

All this means that there is a dialectical relation between subjective and objective interests. Objective interests must always be related to a particular subjectivity occupying a particular position in a given conjuncture: a particular subject can nonetheless miscalculate these interests since they are defined in terms of the conditions actually necessary for its reproduction rather than the subject's own views on these conditions. This dialectic also defines the limits within which one can legitimately attribute interests to other agents. For, whilst external 'interpretation' without regard to an agent's various subjectivities is unacceptable, we can argue 'interdiscursively' that commitment to one subjectivity contradicts the realisation of interests in another of the agent's identities. Examples of these oppositions might include soviet man and democrat, housewife and woman, patriot and proletarian. Whereas the former approach is inherently authoritarian, the latter is at least potentially democratic.

In short, whether one looks at concepts such as 'structural constraint', 'power', or 'interests', it is always necessary to situate them in terms of the relations among social relations. Their meaning in specific conjunctures derives from the overall articulation of elements. Structural constraints comprise those elements in a situation that cannot be altered by agent(s) in a given time period and will vary according to the strategic location of agents in the overall matrix of the formation. This matrix involves a complex hierarchy of potential powers determined by the range and determinacy of opportunities for influencing elements that constitute constraints for other agents. This potential for power depends not only on the relations among different positions in the social formation but also on the organisation, modes of calculation, and resources of social forces. In turn the actual balance of power is determined *post hoc* through the interaction of the strategies or actions pursued by these forces within the limits imposed through the differential composition of structural constraints. The interests advanced or harmed through the exercise of power must also be assessed relationally. For interests depend on the conjunctural opportunities in a given period and hence on the potential balance of power. All this has major implications for calculating political strategies over different time periods and also highlights the importance of a conjunctural, relational approach to such issues as the nature of state power.

CONCLUDING REMARKS

Having adopted an approach that stresses the determinacy of the real world and the overdetermination of particular 'real-concrete' events, it might seem paradoxical to conclude on a note of indeterminacy. But I have emphasised throughout that abstract, simple accounts of such phenomena as capital accumulation, the state apparatus, and the exercise of state power are necessarily indeterminate with reference to more concrete, complex situations, forces, actions, and events. Rather than provide a spuriously definitive general theory of the state apparatus and state power in capitalist societies I have suggested some preliminary guidelines (or protocols) for the construction of a theoretically-informed and realist account of specific phenomena as resulting from the complex synthesis of multiple determinations. This has involved the rejection of all forms of reductionism and subsumption and the substitution of an emphasis on the differential, contingently necessary articulation of various causal chains to produce the 'real-concrete'. In turn this has led to the reformulation of several principles of explanation in Marxist analyses and the problematisation of various phenomena that these analyses tend to take for granted. In particular I have suggested that concepts such as class struggle, the unity of the state apparatus, state power, and class interests should be considered as explanenda rather than an unproblematic principles of explanation. I have also emphasised that many concepts in Marxist analysis must be treated both as contingently necessary principles of explanation and as points of reference for defining conditions of existence and examining their realisation. The implications of this approach have already been outlined in terms of four basic guidelines for an investigation of the state apparatus and state power in capitalist societies. These guidelines emphasise the need for an institutional approach to the analysis of the state apparatuses and a conjunctural, relational approach to the analysis of state power. This need not lead to a rejection of fundamental Marxist insights into the character of the state as a system of political class domination but it does require a careful specification of the conditions in which these insights hold true. At the same time these guidelines provide the theoretical means to combine Marxist analyses with other theoretical concerns lying beyond the issue of the relations of production, their conditions of existence, and their effects. It should be evident from the sketchy, formal nature of the remarks offered in elaboration of these guidelines that there is much theoretical and empirical work still to be done. I hope it will also be evident that these suggestions have some merit for the future development of theories of the state and politics.

References

Note: In compiling these references I have normally given as date of publication either the date of first publication in any language or, in the case of posthumously published works, the date of drafting. This is intended to facilitate the relative dating of different works when comparing the development of authors and/or schools of thought. Where necessary the edition or English translation to which page numbers refer is given in brackets. An asterisk indicates that the work in question is a particularly valuable example of a given approach.

Aaronovitch, Samuel (1956) *The Ruling Class,* London: Lawrence and Wishart

Abendroth-Forum (1977) *Abendroth-Forum: Marburger Gespräche aus Anlass des 70. Geburtstags von Wolfgang Abendroth,* ed. F. Deppe *et al.,* Marburg: Verlag Arbeiterbewegung und Gesellschaftswissenschaft

Abraham, David (1981) *The Collapse of the Weimar Republic:* Political Economy and Crisis, Princeton: Princeton University Press

Adlam, Diana *et al.* (1977) 'Psychology, ideology and the human subject', *Ideology and Consciousness,* 1

Althusser, Louis (1965) *For Marx,* London: Allen Lane

Althusser, Louis (1971) 'Ideology and Ideological State Apparatuses', in *idem, Lenin and Philosophy and Other Essays,* London: New Left Books

Althusser, Louis (1976) *Essays in Self-Criticism,* London: New Left Books

Althusser, Louis and Balibar, Etienne (1968) *Reading Capital,* London: New Left Books, 1970

*Altvater, Elmar (1972) 'Zu einigen Problemen des Staatsinterventionismus', *Prokla,* 3 (Citation from 'Notes on Some Problems of State Interventionism', *Kapitalstate,* 1, 1973, and 2, 1973)

Altvater, Elmar (1975) 'Wertgesetz und Monopolmacht', in Das Argument, Sonderband 6, *Staat und Monopole (I): Zur Theorie des Monopols*

Altvater, Elmar (1977) 'Staat und Gesellschaftliche Reproduktion', in V. Brandes *et al.* (eds.), *Handbuch 5 (Staat)*, Frankfurt: EVA

Altvater, Elmar *et al.* (1974a) 'Entwicklungstendenzen des Kapitalismus in Westdeutschland', *Prokla*, 16

Altvater, Elmar *et al.* (1974b) 'On the Analysis of Imperialism in the Metropolitan Countries: the West German Example', *Bulletin of the Conference of Socialist Economists*, Spring

Altvater, Elmar *et al.* (1976) 'Staat, Akkumulation und soziale Bewegung', in C. Pozzoli (ed.), *Rahmenbedingungen und Schranken Staatlichen Handelns*, Frankfurt: Suhrkamp, pp. 89–114

*Altvater, Elmar and Kallscheuer, Otto (1979) 'Socialist Politics and the "Crisis of Marxism" ', *Socialist Register 1979*

Anderson, Perry (1965) 'Origins of the Present Crisis', in *idem* and R. Blackburn (eds.) *Towards Socialism*, London: Fontana

Anderson, Perry (1976–1977) 'The Antinomies of Gramsci', *New Left Review*, 100

Apel, Hartmut (1976) 'Das Elend der neueren Marxistischen Staatstheorie', *Beiträge zum Wissenschaftlichen Sozialismus*, 6

Arbeitskonferenz München (1974a) 'Programmatische Erklärung der Roten Zellen/AK', *Resultate der Arbeitskonferenz*, 1

Arbeitskonferenz München (1974b) 'Warum Scheitern Marxisten an der Erklärung des bürgerlichen Staates?', *Resultate der Arbeitskonferenz*, 1

Arthur, Chris (1976–1977) 'Towards a Materialist Theory of Law', *Critique*, 7

Aumeeruddy, Aboo *et al.* (1978) 'Labour Power and the State', *Capital and Class*, 6

Autorenkollektiv (1975) 'Probleme der allgemeinen Krise des Kapitalismus', *Marxismus Digest*, 2

Avineri, Shlomo (1968) *The Social and Political Thought of Karl Marx*, Cambridge: Cambridge University Press

Avineri, Shlomo (1972) *Hegel's Theory of the Modern State*, London: Cambridge University Press

Balbus, Isaac (1977) 'Commodity Form and Legal Form: an Essay on the "Relative Autonomy of Law" ', *Law and Society Review*, 2 (iii)

Balibar, Etienne (1975) *Cinq études du matérialisme historique*, Paris: Maspero

Balibar, Etienne (1977) *On the Dictatorship of the Proletariat*, London: New Left Books

Barber, John (1976) 'Stalin's Letter to the Editors of *Proletarskaya revolyutsiya*, *Soviet Studies*, 28 (i)

Barber, John (1979) 'The Establishment of Intellectual Orthodoxy in the USSR', 1928–1934', *Past and Present*, 83

Barghoorn, Frederick (1948) 'The Varga Discussion and Its Significance', *American Slavic and East European Review*, vi, October

Barker, Colin (1978a) 'A Note on the Theory of the State', *Capital and Class,* 4
Barker, Colin (1978b) 'The State as Capital', *International Socialism,* Series 2, 1, July
Bew, Paul *et al.* (1979) *The State in Northern Ireland 1921–72.* Manchester: Manchester University Press
Bhaskar, Roy (1979) *The Possibility of Naturalism,* Brighton: Harvester
Binns, Peter (1980) 'Law and Marxism', *Capital and Class,* 10
Blackburn, Robin (1976) 'Marxism: Theory of Proletarian Revolution', *New Left Review,* 97, May–June
Blanke, Bernhard *et al.* (1974) 'Zur neueren marxistischen Diskussion über die Analyse von Form und Funktion des bürgerlichen Staates: Überlegungen zum Verhältnis von Politik und Ökonomie', *Prokla,* 14/15 (Citation from 'On the Current Marxist Discussion on the Analysis of Form and Function of the Bourgeois State', in J. Holloway and S. Picciotto (eds.) *State and Capital,* London: Edward Arnold)
Blanke, Bernhard *et al.* (1975) *Kritik der Politischen Wissenschaft: Analysen von Politik und Ökonomie in der bürgerlichen Gesellschaft,* Frankfurt: Campus Verlag (citation from the German edition except for Part 5, vol 2, which is cited from *idem,* 1976)
Blanke, Bernhard *et al.* (1976) 'The Relationship between the Political and the Economic as a Point of Departure for a Materialistic Analysis of the Bourgeois State', *International Journal of Politics,* vi (3)
Bobbio, Norberto *et al.* (1976) *Il Marxismo e lo Stato,* Rome: Mondo Operaio Edizioni Avanti
Boccara, Paul (1977) *Etudes sur le capitalisme monopoliste d'état, sa crise et son issue,* Paris: Editions Sociales (3rd, expanded edition)
*Boccara, Paul *et al.* (1976) *Traité d'Economie Politique: le capitalisme monopoliste d'état,* Paris: Editions Sociales (2nd edition, 2 vols.)
Boddy, James and Crotty, Richard (1974) 'Class Conflict, Keynesian Policy, and the Business Cycle', *Review of Radical Political Economy,* vii
Boradjewski, A. (1974) 'Die Besonderheiten des gegenwärtigen kapitalistischen Zyklus (Konferenzbericht)', *Marxismus Digest,* 3
Borkenau, Franz (1939) *The Communist International* (Citation from 1962 edition entitled *World Communism,* Ann Arbor: University of Michigan)
Brandes, Volkhard *et al.* (1977) *Handbuch 5 (Staat),* Frankfurt, EVA
Braunmühl, Claudia von (1973) 'Weltmarktbewegung des Kapitals, Imperialismus, und Staat', in C. von Braunmühl *et al., Probleme einer materialistische Staatstheorie,* Frankfurt, Suhrkamp
Braunmühl, Claudia von (1974) 'Kapitalakkumulation im Weltmarktzusammenhang: zum methodischen Ansatz einer Analyse des bürgerlichen National-staats', *Gesellschaft 1,* Frankfurt: Suhrkamp (a revised version appears as *idem,* 1978)

*Braunmühl, Claudia von (1978) 'On the Analysis of the Bourgeois Nation State within the World Market Context', in J. Holloway and S. Picciotto (eds.) *State and Capital*, London: Edward Arnold

Braunmühl, Claudia von *et al.* (1973) 'Vorwort', in *idem*, *Probleme einer materialistische Staatstheorie*, Frankfurt: Suhrkamp

Braunthal, Julius (1967) *History of the International, 1914–1943*, London: Nelson

*Brunhoff, Suzanne de (1976) *Etat et Capital: recherches sur la politique économique*, Grenoble: Presses Universitaires de Grenoble, and Paris: Maspero (Citation from *The State, Capital, and Economic Policy*, London: Pluto Press, 1978)

Buci-Glucksmann, Christine (1975) *Gramsci et l'Etat*, Paris: Fayard

Buci-Glucksmann, Christine and Therborn, Goran (1981) *Le Défi Social-Démocrate*, Paris: Maspero

Bukharin, Nikolai I. (1916) 'The Imperialist Robber State, *Arbeiterpolitik*, 25, and *Jugend-Internationale*, 6 (Citation from the reprint in V.I. Lenin, 'Marxism on the State', Moscow, 1972)

Bukharin, Nikolai I. (1917) *Imperialism and World Economy*, London: Merlin Press, 1972

Bukharin, Nikolai I. (1920) *Economics of the Transition Period* (Citation from the English translation, *Economics of the Transformation Period*, London: Pluto, 1971)

Bukharin, Nikolai I. (1921) *The Theory of Historical Materialism: a Popular Manual of Marxist Sociology* (Citation from the American translation of the 1926 edition, *Historical Materialism*, Ann Arbor: University of Michigan)

Burdjalov, Felix E. (1978) *State Monopoly Incomes Policy: Conception and Practice (in the context of Great Britain)*, Moscow: Progress (a translation of the revised Russian edition)

Burlatsky, Fyodor (1978) *The Modern State and Politics*, Moscow: Progress

Cammett, John M. (1967) *Antonio Gramsci and the Origins of Italian Communism*, Stanford: Stanford University Press

Cheprakov, V. (1956) 'Die Leninische Theorie von der ungleichmässigen Entwicklung des Kapitalismus und die Zuspitzung der imperialistischen Gegensätze in der Nachkriegsperiode', *Sowjetwissenschaft*, x (8)

Classen, Wolfgang-Dieter (1979) *Probleme einer materialistischer Analyse des bürgerlichen Staates*, Frankfurt: Haag und Herchen

*Clarke, Simon (1978) 'Capital, Fractions of Capital, and the State: 'neo-Marxist' Analyses of the South African State', *Capital and Class*, 5

Claudin, Fernando (1975) *The Communist Movement from Comintern to Cominform*, Harmondsworth: Peregrine

Cobler, Sebastian (1978) *Law, Order, and Politics in West Germany*, Harmondsworth: Penguin

Cohen, Stephen F. (1975) *Bukharin and the Bolshevik Revolution: a Political Biography 1888–1938*, New York, Vintage Books

Colletti, Lucio (1969) *Ideologia e Società*, Rome: Editori Laterza (Citation from the English translation, *Rousseau to Lenin*, London, New Left Books, 1972)

Colletti, Lucio (1975) 'Introduction', in *idem* (ed.), *Karl Marx; Early Writings*, Harmondsworth: Penguin

*Conference Internationale Choisy-le-Roi (1966) *Le Capitalisme monopoliste d'état*, 2 vols., *Économie et politique*, 143–144 and 145–146

Coward, Rosalind and Ellis, John (1977) *Language and Materialism*, London: Routledge and Kegan Paul

*Cutler, Antony *et al.* (1977) *Marx's 'Capital' and Capitalism Today*, vol 1 London: Routledge and Kegan Paul

Cutler, Antony *et al.* (1978) *Marx's 'Capital' and Capitalism Today*, vol 2, London: Routledge and Kegan Paul

Davidson, Alastair B. (1972) 'The Varying Seasons of Gramscian Studies', *Political Studies*, xx (4)

Davidson, Alastair B. (1977) *Antonio Gramsci: Towards an Intellectual Biography*, London: Merlin Press

Day, Richard B. (1981) *The 'Crisis' and the 'Crash': Soviet Studies of the West (1917–1939)*, London: New Left Books

Degras, Jane (ed.) (1956–65) *The Communist International 1919–1943: Documents*, vol 1 1919–1922; vol 2 1923–1928, vol 3 1929–1943, London: Oxford University Press

Delilez, Jean-Pierre (1976) 'L'État et la revolution démocratique de masse', *La Nouvelle Critique*, 93 (274) n.s. avril

Delilez, Jean-Pierre (1977) *L'État du changement*, Paris: Editions Sociales

Della Volpe, Gaetano (1969) *Logica come scienza positiva*, Rome: Editori Riuniti (Cited from the translation, *Logic as a Positive Science*, London: New Left Books, 1980)

Dimitrov, George (1935) 'The Fascist Offensive and the Tasks of the Communist International', in *idem, Selected Speeches and Articles*, London: Lawrence and Wishart, 1951

*Draper, Hal (1977) *Karl Marx's Theory of Revolution: State and Bureaucracy*, in 2 parts, New York: Monthly Review Press

Ebbighausen, Rolf and Winkelmann, Rainer (1974) 'Zur aktuellen politischen Bedeutung der Theorie des staatsmonopolisticihen Kapitalismus und zum Stellenwert einer Kritik ihrer Marx-Rezeption', in R. Ebbighausen (ed.) *Monopol und Staat,* Frankfurt: Suhrkamp

Eicholtz, Dietrich and Gossweiler, Kurt (1968) 'Noch eimmal: Politik und Wirtschaft 1933–1945', *Das Argument*, 47

Engels, Friedrich (1844a) 'The Condition of England: the English Constitution', *MECW*, iii

Engels, Friedrich (1844b) 'Outlines of a Critique of Political Economy', *MECW*, iii

Engels, Friedrich (1845) *The Condition of the Working-Class in England*, *MECW*, iv

Engels, Friedrich (1846) 'The State of Germany: Letter III', *MECW*, vi

Engels, Friedrich (1847) 'The Constitutional Question in Germany', *MECW*, vi

Engels, Friedrich (1850) *The Peasant War in Germany*, *MECW*, x

Engels, Friedrich (1852) *Revolution and Counter-Revolution in Germany*, *MECW*, x

Engels, Friedrich (1872) *The Housing Question*, *MESW*, iii

Engels, Friedrich (1878) *Anti-Dühring: Herr Eugen Duhring's Revolution in Science*, Moscow: Foreign Languages Publishing House, 1954

Engels, Friedrich (1884) *On The Origins of the Family, Private Property, and the State*, *MESW*, iii

Engels, Friedrich (1886a) *Ludwig Feuerbach and the End of Classical German Philosophy*, *MESW*, iii

Engels, Friedrich (1886b) 'Juristen-Sozialismus', *MEW*, 35

Engels, Friedrich (1888) *The Role of Force in History*, *MESW*, iii

Fabre, Jean (1966) 'Capitalisme monopoliste d'état, politique économique et planification, *Économie et politique*, 143–144

Fairley, John (1980) 'French Developments in the Theory of State Monopoly Capitalism', *Science and Society*, 44

Fay, Margaret A. (1978) 'Review of *State and Capital: A Marxist Debate*', *Kapitalistate*, 7

Fine, Ben and Harris, Laurence (1979) *Re-Reading Capital*, London: Macmillan

Fiori, Giuseppe (1970) *Antonio Gramsci: Life of a Revolutionary*, New York: Schocken

*Flatow, Sybille von and Huisken, Freerk (1973) 'Zum Problem der Ableitung des bürgerlichen Staates: die Oberfläche der bürgerlichen Gesellschaft, der Staat, und die allgemeinen Rahmenbedingungen der Produktion', *Prokla*, 7

Funken, Klaus (1973) Überlegungen zu einer marxistischen Staatstheorie', in C. von Braunmühl *et al.*, *Probleme einer materialistischen Staatstheorie*, Frankfurt: Suhrkamp

Galbraith, John K. (1967) *The New Industrial State*, Harmondsworth: Penguin

Genth, Renate and Altvater, Elmar (1976) 'Politische Konzeptionen und Schwierigkeiten der KPI in der Krise – ein Aufriss von Problemen einer Strategie, *Prokla*, 26

Gerns, Willi (1974) *Kapitalismus in der Krise*, Frankfurt: Verlag Marxistische Blätter

Gerstenberger, Heide (1972) 'Elemente einer historisch-materialistischen Staats-theorie', *Kritische Justiz*, 2

Gerstenberger, Heide (1973a) *Zur politischen Ökonomie der bürgerlichen Gesellschaft: die historischen Bedingungen ihrer Konstitution in den USA,* Frankfurt: Athenaeum Fischer Taschenbuch

*Gerstenberger, Heide (1973b) 'Zur Theorie der historischen Konstitution des bürgerlichen Staates', *Prokla,* 8/9

*Gerstenberger, Heide (1975) 'Klassenantagomismus, Konkurrenz, und Staatsfunktionen', *Gesellschaft 3,* Frankfurt: Suhrkamp (Citation from the translation, 'Class Conflict, Competition and State Functions', in J. Holloway and S. Picciotto (eds.) *State and Capital,* London: Edward Arnold)

Gerstenberger, Heide (1976) 'Theory of the State: Special Features of the Discussion in the FRG', in C. von Beyme (ed.) *German Political Studies,* London and Beverley Hills, Sage

Gerstenberger, Heide (1977) 'Zur Theorie des bürgerlichen Staates: der gegenwärtige Stand der Debatte', in V. Brandes *et al.* (eds.), *Handbuch 5 (Staat),* Frankfurt: EVA

Gluschkow, V. (1955) 'The Growth of State Monopoly Capitalism' (Russian), *Voprosy ekonomiki,* 9 (cited in W. Petrowsky, 'Zur Entwicklung der Theorie des staatsmonopolistischen Kapitalismus', *Prokla,* 1, 1971)

Glyn, Andrew and Sutcliffe, Bob (1972) *British Capitalism, Workers, and the Profits Squeeze,* Harmondsworth: Penguin

Goffard, Serge (1976) 'La Question du pouvoir est à l'ordre du jour', *La Nouvelle Critique,* 93 (274) n.s.

Gollan, John (1954) *The British Political System,* London: Lawrence and Wishart

Gough, Ian (1975) 'State expenditure in advanced capitalism', *New Left Review,* 92

*Gramsci, Antonio (1971) *Selections from the Prison Notebooks,* London: Lawrence and Wishart

Gramsci, Antonio (1977) *Selections from Political Writings 1910–1920,* London: Lawrence and Wishart

*Gramsci, Antonio (1978) *Selections from Political Writings 1921–1926,* London: Lawrence and Wishart

Gray, Robert Q. (1977) 'Bourgeois Hegemony in Victorian Britain', in J. Bloomfield (ed.) *Class, Hegemony, Party,* London: Lawrence and Wishart

Gulijew, W. E. (1977) 'Die Relative Selbständigkeit des Staates', *Marxismus Digest,* 32

Gündel, Rudi (1961) *Die zyklische Entwicklung der Westdeutschen Wirtschaft von 1950–1957 unter besonderer Berücksichtigung der Industrieproduktion,* Berlin: Dietz Verlag

*Gündel, Rudi *et al.* (1967) *Zur Theorie des staatsmonopolistischen Kapitalismus,* Berlin: Akademie Verlag

Haak, Ernst *et al.* (1973) *Einführung in die politsche Okonomie des Kapitalismus,* Berlin: Dietz Verlag

Hall, Stuart *et al.* (1978) *Policing the Crisis,* London: Macmillan

Hall, Stuart *et al.* (eds.) *Culture, Media, and Language,* London: Hutchinson

Harris, Lawrence (1976a) 'On Interest, Credit, and Capital', *Economy and Society,* 2 (ii)

Harris, Lawrence (1976b) 'State Monopoly Capitalism and the Capitalist Mode of Production', unpublished paper, CSE Weekend School, London, 5.12.1976

Harris, Lawrence (1977) 'Economic Policy and Marxist Theory', *Marxism Today,* April

Harvey, James and Hood, Katherine (1958) *The British State,* London: Lawrence and Wishart

Heininger, Horst (1975) 'Methodologische Fragen der Analyse des gegenwärtigen Entwicklungsstandes der allgemeinen Krise des Kapitalismus', *Marxismus Digest,* 2

*Hemberger, Horst *et al.* (1975) *Imperialismus Heute: der staatsmonopolistische Kapitalismus in Westdeutschland,* Berlin: Dietz Verlag

Hennig, Eike (1974) 'Lesehinweise für die Lekture der 'politischen Schriften' von Marx and Engels', in E. Hennig *et al.* (eds.), *Karl Marx: Friedrich Engels – Staatstheorie,* Frankfurt: Ullstein

*Herzog, Phillippe (1971) 'Le role de l'état dans la société capitaliste actuelle', *Économie et Politique,* 200–201

Herzog, Phillippe (1972) *Politique économique et planification en régime capitaliste* Paris: Éditions Sociales

Hess, Peter (1971) 'Monopol, Rationalität, und Gleichgewichtiges Wachstum', *Marxismus Digest,* 7

Hess, Peter (1974) 'Fragen der Theorie des Staatsmonopolistischen Kapitalismus und ihre Kritiker', *Blätter für deutsche und internationale Politik,* 8

Hilferding, Rudolf (1909) *Das Finanzkapital: eine Studie über die jüngste Entwicklung des Kapitalismus,* Frankfurt: EVA, 1968 edition

Hindess, Barry (1977) 'The Concept of Class in Marxist Theory and Marxist Politics', in J. Bloomfield (ed.) *Class, Hegemony, and Party,* London: Lawrence and Wishart

Hindess, Barry (1980a) 'Classes and Politics in Marxist Theory', in G. Littlejohn *et al.* (eds.), *Power and the State,* Croom Helm: London

Hindess, Barry (1980b) 'Democracy and the Limitations of Parliamentary Democracy in Britain', *Politics and Power 1,* London: Routledge and Kegan Paul

Hindess, Barry (1980c) 'Marxism and Parliamentary Democracy', in A. Hunt (ed.) *Marxism and Democracy,* London: Lawrence and Wishart

Hindess, Barry and Hirst, Paul Q. (1975) *Pre-Capitalist Modes of Production,* London: Routledge

Hindess, Barry and Hirst, Paul Q. (1977) *Mode of Production and Social Formation*, London: Macmillan

Hirsch, Joachim (1969) 'Funktionsveränderungen der Staatsverwaltung in spätkapitalistischen Industriegesellschaften', *Blätter für deutsche und internationale Politik*

Hirsch, Joachim (1970) *Wissenschaftlich-technischer Fortschritt und politisches System*, Frankfurt: Suhrkamp

Hirsch, Joachim (1972a) 'Ansätze einer Regierungslehre', in G. Kress and D. Senghaas (eds.), *Politikwissenschaft*, Frankfurt: Fischer

Hirsch, Joachim (1972b) 'Zur politischen Ökonomie des politischen Systems', in G. Kress and D. Senghaas (eds.), *Politikwissenschaft*, Frankfurt; Fischer

Hirsch, Joachim (1973) 'Elemente einer materialistischen Staatstheorie', in C. von Braunmühl *et al.*, *Probleme einer materialistischen Staatstheorie*, Frankfurt: Suhrkamp (Citation from the translation, 'Elements of a Materialist Theory of the State', *International Journal of Politics*, vii (2), 1977)

Hirsch, Joachim (1974a) *Staatsapparat und Reproduktion des Kapitals*, Frankfurt: Suhrkamp (Parts 1 and 5 are cited from 'The State Apparatus and Social Reproduction: Elements of a Theory of the Bourgeois State', in J. Holloway and S. Picciotto (eds.), *State and Capital*, London: Edward Arnold, 1978; Part 3 is almost identical to Hirsch, 1974c, and is cited according to the latter)

Hirsch, Joachim (1974b) 'Zum Problem einer Ableitung der Form- und Funktions bestimmung des bürgerlichen Staates', in E. Hennig *et al.* (eds.), *Karl Marx: Friedrich Engels – Staatstheorie*, Frankfurt: Ullstein

*Hirsch, Joachim (1974c) 'Zur Analyse des politischen Systems', *Gesellschaft 1*, Frankfurt: Suhrkamp

*Hirsch, Joachim (1976a) 'Bemerkungen zum theoretischen Ansatz einer Analyse des bürgerlichen Staates', *Gesellschaft 8–9*, Frankfurt: Suhrkamp

Hirsch, Joachim (1976b) 'Remarques théoriques sur l'état bourgeois et sa crise', in N. Poulantzas (ed.) *La Crise de l'État*, Paris: Presses Universitaires de France

Hirsch, Joachim (1976c) 'Thesen zur Funktion und zum Charakter des Staatsinterventionismus im Technologiebereich', in C. Pozzoli (ed.), *Rahmenbedingungen und Schranken staatlichen Handelns*, Frankfurt: Suhrkamp

*Hirsch, Joachim (1977a) 'Kapitalreproduktion, Klassenauseinandersetzungen, und Widersprüche im Staatsapparat', in V. Brandes *et al.* (eds.) *Handbuch 5 (Staat)*, Frankfurt: EVA

Hirsch, Joachim (1977b) 'What is the Fiscal Crisis of the State: on the Political Function of the Fiscal Crisis', paper delivered to the CSE Conference, Bradford, 1977, mimeo

Hirsch, Joachim (1978) 'The Crisis of Mass Integration: on the development of political repression in Federal Germany', *International Journal of Urban and Regional Research*, 2 (ii)

*Hirsch, Joachim (1980a) *Der Sicherheitsstaat*, Frankfurt: EVA

Hirsch, Joachim (1980b) 'On Political Developments in West Germany since 1945', in R. Scase (ed.), *The State in Western Europe*, London: Croom Helm

Hirst, Paul Q. (1977) 'Economic Classes and Politics', in A. Hunt (ed.), Class and Class Structure, London: Lawrence and Wishart

*Hirst, Paul Q. (1979) *On Law and Ideology*, London: Routledge and Kegan Paul

Hirst, Paul Q. (1980) 'Review of Poulantzas' *State, Power, Socialism'*, *Eurored*, 9

Hoare, Quentin and Nowell-Smith, Geoffrey (1971) 'General Introduction', in A. Gramsci, *Selections from the Prison Notebooks*, London: Lawrence and Wishart

*Hochberger, Hunno (1974) 'Probleme einer materialistischen Bestimmung des Staates', *Gesellschaft 2*, Frankfurt: Suhrkamp

Hoffman, David (1972) 'Bukharin's Theory of Equilibrium', *Telos*, 14

*Holloway, John (1979) 'The State and Everyday Struggle', paper presented to Seminar on 'The State in Contemporary Capitalism', Mexico City

*Holloway, John and Picciotto, Sol (1977) 'Capital, Crisis, and the State', *Capital and Class*, 2

Holloway, John and Picciotto, Sol (1978) 'Introduction: Towards a Marxist Theory of the State', in *idem* (eds.), *State and Capital*, London: Edward Arnold

Holloway, John and Picciotto, Sol (eds.) *State and Capital: A German Debate*, London: Edward Arnold

Hood, Christopher *et al.*, 'So you think you know what Government Departments are?' *Public Administration Bulletin*, 27, 1978

Huffschmid, Jorg (1975) 'Begrundung und Bedeutung des Monopolbegriffs in der marxistischen politischen Ökonomie', in Das Argument, Sonderband 6, *Staat und Monopole (I): Zur Theorie des Monopols*, Berlin: Argument Verlag

Hunt, Richard N. (1974) *The Political Ideas of Marx and Engels, vol 1*, London: Macmillan

Inosemzew, N. N. *et al.* (1972) *Die Politische Ökonomie des heutigen Monopolkapitalismus*, Berlin: Dietz Verlag

Jessop, Bob (1977) 'Recent Theories of the Capitalist State', *Cambridge Journal of Economics*, 1 (iv)

Jessop, Bob (1978a) 'Marx and Engels on the State', in S. Hibbin, ed., *Politics, Hegemony, and the State*, London: Lawrence and Wishart

Jessop, Bob (1978b) 'Democracy and Dictatorship: Eurocommunism and the State', *Eurored* 6
Jessop, Bob (1978c) 'Capitalism and Democracy: the best possible political shell?', in G. Littlejohn *et al.* (eds.) *Power and the State*, London: Croom Helm
Jessop, Bob (1979) 'Corporatism, Parliamentarism, and Social Democracy', in P. C. Schmitter and G. Lehmbruch (eds.), *Trends Towards Corporatist Intermediation*, London and Beverley Hills: Sage
Jessop, Bob (1980a) 'The Transformation of the State in Postwar Britain', in R. Scase, ed., *The State in Western Europe*, London: Croom Helm
Jessop, Bob (1980b) 'The Political Indeterminacy of Democracy', in A. Hunt (ed.) *Marxism and Democracy*, London. Lawrence and Wishart
Jessop, Bob (1980c) 'The Capitalist State and Political Practice: review of Nicos Poulantzas, *State, Power, Socialism*', *Economy and Society*, 9 (i)
Jessop, Bob (1980d) 'On Recent Marxist Theories of Law, the State, and Juri-dico-political Ideology', *International Journal of the Sociology Of Law*, 8
Jessop, Bob (1982) *Nicos Poulantzas*, London: Macmillan
Joll, James (1977) *Gramsci*, London: Fontana
Jordan, Dirk (1974a) 'Der Monopolbegriff in System der Kritik der politischen Ökonomie', in R. Ebbighausen (ed.), *Monopol und Staat*, Frankfurt: Suhrkamp
Jordan, Dirk (1974b) 'Der Imperialismus als monopolistischer Kapitalismus: zur Imperialismus-Analyse Lenins als Basis der Theorie des staatsmonopolis-tischen Kapitalismus', in R. Ebbighausen (ed.), *Monopol und Staat*, Frankfurt: Suhrkamp
Jourdain, Henri (1966) 'Capitalisme monopoliste d'état, democratie et social-isme', *Economie et politique*, 143–144
Jung, Heinz (1979) 'Zur privatmonopolistischen Entwicklungsvariante des staatsmonopolistischen Kapitalismus in der BRD', in Das Argument Son-derband 36, *Staat und Monopole (III)*, Berlin: Argument Verlag
*Jung, Heinz and Schleifstein, Josef (1979) *Die Theorie des staatsmonopolis-tischen Kapitalismus und ihre Kritiker*, Frankfurt: Verlag Marxis sche Blätter
Kastendiek, Hans (1980) 'Neo-Korporativismus? Thesen und Analyse-Kon-zepte', *Prokla*, 38
*Katzenstein, Robert (1973) 'Zur Theorie des staatsmonopolistischen Kapital-ismus', *Prokla*, 8/9
Katzenstein, Robert (1974) 'Zur Monopolproblematik. Ein Beitrag zur Diskus-sion um den staatsmonopolistischen Kapitalismus', *Sozialistische Politik*, 28
Khruschev, Nikita S. (1956a) 'Report of the Central Committee to the XXth Congress of the Communist Party of the Soviet Union', *Soviet News Book-let*, 4

Khruschev, Nikita S. (1966b) 'Secret Speech" to 20th Congress of CPSU', in T. H. Rigby (ed.), *The Stalin Dictatorship: Khruschev's 'Secret Speech' and Other Documents*, Sydney: Sydney University Press, 1968

Kinsey, Richard (1979) 'Pashukanis – Law and Marxism', *Head and Hand*, Spring

Klein, Dieter (1974) *Allgemeine Krise und staatsmonopolisticher Kapitalismus*, Berlin: Dietz Verlag

*Kozlov, G. A. (ed.) (1977) *Political Economy: Capitalism*, Moscow: Progress

Kuhlen, Lothar (1975) ' "Ableitung" und "Verdoppelung" in der neueren marxistischen Diskussion über den Staat', in H. Rottleuthner (ed.) *Probleme der marxistischen Rechtstheorie* (Frankfurt: Suhrkamp

Kusminov, L. (1955) *State Monopoly Capitalism* (in Russian), cited in G. Kohlmey, 'Discussion zum Thema staatsmonopolistischer Kapitalismus', *Wirtschaftswissenschaft*, 1958, 12

Kuusinen, O. (ed.) (1961) *Fundamentals of Marxism-Leninism*, Moscow: Foreign Languages Publishing House

Laclau, Ernesto (1975) 'The Specificity of the Political', *Economy and Society*, 4 (i)

*Laclau, Ernesto (1977) *Politics and Ideology in Marxist Theory*, London: New Left Books

*Laclau, Ernesto (1980a) 'Populist Rupture and Discourse', *Screen Education*, 34

Laclau, Ernesto (1980b) 'Togliatti and Politics', *Politics and Power 2*, London: Routledge and Kegan Paul

Laclau, Ernesto and Mouffe, Chantal (1981) 'Socialist Strategy – Where Next?', *Marxism Today*, January

*Laclau, Ernesto and Mouffe, Chantal (1982) *Hegemony and Socialist Strategy*, London: New Left Books

*Läpple, Dieter (1973) *Staat und allgemeine Produktionsbedingungen*, West-berlin: VSA

Läpple, Dieter (1975) 'Staat und politische Organisation: Probleme marxistischen Staatsanalyse', in H. J. Krysmanski and P. Marwedel (eds.) *Die Krise in der Soziologie*, Köln: Pahl-Rugenstein

Läpple, Dieter (1976) 'Zum Legitimationsproblem politischer Herrschaft in der Kapitalischen Gesellschaft', in R. Ebbighausen (ed.), *Burgerlicher Staat und politische Legitimation*, Frankfurt: Suhrkamp

Lenin, Vladimir Illich (1894) 'What the 'Friends of the People' are and how they fight the Social Democrats', *LCW*, 1

Lenin, Vladimir Illich (1908) 'Materialism and Empirio-Criticism', *LCW*, 14

Lenin, Vladimir Illich (1915) 'Socialism and War: the attitude of the RSDLP towards the war', *LCW*, 21

Lenin, Vladimir Illich (1916a) 'A Caricature of Marxism and Imperialist Economism', *LCW*, 23

Lenin, Vladimir Illich (1916b) 'Imperialism and the Split in Socialism', *LCW*, 23

Lenin, Vladimir Illich (1917a) 'A Turn in World Politics', *LCW*, 23

*Lenin, Vladimir Illich (1917b) 'Imperialism: the Highest Stage of Capitalism', *LCW*, 22

Lenin, Vladimir Illich (1917c) 'Tasks of the Proletariat in Our Revolution', *LCW*, 24

Lenin, Vladimir Illich (1917d) 'Report on the Current Situation', *LCW*, 24

Lenin, Vladimir Illich (1917e) 'War and Revolution: a lecture delivered May 14 (27) 1917', *LCW*, 24

Lenin, Vladimir Illich (1917f) 'The Impending Catastrophe and how to Combat it', *LCW*, 25

*Lenin, Vladimir Illich (1917g) 'The State and Revolution', *LCW*, 25

Lenin, Vladimir Illich (1917h) 'Can the Bolsheviks Retain State Power?' LCW, 26

Lenin, Vladimir Illich (1917i) 'Materials on the Revision of the Party Programme', *LCW*, 25

Lenin, Vladimir Illich (1918b) 'The Revolutionary Phrase', *LCW*, 27

Lenin, Vladimir Illich (1918c) 'Report on the Immediate Tasks of the Soviet Government', *LCW*, 27

Lenin, Vladimir Illich (1918d) ' "Leftwing Childishness" and the Petit Bourgeois Mentality', *LCW*, 27

Lenin, Vladimir Illich (1918e) 'Report to the All-Russia Congress of Representatives of Financial Departments of Soviets', *LCW*, 27

Lenin, Vladimir Illich (1918f) 'The Proletarian Revolution and the Renegrade Kautsky', *LCW*, 29

Lenin, Vladimir Illich (1919a) 'Report on the Party Programme', *LCW*, 29

Lenin, Vladimir Illich (1921a) 'The Tax in Kind', *LCW*, 32

Lenin, Vladimir Illich (1921b) 'Report on the Tactics of the RCP (B)', *LCW*, 32

Lenin, Vladimir Illich (1921c) 'The Fourth Anniversary of the October Revolution', *LCW*, 33

Lenin, Vladimir Illich (1922) 'Eleventh Congress of the RCP (B)', *LCW*, 33

*Lewin, Jossif D. and Tumanow, Wladimir A. (1977) *Der politische Mechanismus der Monopoldiktatur*, Berlin: Staatsverlag der DDR

London-Edinburgh Weekend Return Group (1979) *In and Against the State*, London: Conference of Socialist Economists

*London-Edinburgh Weekend Return Group (1980) *In and Against the State*, London: Pluto Press (revised and expanded edition of *idem*, 1979)

Magaline, A. D. (1975) *Lutte de classes et Devalorisation du Capital*, Paris: Maspero, 1975

Maguire, John (1978) *Marx's Theory of Politics*, London: Cambridge University Press

Maier, Lutz and Ivanek, Ladislav (1962) *Unternehmerstaat: Zur Rolle der Staatskonzerne in Westdeutschland,* Berlin: Dietz Verlag

Mancini, F. and Galli, G. (1968) 'Gramsci's Presence', *Government and Opposition,* 4 (iii)

Mandel, Ernest (1978) *From Stalinism to Eurocommunism,* London: New Left Books

Marcuse, Herbett (1971) *Soviet Marxism: a critical analysis,* Harmondsworth: Penguin

Marx, Karl (1842) 'Debates on the Law on Thefts of Wood', *MECW,* 1

Marx, Karl (1843a) *Contribution to the Critique of Hegel's Philosophy of Law, MECW,* 3

Marx, Karl (1843b) 'On the Jewish Question', *MECW,* 3

Marx, Karl (1843c) 'Justification of the Correspondent from the Mosel', *MECW,* 7

Marx, Karl (1844a) 'Contribution to the Critique of Hegel's Philosophy of Law: Introduction', *MECW,* 3

Marx, Karl (1844b) 'Critical Marginal Notes on the Article "The King of Prussia and Social Reform. By a Prussian" ', *MECW,* 3

Marx, Karl (1844c) *Economic and Philosophic Manuscripts of 1844, MECW,* 3

Marx, Karl (1847) *The Poverty of Philosophy, MECW,* 6

Marx, Karl (1850) *The Class Struggles in France, 1848 to 1850, MECW,* 10

*Marx, Karl (1852) *The Eighteenth Brumaire of Louis Bonaparte, MECW,* 11

Marx, Karl (1857) 'Introduction to a contribution to the Critique of Political Economy', in *idem, Grundrisse,* ed. M. Nicolaus, Harmondsworth: Penguin, 1973

Marx, Karl (1858a) *Grundrisse: Introduction to the Critique of Political Economy,* ed. M. Nicolaus, Harmondsworth: Penguin, 1973

Marx, Karl (1858b) 'Die Herrschaft der Prätorianer', *MEW,* 12

Marx, Karl (1959) 'Preface to a Contribution to the Critique of Political Economy', *MESW'* 2

Marx, Karl (1864) *Theories of Surplus Value,* vol 3, London: Lawrence and Wishart, 1972

Marx, Karl (1867) *Capital: a critical Analysis of Capitalist Production,* vol 1, London: Lawrence and Wishart (translated from fourth German edition of 1890)

*Marx, Karl (1871) *The Civil War in France,* in D. Fernbach (ed.) *Karl Marx: the First International and After,* Harmondsworth: Penguin, 1973

*Marx, Karl (1875) 'Critique of the Gotha Programme', in D. Fernbach (ed.) *Karl Marx: The First International and After,* Harmondsworth: Penguin, 1973

Marx, Karl (1885) *Capital: a critical Analysis of Capitalist Production,* vol 2, London: Lawrence and Wishart, 1972 (translated from the second German edition of 1893)

Marx, Karl (1894) *Capital: a critical Analysis of Capitalist Production*, vol 3, London: Lawrence and Wishart, 1972 (translated from the German first edition)

Marx, Karl and Engels, Friedrich (1845–1846) *The German Ideology, MECW*, 5

Marx, Karl and Engels, Friedrich (1848) *Manifesto of the Communist Party, MECW*, 6

Marx, Karl and Engels, Friedrich (1962) *On Britain*, Moscow: Foreign Languages Publishing House

Marx, Karl and Engels, Friedrich (1975) *Selected Correspondence*, Moscow: Progress (third edition)

Marxistische Gruppe Theorie Fraktion (1973) 'Zur Oberfläche des Kapitals', *Cirkular no. 3*, Erlangen: Marxistische Gruppe/Theorie Fraktion

Masson, Gilles (1976) 'L'État du CME et sa transformation démocratique', *Cahiers du Communisme*, 1976, 4

Menshikov, S. (1969) *Millionaires and Managers*, Moscow: Progress

Menshikov, S. (1975) *The Economic Cycle: Postwar Developments*, Moscow: Progress

Middlemas, Keith (1979) *Politics in Industrial Society*, London: Deutsch

Miliband, Ralph (1965) 'Marx and the State', *Socialist Register 1965*, (ed.) *idem* and John Saville, London: Merlin Press

Miliband, Ralph (1969) *The State in Capitalist Society*, London: Weidenfeld and Nicolson

Miliband, Ralph (1970) 'The Capitalist State – Reply to Nicos Poulantzas', *New Left Review*, 59

Miliband, Ralph (1973) 'Poulantzas and the Capitalist State', *New Left Review*, 82

Miliband, Ralph (1975) 'Political Forms and Historical Materialism', *Socialist Register 1975* (ed.) *idem* and John Saville, London: Merlin Press

*Miliband, Ralph (1977) *Marxism and Politics*, London: Oxford University Press

Minnerup, Gunter (1976) 'West Germany Since the War', *New Left Review*, 99

Mouffe, Chantal (1979a) 'Introduction', in *idem* (ed.) *Gramsci and Marxist Theory*, London: Routledge and Kegan Paul

*Mouffe, Chantal (1979b) 'Hegemony and Ideology in Gramsci', in *idem* (ed.) *Gramsci and Marxist Theory*, London: Routledge and Kegan Paul

Mouffe, Chantal and Sassoon, Anne Showstack (1977) 'Gramsci in France and Italy – a review of the literature', *Economy and Society*, 6 (1)

Müller, Wolfgang (1975) 'Momente des bürgerlichen Staates in der griechischen Polis', *Prokla*, 17/18

*Müller, Wolfgang and Neusüss, Christel (1970) 'Die Sozialstaatsillusion und der Widerspruch von Lohnarbeit und Kapital', *Sozialistische Politik*, 6/7 (cited from the translation, 'The Social State Illusion and the Contradiction between Wage Labour and Capital', *Telos*, 25, Winter 1975)

Nairn, Tom (1978) *The Break-Up of Britain*, London: New Left Books

Negri, Antonio (1977) 'Sur quelques tendances de la théorie communiste de l'état la plus récente: revue critique', in ACSES, *Sur L'État*, Brusselles, Contradictions

Neusüss, Christel (1972) *Imperialismus und Weltmarktbewegung des Kapitals*, Erlangen

Nordahl, Richard (1972) 'Stalinist Ideology: the Case of the Stalinist Interpretation of Monopoly Capitalist Politics', *Soviet Studies*, 26 (ii)

Oberlecher, Reinhold (ed.) (1975) 'Deduktion des Staates', *Theorie und Klasse: Blätter für wissenschaftliche Kritik*, 8

*O'Connor, James (1973) *Fiscal Crisis of the State*, New York: St Martin's

Offe, Claus (1969) 'Politische Herrschaft und Klassenstrukturen. Zur Analyse spätkapitalistischer Gesellschaftssysteme', in G. Kress and D. Senghaas (eds.) *Politikwissenschaft*, Frankfurt, EVA (cited after the English translation in Offe, 1972b)

Offe, Claus (1972a) *Strukturprobleme des kapitalistischen Staates*, Frankfurt: Suhrkamp (chapter 2 is cited from the abridged version in Offe, 1973b; chapter 3 is cited from the translation in Offe, 1974; and chapter 7 from the translation in Offe, 1975c)

*Offe, Claus (1972b) 'Political Authority and Class Structure – An Analysis of Late Capitalist Societies', *International Journal of Sociology*, 2 (i)

Offe, Claus (1973a) ' "Krisen des Krisenmanagement": Elemente einer politischen Krisentheorie', in M. Jänicke (ed.) *Herrschaft und Krise*, Opladen: Westdeutscher Verlag (cited from the translation in Offe, 1976a)

Offe, Claus (1973b) 'The Abolition of Market Control and the Problem of Legitimacy', *Kapitalistate*, 1, pp. 109–116, and 2, pp. 73–75

*Offe, Claus (1974) 'Structural Problems of the Capitalist State', in K. Von Beyme (ed.) *German Political Studies*, vol 1, London: Sage, pp. 31–57

Offe, Claus (1975a) *Berufsbildungsreform: eine Fallstudie über Reformpolitik* Frankfurt: Suhrkamp

*Offe, Claus (1975b) 'The Theory of the Capitalist State and the Problem of Policy Formation', in L. Lindberg *et al.* (ed.) *Stress and Contradiction in Modern Capitalism*, Lexington: D. H. Heath

Offe, Claus (1975c) 'Further Comments on Müller and Neusüss', *Telos*, 25 Fall

Offe, Claus (1976a) ' "Crises of Crisis Management": Elements of a Political Crisis Theory', *International Journal of Politics*, Fall

Offe, Claus (1976b) 'Überlegungen und Hypothesen zum Problem politischer Legitimation', in R. Ebbighausen (ed.) *Bürgerlicher Staat und politische Legitimation*, Frankfurt: Suhrkamp, pp. 80–115

Offe, Claus (1978) 'Notes on the Future of European Socialism and the State', *Kapitalistate*, 7, pp. 27–38

➤ Offe, Claus (1980) 'The Separation of Form and Content in Liberal Democratic Politics', *Studies in Political Economy*, 3, Spring

Offe, Claus (1981a) 'The Attribution of Public Status to Interest Groups: the West German Case', in S. Berger (ed.) *Organizing Interests in Western Europe*; London: Cambridge University Press

Offe, Claus (1981b) 'Some Contradictions of the Modern Welfare State', *International Praxis*, 1 (3)

Offe, Claus (1981c) 'Competitive Party Democracy and the Keynesian Welfare State: some reflections on their historical limits', paper prepared for the Conference on 'Organisation Economy Society: Prospects for the 1980s', Griffith University, Brisbane, Queensland, Australia, July 16–19, 1981

*Offe, Claus and Ronge, Volker (1976) 'Thesen zur Begründung des Konzepts des 'kapitalistischen Staates' und zur materialistischen Politikforschung', in C. Pozzoli (ed.) *Rahmenbedingungen und Schranken Staatlichen Handelns*, Frankfurt: Suhrkamp, pp. 54–70 (translated as 'Theses on the ➤ Theory of the State', in *New German Critique*, 1975)

Offe, Claus and Wiesenthal, Helmut (1978) 'Two Logics of Collective Action – ➤ Theoretical Notes on Social Class and Organisational Form', typescript (a revised version appears in M. Zeitlin (ed.) *Political Power and Social Theory*, New York: JAI Press, 1980)

Ölssner, Fred (1971) 'Zur geschichtlichen Rolle und zum Begriff des Monopols', *Marxismus Digest*, 3

Ostrovityanov, K. V. (1948) *Soviet Views on the Post-War World Economy: an official critique of Eugen Varga's 'Changes in the Economy of Capitalism Resulting from the Second World War'*, Washington D.C.: Public Affairs Press

Ostrovityanov, K. V. *et al.* (eds.) (1955) *Political Economy: a textbook* London: Lawrence and Wishart, 1957 (translation of second Russian edition, 1955)

*Pashukanis, Evgeny B. (1929) *Allgemeine Rechtslehre und Marxismus* (3rd German edition) (Cited after the translation, *Law and Marxism: a General Theory*, London: Ink Links, 1978)

Pêcheux, Michel (1975) *Les Verités de la Palice*, Paris: Maspero

Perceval, Louis (1977a) 'L'Etat peut-il être démocratique?' *Economie et Politique*, 272

Perceval, Louis (1977b) 'Comment l'Etat peut devenir démocratique', *Economie et Politique*, 273

Petrowsky, Wenner (1971) 'Zur Entwicklung der Theorie des staatsmonopolistischen Kapitalismus', *Prokla*, 1

Phillips, Paul (1980) *Marx and Engels on Law and Laws*, Oxford: Martin Robertson

Picciotto, Sol (1979) 'The Theory of the State, Class Struggle, and the Rule of Law', in B. Fine *et al.* (eds.), *Capitalism and the Rule of Law*, London: Hutchinson

Poulantzas, Nicos (1964) 'L'examen marxiste de l'état et du droit actuels et la question de l'alternative', *Les Temps Modernes*, 219–220

Poulantzas, Nicos (1965a) 'La Critique de la Raison Dialectique de J-P Sartre et le Droit', *Archives de Philosophie du Droit*, x

Poulantzas, Nicos (1965b) *Nature des Choses et Droit*, Paris: Pichon et Durand-Auzias

*Poulantzas, Nicos (1965c) 'Préliminaires a l'étude de l'hegemonie dans l'Etat', *Les Temps Modernes*

Poulantzas, Nicos (1966a) 'La dialectique hegelienne-marxiste et la logique juridique moderne', *Archives de Philosophie du Droit*, xi

Poulantzas, Nicos (1966b) 'La théorie politique marxiste en Grande Bretagne', *Les Temps Modernes*, 238 (Cited from 'Marxist Political Theory in Great Britain', *New Left Review*, 43, 1967)

Poulantzas, Nicos (1967a) 'A propos de la théorie marxiste du droit', *Archives de Philosophie du Droit*, xii

Poulantzas, Nicos (1967b) 'The Political Forms of the Military Coup D'Etat' (in Greek), *Poreia*, 2, June (reprinted in *Politis*, no 29, 1979) (Cited from the English translation by Grigoris Ananiadis, 1980, mimeo, University of Essex)

*Poulantzas, Nicos (1968) *Political Power and Social Classes*, Paris: Maspero (Cited from the English translation, London: New Left Books, 1973)

Poulantzas, Nicos (1969) 'The Problem of the Capitalist State', *New Left Review*, 58

*Poulantzas, Nicos (1970) *Fascism and Dictatorship*, Paris: Maspero (Cited from the English translation, London: New Left Books, 1974)

Poulantzas, Nicos (1974) *Classes in Contemporary Capitalism*, Paris: Editions Seuil (Cited from the English translation, London: New Left Books, 1975)

Poulantzas, Nicos (1975) *La crise des dictatures*, Paris: Maspero

Poulantzas, Nicos (1976a) 'The Capitalist State: a Reply to Miliband and Laclau', *New Left Review*, 95

*Poulantzas, Nicos (1976b) *The Crisis of the Dictatorships*, Paris: Maspero, second edition with postscript (Cited from the English translation, London: New Left Books, 1976)

Poulantzas, Nicos (1976c) 'Les transformations actuelles de l'état, la crise politique, et la crise de l'état', in *idem* (ed.), *La Crise de l'Etat*, Paris: Presses Universitaires de France

Poulantzas, Nicos (1976d) 'The Crisis of the State' (interview with Henri Weber), *France nouvelle* (Cited from the translation in *Consent*, journal of the University of Essex Communist Society, 1978)

Poulantzas, Nicos (1977) 'The State and the Transition to Socialism', *Critique Communiste*, 16, June (translated in *International 4 (i)*, 1978)

*Poulantzas, Nicos (1978) *State, Power, Socialism*, Paris: Presses Universitaires de France (Cited from the English translation, London: New Left Books, 1978)

Poulantzas, Nicos (1979a) 'Es geht darum, mit der stalinistischen Tradition zu brechen!', *Prokla*, 37

Poulantzas, Nicos (1979b) 'La crise des partis', *Dialectiques*, no 18 (cited from the reprint in *idem, Repères*, Paris: Maspero, 1980)

Poulantzas, Nicos (1979c) 'Is There a Crisis in Marxism?', *Journal of the Hellenic Diaspora*, 6 (iii)

Poulantzas, Nicos (1979d) 'Interview with Nicos Poulantzas', *Marxism Today*, July

Poulantzas, Nicos (1980) *Repères: hier et aujourd'hui – textes sur l'état*, Paris: Maspero

Pozzolini, Alberto (1970) *Antonio Gramsci: an Introduction to his Thought*, London: Pluto Press

Preuss, Ulrich K. (1973) *Legalität und Pluralismus: Beiträge zum Verfassungsrecht der Bundesrepublik Deutschland*, Frankfurt: Suhrkamp

Projekt Klassenanalyse (1972) *Leninismus – neue Stufe des wissenschaftlichen Sozialismus?* Berlin: VSA, 2 vols

Projekt Klassenanalyse (1973) *Materialen zur Klassenstruktur der BRD: erster Teil – Theoretische Grundlagen und Kritiken*, Westberlin: VSA

Projekt Klassenanalyse (1974) *Oberfläche und Staat*, Westberlin, VSA

Projekt Klassenanalyse (1975) *Stamokap in der Krise*, Westberlin, VSA

*Projekt Klassenanalyse (1976) 'Thesen zum Verhältnis von bürgerlicher Gesellschaft und Staat', *Beiträge zum wissenschaftlichen Sozialismus*, 6

Projekt Klassenanalyse (1977) *Der Staat in der BRD*, Hamburg/Westberlin: VSA

— Przeworski, Adam (1977) 'Proletariat into Class: the Process of Class Formation from Karl Kautsky's *The Class Struggle* to Recent Controversies', *Politics and Society*, 7 (4)

— Przeworski, Adam (1980) 'Social Democracy as a Historical Phenomenon', *New Left Review*, 122

Pyadshev, B. (1977) *The Military-Industrial Complex*, Moscow: Progress

Quin, Claude (1976) *Classes sociales et union du peuple de France*, Paris: Éditions sociales

Redhead, Steven (1978) 'The Discrete Charm of Bourgeois Law: A Note on Pashukanis', *Critique*, 9

Reichelt, Helmut (1974) 'Einige Anmerkungen zu Sybille von Flatows and Freerk Huiskens Aufsatz zum Problem der Ableitung des bürgerlichen Staates', *Gesellschaft 1*, Frankfurt: Suhrkamp (Cited from the English translation, 'Some Comments on Flatow and Huisken's Essay 'On the

Problem of the Derivation of the Bourgeois State', in J. Holloway and S. Picciotto (eds.), *State and Capital*, London: Edward Arnold)

*Reinhold, Otto *et al.* (1971) *Der Imperialismus der BRD*, Berlin: Dietz Verlag

Richards, Frank (1979) 'Revisionism, Imperialism, and the State: the Method of *Capital* and the Dogma of State Monopoly Capitalism', *Revolutionary Communist Papers*, 4

Roberts, James W. (1977) 'Lenin's Theory of Imperialism in Soviet Usage', *Soviet Studies*, 29 (iii)

Röder, Karl-Heinz (ed.) (1976) *USA: Aufstieg und Verfall bürgerlicher Demokratie*, Berlin: Staatsverlag der DDR

Ronge, Volker (1974) 'The Politicization of Administration in Advanced Capitalist Societies', *Political Studies*, xxii (1)

Ryndina, M. and Chernikov, G. (eds.) (1974) *The Political Economy of Capitalism*, Moscow: Progress

Sassoon, Anne Showstack (1978) 'Hegemony and Political Intervention', in S. Hibbin (ed.) *Politics, Ideology, and the State*, London: Lawrence and Wishart

*Sassoon, Anne Showstack (1980) *Gramsci's Politics*, London: Croom Helm

Sassoon, Anne Showstack (ed.) (1982) *A Gramsci Reader*, London: Writers' and Readers' Cooperative

Sauer, Dieter (1978) *Staat und Staatsapparat*, Frankfurt: Campus Verlag

Sayer, Derek (1979) *Marx's Method: Ideology, Science and Critique in Capital*, Brighton: Harvester

Schenajew, W. N. (1973) 'Zu Fragen der Monopolisierungsprozesse und der Inflation', in Institut dur Marxistische Studien und Forschungen (ed.), *Der staatsmonopolistische Kapitalismus*, Frankfurt: Verlag Marxistische Blatter

Schirmeister, Caspar (1970) 'Zum Monopol als Herrschaftsverhältnis – aktuelle Aspekte der Leninschen Analyse', *Wirtschaftswissenschaft*, 18 (iv)

Schleifstein, Josef (1973) 'Zur Theorie des staatsmonopolistischen Kapitalismus', *Blätter für deutsche und internationale Politik*, 4

Schlesinger, Rudolf (1949) 'The Discussions on Varga's Changes in the Economy of Capitalism', *Soviet Studies*, 1 (i)

Schmidt, Johann Lorenz (1958) 'Die Wirtschaftskrise in den kapitalistischen Ländern ist unabwendbar', *Einheit*, 13 (v)

Schmidt, Johann Lorenz (1959) 'Uber einige Probleme der Krisen und Zyklen in Monopolkapitalismus', *Konjuktur und Krise*, 3 (ii)

Schmidt, Max (1974) 'Zur Entwicklung des imperialistischen Herrschaftssystems (Thesen)', *Marxismus Digest*, 1

Schubert, Joachim (1973) 'Die Theorie des staatsmonopolistischen Kapitalismus – Kritik der zentralen Aussagen', *Mehrwert*, 4

Schuster, Jürgen (1976) *Parliamentarismus in der BRD*, Berlin: Dietz Verlag

Schütte, Helmuth (1977a) 'Resultate und Kritik der neueren staatstheoretischen Diskussion', *Das Argument*, 104

*Schütte, Helmuth (1977b) 'Staatstheorie als Methodenproblem des historischen Materialismus', in Das Argument Sonderband 16: *Staat und Monopole (II)*, Berlin: Argument Verlag

Schwank, Karl-Heinz (1974) *Staatsmonopolistische Wirtschaftsregulierung in der Gegenwart*, Berlin: Dietz Verlag

Silverman, David and Torode, Brian (1980) *The Material Word: some theories of language and its limits*, London: Routledge and Kegan Paul

➤ Solomos, John (1979) 'The Marxist Theory of the State and the Problems of Fractions', *Capital and Class*, 7

Spriano, Paulo (1979) *Antonio Gramsci and the Party: the Prison Years*, London: Lawrence and Wishart

Stadnichenko, A. (1975) *Monetary Crisis of Capitalism*, Moscow: Progress

Stalin, Joseph (1924) 'The Foundations of Leninism', *SCW*, 6

Stalin, Joseph (1930) 'Political Report of the Central Committee to the 16th Congress of the CPSU (B)', *SCW*, 12

Stalin, Joseph (1934) 'Report to the 17th Party Congress on the Work of the Central Committee of the CPSU (B)', *SCW*, 14

Stalin, Joseph (1939) 'Report to the 18th Congress of the CPSU (B) on the Work of the Central Committee', in B. Franklin (ed.), *The Essential Stalin*, London: Croom Helm, 1973

Stalin, Joseph (1952) 'Economic Problems of Socialism in the USSR', in B. Franklin (ed.) *The Essential Stalin*, London: Croom Helm, 1973

Theret, Bruno and Wieviorka, Michel (1978) *Critique de la théorie du 'Capitalisme monopoliste d'état'*, Paris: Maspero

Therborn, Goran (1978) *What Does the Ruling Class Do When it Rules?* London: New Left Books

Tikos, Laszla (1965) *E. Varga's Tätigkeit als Wirtschaftsanalytiker und Publizist in der Ungarischen Sozialdemokratie, in der Komintern, in der Akademie der Wissenschaften der UDSSR: ein Bericht*, Tübingen: Bohlau Verlag

Togliatti, Palmiro (1957) 'The Present Relevance of Gramsci's Theory and Practice', *Rinascita* (reprinted in *idem, Gramsci and Other Writings*, London: Lawrence and Wishart, 1979)

Tristram, Wolfgang (1974) 'Allgemeine Formbestimmung des bürgerlichen Staates: Zur Kritik des Staatsbegriff in der Theorie des staatsmonopolistischen Kapitalismus', in R. Ebbighausen (ed.) *Monopol und Staat*, Frankfurt: Suhrkamp

Tumanov, Vladimir A. (1974) *Contemporary Bourgeois Legal Thought*, Moscow: Progress

*Tuschling, Burkhard (1976) *Rechtsform und Produktionsverhältnisse*, Frankfurt: EVA

Tuschling, Burkhard (1977) 'Aspekte einer materialistischen Theorie des Rechts und des Staats', in F. Deppe *et al.* (eds.) *Abendroth-Forum,* Marburg: Verlag Arbeiterbewegung und Gesellschaftswissenschaft

Valier, Jacques (1976) *Le Parti Communiste Français et le Capitalisme monopoliste d'Etat,* Paris: Maspero

*Varga, Eugen (1934) *The Great Crisis and its Political Consequences: Economics and Politics, 1928–1934,* London: Modern Books

Varga, Eugen (1946) *Changes in the Economy of Capitalism Resulting from the Second World War* (in Russian), Moscow

Varga, Eugen (1958) 'Probleme des industriellen Nachkriegszyklus und die neue Überproduktionskrise', *Sowjetwissenschaft,* 12 (x)

Varga, Eugen (1963) *Twentieth Century Capitalism,* Moscow: Progress (translated from 1st Russian edition, 1961)

Varga, Eugen (1964) *Politico-Economic Problems of Capitalism,* Moscow: Progress 1968 (translation of Russian edition of 1964)

Vernay, Claude (1968) 'Le capitalisme monopoliste d'état et les perspectives démocratiques', *Economie et politique,* 164–165

Williams, Glyn (1975) *Proletarian Order,* London: Pluto Press

Williams, Mike (1979) 'The Theory of (the) Capitalist State(s) – a Reply to Colin Barker', *Capital and Class,* 9

Winkelman, Rainer (1974) 'Grundzüge und Probleme der Theorie des staatsmonopolistischen Kapitalismus', in R. Ebbighausen (ed.) *Monopol und Staat,* Frankfurt: Suhrkamp

Winkler, J. T. (1977) 'The Corporate Economy: Theory and Administration', in R. Scase (ed.) *Industrial Society: Class, Cleavage, and Control,* London: Allen and Unwin

*Wirth, Margaret (1972) *Kapitalismustheorie in der DDR,* Frankfurt: Suhrkamp

Wirth, Margaret (1973) 'Zur Kritik der Theorie des staatsmonopolistischen Kapitalismus', *Prokla,* 8/8 (Cited from the English translation, 'Towards a Critique of the Theory of State Monopoly Capitalism', *Economy and Society,* 1977, 6 (iii))

Wolfe, Alan (1977) *The Limits of Legitimacy: Political Contradictions of Contemporary Capitalism,* New York: Free Press

Woods, Michael (1977) 'Discourse Analysis: the work of Michel Pêcheux', *Ideology and Consciousness,* 2

*Wygodski, S. L. (1972) *Der gegenwärtige Kapitalismus,* Berlin: Dietz Verlag

Zieschang, Kurt (1956) 'Zu einigen Problemen des staatsmonopolistischen Kapitalismus', *Wirtschaftswissenschaft,* 4 (v)

Name Index

Subject Index

Absolutism, 10, 16, 96, 113–14, 182
Abstraction, 29–30, 71–2, 75, 78,
 158, 212–13, 258
 axes or planes of, 138–40, 181,
 208, 214–18, 228, 247–8, 252,
 259
 degrees or planes of, 23, 82–3,
 137, 138–40, 208, 214–18
Accumulation (*see also* valorisation),
 10, 14, 37, 66, 68–9, 80–1,
 89–94, 97, 103–4, 107–8, 112,
 114–15, 123, 173–7, 218, 226,
 237, 243
 primitive, 25, 28, 89, 114
Administration (*see* executive)
Alliances
 anti-monopoly, 33, 40, 45, 53, 60,
 63, 68–9, 76, 178
 class, 13, 145, 148, 150, 165, 191,
 193, 238
 popular-democratic, 33, 45, 178–9,
 251–2
Allocation (as form of intervention),
 110–11
Althusserianism (*see also*
 structuralism), 130–2, 154–6,
 169, 181, 186, 203
Anti-economism, 192–3, 198, 208
Anti-instrumentalism, 16–17, 145,
 185–6, 223–5

Apparatus (*see also* ideology, mass
 integration, repression)
 economic, 161
 economic state, 67, 176
Articulation (*see also* contingent
 necessity, overdetermination),
 xi–xiii, 75–6, 138–41, 158–9,
 195, 207–9, 213–20, 252, 259
Authoritarian populism, 249–50
Authoritarian statism (*see also* strong
 state), 167, 170–3, 189–90

Bank monopoly capitalism, 33
Base (*see also* materiality,
 reductionism, superstructure), 18,
 20, 22, 26, 85, 132, 143, 151,
 192, 195, 198, 203, 245
 economic, 9–12, 15, 30, 46, 57,
 96, 148, 151
Bonapartism, 13, 16, 17, 27, 30–1,
 169
Bourgeoisie (*see also* capital,
 monopoly capital, power bloc), 9,
 13, 16, 31, 145, 150, 166, 186,
 195, 199
Britain, xii, xv, 8, 13, 15, 17, 21, 78,
 232–3
Bureaucracy, 4–5, 8, 58–9, 105, 111,
 163, 172, 177, 231–2, 233
Bureaucratism, 163, 168

285